OTHER A
THE SCA

MW00782101

1. *The A to Z of Buddhism* by Charles S. Prebish, 2001.
2. *The A to Z of Catholicism* by William J. Collinge, 2001..
3. *The A to Z of Hinduism* by Bruce M. Sullivan, 2001.
4. *The A to Z of Islam* by Ludwig W. Adamec, 2002.
5. *The A to Z of Slavery* & Abolition by Martin A. Klein, 2002.
6. *Terrorism: Assassins to Zealots* by Sean Kendall Anderson and Stephen Sloan, 2003.
7. *The A to Z of the Korean War* by Paul M. Edwards, 2005.
8. *The A to Z of the Cold War* by Joseph Smith and Simon Davis, 2005.
9. *The A to Z of the Vietnam War* by Edwin E. Moise, 2005.
10. *The A to Z of Science Fiction Literature* by Brian Stableford, 2005.
11. *The A to Z of the Holocaust* by Jack R. Fischel, 2005.
12. *The A to Z of Washington, D.C.* by Robert Benedetto, Jane Donovan, and Kathleen DuVall, 2005.
13. *The A to Z of Taoism* by Julian F. Pas, 2006.
14. *The A to Z of the Renaissance* by Charles G. Nauert, 2006.
15. *The A to Z of Shinto* by Stuart D. B. Picken, 2006.
16. *The A to Z of Byzantium* by John H. Rosser, 2006.
17. *The A to Z of the Civil War* by Terry L. Jones, 2006.
18. *The A to Z of the Friends (Quakers)* by Margery Post Abbott, Mary Ellen Chijioke, Pink Dandelion, and John William Oliver Jr., 2006
19. *The A to Z of Feminism* by Janet K. Boles and Diane Long Hoeveler, 2006.
20. *The A to Z of New Religious Movements* by George D. Chryssides, 2006.
21. *The A to Z of Multinational Peacekeeping* by Terry M. Mays, 2006.
22. *The A to Z of Lutheranism* by Günther Gassmann with Duane H. Larson and Mark W. Oldenburg, 2007.
23. *The A to Z of the French Revolution*, by Paul R. Hanson, 2007.
24. *The A to Z of the Persian Gulf War 1990 –1991*, by Clayton R. Newell, 2007.
25. *The A to Z of Revolutionary America*, by Terry M. Mays, 2007.
26. *The A to Z of the Olympic Movement*, by Bill Mallon with Ian Buchanan, 2007.

The A to Z of the French Revolution

Paul R. Hanson

The A to Z Guide Series, No. 23

The Scarecrow Press, Inc.
Lanham, Maryland • Toronto • Plymouth, UK
2007

SCARECROW PRESS, INC.

Published in the United States of America
by Scarecrow Press, Inc.
A wholly owned subsidary of
The Rowman & Littlefield Publishing Group, Inc.
4501 Forbes Boulevard, Suite 200, Lanham, Maryland 20706
www.scarecrowpress.com

Estover Road
Plymouth PL6 7PY
United Kingdom

British Library Cataloguing in Publication Information Available

Library of Congress Cataloging-in-Publication Data

The hardback version of this book was cataloged by the Library of Congress as
follows:

Hanson, Paul R., 1952–
    Historical dictionary of the French Revolution / Paul R. Hanson.
        p. cm. — (Historical Dictionaries of war, revolution, and civil unrest ;
no. 27)
    Includes bibliographical references.
1. France—History—Revolution, 1789–1799—Dictionaries. I. Title. II.
    Series.
DC147.H36 2004
944.04'03—dc22   2004002982

ISBN 0-8108-5593-3 / 978-0-8108-5593-9 (pbk. : alk. paper)

∞™ The paper used in this publication meets the minimum requirements of
American National Standard for Information Sciences—Permanence of
Paper for Printed Library Materials, ANSI/NISO Z39.48-1992.
Manufactured in the United States of America.

For my parents
Jane and Kermit Hanson

Contents

Editor's Foreword

The French Revolution was not the first, nor the last of its kind, but it is certainly the most famous. It is revolution writ large, with all the passions and fears, the nobility and nastiness, the blood and thunder, the revolution that spawns larger-than-life personalities like Danton, Robespierre, and Napoleon and then devours its own children. In this case, the ramifications were exceptionally extensive, spreading throughout much of Europe and being rekindled time and again until it had achieved most of its goals, sometimes several generations later. It is impossible to understand modern European history, or world history, for that matter, without turning back to 1789, when it flared up, considering the previous decades to grasp its origins, and looking further out to witness its formal demise. This makes the *Historical Dictionary of the French Revolution* a landmark of sorts within the steadily growing series of Historical Dictionaries of War, Revolution, and Civil Unrest.

Although more than two centuries have passed, and an almost boundless literature has described it from every possible angle, it helps to collect and sort the basic information once again so interested readers can find what they want without too much difficulty. This is the primary task of the dictionary section, with entries on leading lights and lesser figures, crucial events and turning points, significant institutions and organizations, and some of the economic, social, and intellectual factors. The introduction provides an overall view while the chronology walks us through those turbulent times again. For those who want to extend their excursion in one direction or another, there is a select bibliography, which, although ample and including many of the better works, can only reflect a small if important portion of the literature.

Paul R. Hanson, the author of this volume, has basically two specializations, modern French and European history, and comparative revolution, paying particular attention to the Russian and Chinese revolutions.

These broad interests have informed his study of the French Revolution, on which he has been lecturing and writing for over two decades. His publications, along with articles and papers, include three books: *Provincial Politics in the French Revolution: Caen and Limoges, 1789–1794*; *Revolutionary France*; and *The Jacobin Republic under Fire: The Federalist Revolt in the French Revolution*. For most of his career, since receiving a doctorate at the University of California, Berkeley, Dr. Hanson has been teaching at Butler University in Indianapolis, where he is now Dean of the College of Liberal Arts and Sciences. This historical dictionary will doubtless come in handy for his students, and for untold thousands of students around the world who—while not necessarily enthralled by history in general—suddenly perk up when the topic moves on to one of the most gripping events of all time.

Jon Woronoff
Series Editor

Acknowledgments

I would like to thank Jon Woronoff for asking me to undertake this project, about which I had some apprehension at first. It has been both a pleasure and an adventure to write the dictionary, giving me an excuse to spend a month and a half in Paris at the Bibliothèque Nationale gathering biographical information, and the opportunity to learn a great deal more about the French Revolution as I wrote the entries over the past three years. I would like also to thank Butler University, and in particular Dean Steven Kaplan, for granting me a semester leave in the fall of 2001 to begin serious writing. Three Butler students assisted me in compiling the bibliography: Karleigh Koster, Michelle Kasten, and Courtney Campbell, and I am deeply appreciative of the care they devoted to the task.

Chronology

1786 **26 September** Anglo-French Trade Treaty.

1787 **February–April** First Assembly of Notables. **8 April** Dismissal of Charles-Alexandre Calonne as finance minister. **1 May** Etienne-Charles Loménie de Brienne replaces Calonne. **25 May** Assembly of Notables dismissed after refusing to support Brienne's proposed tax reforms. **26 July** Paris Parlement registers opposition to Brienne reforms. **6 August** Louis XVI issues *lit de justice* to impose reforms. **7 August** Paris Parlement rejects king's *lit de* justice. **14 August** Louis XVI imposes new taxes and exiles Parlement of Paris to Troyes. **Mid-August** Paris demonstrations in support of Parlement. **26 August** Brienne named first minister. **20 September** Brienne reaches compromise with Paris Parlement about new taxes. **28 September** Parlement returns to Paris from Troyes. **November** New Provincial Assemblies begin to meet; Louis XVI agrees to convene Estates-General. **19 November** Edict of Toleration for Protestants. **20 November** Exile of Louis-Philippe Orléans by *lettre de cachet*.

1788 **3 May** Paris Parlement denounces *lettres de cachet*. **8 May** Brienne issues edicts reorganizing judicial courts and reducing the power of the parlements. **May–July** Widespread protests of the May edicts. **June** Assembly of the Clergy reduces its annual *don gratuit* to the monarchy. **7 June** "Day of the Tiles" in Grenoble—popular riots in support of the parlements. **21 July** Convocation of the Estates of Dauphiné at Vizille. **8 August** King convokes Estates-General for 1789. **16 August** Monarchy suspends interest payments on state debt. **25 August** Jacques Necker replaces Brienne. **26 August** Necker restores parlements to former powers. **25 September** Parlement of Paris rules that Estates-General will meet, deliberate, and vote as in 1614, thereby alienating the populace of Paris. **November** Second Assembly of Notables. **5 December** Parlement of Paris agrees to double the representation of the Third Estate in the Estates-General.

1789 January–March Urban riots throughout France. **24 January** Louis XVI issues final regulations for elections to the Estates-General and drafting of *cahiers de doléances*. **January** Publication of Emmanuel-Joseph Sieyès's pamphlet, *What is the Third Estate?* **March–April** Meeting of primary and bailliage assemblies. **27–28 April** Réveillon riots in Paris. **30 April** First meeting of Breton club at Versailles. **5 May** Opening session of the Estates-General. **6 May** Deputies of the Third Estate refuse to meet as a separate chamber. **11 May** Deputies of the Second Estate (nobility) meet as a separate chamber and reject vote by head. **4 June** Death of the dauphin. **13 June** First deputies from the First Estate (clergy) move to join the meeting of the Third Estate. **17 June** Third Estate declares itself a National Assembly. **19 June** First Estate votes to join the National Assembly. **20 June** Tennis Court Oath. **23 June** Louis XVI opposes the declarations of the Third Estate in a Royal Session. **25 June** Paris electors create unofficial municipal council. **27 June** Louis XVI accedes to creation of the National Assembly. **6 July** National Assembly creates a Constitution Committee. **9 July** National Assembly adopts title of Constituent Assembly. **11 July** Dismissal of Necker. **14 July** Fall of the Bastille. **15 July** Paris electors form the Commune and elect Jean-Sylvain Bailly mayor. **16 July** Recall of Necker. **17 July** Louis XVI visits Paris, is greeted by Bailly at the Hôtel de Ville. **20 July–6 August** The Great Fear. **July–September** Municipal revolutions across France. **28 July** First issue of Jacques-Pierre Brissot's *Patriote Français* appears. **4 August** Noble deputies renounce privileges in Constituent Assembly. **26 August** Constituent Assembly adopts Declaration of the Rights of Man and Citizen. **September** Louis XVI refuses to approve the decrees abolishing privilege or the Declaration of the Rights of Man and Citizen. **16 September** First issue of Jean-Paul Marat's *L'Ami du Peuple* appears. **1 October** Banquet of the Queen's bodyguards at Versailles. **5 October** Women of Paris march to Versailles. **6 October** Crowd invades palace at Versailles. Royal family returns to Paris. **19 October** First session of the Constituent Assembly in Paris. **2 November** Church lands nationalized. **9 November** First meeting of the Constituent Assembly in the Manège, near the Tuileries Palace. **30 November** Corsica declared an integral part of France. **14–22 December** Constituent Assembly issues decrees establishing departmental and municipal administrations. **19 December** Sale of *biens nationaux* begins and first *assignats* are issued.

1790 January–February First municipal elections. **20 January** Doctor Joseph-Ignace Guillotin proposes a machine for humane executions to the Constituent Assembly. **4 February** Louis XVI attends Constituent Assembly and deputies swear a civic oath. **13 February** Constituent Assembly abolishes monastic vows and suppresses religious orders. **26 February** France divided into 83 departments. **16 March** Constituent Assembly abolishes *lettres de cachet*. **31 March** Maximilien Robespierre elected president of the Paris Jacobin club for the next month. **April–June** Violence between Catholics and Protestants in Nîmes and Montauban. **5 May** Constituent Assembly decrees the election of judges. **21 May** Paris divided into 48 sections. **19 June** Abolition of nobility. **12 July** Constituent Assembly adopts the Civil Constitution of the Clergy. **14 July** Festival of Federation in Paris. **22 July** Louis XVI accepts Civil Constitution of the Clergy. **5–31 August** Nancy mutiny. **18 August** *Camp de* Jalès counterrevolutionary assembly. **4 September** Necker resigns as finance minister. **7 September** Constituent Assembly orders creation of National Archives. **21 October** Constituent Assembly introduces the tricolor flag. **23 November** New land tax introduced. **25 November** Slave uprising in Saint-Domingue. **27 November** Civil Oath of the Clergy introduced. **21 December** Constituent Assembly orders that a statue be raised to honor Jean-Jacques Rousseau. **26 December** Louis XVI accepts Civil Oath of the Clergy.

1791 January Half of all priests refuse to swear Civil Oath. **13 January** New tax on movable wealth introduced. **February** Election of first constitutional bishops. **19 February** The royal aunts flee France. **24 February** Charles-Maurice Talleyrand administers sacrements to first constitutional bishops. **2 March** Constituent Assembly abolishes guilds. **5 March** Constituent Assembly creates a provisional High Court at Orléans. **10 March** Pope Pius VI condemns Civil Constitution of the Clergy. **28 March** Paris Commune orders closing of Paris Monarchist club. **2 April** Death of Gabriel-Honoré Mirabeau. **4 April** Mirabeau interred in the Panthéon. **13 April** Renewed Papal condemnation of the Civil Constitution of the Clergy. **17 April** Louis XVI celebrates Easter mass with a refractory priest. **18 April** National Guardsmen prevent Louis XVI from leaving Paris for Saint-Cloud. **21 April** Marie-Joseph-Motier Lafayette resigns as Commander of the Paris National Guard, but withdraws resignation the next day. **14 June** Constituent Assembly adopts Le Chapelier Law, prohibiting workers' associations and strikes. **20 June** Royal family flees Paris. **21 June** Royal family apprehended at Varennes. **25 June** Return of the royal family to Paris. **9 July** Constituent Assembly orders *émigrés* to return to France within two months. **11 July** Transfer of Voltaire's ashes to the Panthéon. **15 July** Constituent Assembly declares the king inviolable. **17 July** Massacre on the Champ de Mars in Paris. **18 July** George-Jacques Danton flees to London; Marat goes into hiding. **28 July** Reorganization of National Guard, limiting membership to active citizens. **4 August** Constituent Assembly orders recruitment of first battalions of volunteers. **27 August** Pillnitz Declaration. **29 August–5 September** Elections to the Legislative Assembly. **3 September** Constituent Assembly completes constitution. **9 September** Danton returns to Paris. **13 September** Louis XVI accepts new constitution. **14 September** Annexation of Avignon and the Comtat Venaissin. **30 September** Constituent Assembly adjourns. **1 October** First meeting of Legislative Assembly. **20 October** Brissot calls for military action against *émigrés*. **9 November** Law against *émigrés*, vetoed by Louis XVI. **12 November** Louis XVI invites *émigrés* to return to France. **14 November** Jérome Pétion elected mayor of Paris. **29 November** Legislative Assembly orders refractory priests to swear civic oath or be considered suspect. **19 December** Louis XVI vetoes decree against refractory priests.

1792   January–February Riots in Paris over high price of sugar and coffee. **February–March** Food riots throughout France. **1 February** Internal passports introduced. **9 February** Legislative Assembly orders sequestration of *émigré* property. **1 March** Death of Leopold II of Austria. **10–23 March** First Girondin ministry appointed. **6 April** Legislative Assembly prohibits wearing of religious dress. **20 April** France declares war on Austria. **24 April** Jean-Claude Rouget de Lisle composes *La Marseillaise*. **27 May** Legislative Assembly orders deportation of refractory priests (on denunciation of 20 citizens), vetoed by Louis XVI. **12 June** Dismissal of Girondin ministers. **20 June** Failed assault on Tuileries Palace. **27–28 June** General Lafayette returns to Paris from the front and demands sanctions against Jacobin club. **30 June** Lafayette returns to his army, is burned in effigy in the Palais Royal. **7 July** The "Kiss of Lamourette" in the Legislative Assembly. **11 July** Declaration of *la patrie en danger*. **25 July** Publication of the Brunswick Manifesto.

30 July Legislative Assembly admits passive citizens into the National Guard; Marseille *fédérés* arrive in Paris. **3 August** Petition presented to Legislative Assembly from 47 of 48 Paris sections demanding dismissal of the King. **10 August** Invasion of the Tuileries; fall of the monarchy. **13 August** Transfer of the royal family to the Temple. **19 August** Lafayette deserts French army, is imprisoned by Austrians; Prussian troops invade French territory. **21 August** First use of the guillotine. **23 August** French defeat at Longwy. **27 August** Elections for the National Convention begin. **30 August** Siege of Verdun. **2–6 September** Prison massacres in Paris. **20 September** French victory at Valmy; legalization of divorce. **21 September** National Convention convenes. **22 September** National Convention declares Republic. **10 October** Jacobin club expels Brissot. **25 October–7 November** Girondin attacks on Robespierre, Marat, and Danton. **20 November** Discovery of the king's hidden safe in the Tuileries. **11 December** Trial of Louis XVI begins. **25–26 December** Louis XVI presents his defense. **27 December** Jean-Baptiste Salle proposes *appel au peuple* regarding King's sentence.

1793 15 January Louis XVI found guilty. **16–18 January** National Convention votes death of Louis XVI. **21 January** Execution of Louis XVI. **1 February** France declares war on Great Britain and Holland. **24 February** National Convention orders recruitment of 300,000 volunteers. **25 February** Grocery shops pillaged in Paris. **1 March** National Convention decrees annexation of Belgium. **7 March** France declares war on Spain. **9 March** Designation of first representatives on mission. **10 March** Creation of Revolutionary Tribunal; Vendée rebellion begins. **18 March** Defeat of General Charles-François Dumouriez at Neerwinden. **25 March** Great Britain and Russia ally against France. **27 March–4 April** Treason and defection to Austria of Dumouriez. **5 April** Marat elected president of Jacobin club; National Convention creates Committee of Public Safety. **6 April** Arrest of Louis-Philippe Orléans. **12 April** National Convention orders arrest of Marat. **15 April** Jean-Nicolas Pache, mayor of Paris, demands proscription of 22 Girondin deputies on behalf of 35 of the 48 sections. **24 April** Revolutionary Tribunal acquits Marat. **4 May** National Convention decrees grain *maximum*. **18 May** National Convention creates a Commission of Twelve to investigate plotting by Paris Commune. **24 May** Arrest of Jacques-René Hébert and Jean Varlet. **26 May** Paris Jacobin club calls for insurrection. **27 May** Release of Hébert and Varlet. **29 May** Insurrection in

Lyon ousts Jacobin municipality. **31 May–2 June** Parisian uprising ousts Girondin leaders from National Convention. **June–August** Federalist revolts in provincial cities. **24 June** National Convention adopts constitution of 1793. **25 June** Jacques Roux presents *Enragé* petition to the National Convention. **13 July** Charlotte Corday assassinates Marat. **17 July** Final suppression of all seigneurial dues; execution of Joseph Chalier in Lyon. **6 July** National Convention decrees death penalty for hoarders. **27 July** Robespierre joins Committee of Public Safety. **2 August** Marie Antoinette transferred from the Temple to the Conciergerie. **4 August** Ratification of new constitution by primary assemblies announced. **8 August** National Convention decrees suppression of royal Academies. **23 August** National Convention decrees *levée en masse*. **27 August** Toulon handed over to British navy. **4–5 September** *Sansculottes* uprising in Paris; National Convention declares Terror the "order of the day." **6 September** Jacques-Nicolas Billaud-Varenne and Jean-Marie Collot d'Herbois join the Committee of Public Safety. **9 September** National Convention creates first *armée révolutionnaire*. **17 September** National Convention passes Law of Suspects. **29 September** National Convention decrees General *maximum*. **5 October** Adoption of revolutionary calendar. **10 October** National Convention decrees that government will be revolutionary until the return of peace. **12 October** National Convention decrees that "Lyon is no more." **16 October** Execution of Marie Antoinette. **30 October** National Convention closes women's political clubs. **31 October** Execution of the Girondins. **October–November** deChristianization campaign. **7 November** Execution of Louis-Philippe Orléans. **9 November** Execution of Manon Roland. **10 November** Festival of Liberty in Paris; Notre Dame Cathedral declared a Temple of Reason. **11 November** Execution of Bailly, former mayor of Paris. **23 November** Commune orders closure of all Paris churches. **25 November** Mirabeau's remains removed from the Panthéon. **4 December** National Convention adopts Law of Revolutionary Government (Law of 14 Frimaire). **5 December** Camille Desmoulins publishes first issue of the *Vieux Cordelier*. **19 December** Toulon recaptured from British. **25 December** Robespierre reports to the National Convention on the principles of revolutionary government.

1794 17 January General Louis-Marie Turreau creates *colonnes infernales* in the Vendée. **19 January** British occupy Corsica. **4 February** Abolition of slavery in French colonies. **5 February** Robespierre reports to the National Convention on the principles of political morality. **26 February–3 March** Louis-Antoine Saint-Just introduces the Decrees of Ventôse. **13–24 March** Arrest, trial, and execution of the Hébertistes. **30 March–5 April** Arrest, trial, and execution of the Indulgents. **4 June** Robespierre elected president of the National Convention. **8 June** Festival of the Supreme Being. **10 June** National Convention passes Law of 22 Prairial; beginning of the "Great Terror." **27 July** 9 Thermidor: Overthrow of Robespierre. **28 July** Execution of Robespierre, Saint-Just, Georges Couthon, Augustin Robespierre, and 23 others. **29 August** First public protest in Paris of the *jeunesse dorée*. **8 October** National Convention prohibits meetings of Paris sections. **11 October** Transfer of the remains of Jean-Jacques Rousseau to the Panthéon. **12 November** Closure of Paris Jacobin club following attacks by *jeunesse dorée*. **8 December** Reintegration into National Convention of 73 deputies who had protested Girondin proscriptions. **16 December** Execution of Jean-Baptiste Carrier. **24 December** National Convention abolishes the *maximum*.

1795 **8 February** Marat's remains removed from the Panthéon. **February–June** White Terror, especially in southeast. **21 February** National Convention decrees freedom of religion and separation of church and state. **17–21 March** Food riots in Paris. **1 April** Germinal riots in Paris; deportation of Bertrand Barère, Jacques-Nicolas Billaud-Varenne, and Jean-Marie Collot d'Herbois to Guyana. **10 April** National Convention orders disarming of terrorists. **7 May** Execution of Antoine-Quentin Fouquier-Tinville. **20–22 May** Prairial riots in Paris. **31 May** Suppression of the Revolutionary Tribunal. **8 June** Death of Louis XVII. **17 June** Suicide of the Prairial martyrs. **21 July** Defeat of the *émigré* army at Quiberon by General Lazare Hoche. **22 August** National Convention adopts Constitution of 1795. **5 October** Vendémiaire riots: Napoleon suppresses royalist protests in Paris. **12 October** Elections to the Council of Five Hundred and Council of Ancients. **26 October** National Convention adjourns. **3 November** Directory regime convenes. **16 November** Opening of the Panthéon club.

1796 **19 February** Suppression of *assignats*. **28 February** Closure of the Panthéon club. **2 March** Napoleon appointed commander of Army of Italy. **10 May** Arrest of Gracchus Babeuf. **17 December** General Hoche launches Irish campaign.

1797   **27 May** Execution of Gracchus Babeuf. **4 September** Fructidor coup. **19 September** Death of Lazare Hoche. **17 October** Treaty of Campo Formio.

1798   **11 May** Floréal coup. **19 May** Napoleon launches Egyptian campaign. **23 May** Irish rebellion against English. **24 July** Napoleon's army enters Cairo. **1 August** Admiral Horatio Nelson destroys French fleet. **5 September** Directory adopts Jourdan Law on military conscription.

1799   **March** War of the Second Coalition begins. **18 June** Prairial coup. **23 August** Napoleon leaves Egypt for France. **29 August** Death of Pope Pius VI. **16 October** Napoleon returns to Paris. **23 October** Lucien Bonaparte elected president of Council of Five Hundred. **9–10 November** Coup of 18 Brumaire.

Introduction

The French Revolution remains the most examined event, or period, in world history. It was, most historians would argue, the first "modern" revolution, an event so momentous that it changed the very meaning of the word *revolution*, from "restoration," as in the Glorious Revolution of 1688 in England, to its modern sense of connoting a political and/or social upheaval that marks a decisive break with the past, one that moves a society in a forward, or progressive, direction. No revolution has occurred since 1789 without making reference to this first revolution, and most have been measured against it. One cannot utter the date *1789* without thinking of revolution, and so significant were the changes unleashed in that year that it has come to mark the dividing line between early modern and late modern European history. Kings and emperors ruled Europe prior to 1789. They did not disappear because of the French Revolution, but everywhere in Europe the legitimacy of their rule would be challenged throughout the 19th century by those advocating parliamentary government of some sort.

The Bourbon monarchy ruled France on the eve of 1789, as it had for 200 years. By the end of that year the Bourbon dynasty was widely referred to as the Old Regime, and by late 1792 the monarchy would be toppled and replaced by the first French Republic. The significance of this dramatic change was amplified by the fact that it had occurred in the most powerful nation of Europe. Since the time of Louis XIV (1643–1715) the palace at Versailles had symbolized the grandeur of absolute monarchy. French was the court language of all of Europe, including Russia, and French culture set the standard for the rest of the continent. Moreover, France was the most populous nation in Europe, numbering roughly 25,000,000 inhabitants, and by many standards the most prosperous. Thus, when revolution shook the foundations of the Old Regime in France, shock waves reverberated throughout the western world.

1

It is difficult to overstate the impact of the French Revolution. The Declaration of the Rights of Man and Citizen, first drafted in 1789, stands, along with the American Bill of Rights, as a foundation document for the assertion of universal human rights. The introduction of universal manhood suffrage—first in 1789 for elections to the Estates-General, and then again in 1792 for the election of deputies to the National Convention—marked the first modern experiment with democracy, a political system thought to be impractical by most political theorists to that date. Out of the political upheaval of the 1790s emerged three ideologies that would dominate European politics throughout most of the 19th and 20th centuries: nationalism, liberalism, and socialism. Our tendency to think of political opposition in terms of "left" and "right" derives from the seating arrangement of radical and moderate deputies first evident in the Constituent Assembly. The Jacobin clubs, although they never thought of themselves as a political party, became the prototype for the conspiratorial revolutionary party thereafter. The first revolutionary Terror occurred in 1792–93, and the conservative reaction to violent radicalism that has characterized nearly all revolutions is itself always associated with Thermidor, the name of the month on the revolutionary calendar in which Maximilien Robespierre was toppled from power and executed. Less than two years after the death of Robespierre, Gracchus Babeuf and his Conspiracy of Equals launched a failed movement that is generally interpreted as the first stirring of communism on the European scene. Napoleon Bonaparte was himself a product of the Revolution—he could not have risen to the officer corps in the army of the Old Regime—and while he stifled participatory democracy within France under his rule, his conquering armies spread the reforms of republican France to much of the rest of Europe.

The French Revolution might be compared to Pandora's Box. Although the revolutionaries thought of themselves as acting on the stage of world history, few of them could foresee the far-reaching consequences of the forces they unleashed. But why did this first modern revolution occur in France, and what were its causes?

CAUSES AND ORIGINS OF THE FRENCH REVOLUTION

One might speak of the origins of the French Revolution as lying chiefly in the realm of ideas, and of its causes as largely political, social, and economic. The 18th century is often referred to as the era of Enlightenment, with France lying at the center of that intellectual movement. The thinkers of the Enlightenment, known in France as *philosophes*, were social critics more than philosophers, who directed their critiques against most of the institutions of the Old Regime. François-Marie Arouet, known to contemporaries and to posterity as Voltaire, wrote poetry, plays, novels, historical works, and critical essays. He is most noted for his consistent attack upon religious intolerance and dogmatism. Charles Louis de Secondat, Baron de Montesquieu was the son of a nobleman who eventually succeeded his father as president of the Parlement of Bordeaux. Montesquieu is best known for his critique of absolutism, first suggested in the *Persian Letters* (1721) and more fully developed in his famous work, *The Spirit of the Laws* (1748). In the latter work, Montesquieu advocated a government embodying balance and separation between the executive, legislative, and judicial branches. Virtue for Montesquieu meant justice, and justice required a written body of law and a constitution. Hardly a democrat, Montesquieu saw the aristocracy as the group best able to exercise restraint on monarchical power.

Jean-Jacques Rousseau was more radical than either Voltaire or Montesquieu. He challenged the Enlightenment's faith in progress, and also questioned the *philosophes'* confidence in human reason as the answer to all of society's problems. Rousseau achieved public notoriety at mid-century with the publication of two essays, the first a *Discourse on the Arts and Sciences*, winner of first prize in the 1749 essay contest sponsored by the Dijon Academy, in which he argued that progress in the arts and sciences had led to the moral corruption of man. His second essay, the *Discourse on the Origins of Inequality*, is more famous than the first, though initially it was less popular. In it Rousseau argued that society had corrupted the natural goodness of man and deprived him of his freedom. Inequality was not natural, he asserted, not inherent in the order of things, but rather a social construction, and as such capable of reform. Although this essay presented a scathing indictment of 18th-century European society and government, it also held out hope that man, through the exercise of his free will, might change that society.

Rousseau completed that argument in his most celebrated work, the *Social Contract*, published in 1762. Through the intervention of a "Legislator," someone like Lycurgus or John Calvin, the false social contract, imposed by the strong upon the weak, could be replaced by a true social contract that would substitute natural liberty for moral, or civil, liberty, and replace natural inequality with moral, or civil, equality. Once achieved, the "general will" (not the rule of the majority, necessarily, but in a more abstract sense the voice of the people, thinking of the good of all) would ensure that government worked for the good of the nation and not for individual interests. This vision of an ideal society exercised a powerful influence on the political ideas of the French revolutionaries.

Voltaire, Montesquieu, and Rousseau represent three of the most important figures in the French Enlightenment, but the single most important publication of the Enlightenment was the *Encyclopedia*, edited by Denis Diderot and Jean le Rond d'Alembert. The *Encyclopedia*, published from 1751 to 1772, numbered some 28 volumes, 17 of text and 11 of illustrations. Initially published openly, in 1759 it encountered the wrath of the censor and thereafter was published abroad and smuggled into France. The aspiration of the project, as Diderot put it, was to gather all of human knowledge and present it to the public and for posterity. By this effort to define all human knowledge, and to make public previously private information (such as the techniques of a master craftsman), Diderot and his collaborators implicitly challenged the prerogative of the absolute monarch and the inherently private nature of corporate, privileged society.

By the 1780s there were some 15,000 copies of the *Encyclopedia* in France. It was an expensive collection (not everyone could afford it), but anyone with intellectual pretensions would have had access to a copy in a library or reading society. By its willingness to challenge authority, to question dogma and tradition, to attack ignorance and intolerance, the *Encyclopedia* epitomized the essence of the Enlightenment and helped form the intellectual climate in which the French Revolution occurred.

By presuming to explain both the natural world and the social order, the *Encyclopedia* challenged both the Catholic Church and the absolute monarchy, which claimed to rule by divine right. But there were currents of reform within the Catholic Church as well. Throughout the 18th century, a Jansenist minority within the French church questioned the authority of the papacy and asserted the importance of church councils in deciding matters of doctrine. When Jansenists became the focus of persecution at mid-century, this fed a movement for reform that resonated both within the Catholic Church and throughout the educated elite of France.

While the secular thought of the Enlightenment and the currents of reform within the Catholic Church may be said to have provided a context for revolution, and the inspiration for many of the political ideas put forward during the 1790s, they cannot be said to have caused the Revolution. Few of the *philosophes*, with the possible exception of Rousseau, could be characterized as advocates of violent revolution. None of them believed that democracy was a viable form of government, and even Rousseau, who described in theory a social contract under which the will of the people would prevail, was skeptical that such a political system would be practical in any European country. For the causes of the French Revolution, it is necessary to consider the social, economic, and political tensions in Old Regime society.

Why did the French Revolution happen? The answer, on the most general level, is that Old Regime government just quit working. There were long-term structural problems that weakened the ability of the monarchy to govern effectively, but there were also short-term crises that exposed an inability to act decisively. Many of the structural causes relate to the economic expansion and social change of the 18th century, which also help to explain why the Enlightenment writers found such a receptive audience in France. The years between 1725 and 1775 were growth years for France. Agricultural productivity rose 25 to 50 percent; commercial trade increased astronomically, by approximately 400 percent; industrial production also increased modestly, led by textile production, up 50 to 75 percent. Demographic growth accompanied this economic expansion—population grew by about 30 percent over the course of the century. Economic prosperity accounts for some of this population growth, but the disappearance of the plague from France after 1720, the absence of a major famine after 1709, and the fact that the century was relatively peaceful should also be noted.

The middle decades of the 18th century, in particular, were a time of prosperity and growth, but they also tended to increase social tensions. The economic growth had been fueled in part by the import of silver from the New World, and this produced inflation, a phenomenon that may be taken for granted today, but one that people of the 18th century viewed with great alarm. Between 1726 and 1789 land rents rose 82 to 98 percent, varying from province to province, while agricultural prices rose only 60 percent. Leases, which tended to be long-term, rose dramatically in the 1770s and 1780s, as landlords recouped their losses from earlier years. The cost of living generally rose 62 percent during this period, while wages rose only 25 percent. Both urban workers (a relatively small proportion of the population) and tenant farmers suffered during this inflationary time.

Merchants and large landowners prospered, overall, and urban centers grew in size and vitality. Urban growth contributed to a rise in literacy over the course of the century. Female literacy rose from 14 percent to 27 percent, male literacy rose from 29 percent to 49 percent, and overall literacy rose from 21 percent to 37 percent. There were 21 universities in France in 1789, secondary schooling was widely available, and virtually every major town boasted its own learned academy, where the educated elite could gather to discuss the latest books and their own research. Without this increased reading public, the ideas of the Enlightenment and the political debates between the *parlements* and the monarchy would have had a much diminished impact.

The monarchy itself was plagued by certain structural problems that contributed to the revolutionary crisis. Louis XIV had been a strong king, who ruled without a prime minister. Under Louis XV and Louis XVI there was considerable ministerial infighting, which both tarnished the image of the monarchy and gave rise to accusations of ministerial despotism. The lack of ministerial cooperation proved catastrophic during the financial crisis of the 1780s. Another problem was the increasing insularity of the monarchy, both because Louis XVI tended to select his ministers from within court circles, and because the king disliked travel. How could a king who refused to travel effectively govern a kingdom as diverse as France? There was also the issue of personal character—neither Louis XV nor Louis XVI were the equal of the Sun King.

A final structural problem lay in the inefficient system of taxation. Certainly it was not a rational system but rather a hodgepodge of direct and indirect taxes, and the widespread perception was that the nobility and clergy did not pay their fair share. The tax farming system meant that the royal treasury never received a large portion of the taxes actually collected. In addition, France had no central bank, so that in times of revenue shortfall the monarchy borrowed money on less than favorable terms. Finally, the royal treasury had no official budget—no one really knew how much the government was collecting or spending. This entire system made it very difficult to respond effectively to the financial crisis that hit in 1786.

In the late 1770s the French monarchy sent both financial and material aid to the American colonies in their struggle for independence from the British crown. Louis XVI's finance minister, Jacques Necker, paid for this aid through temporary taxes and short-term loans, scheduled to fall due in the late 1780s and 1790s. When Necker resigned his post in 1781 he published an accounting of the royal budget, which showed a modest surplus in the treasury. Either Necker misread the situation (a definite possibility, given the lack of a unified accounting system) or he lied, for less than five years later it was clear to his successor, Charles-Alexandre Calonne, that the royal treasury was running a 25 percent deficit. For 1787 Calonne projected that interest on the debt would absorb 50 percent of taxes collected, and that 50 percent of the anticipated tax revenue had already been spent in advance.

The crown could neither borrow further, nor levy new taxes. When word began to circulate that the king and his ministers proposed to tax the Church and the nobility, the Parlement of Paris announced that it would oppose such an action. To break the impasse, Calonne convinced Louis XVI to convene an Assembly of Notables in February 1787. Calonne presented to that Assembly an ambitious agenda for reform, but its privileged members were not interested in conceding reforms in the areas of taxation and justice without receiving increased political power in exchange. The fiscal crisis was exacerbated by an economic slump, and the textile treaty that the French government signed with England in 1786, in the hope of selling more wine on the British market, led to a crisis in the French textile sector and a wave of unemployment. As if these problems were not enough, disaster befell the agricultural sector as well. The year 1788 brought the worst harvest since 1709. Recent efforts to introduce free trade in grain only added to the panic, and grain prices rose relentlessly, reaching their peak in July 1789.

A huge national debt, urban unemployment, crop failure, and famine—all of these, combined with the structural weaknesses and contradictions of the monarchy, forced Louis XVI to convoke the Estates-General for the spring of 1789, a step that made revolution all but inevitable.

THE REVOLUTIONARY DECADE

The Estates-General had not met in France since 1614. No living person could remember the last time that they had convened, nor the forms or procedures by which the delegates should be chosen. This fact alone is one compelling reason why the monarchy in France had come to be thought of as an absolute monarchy in the late 17th and 18th centuries. But now, in the face of crisis, the king could not act on his authority alone. Louis XVI appealed to his subjects, particularly the learned among them, for advice regarding the convocation of the Estates-General. Eventually the Paris Parlement issued an opinion, ruling that the delegates to the Estates-General should be elected as they had been traditionally, by order. Under the pressure of public opinion, they ruled that the number of delegates for the Third Estate should be doubled. But they also ruled that voting in the Estates-General should be by order: one vote for the clergy, one for the aristocracy, and one for the Third Estate, thereby neutralizing the advantage that the Third Estate had seemingly gained by the doubling of their representation. Public opinion in Paris opposed this ruling, as did many of the delegates elected by the Third Estate to the Estates-General. Thus, a stalemate developed at Versailles in the weeks following the opening ceremony on 4 May 1789. The majority of delegates to the two privileged orders, the clergy and the aristocracy, refused to accept voting by head, rather than by order, and the majority of the delegates to the Third Estate refused to accept the alternative.

The stalemate was broken on 17 June 1789, when enough moderate clergy and noblemen joined the Third Estate to declare themselves the National Assembly. When Louis XVI ordered the meeting hall of the Third Estate locked three days later, the rebellious deputies swore the Tennis Court Oath, asserting that wherever they might meet, there the nation was represented. Faced with this dramatic gesture, Louis XVI called on the delegates of all three orders to meet together. Some refused to do so, arguing that this would violate the mandate given them by their constituencies. Advisers close to the king urged him to take measures to counter the revolutionary tide. Royal troops began to gather in the region surrounding Paris, and on 11 July 1789 Louis XVI dismissed Jacques Necker from office. Necker was enormously popular in Paris, and its citizens reacted quickly to the news of his dismissal and the reports of troop mobilization. Neighborhood electoral assemblies reconvened and the citizen militia, soon to be known as the National Guard, prepared to defend the city. On 13 July, Camille Desmoulins exhorted a large crowd gathered in the Palais Royal to join with their friends and neighbors and march on the Bastille. Some

80,000 people filled the streets of Paris the following day, marching first to the Invalides military hospital and then to the Bastille, the ominous royal fortress that loomed over the eastern suburbs of the capital. By day's end the Bastille had fallen and its governor, Bernard-René de Launey, lay dead, along with a number of Swiss Guards and 98 citizens. This marked the first violent upheaval of the Revolution.

Events moved quickly in the following weeks. Had protest and resistance been confined to Paris, the monarchy might have regrouped its forces and suppressed it. But Louis XVI did not have the stomach for that, and political upheaval soon spread across the country. By the end of July a majority of the largest towns and cities in France had experienced municipal revolutions, with new town councils replacing the officials of the Old Regime, and creating National Guards both to control popular violence and to counter the presence of royal garrisons. In late July and early August a rural panic swept across much of France, fueled by rumors that aristocrats were hiring brigands to destroy crops in the field, and this Great Fear politicized the countryside and carried the movement to create National Guards into the smaller towns of the provinces.

The Great Fear also had an impact on the deputies of the National Assembly, who voted on the night of 4 August 1789 to abolish the remnants of feudalism and bring an end to the system of privilege. Three weeks later the National Assembly adopted the Declaration of the Rights of Man and Citizen, asserting the sovereignty of the nation and denouncing many of the abuses of Old Regime government and society. Both documents were presented to the king, who refused initially to sign them. More than a month passed, and in the face of political stalemate and a steady rise in the price of bread, the people of Paris grew restive. In early October news reached Paris of a banquet at Versailles at which the queen's bodyguards insulted both the capital and the National Assembly. On 5 October the women of the central market took matters into their own hands and marched en masse to Versailles. They had an audience with Louis XVI that evening, but dissatisfied with his words, invaded the palace the following morning. No harm was done to the king or his family, but later that day they were escorted back to Paris by the women and the National Guard. After a century and a half, Paris had reclaimed the monarchy, which Louis XIV had removed to Versailles to escape the threat of popular upheaval. Louis XVI now signed both the Declaration of the Rights of Man and Citizen and the decrees adopted on the Night of 4 August.

The events of 1789 were both exhilarating and disturbing. They unleashed an enormous energy in the nation, but also created profound new tensions. The deputies of the National Assembly set about the business of redrawing the map of France, installing new political and administrative structures, creating a new judicial system, and reforming the tax code. The country still faced a fiscal crisis, and to pay the national debt the National Assembly voted to confiscate the land owned by the Catholic Church and sell it at public auction. Having deprived the Church of much of its income (not only by the confiscation of its land, but by abolition of the tithe and other seigneurial dues), the deputies thought it reasonable and fair to pay the clergy out of state funds. As civil servants, however, parish priests and other clergy should be expected to swear a Civil Oath. Most bishops and many priests refused to swear that oath, and the schism that this produced within the Church polarized French society. Many who had supported the secular reforms introduced by the National Assembly could not accept this reform of the Church and turned against the Revolution.

Others, both aristocrats and clergy, simply chose to flee France. As their numbers grew in 1790, revolutionaries became increasingly concerned that these *émigrés* represented a threat to the nation, that they would ally themselves with foreign monarchs and lead armies against the new government. Deputies called on Louis XVI to take stern measures against the *émigrés* and the refractory clergy, but he refused to do so. When the National Assembly voted to grant him only a suspensive veto over legislation, rather than an absolute veto, he feared that his ability to rule had been irretrievably undermined. Urged on by conservative advisers, Louis XVI and his family fled Paris on 21 June 1791 in a failed effort to reach a safe haven abroad. The Flight to Varennes, as it is called, did not topple the monarchy immediately. Louis XVI reluctantly signed the constitution, creating a constitutional monarchy, and elections were called for a new Legislative Assembly, to be composed entirely of men who had not previously held national office.

Seeking to force the king's hand, the Legislative Assembly soon declared war on Austria and Prussia. The war went badly for France and foreign troops pushed deep into French territory. Although the popular movement had been briefly discredited and weakened following the Flight to Varennes, that trend did not persist, and popular societies, most notably the Jacobin and Cordelier clubs, gained membership and influence over the course of 1792. They succeeded in toppling the monarchy in the Paris uprising of 10 August 1792. In the weeks that followed, the war turned in France's favor, emboldening the deputies of yet another national assembly, the National Convention, to declare the first French Republic on 22 September 1792.

The National Convention, elected by universal manhood suffrage, ushered in the most democratic phase of the Revolution, but also the period of the Terror. The collapse of political authority in late August, coupled with panic over reports that the Prussians would soon reach the capital, had resulted in a series of prison massacres in Paris in early September. That violence created an immediate rift in the National Convention between moderates, known as Girondins, and radicals, known as Montagnards (many of them members of the Jacobin club). That rift was apparent in the trial of Louis XVI, which ultimately ended in his conviction for treason and execution on 21 January 1793. Thereafter, the deputies could not agree on a new constitution, and the Girondins grew increasingly wary about the undue influence of Paris on national politics and concerned about the dangers of popular democracy. Supported by yet another insurrection in Paris, on 31 May 1793, the Montagnards purged the Girondin leaders from office and took control of the National Convention in June 1793. By that time, however, the young republic was challenged not only by war abroad (with Spain, Great Britain, and Russia now having joined the coalition), but by armed rebellion within France—the counterrevolutionary uprising in the west known as the Vendée, and the federalist revolts in several major cities that erupted in protest of the expulsion of the Girondins. Faced with these threats, the National Convention vested more and more power in the hands of its executive committee, the Committee of Public Safety, which responded to internal rebellion by resorting to revolutionary terror. The leading figure on the Committee of Public Safety was Maximilien Robespierre.

The Committee of Public Safety was successful in leading France to victory on the battlefield, and in stabilizing the domestic economy and bringing inflation under control, but it could not overcome the contradiction of having imposed revolutionary terror in the name of popular democracy. The escalating cycle of revolutionary justice, symbolized by the guillotine, which in the end claimed nearly 40,000 lives, eventually turned the deputies and the people against Robespierre. He fell from power and was executed on 27 July 1794, 9 Thermidor on the new revolutionary calendar.

Both moderates and radicals had conspired to topple Robespierre from power, but in the months that followed it was the moderates, known as Thermidorians, who secured the reins of power. Former terrorists were brought to justice, the most prominent among them either executed or exiled, and in 1795 the Thermidorians adopted a new constitution, less democratic than that adopted, though never enacted, in 1793 by the Montagnards. Fearing both dictatorship and radical democracy, they restored a property requirement for the vote and created a five-man executive branch, called the Directory. The Directory regime featured two legislative bodies, the Council of Ancients and the Council of Five Hundred. Although the legislative accomplishments of the Directory were not negligible, the regime never succeeded in bringing the war to a close, in restoring the economy to vitality, or in bringing stability to France. The directors undermined public confidence in the regime in successive national elections, purging first royalists and then Jacobins from elected office in a futile effort to strengthen the moderate center. Having alienated much of the populace, the directors eventually turned to a military general, Napoleon Bonaparte, to restore strong leadership to the government. Napoleon seized power in a coup on the 18th Brumaire (10 November 1799), bringing the French Revolution effectively to an end.

LEGACY OF THE FRENCH REVOLUTION

Napoleon was in some regards a faithful heir to the Revolution. Although political and civil liberties were stifled within France, the Napoleonic armies carried the reforms and ideals of the Revolution to much of the rest of Europe, over which the Napoleonic Empire would rule for nearly 15 years. In this fashion the influence of the French Revolution extended well beyond French borders, and the remnants of feudalism disappeared from most of western Europe.

The political ideologies that dominated the 19th and 20th centuries — liberalism, socialism, and communism — all emerged from the French Revolution. The exhilaration of popular democracy, and the excesses of revolutionary terror, have both lived on well beyond the 1790s, inspiring both hope and despair among those who contemplate them. The ideals of 1789—Liberty, Equality, and Fraternity—continue to resonate around the world, even if they continue to be elusive for most of the world's inhabitants. Similarly, the Declaration of the Rights of Man and Citizen stands as a foundation document for the assertion of human rights in the world, and its companion document, the Declaration of the Rights of Woman and Citizen, claims those same rights for women. The French revolutionaries also called for an end to slavery and the slave trade, though Napoleon would undo those reforms. Thus, in studying the men and women of the French Revolution, their aspirations, their achievements, and their failures, we come face to face with our own aspirations and our own struggles.

The Dictionary

– A –

ACADEMIES. All of the royal Academies (the *Académie royale de musique*, the *Académie royale de peinture et sculpture*, the *Académie royale des inscriptions et belles lettres*, and the *Académie française*) were suppressed by the **National Convention** on 8 August 1793. Both **Henri-Baptiste Grégoire** and **Jacques-Louis David** spoke eloquently against the old Academies, denouncing them for their strict hierarchy, contrary to the revolutionary spirit of equality; for their intimate relation to the society of **privilege**, which the **Constituent Assembly** had abolished in 1789; and for their domination by an **aristocracy** of letters, also contrary to the ideals of the Revolution. The National Convention created the **Institut National** in October 1795 to replace the royal Academies.

ACTIVE CITIZEN. Under the terms of the **Constitution of 1791**, French citizens (those over the age of 25) were divided into two categories: active and **passive citizens**. Such a distinction was first decreed on 22 December 1789, and governed electoral procedures from that date until the fall of 1792. Active citizens were defined as those adult males, over 25 years of age, who had been resident in their canton for at least one year, were not employed in domestic service, were not bankrupt or insolvent, and who paid a direct tax equal to at least three days' wages. Only active citizens could vote in local and national elections. The percentage of active citizens varied from one city to another, from one region to another, but nationally approximately 61 percent of adult males were classified as active citizens. A decree of 12 June 1790 made status as an active citizen a prerequisite for membership in the **National Guard**. The distinction between active and passive citizens was the focus of heated debate within the **Constituent Assembly**, and **Maximilien Robespierre** was prominent among the minority of deputies who argued that it was in contradiction with the **Declaration of the Rights of Man and Citizen**. After the toppling of the monarchy, on 10 August 1792, the distinction was abolished, and universal manhood suffrage prevailed until the adoption of the **Constitution of 1795**.

AGENTS NATIONAUX. In the aftermath of the **federalist revolt**, during which a number of **departmental administrations** rebelled against the national government, the **National Convention** passed the **Law of 14 Frimaire** (4 December 1793), which reformed some of the institutions of local government. The law reduced the authority of departmental administrations, and made district administrations more prominent. The elected position of *procureur* was abolished at each of the three levels of local administration, and at the municipal and district levels the position of *agent national* was created. Initially, the *agents nationaux* were to be appointed from the ranks of former *procureurs* and *procureurs-syndics*, but in those cases where the revolutionary zeal of those officials was insufficient to the task, they were to be replaced at the discretion of **representatives on mission**. The *agents nationaux* were responsible for supervising the implementation of revolutionary legislation. Those at the municipal level were to report to the district councils, and the district *agents nationaux* were to report directly to the **Committee of Public Safety** once every 10 days. In this fashion, the authority of centralized government was strengthened. Following **Thermidor**, the National Convention made an effort to purge **Jacobins** from these positions, and on 17 April 1795 the positions were abolished.

AGRARIAN LAW. The agrarian law, or *loi agraire*, is a term drawn from Roman history meant to designate any scheme calling for the radical redistribution of land with the aim of achieving the Revolutionary ideal of equality among the peasantry. Such demands did sometimes emerge from the peasantry itself, as in Picardy, but the charge of advocating the agrarian law was also an epithet hurled at the most radical revolutionaries by their conservative opponents. Thus, **Jacques Roux** was accused of advocating the agrarian law in late 1793, and the same was also assumed to be true of the **Conspiracy of Equals**, led by **Gracchus Babeuf**. The Law of 18 March 1793 made advocacy of the agrarian law a capital offense. Some historians have characterized the **Ventôse Decrees** of early March 1794 as tending toward a kind of agrarian socialism, but these laws were never implemented.

AIGUILLON, ARMAND-DÉSIRÉ DUPLESSIS-RICHELIEU (1761–1800). The Duc d'Aiguillon inherited the title of his father, who had served Louis XV as foreign secretary and as royal governor of Brittany. Armand-Désiré served in the light cavalry of the king's royal guard before assuming the rank of colonel in the Royal-Pologne cavalry regiment in 1788. He detested **Marie Antoinette**, however, whom he blamed for removing his father from official position, and had no confidence in the ability of **Louis XVI** to lead France out of its crisis. After Louis XVI himself, the Duc d'Aiguillon was the second wealthiest man in the kingdom.

Aiguillon represented the **aristocracy** of Agen at the **Estates-General**. He sat among the liberal nobility, and is best known for being the second speaker to rise, after **Louis-Marie Noailles**, on the **Night of 4 August**, to renounce his **seigneurial dues**. The gesture was all the more significant in his case, given his enormous land holdings. Aiguillon did insist that there should be some indemnity paid to seigneurial lords, since the dues were after all a form of property, but he suggested that the indemnity be quite modest. He was among the leaders of the **Breton club**, favored a single chamber for the legislature, and opposed an absolute veto for the king. For all of this he was widely reviled by conservative aristocrats, and his enemies accused him of supporting, if not indeed participating in, the march to **Versailles** during the **October Days**.

Aiguillon shifted toward the center after the king's flight to **Varennes** in June 1791, and returned to military duty after the **Constituent Assembly** dissolved, serving as marshal in the Army of the Rhine. In the days following the **uprising of 10 August 1792**, he was denounced as a supporter of **Marie-Joseph-Motier Lafayette** and went into exile. Aiguillon went first to London, but then lived in Germany with his friends the **Lameth** brothers, while staying aloof from *émigré* politics. After **Brumaire** his name was removed from the lists of *émigrés*, and he was preparing to return to France when he died in Hamburg.

AMAR, JEAN-PIERRE-ANDRÉ (1755–1816). Amar was born in Grenoble, where his father was a *directeur de la monnaie*. He studied law, became an *avocat* before the Parlement of Grenoble, and in 1786 secured a position as *trésorier du bureau des Finances* in that same city. Amar served on the Grenoble district administration between 1790 and 1792, and was elected in that year to the **National Convention** from the Isère. Amar sat with the **Montagnards**, voted for death in the trial of **Louis XVI**, and joined the **Cordelier club**. In June 1793 he was elected to the **Committee for General Security**, and served for more than a year as one of that body's most influential members. He wrote the indictment of the proscribed **Girondin** deputies in October 1793, and in 1794 drew up the charges against **François Chabot**, Claude Basire, and **Philippe Fabre d'Eglantine**. In April 1794 he presided over the Convention when the honors of the **Panthéon** were accorded to the remains of **Jean-Jacques Rousseau**. Amar supported the coup of 9 **Thermidor** but played no public role in those events, and found himself under attack as a **Terrorist** shortly thereafter. He was finally arrested in April 1795, but amnestied at the end of the year when the National Convention dissolved. Amar was implicated in the **Conspiracy of Equals**, led by **Gracchus Babeuf**, but acquitted by the High Court at Vendôme, after which he withdrew from public life and immersed himself in mysticism.

APPEL AU PEUPLE. The "appeal to the people" refers, in general terms, to any call for a popular referendum to decide an important issue, as in the 1793 referendum on the proposed constitution. More specifically, it refers to the **Girondin** proposal during the trial of **Louis XVI** that the king's sentence be determined by an *appel au peuple*. The debate over the *appel au peuple* was the most important and sustained confrontation between Girondins and **Montagnards** during the king's trial. A number of deputies gave lengthy and impassioned speeches, most notably **Pierre-Victurnien Vergniaud** and **Maximilien Robespierre**. The Girondins argued that only by such a referendum could the **sovereignty** of the people be given expression on this most important issue. The Montagnards countered that the people had already spoken in the **uprising of 10 August 1792** that had toppled the monarchy, and that the Girondin proposal was an attack on **Paris** and a transparent effort to save the life of the king. On 15 January 1793 the proposal was decisively defeated, and two days later Louis XVI was sentenced to death by a much narrower margin.

ARISTOCRACY. In common usage the term is used interchangeably with nobility. The aristocracy, some 250,000 individuals, constituted the Second Estate in Old Regime society. The oldest aristocratic families, sometimes referred to as the sword nobility, traced their lineages back to the Middle Ages and owed their status to service performed for the king on the field of battle. From the early 17th century onward, a second category of aristocracy, sometimes referred to as the robe nobility, came into existence by virtue of service in the royal bureaucracy or judiciary. The **privileges** enjoyed by the aristocracy were widely attacked in the *cahiers de doléances* of the **Third Estate**, and were symbolically abolished on the **Night of 4 August** (1789). Aristocratic privilege was systematically dismantled in subsequent legislation, and on 23 June 1790 the aristocracy/nobility was itself formally abolished. Now stripped of their noble titles, aristocrats came to be referred to as *ci-devants*. Many soon chose to join the growing ranks of the *émigrés*, some were executed during the **Terror** simply because they had once been aristocrats, while others weathered the revolutionary storm relatively unscathed. The term *aristocrate*, however, came to have a broader meaning in the years following 1790, taking on a moral or political sense. It came to refer to anyone who opposed the Revolution, or to those who tried to exercise an unwarranted dominance over others.

ARMÉES RÉVOLUTIONNAIRES. The *armées révolutionnaires*, or "people's armies," were mainly organized in the fall of 1793 to enforce the policies of the **Terror** in the provinces. They were not associated with the national army, but were created in **Paris** at the initiative of **popular societies** or representatives in accordance with a law drafted by the **National Convention** on 5 September 1793. This law was itself a response to the Parisian **uprising of 4–5 September 1793**, in which the **sans-culottes** demanded the extension of price controls to other staple goods in addition to grain, and the declaration of terror as "the order of the day." The historian Richard Cobb identified some 56 *armées révolutionnaires* in the provinces in addition to a Parisian army. They were generally small forces, often numbering less than a hundred men, although the Parisian army may have been as large as 6,000 and the people's army of the department of the Lot, in southwestern France, numbered approximately 3,200. Their membership was drawn principally from the ranks of the common people, and they were paid a generous daily wage.

The chief mission of these armies was to see that the **maximum** was enforced, and that urban food markets and military commissaries were adequately supplied. They also played a role in the **deChristianization** campaign launched in the winter of 1793–94. The Parisian army, under the command of **Charles-Philippe Ronsin**, participated in the campaign against the **Vendée** rebellion, as well as in the repression of the **federalist revolt** in **Lyon**. Their supporters viewed the *armées révolutionnaires* as an expression of direct democracy, while their critics were alarmed by their sometimes violent extremism and anarchic tendencies. When revolutionary government was reorganized by the **law of 14 Frimaire** (4 December 1793), the people's armies were abolished. It would be some months, however, before the last of them were disbanded.

ASSEMBLY OF NOTABLES. There were actually two Assemblies of Notables (22 February to 25 May 1787, and 6 November to 12 December 1788), convened by **Louis XVI** to address the intractable fiscal crisis that confronted the monarchy at the end of the Old Regime. The first Assembly of Notables (*Assemblée des Notables*) gathered under the direction of **Charles-Alexandre Calonne**, the controller-general of the crown. There were 144 delegates, including the princes of the blood, archbishops and bishops, a number of prominent nobles, judges from the parlements, royal officials, members of provincial assemblies, and mayors of several large towns. Nearly all were members of the **aristocracy**.

Calonne proposed to the Assembly a series of fundamental reforms, including the creation of provincial assemblies, conversion of the *corvée* (forced labor service) to a tax payment, liberalization of the grain trade, and the introduction of a new land tax to be borne equally by all landowners, whether commoner, noble, or **clergy**. When the notables balked at these proposals, Calonne appealed to the public for support, which infuriated the Assembly. In consequence, Calonne was dismissed by the king on 7 April and replaced by **Etienne-Charles Loménie de Brienne**. Loménie modified the proposals slightly, and ultimately succeeded in persuading the Assembly to adopt many of them. But the notables stood firm in their opposition to the land tax, which they insisted could only be approved by an **Estates-General**.

After **Jacques Necker** persuaded the king to convene the Estates-General in August 1788, the second Assembly of Notables was called to rule on its composition. The second Assembly numbered 147 delegates, composed essentially in the same manner as the first. It took a very traditional position, ruling that representation should be equal for each of the three estates, that each estate should meet separately, and that each should have one vote. The ruling was viewed by commoners as a defense of elite **privilege**, and set off a spirited pamphlet debate in the first months of 1789.

ASSIGNATS. First issued in December 1789 as a form of government bond, guaranteed by land confiscated from the Catholic Church, by late 1790 the *assignats* had effectively become a circulating paper currency. Initially, 400,000,000 *livres* of *assignats* were issued to creditors of the state, in 1,000 *livre* denominations, to be exchanged for *biens nationaux* of equal value or redeemed with the state at 5 percent interest. In this fashion, both the national debt and the *assignats* themselves were to be liquidated. In the midst of political upheaval, however, neither the economy nor royal tax revenue improved as quickly as the deputies of the **Constituent Assembly** had hoped, and in the fall of 1790 **Gabriel-Honoré Mirabeau** proposed that an additional 400,000,000 *livres* of *assignats* be issued. In subsequent years additional *assignats* were issued, so that by January 1793 some 2.3 billion *assignats* were in circulation. They were also issued in increasingly smaller denominations: 50 *livres* in October 1790, 5 *livres* in May 1791, 10 *sous* in January 1792. As a result, the *assignats* depreciated rapidly in value, and people began to hoard metallic currency. In January 1791 a 100 *livres* note was valued at 91; in January 1792 at 72; in January 1793 at 51, and in July 1793 at 23. Only during the year of the **Terror** was that rapid inflation brought temporarily under control. It returned with a vengeance under the **Directory**, however, and in December 1795 the **Council of Five Hundred** introduced legislation to gradually withdraw the *assignats* from circulation. They were completely abolished in May 1797.

– B –

BABEUF, FRANÇOIS-NOËL (1760–1797). Babeuf was the son of a collector of the salt tax, formerly a soldier, who abandoned his family to flee debts. Growing up in poverty, Babeuf was self-taught and began work at the age of 14, first as a laborer on the Picardy canal, and then as a *commissaire à terrier*, responsible for verifying the dues and duties owed to seigneurial landowners. Babeuf spent time in **Paris** early in the Revolution, but returned to Roye, in Picardy, where he published a newspaper, the *Correspondant Picard*, and organized popular resistance to the collection of **seigneurial dues**. He served as both a district and a departmental administrator in the Somme between 1791 and 1793, but did not get on with his colleagues and faced numerous charges of libel for his newspaper writings (a point of pride, it seems, for Babeuf).

Following several acquittals, and a few short stints behind bars, Babeuf spent eight months in prison between November 1793 and July 1794. After his release from prison and the fall of **Maximilien Robespierre**, Babeuf began publication of a new newspaper that shortly became known as the *Tribun du Peuple*. At about this same time he took the first name of Gracchus, after the Gracchi brothers, both of them Tribunes who had championed the cause of the plebeians and called for land reform under the Roman Republic. As the **Thermidorian** reaction set in, Babeuf grew more and more critical of the government and soon found himself incarcerated once again, this time in Arras. There he met **Filippo Michele Buonarroti** and encountered the writings of the abbé Morelly, among other **Enlightenment** figures. He was released in October 1795 and returned to Paris to resume publication of the *Tribun du Peuple*. The newspaper had a modest, but national, circulation and appealed in particular to former **Jacobins** and the widows of former Jacobins killed during the **White Terror**. Babeuf also helped to found the new **Panthéon club**, which attracted a number of former *Conventionnels*, including **Robert Lindet** and **Jean-Pierre Amar**.

When police closed down the Panthéon club, Babeuf took his movement underground in what eventually came to be known as the **Conspiracy of Equals**. Babeuf never attracted a broad popular following in Paris, but the group did have a vague plan to overthrow the **Directory**, and for this it was denounced in May 1796 by a police spy who had infiltrated the organization. **Lazare Carnot** chose to prosecute the case aggressively, and 65 conspirators were brought to trial before the High Court of Vendôme in early 1797. Only Babeuf and Augustin Darthé were sentenced to death. Seven others, including Buonarroti, were sentenced to deportation, while 56 were acquitted. Babeuf spoke eloquently in his own defense, citing **Rousseau**, Diderot, Mably, and Morelly from memory. His insistence that the ideals of 1789 had been abandoned and that political equality could only be realized in a society in which social and economic equality had also been achieved, have earned for Babeuf a reputation as the first European communist.

BAGARRE DE NÎMES. The *bagarre*, or brawl, of Nîmes was a violent upheaval pitting Catholics against **Protestants** in the eighth largest city of France in June 1790. It is indicative of the tension that still persisted between Catholics and Protestants in many parts of France on the eve of the Revolution, and of the degree to which that hostility often colored revolutionary politics. The region around Nîmes was a Huguenot stronghold in the 17th century, prior to the 1685 revocation of the Edict of Nantes, which had accorded toleration to Protestants since 1598. In 1787 **Louis XVI** issued a new **Edict of Toleration**, once again granting civil rights to Protestants, but in 1789 it remained an open question whether Protestants were eligible for election to the **Estates-General** or to other local administrative bodies created later that year. The question was decided in favor of Protestants, and a Protestant pastor, **Jean-Paul Rabaut Saint-Etienne**, was the first deputy elected by the **Third Estate** of Nîmes.

For Nîmes Protestants, then, the Revolution promised an improvement in their status, and increased opportunities to participate in public life, which prominent Catholic families in the region viewed as a threatening development. In Nîmes, the opposition between royalists and revolutionaries was accentuated by a Catholic/Protestant antipathy. The creation of **National Guard** companies and the election of local administrations became arenas for both political and religious contestation. In June 1790 that contestation erupted into violence as electors gathered in Nîmes to elect the first **departmental administration**. Protestant guardsmen poured into Nîmes by the thousands, and in the end between 200 and 300 Catholics were massacred, making the *bagarre* the single most violent incident in France between 1789 and 1791. As a result, local Protestants gained control of departmental politics, while devout Catholics in the region turned toward counterrevolutionary movements.

BAILLY, JEAN-SYLVAIN (1736–1793). Bailly was a celebrated literary figure and scientist. He published his first tragedies at the age of 16, and in 1783 his five-volume *History of Astronomy* secured his election to the *Académie Française*. His membership in the French Academy of Science dated from 1763. Bailly presided over the electoral assembly of his district in 1789, and represented the **Third Estate** at the **Estates-General**. He was elected president of the National Assembly on the day of its declaration, 17 June, and on 20 June was the first deputy to swear the **Tennis Court Oath**. On 15 July he was elected the first mayor of **Paris**, and two days later received **King Louis XVI** at the Hôtel de Ville, presenting the king with a tricolor **cockade**, the revolutionary symbol of the new unity between Paris and the Bourbon monarchy. He addressed the crowd with these famous words: "Whereas Henri IV conquered his people, here it is the people who have reconquered their king."

Bailly was an enormously popular mayor of Paris, but exactly two years to the day after his triumphal reception of the king before the Hôtel de Ville that popularity was shattered by the massacre on the **Champ de Mars**. Faced with a rebellious crowd gathering signatures for a petition to depose the king, Bailly declared martial law. Dozens of demonstrators were killed when General **Lafayette** ordered the **National Guard** to open fire. In the face of growing public criticism, Bailly resigned as mayor in November and left Paris for Nantes. He lived there quietly until 10 September 1793, when he was arrested shortly after the declaration of the first **Law of Suspects**. Bailly testified at the trial of **Marie Antoinette**, and in November came to trial himself, charged with opposing the will of the people. He was found guilty and executed on 12 November 1793.

BARA, JOSEPH (1779–1793). Bara was a revolutionary martyr, immortalized in the unfinished painting of **Jacques-Louis David**. At the age of 13 Bara joined the republican volunteers sent to combat the rebels of the **Vendée**. Caught in an ambush, Bara and his fellows were ordered by the rebels to yell out "Long live the King." When Bara responded, "Long live the Republic," he was cut down in a hail of bullets. The **National Convention** decreed that Bara be accorded the Honors of the **Panthéon**, and ordered that his picture be sent to all primary schools, as a lesson to the students about republican duty. A virtual cult of Bara grew up, featuring poems, plays, and patriotic hymns, including **Marie-Joseph Chénier's** *Chant du Départ*.

BARBAROUX, CHARLES-JEAN-MARIE (1767–1794). Barbaroux's father was a **Marseille** merchant who died in Guadeloupe, where he had gone to try to recoup his fortune. Charles studied physics at an Oratorien school, before going on to study law in Aix-en-Provence. After completing his law degree he went to **Paris**, where he took a course in optics from **Jean-Paul Marat**. Barbaroux returned to Marseille on the eve of the Revolution, and quickly emerged as one of the city's young firebrands. He was among the founders of the Marseille **Jacobin club**, and in the aftermath of violent protests in 1789 ardently defended local patriots against their detractors. In 1790 he was elected secretary of the Marseille municipal council, a significant post for one so young.

Early in 1792 the council sent him as a special envoy to report on recent troubles in Arles to the **Legislative Assembly**. He remained in Paris for some months, attending Jacobin club meetings and frequenting the home of **Jean-Marie** and **Manon Roland**. In July 1792 it was Barbaroux who summoned the Marseille volunteers to Paris to lead the charge against the **Tuileries palace** on 10 August. Barbaroux was elected to the **National Convention** from the Bouches-du-Rhône. He soon abandoned the Jacobin club, however, and joined Roland and the **Girondins** in their attacks on the **Montagnards**. In the aftermath of the **September Massacres,** he once again called on Marseille volunteers to march to Paris, although this time not to join the militant **sans-culottes**, but rather to protect the deputies of the Convention from them. He voted for death in the trial of **Louis XVI**, but joined the Girondins in calling for an *appel au peuple* to decide the king's fate. In April 1793 he supported the indictment of Marat, which secured his spot among the 29 deputies proscribed on 2 June. Barbaroux fled to **Caen** with a number of other deputies, and from that haven issued an appeal to his constituents calling for rebellion against Paris. In that pamphlet he called for the creation of a "republic of the Midi," lending credence to the charge of **federalism** leveled against those departments that rose in revolt. After the revolt collapsed, Barbaroux fled, via Brittany, to **Bordeaux**, where he went into hiding with **Jérome Pétion** and **François Buzot**. When the three were discovered in June 1794, Pétion and Buzot committed suicide, while Barbaroux went to the **guillotine** in Bordeaux.

BARÈRE, BERTRAND (1755–1841). Barère was among the original members of the **Committee of Public Safety**. Born in Tarbes, near the Pyrenees, he studied law in **Toulouse** and in 1775 became an *avocat* before the Parlement of Toulouse. Like many lawyers of the day, he also pursued a literary career. Barère was elected to the **Estates-General** from Bigorre as a deputy for the **Third Estate**. He was initially a constitutional monarchist, and from April 1789 to October 1791 published a newspaper, *Le Point du Jour*. He was elected to the **National Convention** in 1792 from the Hautes-Pyrénées. Barère was responsible on the Committee of Public Safety for foreign affairs, military affairs, and the navy. Although he participated in the coup of 9 **Thermidor** that ousted **Maximilien Robespierre**, Barère was later denounced by the **Thermidorians** and tried along with **Jacques-Nicolas Billaud-Varenne** and **Jean-Marie Collot d'Herbois**. Sentenced to deportation, he escaped and hid in the countryside near **Bordeaux**. He was elected to the Chamber of Deputies during the Hundred Days and exiled as a regicide in 1816.

BARNAVE, ANTOINE-PIERRE-JOSEPH-MARIE (1761–1793). Barnave was born into a **Protestant** family in Grenoble, where his father was a *procureur au Parlement*. Antoine followed his father's footsteps in the study of law and obtained a position as *avocat au Parlement*, also in Grenoble. He was elected to the **Estates-General** by the **Third Estate** of Grenoble, and when **Trophime-Gérard Lally-**

Tollendal condemned the 18 July killings of Louis Bertier de Sauvigny and Joseph Foulon by an angry crowd, it was Barnave who uttered the famous reply, "Was their blood, then, so pure?"

Barnave was a dominant figure in the **Constituent Assembly** in 1790, along with **Adrien Duport** and the **Lameth** brothers, and played an important role in the **Jacobin club** during that period as well. He supported the creation of a strong constitutional monarchy, and was denounced by deputies on the left for his support of the slaveholding planters of **Saint-Domingue**. After the king's flight to **Varennes**, Barnave was sent along with **Jérome Pétion** to escort the royal family back to **Paris**. His detractors accused him of cultivating a friendship with the queen during that journey, an accusation later substantiated by the discovery that he remained in correspondence with **Marie Antoinette** for the next five months. In one of his final speeches before the Constituent Assembly, he defended the principle of royal inviolability.

When the Constituent Assembly dissolved, Barnave returned to Grenoble, where he was arrested on 19 August 1792 after the discovery of incriminating documents in the royal chambers. He remained in prison in Grenoble for 15 months, before being returned to Paris in November 1793 for trial and execution.

BARRAS, PAUL-FRANÇOIS-JEAN-NICOLAS (1755–1829). Barras was born into an old noble family in southeastern France. He was educated by nuns, and at the age of 16 joined the Regiment of Languedoc, with which he embarked for Pondichéry in 1776. He was shipwrecked en route, however, and arrived in 1777 just in time to see the French forces defeated by the British. He returned to France in 1780, having attained the rank of lieutenant. In 1783 he resigned his military commission, and led a rather shiftless life in **Paris** for the next six years. Barras was present at the storming of the **Bastille**, but not as a participant. He returned to Provence late in 1789 and was elected to the **departmental administration** of the Var.

In 1792 Barras was sent from the Var as a deputy to the **National Convention**. He sat with the **Montagnards**, voted for death in the trial of **Louis XVI**, and in the spring of 1793 was sent on a recruitment mission to the southeast with **Louis-Stanislas Fréron**. The two remained in the region for some months, eventually overseeing the repression of the **federalist revolt** in **Marseille**, and the recapture of **Toulon** from the British at the end of the year. Barras and Fréron were criticized by some for the harsh reprisals that they ordered against the rebels, but they defended themselves successfully against those charges. In Toulon Barras met the young **Napoleon Bonaparte**, and ordered his promotion to the rank of captain.

When Barras returned to Paris in early 1794 he received a cool reception from the **Committee of Public Safety**. He appears not to have played a substantial role in the conspiracy against **Maximilien Robespierre**, but was named commander of Parisian forces on 9 **Thermidor**, and as such led the troops that ultimately apprehended Robespierre and the others at the Hôtel de Ville. Barras would exercise a similar role, alongside General Bonaparte, in the repression of the **Vendémiaire uprising** in 1795. He would subsequently be elected to the **Council of Five Hundred**, and then was elected the last of the five directors. Barras was the only one of the directors to hold that post throughout the life of the regime. He was by then a man of great wealth, which he displayed ostentatiously at lavish banquets at his château at Grosbois. He cultivated military suppliers, such as Gabriel Ouvrard, and arranged sexual liaisons to secure his power and influence (**Josephine de Beauharnais** had been his mistress before marrying Napoleon).

Barras orchestrated the **Fructidor coup** in 1797, along with his fellow directors **Jean-François Reubell** and **Louis La Révellière**, but later claimed to have opposed the **Floréal coup** against the Jacobins in 1798. As the **Directory** regime fell into crisis, Barras entered into negotiations with **Louis XVIII** regarding a possible restoration of the monarchy, but those overtures came to nothing. He was curiously inactive on the eve of **Brumaire**, and simply tendered his resignation when Napoleon seized power. Barras was in and out of exile over the next 15 years, often persecuted by his former protégé.

BASTILLE. The Bastille was a royal fortress and prison on the eastern edge of **Paris**, which stood as the most potent symbol of monarchical despotism at the end of the Old Regime. Built in 1370, it functioned both as a garrison, to control the potentially unruly populace of the *faubourg* **Saint-Antoine**, and as a royal prison, although in 1789 it held only seven prisoners. Over the course of the century, however, its inmates had included such literary luminaries as **Voltaire**, Denis Diderot, and **Pierre-Augustin Caron de Beaumarchais**, and the celebrity of its victims enhanced the darkness of the Bastille's reputation.

The storming of the Bastille, on 14 July 1789, was the first great *journée* of the Revolution. The instigating event was the dismissal of **Jacques Necker**, on 11 July, but Parisians were also troubled by reports that royal troops were gathering in the environs of the city. On 12 July, a Sunday, **Camille Desmoulins** exhorted a crowd in the **Palais Royal** to take action, and on the following day the electors of Paris voted to create a bourgeois militia of some 48,000 men. The first pressing question was how to arm such a militia. Thus, on 14 July a large crowd marched first to the **Invalides** military hospital, where guns could be found, and then to the Bastille, in the hope of finding powder and ammunition. The governor of the Bastille, Bernard-René de Launey (who was actually born at the Bastille, and whose father had been governor before him), invited delegates of the crowd inside the fortress to negotiate, ordering the **Swiss guards** not to fire on the crowd gathered outside. Negotiations dragged on, however, and the crowd soon numbered some 80,000. Some reports suggested that de Launey lost his nerve and changed his orders, but at any rate shots were fired in the early afternoon and the crowd laid siege to the fortress, soon aided by four cannons brought from the Invalides. At 5:00 p.m. de Launey capitulated, fearful that the garrison would be massacred. As it was, six defenders of the Bastille died in the battle, and 98 of the besiegers were killed. De Launey was arrested, but while en route to city hall he was seized by the crowd and killed.

Three days later **Louis XVI** traveled to Paris from **Versailles** to accept the revolutionary **cockade** and recognize the new municipal authorities, thereby acknowledging the people's victory. Necker was soon restored to office, and the **Constituent Assembly** commissioned **Pierre-François Palloy** to demolish the old fortress. 14 July 1789 came to mark the beginning of the French Revolution, and *Bastille Day* is today the French national holiday.

BATZ, JEAN-PIERRE (1760–1822). Baron de Batz, born into a noble family, was a financier under the Old Regime, credited with creating the first life insurance company in France. He was a delegate for the aristocracy to the **Estates-General**, where he occupied himself principally with financial matters, in particular expressing strong opposition to the creation of *assignats* as a means toward solving the national debt. The Baron left France after the dissolution of the **Constituent Assembly**, but returned during the trial of **Louis XVI** and allegedly conspired with the Spanish ambassador to bribe deputies to vote for acquittal. He also made plans, never implemented, to rescue the king on his route to the scaffold. Batz was implicated, along with **François Chabot** and **Philippe Fabre d'Eglantine**, in the financial scandal of the East India Company in early 1794, but managed to elude arrest. He was briefly imprisoned, however, for his role in the royalist uprising of **Vendémiaire** 1795. He escaped from jail and lived quietly thereafter. Under the Restoration, Batz was accorded the rank of *maréchal de camp* and decorated with the Cross of Saint Louis.

BAUDOT, MARC-ANTOINE (1765–1837). Baudot, the son of a tenant-farmer employed on a noble estate, received a medical education and began a career as a doctor in Charolles before the Revolution. He was elected as a substitute deputy to the **Legislative Assembly** from the Saône-et-Loire, and took up his seat in July 1792. Two months later that same department elected him to the **National Convention**. Baudot sat with the **Montagnards**, was close to **Georges Danton**, and voted for death in the trial of **Louis XVI**. He went frequently on mission to the departments and the armies in 1793–94. As an advocate for the poor, and an ardent **deChristianizer** as well as an enemy of the **aristocracy**, Baudot's missions tended to arouse controversy. Sent to **Bordeaux** along with **Claude Ysabeau** in August 1793, during the **federalist revolt**, the two found themselves treated rather roughly and run out of town. In May 1795 the citizens of Strasbourg denounced Baudot for excesses committed while on mission to that city in 1794, charges which he evaded by fleeing to Venice until being amnestied later that year. It should be noted, however, that during that 1794 mission to the Army of the Rhine, Baudot participated valiantly in several battles, an unusual act for a deputy on mission. Baudot took a post in the Ministry of War in July 1799, but resigned after the **Brumaire** coup and held no position under the Empire. He was exiled as a regicide in 1816.

BEAUHARNAIS, JOSEPHINE DE (1763–1814). Josephine de Beauharnais was the only French woman ever to hold the title of Empress of France. She was born Marie-Josephe-Rose de Tacher de la Pagerie, on the isle of Martinique, the daughter of an aristocratic sugar planter. In 1779 she married Alexandre, Vicomte de Beauharnais, and they had two children, Eugène and Hortense, before formally separating in the mid-1780s. The Revolution brought them back together again, if only briefly. Alexandre was arrested in March 1794, charged with treason, and sent to the **guillotine** on 24 July, a fate that Josephine narrowly escaped, although she was also arrested.

Social life in **Paris** revived after the **Terror**, and Josephine soon met **Napoleon Bonaparte** at the salon of Madame **Tallien**. They were married on 9 March 1796, two days before Napoleon left for the Army of Italy. While Napoleon was away at war, Josephine kept the company of **Paul Barras**, her former lover, and perhaps others, but by all accounts Napoleon loved her deeply, and their marriage was a happy one while they were together. At his own coronation as emperor on 2 December 1804, Napoleon crowned Josephine as empress of France. The couple failed to have a son, however, and in January 1810 the marriage ended in divorce. Josephine retired to her estate at Malmaison, west of Paris, but continued to have an indirect influence on imperial affairs. Her son, Eugène, became Viceroy of Italy and her daughter, Hortense, married Napoleon's brother, Louis, and became Queen of Holland.

BEAUMARCHAIS, PIERRE-AUGUSTIN CARON DE (1732–1799).
Beaumarchais was born the son of a **Paris** watchmaker, a trade that he pursued himself with some success early in his life. He taught music to the daughters of Louis XV, married well, and in the 1760s entered the world of finance and overseas trade. The death of a close friend, Joseph Pâris-Duverney, landed Beaumarchais in debtor's court in the early 1770s, and in the face of his legal troubles he published a series of *mémoires judiciaires*, which became his first literary successes and placed him at the center of several *causes célèbres* over the course of the following decade.

Beaumarchais served both Louis XV and **Louis XVI** as a secret agent in foreign affairs, and independently sold arms to American colonists during the American War of Independence. He is best known for his two plays, *Le Barbier de Seville* (1775) and *Le Mariage de Figaro* (1784). The first enjoyed considerable success on the stage of the Comédie Française, but the second was not performed for several years due to the opposition of the king and queen, who were displeased by the play's pointed barbs directed against the **aristocracy**. This censorship only increased the public's anticipation, and the play was an enormous success when first performed at **Versailles**. Aristocrats laughed heartily at their own pillorying, but while some have seen in this play a first act of the Revolution, it must be observed that by play's end the social hierarchy has been restored and the main characters all occupy their proper places.

Beaumarchais also edited an edition of the collected works of **Voltaire**. He continued to participate in the arms trade during the early years of the Revolution, and was briefly arrested just on the eve of the **September Massacres**. Friends helped to secure his release, and he spent the next three years as an *émigré* in London and Germany. Beaumarchais returned to France under the **Directory**, and died in Paris six months before **Napoleon Bonaparte** came to power.

BELGIUM. The Austrian Low Countries, known today as Belgium, were the possession of the Hapsburg monarchy until 1792. In the last decades of the 18th century, however, the region was much influenced by the ideas of the **Enlightenment** and the American War of Independence. A movement for reform and independence developed among Belgians, but was repressed by Emperor Joseph II of Austria. The leader of the Belgian patriots was **Jean-François Vonck**. After 1789, Vonck and his supporters looked for assistance from revolutionaries in France.

With the declaration of war between France and Austria in April 1792, the Belgian provinces became a key battleground, and by the end of the year French troops had occupied much of Belgium. The situation was complicated, however. French was spoken in the southern portion of Belgium, while in other parts of the country Flemish and Dutch were dominant. General **Charles Dumouriez**, commander of the French forces, was a staunch advocate of Belgian independence, but many of the deputies in the **National Convention** favored annexation of Belgium. Belgians were divided on this issue, too, though scattered plebiscites in the spring of 1793 tended to support annexation. Austria temporarily retook Belgium with the treason of Dumouriez in April 1793, but French armies regained the advantage and in 1795 nine new departments were created out of an enlarged Belgian territory. This remained the situation until the fall of **Napoleon Bonaparte**. At the Congress of Vienna, in 1815, the Belgian provinces were restored to Austria, and in 1830 Belgium gained its independence.

BERGASSE, NICOLAS (1750–1832). Bergasse was the son of a wealthy **Lyon** merchant. After studying law he became a prominent *avocat* in **Paris**, where he frequented the salon of Claude Helvétius and publicized the theories of Franz Mesmer. From 1786 to 1788, Bergasse represented the husband in the celebrated Kornmann case, one of the most notorious of the *causes célèbres* of the late Old Regime. Although he lost the case, Bergasse's brilliant and eloquent defense attracted enormous public attention (the playwright **Pierre-Augustin Caron de Beaumarchais** was implicated as a suspected lover of Kornmann's wife), and seemingly challenged not only the Old Regime legal system, but monarchical despotism as well.

Bergasse was elected to the **Estates-General** by the **Third Estate** of Lyon, and adopted a very conservative position on the constitutional committee, opposing the **Declaration of the Rights of Man and Citizen**. He resigned from the committee in September 1789, and left the Assembly after the **October Days**. In 1790 he lobbied against the sale of Church lands and the creation of *assignats*, and after the flight to **Varennes** became a legal adviser to **Louis XVI**, even drafting a monarchical constitution in July 1792. When this became known, following 10 August, Bergasse went into hiding. He was arrested near the Spanish border in January 1794, but managed to delay his return to Paris until after **Thermidor**, thereby avoiding trial and almost certain execution. He retired from public life thereafter.

BERGEOING, FRANÇOIS (1750–1829). Bergeoing was the son of a doctor/surgeon, and after studying at the *collège des Jésuites* he went on to follow in his father's footsteps in the medical profession. In 1790 he was elected mayor of Saint-Macaire, and two years later was sent from the Gironde as a deputy to the **National Convention**. He voted for imprisonment rather than death in the trial of **Louis XVI**, but voted against the **Girondin** proposal for an *appel au peuple*. Bergeoing supported the impeachment of **Jean-Paul Marat**, and sat on the **Commission of Twelve**, both of which enraged Parisian **sans-culottes**. He was proscribed on 2 June 1793 and placed under house arrest, but escaped and fled to **Caen**, where he published a report on the findings of the Commission of Twelve and actively encouraged his constituents to rebel against the **Montagnard** Convention. After the collapse of the **federalist revolt**, he went into hiding and eluded arrest (rather surprising, since he hid in his hometown of Saint-Macaire). Bergeoing returned to the National Convention in March 1795, and joined **Paul-François Barras** in putting down the royalist **Vendémiaire uprising** in late 1795. He was elected to the **Council of Five Hundred** in 1795 from the Pas-de-Calais, allied himself politically with Barras, and spent time in the company of **Benjamin Constant** and **Germaine de Staël**. Bergeoing retired from political life after **Brumaire**, and returned to the Gironde.

BERNARDIN DE SAINT-PIERRE, JACQUES-HENRI (1737–1814). Born in Le Havre to a family of the **aristocracy**, Bernardin de Saint-Pierre served as an officer and military engineer, and was a friend and follower of **Jean-Jacques Rousseau**. He traveled widely and wrote several works in the last decades of the Old Regime, but is best known for his sentimental novel, *Paul et Virginie*, published in 1788. The two protagonists of the novel, its title characters, were fatherless children who grew up on the island paradise of the Ile de France (Mauritius). Theirs was a story of unconsummated love and tragic death, but also of youthful virtue as yet uncorrupted by European civilization. The novel was enormously popular during the decade of the Revolution, appearing in 30 separate editions and inspiring plays, an opera, and decorative jewelry. Bernardin used his profits from the sales to buy a house in the *faubourg* Saint-Marcel in **Paris**, but took no active role in the events of the Revolution. **Napoleon Bonaparte** admired his work and gave him both a pension and a seat in the Académie Française.

BIENS NATIONAUX. The "national lands" were properties confiscated over the course of the Revolution from the Catholic Church, from the royal family, and from *émigrés* and other political suspects. Faced with a financial crisis, the **Constituent Assembly** voted on 2

November 1789, at the initiative of Bishop **Charles-Maurice Talleyrand**, to place the property of the Church, estimated to have been some 10 percent of total landholdings in France, at the disposal of the nation. These properties were to be sold to the creditors of the state in exchange for the *assignats* that they had been issued, thereby liquidating the national debt.

There were, in effect, three classes of *biens nationaux*: the Church lands, confiscated by decrees issued on 2 November 1789, 13 May 1790, and 16 July 1790; royal properties, confiscated by decrees issued on 19 December 1789 and 9 March 1790; and the properties of *émigrés*, confiscated by decrees issued on 9 February 1792 and 17 July 1792. Similarly, the sale of *biens nationaux* was governed by two sets of decrees: the law of 14–17 May 1790, which stipulated that confiscated properties would be sold at auction to the highest bidder; and laws of 3 June to 25 July 1793, which stipulated that the properties were to be broken up into small parcels, and allowed payments to be spread over 10 years. There had been no intention to favor the wealthy by the first legislation (indeed, in the event of equal bids, the parcel was to go to a collection of bidders rather than a single individual if that were an option), but the later legislation was clearly designed to foster distribution of land among poorer **peasants**. Throughout the decade there was tension between the goal of liquidating the national debt, which called for maximizing the return on the sale of *biens nationaux*, and the revolutionary ideal of equality, which called for selling the lands in small parcels. There was also a tension in the way that purchasers of *biens nationaux* were viewed over the decade: sometimes as patriotic supporters of the revolutionary government; but at other times as speculators who managed to strike a good deal through their political connections.

The overall impact of the sale of *biens nationaux* is difficult to assess, since the evidence is voluminous and variable from one part of the country to another. The sales did not solve the national debt, but they did help. The lands confiscated from the Church remained forfeit under the terms of the Concordat, but some *émigré* nobles regained their property after 1815. The value of the property sold may have been as high as six billion *livres*, although given the inflation of the revolutionary decade this is a difficult figure to assess. By virtue of the sales, the number of landed properties in France may have doubled. It has generally been argued that the **bourgeoisie** and already wealthy landowners gained most from the sale of *biens nationaux*, but recent studies have shown that a substantial number of poor and middling peasants also benefited. The consensus among historians is that the sale of these lands served to perpetuate the pattern of small-scale landholding that prevailed in most of the French countryside well into the 20th century.

BILLAUD-VARENNE, JACQUES-NICOLAS (1756–1819). Born in La Rochelle, Billaud-Varenne studied law in Poitiers and joined his father's law practice. He grew estranged from his parents in the 1780s, however, and moved to **Paris**. There he wrote a three-volume work, *Despotisme des Ministres de France*, that was published anonymously in 1789. Billaud's obsession with despotism and conspiracy, a characteristic trait throughout his revolutionary career, is apparent in this work. He became very active in Parisian politics in the early years of the Revolution, and sat on the insurrectionary **Commune** in the days leading up to the **uprising of 10 August 1792**. Elected to the **National Convention** from Paris, he sat with the **Montagnards** and voted for the death of **Louis XVI**. Billaud was pressed onto the **Committee of Public Safety** by the Parisian **sans-culotte** movement following demonstrations against rising prices in September 1793. He was devoted to the "unity of action" of the revolutionary government and in **Thermidor** actively opposed **Maximilien Robespierre** because of the latter's apparent ambition for personal power. Billaud was among the most radical of the deputies on the Committee of Public Safety, and in April 1795 was denounced as a terrorist and deported to Guyana. He left Guyana for Haiti in 1816, refusing to live as a subject of **Louis XVIII**, even at a distance. Billaud's final words, reportedly, were "My bones, at least, will find repose in this land that desires liberty."

BIROTTEAU, JEAN-BONAVENTURE-BLAISE-HILARION (1758–1793). Birotteau's father was an *avocat*, as was he, in the town of Perpignan. He was elected to the municipal council of Perpignan in 1789, and subsequently served as secretary of the district administration. In 1792 he was elected from the Pyrénées-Orientales to the **National Convention**. Birotteau sat with the **Girondins**, and was immediately named to the commission charged with investigating the **September Massacres**. Their report concluded that innocent people had been killed in the prisons, and that more thorough investigation should proceed. This prompted Birotteau to call for the creation of a departmental guard to protect the Convention, a proposal that was wildly unpopular in **Paris**. Birotteau voted for death in the trial of **Louis XVI**, but with the sentence to be suspended. He was an undisciplined deputy, frequently making allegations that he could not substantiate. He supported the indictment of **Jean-Paul Marat** and was proscribed from the Convention on 2 June 1793. Birotteau fled Paris for **Lyon**, where he addressed an insurrectionary assembly and actively encouraged revolt. As the revolt crumbled in Lyon, he left for **Bordeaux**, where he was apprehended and executed immediately, having already been declared an outlaw.

BOISSY D'ANGLAS, FRANÇOIS-ANTOINE (1756–1826). Born into a **Protestant** family in the Ardèche region of south central France, Boissy d'Anglas pursued a legal career and secured a position as *avocat* before the **Parlement of Paris** in the late 1780s. He was widely known on the eve of the Revolution for his critique of royal absolutism and defense of Protestants. He was elected to the **Estates-General** by the **Third Estate** of Annonay, and to the **National Convention** from the Ardèche. A man of moderate politics, Boissy played an active role in drafting the **Constitution of 1795**, which confirmed the creation of a republic of property owners. For his refusal to reintroduce the ***maximum*** in the face of food shortages in 1795, he earned the nickname in the Parisian faubourgs of *Boissy-Famine*. Boissy d'Anglas was elected to the **Council of Five Hundred**, but was purged from office in the **Fructidor coup** of 1797. He later served the regimes of both **Napoleon Bonaparte** and **Louis XVIII**.

BONAPARTE, LUCIEN (1775–1840). The younger brother of **Napoleon**, and like him, he was a student at the *collège* of Autun and then the military academy at Brienne. Their father was granted minor noble status by the French crown in 1771 for his support of **Pascal Paoli** in the Corsican rebellion against Genoa. The Bonapartes broke with Paoli in 1793, however, accusing him of delivering Corsica to the British. Lucien, who had joined the **Jacobin club** in Ajaccio early in the Revolution, fled to southern France in 1793 and continued his Jacobin activity there. He was briefly imprisoned in Aix-en-Provence during the summer of 1795, but his brother secured his release and a position as a commissioner of war to the Army of the Nord. Lucien later joined Napoleon in the Italian campaign. In 1798 he was elected to the **Council of Five Hundred** from the new department of Liamone (formerly Corsica). As president of the Council of Five Hundred in 1799, he played a pivotal role in the coup of **Brumaire**. Lucien subsequently served in the Tribunat, and then as minister of the interior. He was named ambassador to Spain in 1801, returned to **Paris** in 1802 and played a role in the negotiation of the Concordat, and after that was named to the Senate. After 1804 he lived mostly in Italy, having quarreled with the emperor. He fell into the hands of the British while traveling to America in 1810, was placed under a kind of house arrest until 1814, but was allowed to return to Rome after Napoleon's final abdication.

BONAPARTE, NAPOLEON (1769–1821). Born into a Corsican family of minor nobility, Napoleon Bonaparte went with this brother, **Lucien Bonaparte**, to study in France, first at the *collège* of Autun, then the military academy at Brienne, and finally at the Ecole Militaire in **Paris**. He was assigned to the artillery in 1785, stationed at Auxonne, in Burgundy. Napoleon returned frequently to Corsica, however, and supported his family's alliance with **Pascal Paoli** in the cause of Corsican independence.

Napoleon embraced the ideals of the Revolution in 1789 and did not choose to emigrate, as many of his fellow officers did. He was in Corsica from September 1789 until May 1791, and then again from September 1791 until May 1792, but was in Paris for the **uprising of 10 August 1792**, which impressed upon him the capacity of the crowd to bring down a government. Later that year he led a failed Corsican expedition against Sardinia, and then fled with his family to southern France. He rejoined the republican army at the siege of **Toulon**, where he met **Augustin Robespierre** and **Christophe Saliceti**, both deputies in the **National Convention**. It was here at Toulon that Napoleon first began to make his mark.

In 1794 he was assigned to the general staff in Italy as a brigadier-general. Napoleon came under suspicion following 9 **Thermidor**, both for his early **Jacobin** sympathies and for his personal contact with the younger Robespierre. When offered a command in the **Vendée** he declined, preferring not to lead soldiers into combat against their countrymen. The **Vendémiaire** uprising of October 1795, in which he commanded the troops defending the National Convention, gave him the opportunity to return to the national limelight. Shortly thereafter he married **Josephine de Beauharnais**, and was then assigned to rehabilitate the Italian army. He did so with considerable élan, restoring the morale of his troops and turning the front into a major theater. In October 1797 France signed the treaty of Campo-Formio with Austria, which ceded control over **Belgium**.

Emboldened by his successes in Italy, Napoleon conferred with the **Directory** in regard to strategy against Great Britain. Rather than risk a sea attack against England or Ireland, he proposed the **Egyptian campaign**, which embarked in May 1798. The campaign was a military disaster, with most of the ships sunk by the British navy in Alexandria harbor and the army eventually ravaged by disease, but it did yield important scientific and cultural discoveries. Napoleon returned surreptitiously to France in August 1799, fearful that his setbacks in Egypt would have scuttled his reputation. Instead, he found his status as military hero untarnished, and discovered an unstable political situation into which he might easily insert himself. Allying himself with **Emmanuel-Joseph Sieyès** and his brother Lucien, then president of the **Council of Five Hundred**, Napoleon seized power in the coup of 18 **Brumaire**, installing himself first as consul, then consul for life (1800), and finally as emperor (1804). French military conquest throughout Europe under Napoleon did much to extend the influence of Revolutionary institutions, even as Napoleon's regime within France did much to stifle the civil liberties and political freedoms that the Revolution had championed. Napoleon suffered final military defeat at Waterloo in 1815, and died in exile on the island of Saint Helena.

BONNEVILLE, NICOLAS (1760–1828). Bonneville, whose father was a *procureur du roi*, grew up in Evreux, where **François Buzot** was among his childhood friends. He attended *collège* in Evreux, but when he refused to speak critically of **Jean-Jacques Rousseau** in public he was forced to leave town for **Paris**. Bonneville was an intellectual of the

first order at the end of the Old Regime, and was the principal translator of German romantic works into French. He was an elector in Paris
in 1789, very active in the events of July, and was among the first to call
for the creation of a bourgeois militia, what eventually became known
as the **National Guard**. In early 1790 Bonneville joined with **Claude
Fauchet** to found the **Cercle Social**, one of the most important of the
Paris clubs and debating societies of that period. He was known as a
progressive reformist in 1791–92 and denounced by his enemies as a
radical socialist, a reputation enhanced by the publication of *L'Esprit
des Religions* in 1791. Bonneville was among the few to call publicly
for the creation of a republic immediately after the king's flight to
Varennes.

Bonneville became increasingly associated with the **Girondin**
deputies. He published a number of their pamphlets through the press
of the Cercle Social, and was the official printer for **Jean-Marie
Roland**. He was arrested after 2 June 1793, but released upon the intervention of **Jean-Paul Marat**, who thought him crazy. Bonneville
took refuge in Evreux and lived there quietly until after 9 **Thermidor**. He resumed publication thereafter, though never with the success of the early 1790s. When he compared **Napoleon Bonaparte** to
Cromwell in one of his publications, his press was shut down.
Thomas Paine helped his family to emigrate to the United States under the Empire, but Bonneville himself could never leave Paris for
long. In the 1820s he opened a bookstore in Paris and cultivated the
acquaintance of a new generation of Romantic writers.

BORDEAUX. Bordeaux was the third largest city in France at the beginning of the Revolution, behind **Paris** and **Lyon**, and just slightly
ahead of **Marseille**, with a population of 109,000. It was the most
important Atlantic seaport in France, made prosperous by the export
of the fine wines produced in the city's hinterland, and by its role in
the trans-Atlantic trade in slaves and sugar. The city is significant in
the history of the Revolution because so many of the leaders of the
Girondin faction in the **National Convention** hailed from Bordeaux and its department, the Gironde. Bordeaux also became one
of the centers of resistance to the **Montagnard** government during
the **federalist revolt**. Over 300 people were executed during the
Terror in Bordeaux, most often because of their support for the re-

volt. After **Thermidor** the city became known as a haven for the *jeunesse dorée* and those favoring a restoration of the monarchy. Bordeaux's economy was shattered by the revolutionary and Napoleonic wars, and the city never recovered its mid-18th-century prosperity.

BOUCHE DE FER. The *Bouche de Fer* was the newspaper of the **Cercle Social** in **Paris**, appearing three times each week from October 1790 until its suppression in July 1791, shortly after the **Champ de Mars** massacre. The paper was edited by **Nicolas Bonneville**, and generally recorded the minutes and debates of Cercle Social meetings. **Claude Fauchet**, **Etta Palm d'Aelders**, and **Marie-Jean Condorcet** were all regular contributors. The newspaper took its name from a Cercle Social custom, whereby members could deposit comments or notices into an iron box shaped like a lion's head located at the club's meeting hall. These comments would then be printed in the newspaper.

BOUCHOTTE, JEAN-BAPTISTE-NOEL (1754–1840). Born into a bourgeois family, his father was a military clerk. Bouchotte became a captain of cavalry in the royal army, and played a crucial role in preventing the town of Courtrai from falling into Austrian hands at the time of the defection of General **Charles Dumouriez** in March 1793. In April the **National Convention** named him minister of war, despite **Girondin** opposition. Bouchotte worked closely with the **Committee of Public Safety** to restructure the army. He staffed the Ministry itself with Parisian **sans-culottes**, and promoted such future military talents as Pierre Augereau, Jean-Baptiste Kléber, André Masséna, Jean-Baptiste Bernadotte, and **Napoleon Bonaparte**. He republicanized the army by sending Parisian newspapers to the front, circulating copies of the **Constitution of 1793**, and sponsoring revolutionary festivals among the troops. Bouchotte was accused as a **terrorist** after 9 **Thermidor**, imprisoned for just over a year, and retired to private life upon his release. Napoleon refused to return him to active duty, but did give him a military pension.

BOURDON, LOUIS-JEAN-JOSEPH-LÉONARD (1754–1807). Léonard Bourdon was a complicated figure, extolled for his dedication to educational reform and decried for fanatical Jacobinism while on mission to the provinces in 1792–93. His father was a *conseiller du roi*, dismissed from his post and briefly imprisoned in the **Bastille** for allegedly having published proposed plans for reform without royal permission. Léonard studied law himself, and also attained the position of *conseiller du roi*. He appears to have spent much of the 1780s as counsel to the Benedictine congregation of Saint Maur, which was particularly involved in educational efforts. In 1790 Bourdon founded a school for young men in **Paris**, which thrived and drew much acclaim for some years, and published on national educational issues. He was present at the storming of the Bastille, became a militant in the Gravilliers section of the capital, and joined the Paris **Jacobin club**. Bourdon played a prominent role in the **uprising of 10 August 1792**. Later that month he was sent to escort a group of prisoners from Orléans to Versailles. Not only did the mission end with the massacre of the prisoners by an angry crowd in Versailles, Bourdon was also accused of having looted the prisoners of their valuables. He was also accused, in Paris, of stealing money intended for the purchase of grain.

Despite these controversies, he was elected to the **National Convention** from the Loiret, though there was confusion in the election between his name and that of Louis-François Bourdon, who ended up being elected from the Oise. He sat with the **Montagnards** and voted for death in the trial of **Louis XVI**. In March 1793 Bourdon was sent on mission for military recruitment, and once again he generated controversy and conflict. He stopped first in Orléans, where his violent words sparked a riot among the local **National Guard**, during which he was attacked, leading eventually to the trial and execution of nine men. Bourdon went on to the departments of the Jura and the Côte-d'Or, where he ordered harsh measures against local authorities suspected of supporting the **federalist revolt**, and later supported the **deChristianization** campaign. Although he and **Maximilien Robespierre** disliked each other, Bourdon played no active role in the coup of 9 **Thermidor**. He remained a staunch republican thereafter, but was denounced in 1795 by the citizens of both Orléans and Dijon, and spent some months imprisoned in the fortress of Ham.

Under the **Directory** he was named first to a position responsible for overseeing the provisioning of Paris, and in 1798 was sent as a commercial agent to Hamburg. His bad reputation having preceded him, Bourdon did not remain long in Hamburg. After **Brumaire**, Bourdon served for a time as chief administrator of the military hospital in **Toulon**, and in 1807 was named director of all military hospitals. He died in 1807 while accompanying the army on a campaign in Prussia.

BOURGEOISIE. The standard interpretation of the French Revolution through much of the 20th century, the so-called Marxist interpretation, argued that the Revolution was initiated by a burgeoning capitalist bourgeoisie, frustrated both by the economic constraints of the Old Regime and by the system of **privilege** that denied to them the political influence enjoyed by the **aristocracy**. That argument was effectively dismissed by revisionist historians writing in the 1960s and 1970s, who observed that there existed no identifiable capitalist bourgeois class in 18th-century France, and that the social distinction between bourgeois commoners and aristocrats had grown quite fuzzy by 1789.

There was a legal category of bourgeois under the Old Regime. These were men who resided in free towns (from the root word "bourg") and who lived on the interest income from their investments. One might also include in the Old Regime bourgeoisie a large number of officeholders in the royal bureaucracy, a growing legal profession, and an array of other urban professionals. It is more difficult to argue that they possessed any consciousness of belonging to a bourgeoisie, and many of them aspired to achieve noble status.

On the other hand, the writings of men such as **Emmanuel-Joseph Sieyès** explicitly attacked the privileges of the aristocracy and **clergy** and championed those who belonged to the **Third Estate** as the productive members of society. It is clear as well that the delegates of the Third Estate to the **Estates-General** in 1789 felt considerable resentment toward most of the delegates of the privileged orders. With the **Night of 4 August** and the **Declaration of the Rights of Man and Citizen** the marks of distinction of a privileged society were swept aside and the equality of all citizens, as individuals, was asserted. Did this represent the triumph of the bourgeoisie? Perhaps not. But it is hard to deny that it laid the foundations for 19th-century European society, in which status would be measured by wealth rather than birth, a society that most observers, both contemporary and later, have described as bourgeois.

BOURGES. Bourges is the departmental seat of the Cher, best known for its magnificent Gothic cathedral, built in the 12th and 13th centuries. Bourges is of significance during the Revolution as the proposed site for an alternative **National Convention** during the **federalist revolt**. **Girondin** deputies and many departmental administrators complained throughout 1792–93 that the deputies of the National Convention could not deliberate freely in **Paris**, that they might even be in danger from the militant **sans-culottes** of the capital. After the 2 June 1793 proscription of the Girondin leaders, federalist rebels charged that the Convention had been violated, and the federalist authorities in **Marseille** called for substitute deputies to convene in Bourges, because it was a neutral site, centrally located, without a large and menacing urban population. The proposal was never enacted.

BOYER-FONFRÈDE, JEAN-BAPTISTE (1765–1793). Boyer-Fonfrède was the son of a wealthy **Bordeaux** merchant, with substantial property holdings in **Saint-Domingue**. Jean-Baptiste also pursued a career in commerce, and was in Holland representing the family business on the eve of the Revolution. He was married to the sister of **Jean-François Ducos**. The political turmoil of 1789 brought Boyer-Fonfrède back to Bordeaux, where he quickly embraced patriotic ideas. He was among the founders of the local **National Guard**, spoke out against the Bordeaux Parlement as a den of **privilege**, and joined the **Jacobin club** in Bordeaux as well. His family wealth enabled him to buy a substantial number of *biens nationaux*, the lands confiscated from the Church. In 1792 he was elected to the **National Convention** from the Gironde, but unlike most of his colleagues from that department voted for death in the trial of **Louis XVI**, and against the *appel au peuple*.

Boyer-Fonfrède tried to play a conciliatory role in the National Convention between the feuding **Girondins** and **Montagnards**, but his politics were closer to his fellow Girondins. On 6 April he called for the arrest of **Louis-Philippe Orléans**, following the treason of **Charles Dumouriez**, and on 12 April he proposed the indictment of **Jean-Paul Marat**. In early May he presided over the Convention, and on 18 May was named to the **Commission of Twelve**, called to investigate the insurrectionary actions of the **Paris** sections. He refused to sign the Commission's order for the arrest of **Jacques René**

Hébert, however, and this spared him from proscription on 2 June 1793. In the weeks that followed, Boyer-Fonfrède demanded due process for those who were proscribed and arrested, denounced the violation of private letters, and participated in discussions of the new constitution. He also counseled the Bordelais against rebelling against the authority of the National Convention. He remained at his post until 3 October, when he was named in the indictment of the Girondin deputies drawn up by **Jean-Pierre Amar**. Boyer-Fonfrède was tried, convicted, and executed later that month. One hundred years later, Auguste Kuscinski would write that Boyer-Fonfrède should be considered a martyr to liberty.

BREAD RIOTS. Bread riots were the most common form of popular protest under the Old Regime, and historians have long argued that these riots were inherently political, a reactive protest against the increasing power of the absolutist monarchy. At times of scarcity or rising prices (generally the two coincided), bread riots would target either the suppliers of grain or the shops of bakers. Rioters demanded that prices be lowered, sometimes seized flour or bread and sold it at what they deemed a fair price, and resorted to damaging property if they encountered resistance. **Women** generally played the most prominent role in these protests. In 1775, after Anne-Robert-Jacques Turgot introduced free trade in grain, bread riots were so extensive in the **Paris** basin that they came to be known as the Flour War.

Bread riots played a particularly potent political role in the summer of 1789. After two successive poor harvests, flour and bread prices reached the highest mark of the century to that date in July. Those who stormed the **Bastille** on 14 July were concerned not only by the news coming from **Versailles**, but also by the spiraling prices of grain and bread, especially since bread was the single most important item in the diet of most people. A spike in the price of bread was also an important instigating factor in the women's march to Versailles during the **October Days** of 1789. Indeed, concern over the price of food was a contributing factor in virtually all of the revolutionary *journées* in Paris during the 1790s, and ensuring an adequate supply of grain, at a reasonable price, especially in urban markets, remained a paramount concern of the revolutionary government throughout the decade. *See also* GRAIN *MAXIMUM*.

BRETON CLUB. The Breton club is considered the forerunner of the **Jacobin club**. On the eve of the opening of the **Estates-General**, a group of deputies from Brittany met in a private home or café to discuss the momentous occasion. No formal records of their meetings were kept, but memoirs and diaries suggest that by June 1789 their gatherings had attracted a number of progressive deputies from outside of Brittany, including **Antoine-Pierre Barnave**, **Adrien Duport**, **Gabriel-Honoré Mirabeau**, **Emmanuel-Joseph Sieyès**, and **Maximilien Robespierre**. The deputies meeting as the Breton club played an influential role in the declaration of a National Assembly and the strategy of the **Third Estate** leading up to the royal session of 23 June. Plans for the **Night of 4 August** may also have taken shape at its meetings. After the **Constituent Assembly** moved to **Paris** in October 1789, the Breton club ceased to exist, with the Jacobin club soon emerging to take its place.

BRISSOT, JACQUES-PIERRE (1754–1793). Brissot was the son of a food-shop proprietor in Chartres. He attended *collège* in Chartres, where **Jérome Pétion** was among his fellow students, and went on to study law. Brissot would pursue his career, however, in journalism and publishing, moving back and forth between the high and low literary cultures of the late **Enlightenment** in France and England. He collaborated with an English newspaperman by the name of Swinton in the late 1770s and early 1780s, but encountered difficulties both with his creditors and the censors in France. Those difficulties landed him in the **Bastille** in 1784, and Brissot would later be accused of having secured his freedom by agreeing to serve as a police spy in the literary and publishing circles of **Paris**. In 1788 he made a trip to the United States, where he was profoundly influenced by the ideals of the young republic. Upon his return, late that year, he joined with **Gabriel-Honoré Mirabeau** and Etienne Clavière to found the **Society of the Friends of Blacks**.

Brissot was swept up by the events of 1789, and his *Le Patriote français* was among the first **newspapers** to commence publication, on 6 May 1789. The newspaper brought him fame and popularity, and on 14 July the conquerors of the Bastille brought the keys of the dungeon to present to him. Brissot was elected to the municipal council of Paris in 1789, but it was principally through his newspaper that he exercised political influence. His advocacy of the rights of Blacks was controversial, however, with some accusing him of acting as an agent of the British in that regard.

On 10 July 1791, following the flight to **Varennes**, Brissot gave a powerful speech at the **Jacobin club** against the inviolability of the king. He is credited with drafting the petition that circulated the following week on the **Champ de Mars**. In September he was elected from Paris to the **Legislative Assembly**, and in October presided over the Paris Jacobin club. Brissot was a dominant figure in the Legislative Assembly, at the peak of his influence, and he was among the first deputies to call for a declaration of war against those European powers hostile to the Revolution. In this he was opposed by **Maximilien Robespierre**, but Brissot and his allies prevailed and on 20 April 1792 war was declared against Austria. Brissot now exercised great influence among the king's ministers, but when the war went badly his popularity waned among Parisians and at the Jacobin club. Brissot and his supporters (called Brissotins in 1791–92, but **Girondins** by 1793) were ambivalent about the growing popular movement calling for an end to the monarchy, and Brissot himself was slow to denounce General **Lafayette**, who proved to be a traitor to the Revolution in the summer of 1792.

When new national elections were called, after 10 August 1792, Brissot was no longer a viable candidate in Paris, and instead was elected to the **National Convention** from the Eure-et-Loir. The **September Massacres** drove a further wedge between him and Robespierre, and in October Brissot was expelled from the Jacobin club. He voted for death in the trial of **Louis XVI**, but as a suspended sentence, and also supported the *appel au peuple*. Increasingly unpopular among Parisians, Brissot found himself denounced on all sides, as a former police spy, as a sympathizer to the condemned king, as an intriguer with the traitorous General **Charles Dumouriez**. In May 1793 he published a pamphlet demanding that the Jacobin club be closed down and that the Paris municipal council be disbanded. It is thus not surprising that he was among those deputies proscribed on 2 June 1793. Brissot fled Paris, but was arrested in Moulins and returned to the capital to be tried with the other Girondins. He wrote his memoirs in prison, while awaiting trial, and went to the **guillotine** on 31 October 1793.

BRUMAIRE. On 18–19 Brumaire VIII (9–10 November 1799), **Napoleon Bonaparte** overthrew the **Directory** in a planned coup and introduced the regime of the Consulate. Throughout its four-year existence, the Directory had been plagued by political instability, with royalist and **Jacobin** deputies purged from office in successive years as liberal republicans tried to fashion a workable centrist government. The result was the alienation of the electorate rather than political stability. By 1799 a group of leading political figures—including **Emmanuel-Joseph Sieyès**, **Paul-François Barras**, **Joseph Fouché**, and **Charles-Maurice Talleyrand**—had decided to turn to a military general to reestablish order and assert strong leadership. The first choice of Sieyès was in fact General Barthélemi-Catherine Joubert, but General Joubert died on the field of battle before the plot could be hatched. Napoleon, recently returned from Egypt, was an attractive second choice because his brother, **Lucien Bonaparte**, presided over the **Council of Five Hundred**.

The pretext for the coup was an alleged Jacobin plot against the Republic. On 18 Brumaire the **Council of Ancients** and the Council of Five Hundred were informed of the plot and asked to appoint Napoleon commander of the army in **Paris**, an appointment that was technically illegal. The two assemblies were then called into special session the following day at the palace of Saint Cloud, just across the Seine to the west of the city. The plan was to ask the deputies to approve in principle constitutional revisions that would end the Directory and create a new regime, the Consulate, in which three consuls (one of them Napoleon) would replace the five directors. Surrounded by armed troops, the Ancients quietly acquiesced to the demand, but in the Council of Five Hundred Jacobin deputies hooted Napoleon, and called for the arrest of the tyrant. Shaken by this unexpected hostility, Napoleon nearly fainted and was ushered out of the palace by his brother. He soon recovered and ordered troops back into the meeting hall, producing the rather comical scene of deputies climbing out the windows and fleeing across the grounds in their togas.

A new constitution was drafted within six weeks, and on 25 December 1799 the Consulate was declared. Sieyès and **Pierre-Roger Ducos**, both of whom had been directors, joined Napoleon as consuls. Napoleon, however, was named first consul, a position of power that he never relinquished.

BRUNSWICK MANIFESTO. The Brunswick Manifesto was issued on 25 July 1792 in the name of the Duke of Brunswick, commander of the combined armies of Prussia and Austria. **Axel von Fersen** played a role in drafting the manifesto, which announced that the allied armies had invaded French territory with the aim of restoring the authority of **Louis XVI**. It called on all French citizens to submit to royal authority, and in particular warned the people of **Paris** that if harm were done to any member of the royal family, those responsible would be duly punished and the city itself would be destroyed. Far from casting fear into the hearts of Parisians, the Brunswick Manifesto incited a patriotic fervor in the capital that led to the storming of the **Tuileries** Palace and the fall of the monarchy on 10 August 1792. The Duke of Brunswick was said to have regretted the harsh tone of the manifesto for the rest of his life.

BUONARROTI, FILIPPO MICHELE (1761–1837). Buonarroti was born into a noble Tuscan family and became a protégé of Grand Duke Leopold of Tuscany, brother of **Marie Antoinette** and the future Emperor Leopold II. When Filippo embraced the ideals of 1789, the grand duke ordered his exile. Buonarroti traveled to **Corsica**, where he published a newspaper, *Ami de la Liberté italienne*, and administered lands confiscated from the Catholic Church. Late in 1792 he went to France, in the company of **Christophe Saliceti**, and became a naturalized French citizen. Through Saliceti he met **Augustin Robespierre**, and the two of them helped obtain for Buonarroti a variety of posts and missions in 1793–94. He was denounced as a **Jacobin** after 9 **Thermidor**, arrested, and imprisoned. While in prison he met **Gracchus Babeuf**. Buonarroti was among the founders of the **Panthéon club**, and an active propagandist for the **Conspiracy of Equals**, the history of which he would publish in 1828. He was tried along with Babeuf, and sentenced to deportation. Buonarroti lived principally in Geneva until 1815, and thereafter became very active in the revolutionary Carbonari of southern Europe. He returned to France after 1830, became a sort of mentor to Louis Blanc and Auguste Blanqui, and was arrested a final time for his subversive activities in October 1833, at the age of 72.

BURKE, EDMUND (1729–1797). Edmund Burke was an Irishman by birth and a lawyer by training, and sat among the Whig deputies in the British House of Commons. Burke supported the American colonies in their war for independence, and was an advocate of reform in England, including recognition of the rights of Catholics in Ireland. But in 1790 he grew alarmed at public pronouncements of support for the recent revolutionary events in France, and in November 1790 published his *Reflections on the Revolution in France*, recognized immediately and for many years thereafter as an eloquent expression of the ideology of **counterrevolution**.

Burke condemned the Revolution as a blind incarnation of the abstract philosophy of the **Enlightenment** and its assertion of human universals. He argued that the elections to the **Estates General**, and the violence that followed, represented a repudiation of the organic social order of France and a rejection of its historic tradition. This, he insisted, was a formula for disaster, one that the British must avoid at all cost. He denounced, in particular, the violence of the **October Days**, and the **confiscation of Church lands**, and predicted that the Revolution would lead inevitably to atheism and military dictatorship.

Burke's *Reflections* were an immediate best seller and turned **public opinion** in Great Britain decidedly against the French Revolution. But his views also aroused a spirited response, most notably **Thomas Paine's** *Rights of Man*, which sold even more copies than Burke's book. Paine argued that Burke had overstated the extent of popular violence and exaggerated both the virtues of traditional institutions and the capacity of the monarchy for gradual reform. He offered, in addition, a defense of the **Declaration of the Rights of Man and Citizen**. The events of the **Terror**, however, and the eventual rise of **Napoleon Bonaparte** to power seemed to vindicate Burke's critique, and his *Reflections on the French Revolution* have stood for two centuries as a most cogent ideological refutation of the ideals of 1789.

BUZOT, FRANÇOIS-NICOLAS-LEONARD (1760–1794). Buzot's father was a *procureur au bailliage* in Evreux, and his mother also came from a robe nobility family. François attended school in Evreux, went on to study law (most likely in **Paris**), and in 1786 was named a *conseiller au bailliage et siège présidial* in Evreux. He was sent as a delegate for the **Third Estate** to the **Estates-General**, and sat on the left in the **Constituent Assembly**, alongside deputies such as **Jérome Pétion**, **Pierre-Louis Prieur**, and **Maximilien Robespierre**. He attended meetings of the **Breton club**, and joined the **Jacobin club** very early. Buzot spoke seldom in the Constituent Assembly, but in May 1791 did propose the creation of a two-chamber legislature, an idea favored by no one else except for **Joseph Sieyès**. In late 1791 Buzot returned to the Eure as president of the departmental Criminal Tribunal. For the next year he maintained a correspondence with **Manon Roland**, and when he returned to Paris in 1792 as a deputy from the Eure to the **National Convention** Buzot was very close to both Madame Roland and her husband.

Buzot sat with the **Girondins** in the Convention, and was among the most vocal deputies in condemning Paris for the **September Massacres**. Prompted by **Jean-Marie Roland**, he called for a departmental guard to protect the Convention. As the trial of **Louis XVI** approached, Buzot proposed that anyone who advocated the restoration of the monarchy be punished by death. So prominent was he in his public rhetoric that the term "Buzotins" was sometimes substituted for "Brissotins" in the radical press. In the trial of the king, he voted for death, but with a suspended sentence, and for the *appel au peuple*. When the sections of Paris called for a **grain *maximum*** in February 1793, Buzot, a supporter of free trade, brushed the demand aside with the observation that Paris had nothing to complain about, since it produced no grain itself. He opposed the creation of the **Revolutionary Tribunal** and the **Committee of Public Safety** in the spring of 1793, but while he spoke in support of the indictment of **Jean-Paul Marat**, he abstained when the matter came up for a vote. In April 1793 he called for the closing of the Jacobin club, and in May suggested that the Convention be moved to a smaller town.

Buzot was among the deputies proscribed on 2 June 1793. He fled first to Evreux, then on to **Caen**, and actively encouraged revolt against Paris in both towns. When the **federalist revolt** collapsed, he fled to Brittany and then to the Gironde, where he hid near St. Emilion with Pétion and **Charles Barbaroux**. Buzot wrote his memoirs while in hiding. He and Pétion killed themselves when their hideout was discovered in June 1794. The National Convention ordered that his house in Evreux be razed.

– C –

CAEN. Caen is the departmental seat of Calvados, and the center of the Old Regime province of Lower Normandy. Celebrated as the home of William the Conqueror, its importance in the Revolution is twofold. In June 1793 the city became one of the centers of the **federalist revolt**, and a number of the **Girondin** deputies took refuge in the city after their proscription, and encouraged its citizens in their rebellion against **Paris**. The revolt in Caen crumbled after a single desultory battle near the town of Vernon, but on the same day as that battle, **Charlotte Corday**, a resident of the city, plunged a knife into the breast of **Jean-Paul Marat**, thereby earning for Caen its second point of notoriety.

CAHIERS DE DOLÉANCES. The *cahiers de doléances*, or grievance lists, were drafted by the local assemblies that met in the first months of 1789 to elect deputies to the **Estates-General**. The *cahiers* were meant to accompany the deputies to **Versailles** as a kind of mandate, an expression of concerns, complaints, and demands for reform. Thousands of these *cahiers* were drafted, and most of them survive in the National Archives, a virtual record of the grievances of Frenchmen on the eve of the Revolution and a measure of the degree to which revolutionary sentiments were held across France prior to the events of the summer of 1789.

The *cahiers* delivered to Versailles were drawn up by assemblies at the local administrative level of the *bailliage*. Model *cahiers*, many of them drafted in **Paris**, often circulated throughout the country in advance of those assemblies. For the **Third Estate**, the *bailliage* assembly might well have been preceded by two or three prior assemblies, with revisions being made at each stage of the process. The voices and concerns of poor **peasants** and urban workers, then, were only indirectly expressed. The final assemblies were dominated by literate elites, especially lawyers. For the Second Estate, the **aristocracy**, all were entitled to attend *bailliage* assemblies, and the *cahiers* were thus a more direct expression of noble concerns. Among the First Estate, the **clergy**, the hierarchy participated directly in *bailliage* assemblies, whereas the lower clergy went through a two-stage process. The upper clergy tended to speak with a unified voice, while the assemblies of the lower clergy were sometimes extremely contentious.

The *cahiers* thus represent a nuanced and complicated body of evidence, enormous in their scope, difficult to interpret. The recent works of John Markoff and Gilbert Shapiro represent the most comprehensive effort to date to analyze and interpret the *cahiers de doléances*, so vast as to defy summary here. It should be noted, however, that beyond what the *cahiers* said, the very process of assembling the people to draft them constituted a political mobilization of the populace. Having been asked by the king to give voice to their concerns, the people of France expected to be heard. *See also* PEASANTRY; SEIGNEURIAL DUES.

ÇA IRA. *Ça ira* was the first popular song of the Revolution. If the **Marseillaise** became the official national song of the French Republic, the *Ça ira* was its revolutionary anthem. It came into popularity at the time of preparations for the first **Festival of Federation**, in July 1790. The Festival was scheduled for 14 July, the anniversary of the storming of the **Bastille**, on the **Champ de Mars**. When rumors began to circulate that the site would not be ready on time, thousands of Parisians, of all social classes, streamed to the Champ de Mars to lend a hand. Even **Louis XVI** turned a spadeful of dirt. It was an extraordinary scene of revolutionary fraternity, and the *Ça ira* emerged as the working song of the people. The song was sung to a spritely tune, and had an optimistic air about it: the second line promised that "good times will come." But it also expressed the latent social tensions of the day, as in the refrain: "ça ira, Hang the aristocrats!" *See also CARMAGNOLE.*

CALENDAR. *See* REVOLUTIONARY CALENDAR.

CALONNE, CHARLES-ALEXANDRE (1734–1802). Calonne was a native of Douai, trained in law. Early in his career he obtained the post of *procureur* at the Parlement of Flanders, later was appointed as *maître des requêtes* in the royal bureaucracy, and then became an intendant, first in Metz (1766) and later in Flanders (1778). In 1783 he replaced **Jacques Necker** as *Contrôleur Général des Finances*. Calonne did all that he could to ingratiate himself at Court, hosting lavish parties and even paying the debts of the king's brother, the Count of Artois. He took only cautious measures, however, to address the growing financial problems of the crown, and in February 1787 was forced to convene an **Assembly of Notables** to deal with the crisis. When the Assembly refused to endorse Calonne's proposal for a new, unified property tax, the king dismissed him at the queen's urging. Calonne left immediately for London, and from there carried on a polemical debate with Jacques Necker, dismissing the latter's 1783 account of the royal treasury as completely inaccurate. After the Revolution began, Calonne joined the *émigrés*, first in Turin and then in Coblenz, placing his private fortune at their disposal. He tried to function as a sort of prime minister among the constantly feuding *émigrés*, but to little effect. Just before his death, **Napoleon Bonaparte** granted Calonne permission to return to France.

CAMBON, PIERRE-JOSEPH (1756–1820). Cambon's father was a **Protestant** merchant in Montpellier, and Pierre followed in that path. He was elected to the Montpellier municipal council in the first year of the Revolution, and was among the founders of the **Jacobin club** in that city. Elected to the **Legislative Assembly** and the **National Convention** from the Hérault, he served on the **Committee of Public Safety** from April 1793 until after **Thermidor**. Along with **Robert Lindet**, Cambon was responsible for food supply and for most of this period served as the effective minister of finances for France. Attacked by **Louis-Antoine Saint-Just** before Thermidor, and by **Jean-Lambert Tallien** afterward, Cambon later defended the policies of the Committee of Public Safety during the **Terror**. During the **Prairial Uprising** of 1795, Cambon was proclaimed mayor of **Paris** by the insurgents. Subsequently denounced, he retired to the Hérault, where he narrowly escaped death at the hands of royalist assassins. In 1816 Cambon was exiled as a regicide.

CARMAGNOLE. The *Carmagnole* was among the most popular of revolutionary songs. Unlike the *Marseillaise*, composed by **Jean-Claude Rouget de Lisle** as a marching song for the army, or the *Ça Ira*, the melody of which is reminiscent of an opera aria, the tune of the *Carmagnole* has its origins in popular folk music. Some sources suggest that the song, and the dance that accompanied it, first appeared in Provence among the migrant laborers who came from the Piedmont to pick grapes and olives. The song may have made its way to **Paris** with the **Marseille** volunteers in July 1792. The revolutionary lyrics to the song make direct reference to events and circumstances in Paris following 10 August 1792, and the song's derisive references to **Marie Antoinette** gained for it the alternative title of *Madame Véto*. It was enormously popular among Parisians through the **Terror**, but was banned by **Napoleon Bonaparte** when he came to power. The *Carmagnole* reemerged as part of the republican tradition, however, in both 1830 and 1848.

CARNOT, LAZARE-NICOLAS-MARGUERITE (1753–1823). Known to posterity as the "Organizer of Victory," Carnot served on the **Committee of Public Safety** as a military expert and strategist. Schooled at the Oratoriens *collège* of Autun, he went on to military school in **Paris**. In 1773 he entered the ranks of military engineers as a lieutenant. Carnot was an ardent critic of the social structure of the Old Regime, especially the rule of **privilege** and the limits to military advancement for a commoner. He was a member of the Rosati literary academy in Arras, where he met **Maximilien Robespierre**, and in 1784 won an award from the Dijon Academy for his *Eloge du maréchal de Vauban* (Vauban was the great fortress builder of Louis XIV). Carnot was elected from the Pas-de-Calais to both the **Legislative Assembly** and the **National Convention**. He sat with the **Montagnards**, but did not attend the **Jacobin club**. He frequently went on mission to the armies, and in August 1793 was elected to the Committee of Public Safety, with principal responsibility for military affairs. The republican armies fared well under his leadership, and he was the only member of the Great Committee to be reelected after **Thermidor**. Carnot was elected to the **Council of Ancients** in 1795, served as a director, and in that role moved aggressively against **Gracchus Babeuf** and his fellow conspirators in May 1796. Carnot was proscribed as a rightist in the **Fructidor coup** of 1797, returned after **Brumaire** to serve briefly as minister of war, was elected to the Tribunat in 1802, and was its only member to vote against the declaration of the Empire. He retired to private life in 1807, and in 1816 was exiled as a regicide. *See also* DIRECTORY.

CARRA, JEAN-LOUIS (1742–1793). Carra, whose father was a clerk for a seigneurial landowner, had a difficult childhood, fleeing France briefly for Germany and Moldavia when he fell under suspicion of theft. When he returned to France he obtained a job at the royal library through the good offices of the Cardinal du Rohan. In 1789, he and **Louis-Sébastien Mercier** founded a **newspaper**, *Les Annales patriotiques*, and it would be in this realm, rather than as a politician, that Carra would exercise his greatest influence during the Revolution. His newspaper was an important vehicle of communication between the **Jacobin club** of **Paris** and the clubs in the provinces, and he supported in its pages **Jacques Brissot's** calls for a declaration of war against Austria. Carra was elected to the **National Convention** in 1792 from the Saône-et-Loire, and at about this same time **Jean-Marie Roland** secured for him a position at the National Library. Although he sat with the **Girondins**, he voted for death in the trial of **Louis XVI**. Carra remained aloof from the political feuds of 1792–93, but in the summer of 1793 he was denounced by **Maximilien Robespierre** and **Jean-Paul Marat** for having called for the Duke of Brunswick to be placed on the French throne. Even though his offense had occurred back in July 1792, he went to trial with the Girondin deputies and was executed with them in October 1793. *See also* BRUNSWICK MANIFESTO.

CARRIER, JEAN-BAPTISTE (1756–1794). Carrier's father was a tenant farmer on the land of a nobleman in south central France. Jean-Baptiste was educated in a Jesuit *collège* in Aurillac, where his parents intended for him to pursue a clerical career. Instead he took a job as a legal clerk in the office of a relative, and in 1779 left for **Paris** to study law. He returned to Aurillac in 1785 as a *procureur au bailliage* and in that same year married the daughter of a local merchant. In 1789 he joined the Aurillac **National Guard**, and soon joined the local **Jacobin club** as well, but appears not to have held political office until his election to the **National Convention** from the Cantal in 1792. There he sat with the **Montagnards** and voted for death in the trial of **Louis XVI**.

In July 1793, Carrier was sent on mission to Normandy to assist in the repression of the **federalist revolt**. He continued on to Brittany, where he confined the bishop of Rennes on the island of Mont Saint-

Michel, and then on to **Nantes**, which had just recently been under siege by the rebels of the **Vendée**.

Carrier's orders were to combat the Vendée rebellion with the most energetic means possible. The result was one of the most gruesome episodes of the **Terror**. Urged on by local radicals, Carrier ordered the mass execution of more than 3,000 captured rebels, many of them priests, some by drowning in the Loire, others before firing squads. Most were killed without trial, a decree of the Convention having declared "outside the law" anyone caught bearing arms against the Republic. Carrier was recalled to Paris in early 1794, after **Marc-Antoine Jullien, fils** reported on his excesses directly to **Maximilien Robespierre**. He remained active in the Jacobin club, survived the **Thermidor** coup, and even managed to secure the ousting of **Jean-Lambert Tallien** from the Jacobin club.

In October 1794, however, repeated denunciations forced the Convention to name a commission to investigate Carrier's alleged crimes, and in December he was brought to trial along with several members of the Nantes revolutionary committee. Two of them accompanied Carrier to the **guillotine** on 16 December 1794, the jury unpersuaded by Carrier's insistence that he had simply followed the orders of the **Committee of Public Safety**. To this day, the name of Carrier and the *noyades* of Nantes are emblematic of the excesses of the Terror.

CARTEAUX, JEAN-FRANÇOIS (1751–1813). Carteaux was the son of a marshal in the royal army, and he followed in his father's footsteps. In July 1789 he was an aide to General **Lafayette**, and was soon promoted to the rank of lieutenant. As a cavalry officer in the **Paris National Guard**, Carteaux's actions in the **uprising of 10 August 1792** prevented reinforcements from reaching the defenders of the **Tuileries** Palace. Consistent and regular promotions brought him to the rank of brigadier-general by July 1793, when he led republican troops against the **federalist rebels** of **Marseille**, entering the city in August. The **National Convention** voted him a commendation and promoted him to Commander in Chief of the Army of the Midi. Two representatives on mission, **Paul Barras** and **Louis-Stanislas Fréron**, were less confident of his abilities, however, and reassigned him well away from **Toulon**, to the Army of Italy. Carteaux was arrested in December

1793, and remained in prison until after **Thermidor**. He served in a number of different posts under the **Directory**, though without special distinction, and retired to private life in 1803.

CAUSES CÉLÈBRES. In the final decades of the Old Regime, a series of *causes célèbres* captured the attention of the educated public, particularly in **Paris**, and had a profound effect on **public opinion** on the eve of the French Revolution. These *causes célèbres* included the Calas affair, long championed by **Voltaire**; a series of sensational trials involving the playwright **Pierre-Augustin Caron de Beaumarchais**; the **Diamond Necklace Affair**; the Kornmann case; and a host of others. The details of these trials became known to the public through the publication of lawyers' briefs (*mémoires judiciaires*), which were exempt from royal censorship and published in runs of up to several thousand. In this way, the foibles of private lives became public concerns, and the exposure of the frailties and deceits of the social elite (even including the royal family) helped to turn public opinion against the legitimacy of social hierarchy and the Old Regime system of **privilege**.

CAZALÈS, JACQUES-ANTOINE-MARIE (1758–1805). Born into a family of provincial nobility, his father was a *conseiller au Parlement* in **Toulouse**. Cazalès pursued a military career, joined the Dragoons of Jarnac in 1773, and rose to the rank of captain and squadron commander by 1779, stationed in Flanders. He was elected as a representative of the **aristocracy** to the **Estates-General**, and was among the principal voices opposing the reunion of the three orders. When the king decreed that reunion on 23 June, Cazalès spoke out in opposition to voting by head. After the fall of the **Bastille**, on 14 July, Cazalès left **Paris** to return home, but was stopped en route and obliged to resume his post. He was a frequent and eloquent speaker in the **Constituent Assembly**, often citing **Enlightenment** thinkers to support his conservative positions, and served on the Finance Committee. Cazalès warned the Assembly against requiring the **Civil Oath of the Clergy**, voted against the creation of *assignats*, and protested the abolition of nobility. He resigned his seat definitively on 9 July 1791 and emigrated to Coblenz, but returned home after a cool reception among the *émigrés*. Cazalès emigrated again following 10 August 1792, to England, and accompanied the English squadron at **Toulon** in late 1793. He returned to England thereafter, wrote a *Defense of Louis XVI*, and refused to serve under **Napoleon Bonaparte**. He died in southern France.

CERCLE SOCIAL. The Cercle Social was among the most important political clubs in **Paris** between 1790 and 1793, and functioned after 1791 as a publishing house as well. Founded by **Nicolas de Bonneville** and **Claude Fauchet**, the club, whose full title was the Confederation of the Friends of Truth, drew as many as 5,000 people to its meetings in the **Palais Royal**. Fauchet would typically lead off those meetings with an analysis of some aspect of **Jean-Jacques Rousseau's** *Social Contract*, and in both its meetings and its publications the Cercle Social constituted one of the principal venues linking the ideas of the **Enlightenment** to the politics of the Revolution. Other clubs, including the **Jacobin club**, denounced it for its extremism.

Prominent members of the Cercle Social included **Camille Desmoulins**, **Marie-Jean Condorcet**, **Jacques-Pierre Brissot**, and **Jean-Baptiste Louvet**. Through its **newspaper**, the *Bouche de Fer*, the club was perhaps the most important advocate of democratic politics in 1791, and in a July 1791 speech at the Cercle Social, Condorcet was the first prominent figure to call for the declaration of a republic. The club itself was closed down in the aftermath of the **Champ de Mars** massacre, but the publishing house continued, becoming by 1792–93 the virtual house organ of the **Girondin** deputies. With the proscription of the leading Girondins in June 1793, the Cercle Social faded from the revolutionary scene.

CERTIFICATS DE CIVISME. The *certificats de civisme* were official documents attesting to the bearer's civic virtue. They were first required of foreigners in early 1793, and municipal authorities were charged with issuing them. The signatures of six citizens in good standing were required before a *certificat* could be issued. Thereafter, these cards became required of individuals holding public office or exercising certain occupations, such as teachers, and in the spring of 1793 **committees of surveillance** were formed throughout the country to oversee the issuance of these *certificats*. **Jacobin clubs** exercised substantial influence in the formation of those committees of surveillance, and the *certificats* came to function as internal passports. With the passage of the first **Law of Suspects** in September 1793, to be denied a *certificat de civisme* meant essentially to be considered a suspect. Ex-priests and ex-nobles were routinely so defined, but simply to have been considered an advocate of **federalism** was enough to warrant the denial of a *certificat*. Issuance of these cards thus became intensely politicized, often arbitrary, and the abuse of this authority became an important issue in eventual attacks upon the committees of surveillance. When the **Terror** came to an end after **Thermidor**, the practice of issuing *certificats de civisme* gradually came to an end as well.

CHABOT, FRANÇOIS (1756–1794). Chabot's father was a cook at the *collège* in Rodez where François received his early education. Chabot went on to pursue a monastic vocation, received his tonsure in March 1772, and joined the Order of Capucins in Rodez. In his role as caretaker of the monastery, Chabot had access to works of **Enlightenment** philosophy that were troubling to him, and by 1788 the Bishop of Rodez had forbidden him to preach in the diocese. After 1789 he abandoned his monastery as soon as clerical orders were suppressed, swore the constitutional oath, and became vicar-general to **Henri-Baptiste Grégoire** at Blois, an appointment that Grégoire claimed later to regret. In 1791 Chabot was elected to the **Legislative Assembly** from the Loir-et-Cher and sat on the far left. By the summer of 1792 he was actively calling for **Louis XVI** to be removed from the throne, and rallied the people of the *faubourgs* for the **uprising of 10 August 1792**. He was sent by the Assembly to try to halt the **September Massacres**, and managed to save a single abbot.

Chabot was re-elected from the Loir-et-Cher to the **National Convention**, and now adopted the dress of the **sans-culottes**. He voted for death in the trial of Louis XVI, was named to the **Committee of General Security** in January 1793, and in the early spring went on mission for military recruitment to southern France. In May he preached in a **Toulouse** church on the subject of Jesus as a sans-culotte. Although Chabot had spoken critically of **Marie-Jean Condorcet** early in the year, for his proposed constitution, and had denounced many of the other **Girondin** deputies, he returned to **Paris** in late May and played something of a mediating role in the insurrection of 31 May to 2 June 1793. He was sent on mission to Amiens in July 1793 to quell troubles in that town, but failed miserably in his mission and was forced to flee. Chabot now became an ardent **de-Christianizer** and in November renounced his priesthood. This may have been prompted by his marriage to Léopoldine Frey, whose brothers allegedly paid Chabot a dowry of 200,000 *livres* to marry their sister, perhaps in an effort to deflect suspicion from their involvement in the *Compagnie des Indes* scandal. Chabot tried to protect himself by denouncing others involved in the plot, but was arrested in January 1794 and went to trial in April along with the Dantonists. The *Compagnie des Indes* plotters defended themselves badly, by accusing each other, and all went to the **guillotine**. *See also* CLERGY.

CHALIER, JOSEPH (1747–1793). Little is known about Chalier's family or youth. He was born near Briançon in the French Alps, at one time a part of Piedmont, into a family of lawyers. Chalier moved to **Lyon** in the 1760s to complete his education, finding employment as a tutor for the children of wealthy merchants. Through the patronage of one of those families he undertook a commercial career for himself in the 1780s. He was in **Paris** at the time of the storming of the **Bastille**, but returned to Lyon and was elected a municipal *notable* in February 1790. Along with **Jean-Marie Roland**, he played a principal role in the democratization of Lyonnais politics, and in November 1790 was elected as an officer on the municipal council. Late in 1791 Chalier appears to have been overzealous in carrying out domiciliary visits in search of arms, and the **departmental administration** dismissed him from office. He went to Paris to plead his case before the **Legislative Assembly**, but it was not until 15 August 1792 that it ruled in his favor. In the meantime the monarchy had fallen and Chalier had developed close ties with the Paris **Jacobin club**.

He returned to Lyon determined to radicalize politics there, stood as a candidate in the mayoral election, but lost, settling for a position as president of the district tribunal. The municipal council was dominated by a slate of his supporters, however, and Chalier stood at the center of the polarization of Lyon politics in 1793. The moderate mayor was ousted from office in February 1793, and in the months that followed, Chalier and his Jacobin supporters heightened the tone of their rhetoric directed against **aristocrats** and wealthy merchants. Fearful moderates mobilized their supporters through the sectional assemblies of Lyon, and in a violent insurrection on 29 May 1793 reclaimed control of municipal government. Chalier was arrested, brought to trial in July (in the midst of the **federalist revolt**), and executed on 16 July 1793. He immediately took his place in the pantheon of Jacobin martyrs, alongside **Jean-Paul Marat** and **Louis-Michel Lepelletier de Saint-Fargeau**.

CHAMP DE MARS. The Champ de Mars, or *Field of Mars*, was a large open space at the western edge of **Paris**, not far from the **Invalides**. Today the Eiffel Tower stands at one end of the Champ de Mars, and the Ecole Militaire at the other. The Champ de Mars is of significance in the Revolution because of two important events. The first of these was the **Festival of Federation**, held on the initial anniversary of the fall of the **Bastille**. Plans for the festival called for a huge amphitheater to be constructed on the site, and this ambitious construction project brought thousands of Parisians, including **Louis XVI** himself, to the Champ de Mars to lend a hand. The weeks leading up to the event, and the festival itself, which brought representatives of the **National Guard** from every department in the nation, were a remarkable display of social harmony and revolutionary fraternity.

One year later, however, the Champ de Mars became the site of conflict and tragedy. Following the king's flight to **Varennes**, in June 1791, both the **Cordelier club** and the **Cercle Social** issued calls for the declaration of a republic. A petition to that effect, when presented before the **Jacobin club** on 16 July, produced the split that led to the creation of the **Feuillants**. When the **Constituent Assembly** rebuffed the demands of the petition, the Jacobins backed away and the Cordeliers took up the initiative. François Robert drafted a new petition, explicitly republican, and a call went out summoning Parisians to the Champ de Mars on 17 July 1791 to sign the petition. Early in the day, however, the mayor of Paris, **Jean-Sylvain Bailly**, had declared martial law, and the crowd of some 50,000 that gathered on the Champ de Mars was met by the **National Guard**, commanded by General **Lafayette**. Lafayette ordered the crowd to disperse. When they failed to do so, after an unknown provocation, Lafayette's troops opened fire, killing as many as 50 and wounding over 100, in what soon came to be known as the Champ de Mars massacre.

The immediate aftermath of the Champ de Mars massacre saw the repression of the popular movement in Paris. Dozens of radicals were arrested, and many others went into hiding. **Georges Danton** fled to England. The Cordelier club suspended its meetings, while the Cercle Social ceased to exist as a club. In the long run, though, the violence of 17 July and the repression that followed led to the disgrace of both Bailly and Lafayette, and an increased radicalism in the popular movement in Paris.

CHAMPION DE CICÉ, JÉRÔME-MARIE (1735–1810). Champion de Cicé was educated at the *collège* of Plessis, and went on to earn his Doctorate in theology at the Sorbonne. In the 1770s he served as Bishop of Rodez and was named Archbishop of **Bordeaux** in 1781. He was a delegate to the first **Assembly of Notables** in 1787, where he opposed the reforms proposed by **Charles Calonne** and favored the return of **Jacques Necker** to office. Champion de Cicé was elected from the **clergy** to the **Estates-General**, and was among the first clerics to join the **Third Estate**. He served on the constitutional committee in the **Constituent Assembly**. On 3 August 1789 **Louis XVI** appointed him *Garde des Scéaux*, which displeased deputies on both the left and the right. In that function he urged the king to delay the publication of important decrees, including the **Declaration of the Rights of Man and Citizen** and the abolition of **seigneurial dues**, which enraged patriots. He encouraged Louis XVI to sign the legislation introducing the **Civil Constitution of the Clergy**, but then refused to swear the civil oath himself. He joined the **Monarchist club** in 1790, and in November of that year resigned his position in the Constituent Assembly. When the Assembly disbanded he emigrated, first to Brussels, then to Holland and finally to England. Champion de Cicé returned to France in 1801, was named Archbishop of Aix-en-Provence the following year, and in 1808 was awarded the title of Count of the Empire.

CHARITY. The abolition of **privilege** on the **Night of 4 August 1789** also effectively eliminated many of the sources of charity that had existed under the Old Regime. The **confiscation of Church lands** in November 1789 marked an additional blow to charity, since the Church had operated most of the **hospitals** serving the poor. In August 1792 the abolition of religious orders completed the dismantling of virtually all of the institutions that had directed charity toward the poor prior to the Revolution.

The **Constituent Assembly** was mindful of the problems thus created, and in May 1790 called for the creation of *ateliers de charité*, public workshops. These were unpopular with the middle classes, however, and never adequately funded or organized. In March 1793 the **National Convention** passed legislation creating a system of public assistance, but the crisis brought on by war and **counterrevolution** rendered that legislation largely ineffective. October 1793 brought additional decrees outlawing both begging and almsgiving. The government was relatively successful at controlling prices and securing the food supply under the **Terror**, but with the abandonment of the *maximum* following **Thermidor** the sick and indigent fell easy prey to the harsh winter of 1795.

Under the **Directory**, a system of public charity was finally put in place with some success. Legislation passed in November 1796 established *bureaux de bienfaisance* in every commune, responsible for providing home relief, and funding for state hospitals was increased. One month later, legislation placed abandoned children under the care of the state. Late in the decade, the prohibition against congregations of nursing sisters was lifted.

CHARRIER, MARC-ANTOINE (1755–1793). Charrier was the son of a royal notary. He studied law in **Toulouse**, but then served as an officer in the Bourbonnais regiment, participating in the 1769 Corsican campaign, before returning to Toulouse to take up a career in law. In 1789 he was elected to the **Estates-General** as a delegate for the **Third Estate**. He was present at the swearing of the **Tennis Court Oath**, but adopted mostly conservative positions in the **Constituent Assembly** and opposed the constitution presented in September 1791. When the Assembly disbanded, he emigrated to Coblenz, but returned to France shortly thereafter to take up leadership of royalist bands in the Lozère. The **Legislative Assembly** ordered his arrest in April 1792, but he went into hiding and took up arms, scoring several victories in battle over the next year at the head of his **peasant** army. His army was finally defeated in June 1793, and Charrier was executed in Rodez the following month.

CHÂTELET. The Châtelet was the main civil and criminal court in **Paris** on the eve of the Revolution, but also the name of a notorious debtors and criminal prison on the right bank of the Seine River. During the first year of the Revolution, the Châtelet had jurisdiction over the new offense of *lèse nation*, and was also charged with bringing to justice those responsible for the violence of the **October Days**. That investigation, in particular, made the court the focus of considerable political controversy, and it was abolished by the decree of 25 August 1790. The Châtelet prison survived, and was the scene of some 200 killings during the **September Massacres** of 1792.

CHAUMETTE, PIERRE-GASPARD (1763–1794). Chaumette was one of the most popular orators of the **Palais Royal** and a leading figure in the Parisian **sans-culotte** movement. His youth was a tumultuous one. He was the son of a shoemaker in Nevers; was expelled from school in 1776; worked as a cabin boy, a copyist, and a clerk to a prosecutor; was self-taught in medicine and surgery; and became a teacher himself on the eve of the Revolution. In 1789 Chaumette moved to **Paris**, where he joined the **Cordelier club** and worked on **Louis Prudhomme's** *Journal des Révolutions*. He sat on the Insurrectionary Commune in August 1792, was unjustly accused of being involved in the **September Massacres**, and in December was named prosecutor in Paris. In 1793 Chaumette took the name *Anaxagoras*, after an alleged atheist hung during the time of Pericles. Although excoriated by many as a radical **deChristianizer**, Chaumette was very much a moralist and egalitarian, and an advocate for social reform. He was active in the **uprisings of 4–5 September 1793**, supported the **Law of Suspects** that was passed shortly thereafter, and is generally credited with the creation of the mobile **guillotine**. He was associated with **Jacques Roux** and the *enragés*, and was arrested at about the same time as **Jacques Hébert**, although Chaumette was tried separately and executed on 13 April 1794.

CHÉNIER, ANDRÉ (1762–1794). André Chénier was born in Constantinople, the son of a French textile merchant and an aristocratic mother with Greek bloodlines. His father, Louis, fell on economic hard times in 1765 and took the family back to France. André went to live with an aunt in Carcassonne, where he spent the next seven years, while his father traveled to Morocco in the French diplomatic corps. André joined his mother in **Paris** in 1773, attended the *collège* of Navarre at his father's insistence, made the acquaintance of the wealthy Trudaine brothers, and through them and his mother's **salon** made an entrée into Parisian society. He wrote his first poetry in these years, but left Paris in 1783 for a post as a gentleman cadet with an infantry company. His military career lasted barely a year.

Chénier returned briefly to Paris, then traveled to Switzerland and Italy, writing poetry that blended contemporary themes with allusions to classical Rome. Short of funds, he went to London in 1787 as personal secretary to the French ambassador, returning to Paris only in May 1790. André joined the **Society of 1789**, and began publishing pamphlets and **newspaper** articles critical of the **Jacobin club**, of which his brother was a member. Marie-Joseph felt obliged to respond in print to his brother's polemics, in part because André signed his articles with his last name only, and as Marie-Joseph was at this time much the better known of the two he worried that Parisians might take the anti-Jacobin diatribes to be his own. André did not lay his pen down, however, continuing to write biting criticism of the violent militancy of the **sans-culottes**, and denouncing by name leaders such as **Maximilien Robespierre**, **Jacques-Pierre Brissot**, and **Jérome Pétion**. With his hopes for a viable constitutional monarchy dashed by the **uprising of 10 August 1792**, Chénier went into hiding, eventually seeking refuge in **Versailles**. After the assassination of **Jean-Paul Marat**, he composed an *Ode à Charlotte Corday*. André Chénier was arrested on 7 March 1794 and went to the **guillotine** on 25 July, just two days before Robespierre. He continued to write poetry while in prison, but his collected poems remained unpublished until 1819.

CHÉNIER, MARIE-JOSEPH (1764–1811). Chénier, like his older brother **André Chénier**, was born in Constantinople. He had a brief, and unremarkable, military career, but made his mark as a playwright, most notably with *Charles IX, ou l'école des rois*, a strongly anti-monarchical and anti-clerical play that opened in **Paris** in the fall of 1789, with **François-Joseph Talma** in the lead role. Among his other plays were *Henri VIII*, *Jean Calas*, and *Caïus Gracchus*. Chénier joined the **Jacobin club** in 1791, was elected to the **National Convention** from the Seine-et-Oise, and later sat in the **Council of Five Hundred**. He composed the lyrics to a number of patriotic hymns, the most celebrated of which was *Le Chant du départ*. In the spring of 1794 Chénier offended **Maximilien Robespierre** with his play *Timoléon* and its references to tyranny. He similarly offended the Emperor **Napoleon Bonaparte** in 1806 with his play *Epitre à Voltaire*, which forced him to retire from public life.

CHOUANS. The *chouans* were royalist rebels, mostly **peasants**, centered in Brittany. Their movement, known as *chouannerie*, was the most extensive peasant rebellion of the Revolution and at its height, in 1794, spread east into Normandy, affecting portions of 10 departments. Unlike the rebels of the **Vendée**, however, the *chouans* never coalesced into a unified military campaign, surviving instead as more of a scattered and sporadic guerrilla movement. *Chouans*, named perhaps for the local screech owl whose call they imitated, first appeared in 1792 and grew in response to the military recruitment ordered in the spring of 1793. They operated mainly in rural areas, attacking republican patrols, capturing grain convoys, persecuting elected officials and constitutional priests. Rarely did they come together into large forces, but both **Joseph Puisaye** and Georges Cadoudal attempted to link the *chouannerie* to the *émigré* forces supported by the British, though without success. The *chouans* were a persistent thorn in the side of the revolutionary government, however, limiting its effective control in the West to the urban areas. *Chouannerie* was dealt a severe blow in 1796 by forces under the command of General **Lazare Hoche**, but not until after the 1801 Concordat, negotiated with the Catholic Church by **Napoleon Bonaparte**, were the peasant rebels truly pacified.

CIVIL CONSTITUTION OF THE CLERGY. The Civil Constitution of the Clergy was adopted by the **Constituent Assembly** on 12 July 1790 to restructure and reorganize the Catholic Church in France. Following the abolition of **privilege** on the **Night of 4 August**, and the subsequent decision in November 1789 to convert Church property into *biens nationaux*, there was general agreement among the deputies about the need for reform of the Church, and an ecclesiastical committee was formed to draft legislation. Few deputies foresaw the deep divisions that the Civil Constitution of the Clergy would create among French citizens in the years that followed.

The main features of the legislation were as follows. The number of bishops was reduced from 136 to 83, one per department, with bishops now to be elected rather than appointed. The number of parishes was also reduced, their distribution to be determined rationally. Given the confiscation of Church land, both bishops and priests were to be salaried employees of the state. The legislation included a scale of salaries, much narrower in range than those that had prevailed under the Old Regime. As state officials, priests and bishops would be required to swear an oath of loyalty, the **Civil Oath of the Clergy**.

The supporters of the Civil Constitution of the Clergy, influenced no doubt by **Jansenism**, insisted that they had acted in the best interest of the Church, intent only on removing past abuses. Opponents of the legislation argued that it flaunted the authority of the Papacy, and many of the faithful objected to the election of priests, arguing that nothing would prevent **Protestants** from participating in those elections. Many **clergy** hoped for guidance from Rome, but none was forthcoming, and **Louis XVI** reluctantly signed the legislation on 26 December 1790. Three months later **Pius VI** denounced the legislation and threatened those who swore the oath with excommunication. Thus, the Civil Constitution of the Clergy produced a virtual schism within the French church, and contributed much to the contours of counterrevolutionary opposition over the following decade. *See also* CLERGY.

CIVIL OATH OF THE CLERGY. The Civil Oath of the Clergy was the most controversial element of the **Civil Constitution of the Clergy**, and the most divisive. It seemed logical to the deputies of the **Constituent Assembly** that the **clergy**, who like themselves would now be salaried officials of the state, should swear the same oath as other public officials, pledging "fidelity to the nation, the law, the king and the constitution." For many clergy, however, this oath posed a crisis of conscience, for it presented the possibility that their first loyalty to God might come into conflict with a sworn loyalty to a temporal authority.

The requirement of the Civil Oath immediately accentuated the split between the upper and lower clergy that had become apparent during elections to the **Estates-General**. During the first months of 1791, approximately 60 percent of parish priests swore the oath, whereas only seven of 83 bishops swore the oath. After **Pope Pius VI** denounced the Civil Constitution in March 1791, a number of parish priests retracted their oath, so that in the end approximately 50 percent of parish priests swore the oath. Those who refused, or who retracted, known as refractory priests, were removed from their posts, to be replaced by election, but were initially allowed to perform priestly functions. The geographic pattern of the Civil Oath is an interesting one: those departments with the highest numbers of juring priests tended to support **Jacobin** policies in 1792–93, while departments with high numbers of refractory priests, as in the **Vendée** and much of Brittany, supported counterrevolutionary rebellion. Voting patterns in 19th-century elections also tended to reflect the geographic patterns of the Civil Oath.

The rivalry between juring and refractory priests produced conflict among their respective supporters, and on 27 May 1792 the **Legislative Assembly** adopted legislation decreeing that refractory clergy could be deported at the request of 20 **active citizens**, and in late August that decree was amended to require the demand of only six citizens. One year later the **National Convention** decreed that all refractory priests were subject to deportation. The persecution of refractory clergy continued through the **Terror**, until the law of 7 Fructidor V (24 August 1797) repealed the legislation of 1792 and 1793. Within days, however, the **Fructidor coup** reversed that decision, and persecution of refractory clergy resumed until the negotiation of the Concordat in 1801.

CLERGY. The Catholic clergy constituted the First Estate in Old Regime France. The clergy numbered about 150,000 members, less than 1 percent of the total population. About 60,000 were members of the secular clergy (parish priests, vicars, bishops), while the remainder constituted the regular clergy, members of religious orders that would be abolished during the Revolution. One should also distinguish between the lower clergy, the vast majority, and the upper clergy, numbering about 10,000, who constituted the hierarchy of the Church (archbishops, bishops, abbots, and prioresses). The upper clergy enjoyed benefices and often lived in an opulence similar to that of the wealthy **aristocracy** (indeed, most of them were aristocrats), while the lower clergy lived more modestly, according to the means of the parish or community that they served.

The poor parish priests often resented the wealth of the hierarchy, and the division between upper and lower clergy made the electoral assemblies of the First Estate among the most contentious of 1789. At the **Estates-General**, disgruntled parish clergy were among the first to rally to the **Third Estate** at **Versailles**. The adoption of the **Civil Constitution of the Clergy**, in late 1790, produced a new split among the clergy. Most of the upper clergy refused to support it, while about 50 percent of the parish priests accepted the Civil Constitution by swearing the **Civil Oath**. Some clergy became ardent supporters of the Revolution, with a few going so far as to renounce their vows, while others joined the ranks of the **counterrevolution**. During the Year II, several thousand of the clergy chose to marry. Overall, the reorganization of the Church during the early Revolution, and the **deChristianization** campaign that followed, decimated the numbers of the clergy, a blow from which the Catholic Church in France never fully recovered.

CLERMONT-TONNERRE, ANNE-ANTOINE-JULES (1749–1830).
Clermont-Tonnerre's father was a duke and peer of France, who went to the **guillotine** in **Paris** two days before **Maximilien Robespierre**. His brother was executed in **Lyon** two days after the collapse of the **federalist revolt** in that city. Anne-Antoine-Jules was educated at the seminary of Saint-Sulpice and went on to complete a doctorate in theology at the Sorbonne. His father was a grand master in the **Freemasons**, and he himself was a member of the Academy of Sciences, Arts, and Belles-lettres in Châlons, where he was appointed bishop in 1782. In 1789 Clermont-Tonnerre was elected to the **Estates-General** as a delegate for the **clergy**. In April 1790 he signed a declaration in favor of Catholicism as the official religion of France, and opposed the **Civil Constitution of the Clergy** that was passed later that year. He emigrated to Germany after the **Constituent Assembly** dissolved.

Clermont-Tonnerre was reappointed to the bishopric of Châlons in 1817, but did not take up the post, and was named archbishop of **Toulouse** in 1820. Two years later, he was made a cardinal.

CLERMONT-TONNERRE, STANISLAS-MARIE-ADELAIDE (1757–1792). Stanislas Clermont-Tonnerre was the cousin of Anne-Antoine. His father was a *maréchal de camp* and first chamberlain to the king of Poland. Clermont-Tonnerre studied at the *collège* of Pont-à-Mousson and then the *collège* of Plessis in **Paris**. He followed a military career before the Revolution, rising to the rank of colonel in the Royal-Navarre Regiment. He was a member of the **Committee of Thirty**, drew up the *cahier de doléance* for the nobility of Meaux, and was sent as a delegate to the **Estates-General** by the **aristocracy** of Paris. Clermont-Tonnerre was one of the 47 aristocrats who joined the **Third Estate** in June, was among the most active orators in the **Constituent Assembly**, twice presided over that body, and sat on the important Constitutional Committee. He was close to **Jean-Joseph Mounier**, **Trophime-Gérard Lally-Tollendal**, and **Pierre-Victor Malouet**, with whom he founded the **Monarchist club** in Paris. He protested the abolition of nobility, but favored full civil and political rights for non-Catholics, and supported a suspensive veto for the king. He was an active pamphleteer during the early years of the Revolution. Clermont-Tonnerre plotted with Bertrand de Molleville, Lally-Tollendal, and Malouet to save **Louis XVI** on 10 August 1792, but they were recognized on the street and pursued into the hôtel of Madame de Brassac, where Clermont-Tonnerre was killed.

CLUB DE CLICHY. The Club de Clichy was a loose right-wing assemblage that emerged late in 1794, so named because those attending met at the home of J. Gérard-Desrivières on the *rue de Clichy*, in one of the more fashionable neighborhoods of **Paris**. The members were drawn together more by what they opposed than by a common program or political ideal. Included among them were deputies who had participated in 9 **Thermidor**, former **Girondins** who had been imprisoned during the **Terror**, constitutional monarchists, and outright royalists. They came together in order to prevent any resurgence of Jacobinism or what they tended to refer to as anarchism.

The closing of the **Jacobin club** in November 1794 weakened the common enemy that had united the Clichyens, and a number of moderate republican deputies left the club. Controversy over the decree of two-thirds and the failure of the **Vendémiaire** uprising in 1795 attracted new membership and **Lazare-Nicholas Carnot**, one of the first directors, gave cautious support to the club. Staunch royalists within the club did make contact with agents of the Comte de **Provence**, but members of the club on the whole did not favor restoration of the monarchy. The elections of 1797 brought a surge in membership, with meetings often attracting as many as 300. But the **Fructidor coup** carried out by the **Directory** purged a number of Clichyens from office, and the club disappeared by the end of the year.

COCKADES. The tricolor cockade was among the first symbols of the French Revolution. After the fall of the **Bastille**, in July 1789, the white of the Bourbon monarchy was joined to the red and blue colors of **Paris** to create the new tricolor symbol of the nation, soon to appear on flags, banners, sashes, and cockades. The cockades themselves, made from either wool or ribbon, were from two to five inches in diameter and were worn on the hats of men and the clothing of **women**. At a banquet on 1 October 1789, at **Versailles**, the queen's bodyguards were reported to have removed their tricolor cockades, stomped them underfoot, and replaced them with the black cockades of the Austrian monarchy, an incident that led to the women's march of the **October Days**. The cockades soon became a symbol of revolutionary patriotism, and a decree of 21 September 1793 mandated that all women wear a tricolor cockade in public, lest they be denounced as suspects and be punished by a week in prison. After 9 **Thermidor**, the public prominence of the cockades as a revolutionary symbol gradually declined.

COLLOT D'HERBOIS, JEAN-MARIE (1749–1796). Collot d'Herbois was the son of a **Paris** goldsmith. Schooled at the Oratoriens, he left at the age of 15 to join a marionette troupe. He traveled widely in France in the 1770s and 1780s as an actor, playwright, and theater director. After a disappointing stint as theater director in **Lyon** in 1787, he returned to Paris and acted often at the **Palais Royal**. Collot was active in Paris politics after 1789, joining both the **Cordelier club** and the **Jacobin club**. He sat on the insurrectionary **Commune** in August 1792 and was elected to the **National Convention** from Paris. Collot went on numerous recruitment missions to the provinces in 1793, and along with **Jacques-Nicolas Billaud-Varenne** was elected to the **Committee of Public Safety** after the **sans-culotte** uprising of September 1793. In October he was sent on mission to Lyon, where he clashed with **Georges Couthon**. Collot is generally held responsible, along with **Joseph Fouché**, for the harsh repression of the **federalist revolt** in Lyon, where nearly 1,900 rebels were executed. During this same period he wrote his *Instruction...*, often cited as a **terrorist** manifesto. As president of the National Convention in July 1794, Collot played a key role in the 9 **Thermidor** coup against **Robespierre**. Denounced as a terrorist in March 1795, Collot was tried and deported to Guyana, where he died of fever within a year.

COLONNES INFERNALES. Following the defeat of the main rebel army in the **Vendée** on 23 December 1793, at Savenay, General Louis-Marie Turreau, who had recently been appointed commander of the Army of the West, adopted a "scorched earth" policy in order to eliminate what remained of the rebel forces. Such a policy had been implicitly approved by the 1 August 1793 decree of the **National Convention**. General Turreau organized his troops into two armies of 12 columns each, positioned them at the eastern and western extremes of the rebel zone, and ordered them to proceed toward each other, putting to the bayonet all those they encountered who had taken up arms against the Republic, and putting to the torch all villages and towns, except 13 designated as patriotic. The campaign began on 21 January 1794, the first anniversary of the execution of **Louis XVI**, without explicit approval from **Paris**. Thousands were killed in the following months, including **women** and children, the precise numbers being impossible to calculate. Far from ending the rebellion, the *colonnes infernales* had the opposite effect and increased **peasant** opposition in the Vendée. On 13 May the Convention recalled and sacked Turreau, and the rebellion in the West continued on to the end of the decade.

COMMISSION OF TWELVE. The Commission of Twelve (*Commission des Douze*) was created on 18 May 1793, on the proposal of

Bertrand Barère, then a member of the **Committee of Public Safety**, to investigate the alleged conspiracy taking shape among the **Paris** sections against the **National Convention**. Twelve deputies were named to the Commission on 20 May, nearly all of them drawn from the **Girondin** faction. The Commission immediately subpoenaed the minutes of all 48 of the Paris sections; called **Pierre-Gaspard Chaumette**, **Dominique-Joseph Garat**, and **Jean-Nicolas Pache** to testify before it; and soon ordered the arrest of **Jacques-René Hébert** and **Jean Varlet**. On 25 May, representatives of the sections and the **Paris Commune** demanded the release of those arrested, prompting **Henri-Maximin Isnard**, then presiding over the Convention, to threaten Paris with annihilation. This intemperate remark provoked the mobilization of Parisian militants, and under their pressure the Convention voted on 27 May to dissolve the Commission of Twelve, only to reinstate it the very next day. The Commission was permanently dissolved during the *journée* of 31 May, and a number of its members were proscribed from the National Convention on 2 June 1793, which marked the political ascendancy of the **Montagnard** deputies.

COMMITTEE OF GENERAL SECURITY. The Committee of General Security (*Comité de Sûreté Générale*) was the second of the "Great Committees" of the **Terror**, along with the **Committee of Public Safety**. Unlike the Committee of Public Safety, the Committee of General Security had predecessors under earlier National Assemblies: the *Comité des recherches* (Search Committee) under the **Constituent Assembly**, and the *Comité de surveillance* (Committee of Surveillance) under the **Legislative Assembly**. The **National Convention** chose to continue that committee, and renamed it in October 1792.

The Committee of General Security, as with those committees that preceded it, was principally charged with surveillance of state security, correspondence with authorities in the departments, supervision of internal passports, and the prosecution of foreign agents and counterfeiters. During the first months of the National Convention, it was a large committee, with as many as 30 members. **Montagnard** deputies dominated in the fall of 1792, but the **Girondins** made a concerted effort in January 1793 to wrest control from their rivals. This produced a backlash, however, and following the execution of

Louis XVI the committee was reduced in size to 12 members, nearly all of whom were Montagnards. From that time until the end of 1795, the Committee of General Security never exceeded 16 members.

The Committee of General Security was essentially a police committee, secondary to the Committee of Public Safety (created in April 1793), whose superior authority was formalized by the **Law of 14 Frimaire**. The Committee of General Security was responsible for overseeing the machinery of revolutionary justice within **Paris**, and at the peak of the Terror employed over 100 people to carry out that task. It did not send **representatives on mission** into the provinces (that responsibility fell to the Committee of Public Safety), but it did maintain regular correspondence with the revolutionary committees in the departments. To carry out that task, the committee divided into four, each group maintaining contact with a specific region of the country. To some degree, the responsibilities of the two great committees overlapped, and they in fact met together once each week. By spring 1794, however, there was clear rivalry, even tension, between the two committees, and several members of the Committee of General Security (most notably **Jean-Pierre-André Amar** and **Marc-Alexis Vadier**) played an active role in the 9 **Thermidor** coup against **Maximilien Robespierre**.

After Thermidor the committee was enlarged somewhat, and one quarter of its membership changed regularly in a monthly rotation. It now supervised the release of prisoners arrested during the Terror, while continuing its former duties. The Committee of General Security played no active role in the **White Terror**, and ceased to exist when the National Convention dissolved in late 1795.

COMMITTEE OF PUBLIC SAFETY. The Committee of Public Safety (*Comité de Salut Public*) functioned as the executive power in the French government from April 1793 until October 1795. Up until the **uprising of 10 August 1792**, of course, the king was the executive, and the situation remained ambiguous until the execution of **Louis XVI** on 21 January 1793. At that time, the **National Convention** began to discuss the need for some sort of Committee of General Defense, and such a committee did function in an ad hoc fashion through the first few months of the year. In March, with the defeat at Neerwinden and the first manifestations of the **Vendée rebellion**, the need for a more streamlined and formal structure became apparent, and on 6 April 1793 the deputies voted to create the Committee of Public Safety.

The first committee was composed of nine members, renewable monthly, who met in closed session, a departure from past practice. Its responsibilities were essentially to oversee the activities of ministers, to manage all areas related to national defense, and to report to the Convention each week. The dominant figures on this first committee were **Georges-Jacques Danton**, **Bertrand Barère**, and **Pierre-Joseph Cambon**. The **uprising of 31 May–2 June 1793**, and the proscription of the **Girondin** deputies, changed the political complexion of the National Convention, and the **federalist revolt** in the provinces added to the national crisis. As a result, the Committee of Public Safety was expanded slightly and its membership altered in July 1793. The committee now numbered 10, with Danton leaving and **Maximilien Robespierre** joining. Two additional members were added in September, and that committee, often referred to as the "Great Committee," remained virtually intact and ruled France until 9 **Thermidor**.

The 12 members of the Great Committee, with their areas of responsibility, were as follows: Maximilien Robespierre, who served as chief spokesperson for the committee before the National Convention and took responsibility for matters of policy, police, and religion; **Louis-Antoine Saint-Just**, Robespierre's closest ally on the committee, with responsibility for war planning and political policy; **Georges Couthon**, also responsible for political policy and for police matters; **Bertrand Barère**, responsible for education, social welfare, and diplomacy, also served as a liaison to the Convention; **Jacques-Nicolas Billaud-Varenne**, responsible for corresponding with **representatives on mission** and departmental authorities; **Jean-Marie Collot d'Herbois**, closely allied with Billaud-Varenne, had responsibilities in the same areas; **Robert Lindet**, responsible for food supply to the armies and cities; **Lazare-Nicholas Carnot**, responsible for war strategy and personnel; **Claude-Antoine Prieur-Duvernois**, responsible for arms procurement and gunpowder manufacture; **Pierre-Louis Prieur**, generally on mission to the army or to the departments; **André Jeanbon Saint-André**, also frequently on mission, and responsible for naval affairs; **Marie-Jean Hérault-**

Séchelles, responsible for diplomacy, but arrested, tried, and executed in April 1794.

The powers of the Committee of Public Safety steadily expanded from July 1793 through July 1794. On 28 July 1793, it was given authority to issue arrest warrants for suspects. In September it assumed the power to nominate members of the other important committees, including the **Committee of General Security**. The 10 October 1793 decree, by which the Convention proclaimed the government to be revolutionary until peace was declared, gave the committee the authority to nominate generals and oversee the war effort. In November the committee was given explicit control of representatives on mission, although they had reported back to the committee since early in the summer. The **Law of 14 Frimaire** formalized the executive power of the Committee of Public Safety and placed foreign policy under its purview. Over the next six months, the staff of the committee grew from 67 to 418, a clear indication of its expanding duties. In April 1794 the Convention voted to abolish ministries, thereby increasing the committee's power, and also increased the police powers of the committee, thereby reducing the power of the Committee of General Security.

That shift no doubt increased the rivalry between the two great committees, and may have impelled certain members of the Committee of General Security to join in the conspiracy against Maximilien Robespierre. Within the Committee of Public Safety, Billaud-Varenne and Collot d'Herbois, as its most radical members, also joined in the plot to remove Robespierre from power. The arrest of Robespierre, Saint-Just, and Couthon on 9 Thermidor, and their execution the following day, obviously altered the composition of the Committee of Public Safety, but it did not bring its influence to an end. The committee retained its authority over foreign policy and the war effort, but saw its police powers curtailed, as the **Terror** over which it had ruled drew to a close. Membership on the committee now rotated each month, as had originally been intended, and between August 1794 and the dissolution of the National Convention in October 1795 more than 60 different deputies served in its ranks.

Controversy over the Committee of Public Safety and its place in the history of the Revolution began even before it disappeared. It is credited, on the one hand, for overseeing the defense of the country and guiding France to victory in war over virtually all of the other nations of Europe. But, on the other hand, it is condemned for overseeing the machinery of the Terror and putting in place what has often been characterized as a **Jacobin** dictatorship. Whether the former required the latter lies at the heart of the debate.

COMMITTEE OF THIRTY. The Committee of Thirty (*Comité des Trente*) was perhaps the most influential of the informal clubs or societies that existed in **Paris** on the eve of the Revolution. As early as November 1788 the Committee of Thirty began meeting as often as thrice weekly at the home of **Adrien Duport**, a *conseiller* at the **Parlement of Paris**. A number of influential figures participated in these meetings, including **Louis-Marie Noailles, Louis-Michel Le Peletier de Saint-Fargeau**, the three **Lameth** brothers, **Louis-Alexandre La Rochefoucauld, Marie-Joseph-Motier Lafayette, Pierre-Samuel Dupont de Nemours, Gabriel-Honoré Mirabeau, Marie-Jean Condorcet, Emmanuel-Joseph Sieyès**, and **Guillaume Target**. The Committee brought together liberal **aristocrats** as well as prominent leaders of the Paris **Third Estate**. They helped to finance and disseminate a number of important pamphlets in the months leading up to the convocation of the **Estates-General**, including those by Sieyès and Target, and also sponsored the circulation in the provinces of model *cahiers de doléances*. The Committee of Thirty, which actually numbered more than 50 members, may have been so named because some 28 of its regular attendees were elected to the Estates-General, where they played an active role among the liberal leadership of the assembly.

COMMITTEES OF SURVEILLANCE. Committees of surveillance (*comités de surveillance*) emerged, largely spontaneously, immediately after the **uprising of 10 August 1792**, when the **Legislative Assembly** charged municipal governments with the task of overseeing public order. The most prominent of these committees was that created by the **Paris Commune**, later assigned principal responsibility, or blame, for the **September Massacres**. In large cities, each section created a committee of surveillance in this period. The election of the **National Convention**, and the 20 September 1792 victory at **Valmy**, calmed public fears substantially and these first committees largely disappeared.

By spring 1793, however, the combined danger of war and rebellion prompted the National Convention to pass the law of 21 March, which mandated the creation of committees of surveillance in every commune of France. Large cities were to have one committee for every section. Committees were to be composed of 12 members, chosen by election, and their principal task was to compile lists of foreigners residing in their town or section, and to issue *certificats de civisme* to those for whom six citizens would vouch. Local **Jacobins** tended to dominate the committees.

The **Law of Suspects**, passed on 17 September 1793, broadened the powers and responsibilities of the committees of surveillance, which were now charged with compiling lists of suspects and arresting them. In areas that had participated in the **federalist revolt**, or cities near the **Vendée rebellion**, such as Nantes, the committees were particularly active. **Representatives on mission** often took responsibility for overseeing their activities, and relied heavily on the committees for information about the local scene. The **Law of 14 Frimaire** further defined the purview of the committees of surveillance, making them now responsible for enforcing revolutionary legislation and directing them to report each 10 days to the newly created *agents nationaux*. Committees were henceforth to be appointed, by representatives on mission, not elected.

The committees of surveillance, sometimes called revolutionary committees, thus played a pervasive role in the machinery of the **Terror**. In addition to overseeing revolutionary justice, they also supervised the enforcement of the *maximum* and the administration of food procurement policies. They were often overzealous in the exercise of their duties, and not surprisingly became a focus of the reaction that followed **Thermidor**. The law of 24 August 1794 eliminated committees of surveillance in small towns, and stipulated that their membership should be regularly rotated. Their powers were progressively restricted, until they disappeared completely with the enactment of the **Constitution of 1795**.

COMPAGNIE DES INDES. The *Compagnie des Indes* lent its name to an investment scandal in 1794, but its history spans nearly all of the 18th century. In its first incarnation it appeared in 1718–1719 as part of the overseas colonial investment system devised by John Law.

Over the course of the century, the company's fortunes waxed and waned, and in the 1770s it lost its monopoly over trade with the Far East. But in 1784 the monopoly of the *Compagnie des Indes* over all trade east of the Cape of Good Hope was once again recognized by the monarchy, largely through the good offices of **Charles-Alexandre Calonne**.

When the **Constituent Assembly** abolished **privilege** in 1790, the *Compagnie des Indes* once again lost its trade monopoly. It continued to operate, now as a publicly traded company, but as the political climate grew less tolerant of merchants and capitalists in 1793, the fortunes of the enterprise declined and in August 1793 the **National Convention** ordered its liquidation. The scandal that was exposed in 1794 involved **Baron Jean-Pierre de Batz** and a handful of **Montagnard** deputies who hoped to profit from the liquidation by manipulating the price of shares and then buying them up cheaply. **François Chabot** was implicated, along with **Philippe Fabre-d'Eglantine** (who was probably innocent), and an array of others with links, on the one hand, to the **Indulgents** and, on the other, to the supporters of **Jacques-René Hébert**, both of them groups that the **Committee of Public Safety** was eager to eliminate. Baron de Batz escaped arrest, but both Chabot and Fabre went to the **guillotine** in April 1794. The *Compagnie des Indes* was subsequently liquidated, its assets seized by the government. The descendants of shareholders continued to seek restitution from successive French governments through the late 19th century.

CONCIERGERIE. The Conciergerie, located on the Ile de la Cité, was the oldest prison in **Paris**, dating from the 14th century. Under the Revolution it was perhaps the most deplorable of the city's prisons—overcrowded, damp, humid, and rat infested. During the **September Massacres**, 378 of the 508 inmates incarcerated there lost their lives. In 1793 the **Revolutionary Tribunal** was installed in the nearby Palace of Justice, and the most celebrated victims of the **Terror** in Paris passed through the cells of the Conciergerie. These included **Marie Antoinette**, most of the proscribed **Girondins**, **Jacques-René Hébert**, **Georges Danton**, **Camille Desmoulins**, **Manon Roland**, **Jean-Sylvain Bailly**, and **Maximilien Robespierre**.

CONDORCET, MARIE-JEAN-ANTOINE-NICOLAS (1743–1794).

The Marquis de Condorcet was born into an old noble family of the Dauphiné. His father was a captain in the army and would have preferred that his son pursue a military career as well, but Condorcet had an aptitude for science. He was schooled by the Jesuits in Reims, and then went on to study mathematics, physics, philosophy, economics, and politics at the *collége* of Navarre in **Paris**. He was elected to the French **Academy** of Science in 1769 at the remarkably young age of 26, and in 1782 he entered the Académie Française. Condorcet represents one of the rare personal links between the intellectual world of the French **Enlightenment** and the political world of the French Revolution.

Condorcet was involved in revolutionary politics from the outset. He joined the Club of 1789, one of the forerunners of the **Jacobin club**, and in September 1789 was elected to the municipal council of **Paris**. In April 1790 he spoke before the **Constituent Assembly**, calling for an end to the property requirement for election to national office, and in a July 1791 speech before the **Cercle Social** he was among the first to call publicly for the declaration of a republic. Condorcet was also among the few male voices in this period to call for full citizenship rights for **women**. In 1791 he was elected from Paris to the **Legislative Assembly**, where he devoted much of his energy to a report on public education, which he viewed as essential to the cultivation of republican citizenship. He presided over the Assembly in late July 1792, and took a principal role in drafting the official report to the nation on the events of 10 August 1792.

Condorcet was then elected to the **National Convention** from the Aisne, and distanced himself somewhat from the **Girondin** deputies with whom he has often been associated. He was critical of **Jean-Baptiste Louvet's** denunciation of **Maximilien Robespierre**, and refused to support the indictment against **Jean-Paul Marat** in April 1793. Condorcet questioned the authority of the Convention to try **Louis XVI**, and voted against death as a sentence out of principled opposition to capital punishment. He is generally credited with drafting the "Girondin" constitution, presented to the Convention in February 1793 but never adopted. He voted with the **Montagnard** deputies to suppress the **Commission of Twelve**, and made no protest of the events of 31 May–2 June 1793. He did, however, publish a pamphlet that was quite critical of the Montagnard **constitution** that was adopted on 24 June 1793, and it was chiefly for this that he was denounced by **François Chabot** on 8 July. Condorcet went into hiding in the home of a friend, Madame Vernet, and in the following months wrote one of his most important philosophical treatises, *Equisse d'un tableau historique des progrès de l'esprit humain*. He left the refuge of Madame Vernet's home when he grew fearful that his continued presence was about to jeopardize her own safety. Plans went awry on the journey to his next haven, however, and when Condorcet sought shelter in an inn he was recognized and arrested. He died the next day in jail, probably from the poison that he carried with him.

CONFISCATION OF CHURCH LANDS. On 2 November 1789 the **Constituent Assembly** voted to confiscate income-producing property of the Church, a proposal first made by **Charles-Maurice Talleyrand-Périgord**. The legislation, which aimed at resolving the financial crisis of the government, had far-reaching implications. The confiscated land and other properties would soon be declared *biens nationaux*, and put up for sale at public auction. The creation of *assignats* to facilitate that process triggered a spiral of inflation from which no revolutionary regime fully escaped. By virtue of the confiscation of Church lands, the **clergy** effectively became civil servants, and as such were required to swear the **Civil Oath of the Clergy**, which nearly all bishops and roughly 50 percent of parish priests refused to do. This division within the Catholic Church contributed to the **counterrevolution** that would plague the First French Republic throughout its existence. Thus, the confiscation of Church lands could be said to have created more problems than it solved. Its most enduring legacy, through the sale of *biens nationaux* at public auction, was to perpetuate the predominant pattern of small-scale **peasant** landholding in the French countryside.

CONFRATERNITIES. Confraternities had long existed in most towns and cities of France, particularly in the Midi. They were lay societies organized around parish churches, grudgingly tolerated by the hierarchy of the Catholic Church. Each confraternity elected officers, maintained a membership roll, and recorded minutes of meetings. They drew their members from all levels of society, rich and poor, and each confraternity typically contributed to a different **charity** or form of public assistance in the town. Along with **freemasonry**, the confraternities of Old Regime France constituted an important vehicle for popular sociability that contributed to the vitality of **popular societies** and **Jacobin clubs** during the Revolution. Indeed, political clubs often adopted the institutional forms and procedures of the confraternities that had existed in their communities. Confraternities were suppressed by law in 1792, but reappeared in many towns after the Revolution.

CONSCRIPTION. The idea of a conscript army was considered by the **Constituent Assembly** as early as September 1789 but was rejected at that time. Instead, the government drew volunteers from the **National Guard** to increase the ranks of the military. The **Legislative Assembly**, too, relied on volunteers, even after declaring the *patrie en danger* in July 1792. More aggressive recruitment in the spring of 1793 did ignite resistance in some parts of France, contributing to the **Vendée rebellion** in the West, for example, but true conscription had still not been introduced. In August 1793, under pressure from the **Paris Commune**, the **National Convention** decreed a *levée en masse*, which made military service obligatory for bachelors and widowers without children between the ages of 18 and 25. This increased the size of the army by nearly 750,000 troops.

From 1794 to 1797, however, the size of the army fell from nearly one million soldiers to fewer than 400,000. This was an untenable situation, and the **Directory** finally did introduce a true system of conscription. The Jourdan Law, proposed by **Jean-Baptiste Jourdan** in the **Council of Five Hundred**, decreed that military service was obligatory for all able-bodied males over the age of 20. In the future, no Frenchman could hold public office, or exercise full civil rights, if he had not fulfilled his military obligation. A first call-up of conscripts was ordered in September 1798, mobilizing 200,000 soldiers. An additional call-up in April 1799 allowed the controversial provision that conscripts might send a substitute to fulfill their duty, but the call-up of all eligible conscripts in June 1799 would have rendered potential substitutes scarce. When the French government attempted to apply the Jourdan Law in **Belgium** in late 1798, it led to insurrection. There were sporadic riots against conscription in France as well, but the Jourdan Law regulated French military service for the next century.

CONSPIRACY OF EQUALS. The Conspiracy of Equals (*Conspiration des Egaux*) was a radical plot aimed at overthrowing the regime of the **Directory**. The principal leader of the plot was **Gracchus Babeuf**, who in 1795 had helped to found the **Panthéon club** in **Paris**. When authorities shut down the Panthéon club in February 1796, Babeuf and others decided to take their movement underground, and the Conspiracy of Equals was born. By March an insurrectionary committee had been formed, including Babeuf, **Sylvain Maréchal**, and Félix Le Pelletier. **Filippo Michele Buonarroti** soon joined the committee, as did Augustin-Alexandre Darthé. The conspiracy was more substantial on paper than in reality, although a network of potential supporters did exist based on the membership of the Panthéon club and the list of more than a thousand subscribers to Babeuf's newspaper, *Le Tribun du Peuple*. The plan was to organize insurrectionary cells in each of the 12 *arrondissements* of Paris, and to launch an uprising against the government on a prearranged date. The plot was never hatched. A police spy by the name of Grisel infiltrated the movement and betrayed it to the government, which was gravely concerned about the threat of popular upheaval in the midst of what had been the harshest winter in living memory. Babeuf, Buonarroti, Darthé, and some 50 others were arrested on 10 May 1796.

The program of the Conspiracy of Equals had been enunciated both in the pages of *Le Tribun du Peuple* and in a *Manifesto of Equals*, written by Maréchal and published in the spring of 1796. Babeuf argued that the **Thermidorians** had abandoned the ideals of 1789, and that social and political inequality were rapidly increasing in French society under the Directory. He and Maréchal called for a society of true equality, based on equal landownership and a fair distribution of goods. This somewhat vague ideal was to be achieved through a popular insurrection, followed by a period of revolutionary dictatorship. Should the insurrection succeed, Babeuf promised to enact the **Constitution of 1793**.

The Directory took 10 months to prepare its case against Babeuf and the others, and then tried them before a High Court in the small town of Vendôme outside Paris. The trial took three months and went badly for the government. Babeuf defended himself eloquently and with emotion, and in the end none of the defendants were found guilty of conspiracy, only seven were found guilty of any charge, and only Babeuf and Darthé were sentenced to death, for the crime of having urged the adoption of the Constitution of 1793. Buonarroti was sentenced to deportation and lived to revive the tradition of conspiratorial revolution and socialist ideals associated with Babeuf by publishing a history of the Conspiracy of Equals in 1828.

CONSTANT, BENJAMIN (1767–1830). Benjamin Constant was born in Lausanne, the son of a Swiss officer and businessman. He was educated at the University of Edinburgh, and in 1788 became chamberlain to the duke of Brunswick-Wolfenbüttel, in northern Germany. Court life bored him, however, and after meeting **Germaine de Staël** in Switzerland in late 1794 he made up his mind to move to France. Shedding his youthful cynicism, Constant now committed himself to a life of political activism. He gained French citizenship in 1797 and in that same year was elected to the municipal council of Luzarches, a small town just 20 miles north of **Paris**. He also published a number of political essays and pamphlets in 1796–97. Constant initially embraced the radicalism of the **Jacobin** revolution, but under the **Directory** he moderated his views, and his writings expressed in theory the difficult balance between republican extremism and royalist conservatism that the Directory regime never managed to achieve in practice. In his political moderation, he stands as a founder of French liberalism. After **Brumaire** he served in the Tribunat, but along with de Staël he became an antagonist to **Napoleon Bonaparte's** imperial ambitions and both went into exile after 1802. It was over the next decade and a half that Constant did most of his writing, both essays and fiction. He is best known for his psychological novel, *Adolphe*. His most substantial political work, *Fragments d'un ouvrage abandonné sur la possibilité d'une constitution républicaine dans un grand pays*, was not published until 1991.

CONSTITUENT ASSEMBLY. On 9 July 1789, the delegates to the **Estates-General**, having previously declared themselves a National Assembly, officially adopted the title of Constituent Assembly (*Assemblée Constituante*). Some delegates now chose to leave **Versailles**, asserting that they had been elected to a body that no longer existed, but most chose to remain. The Constituent Assembly adopted the **Declaration of the Rights of Man and Citizen**, initiated the abolition of

seigneurial dues and other forms of **privilege**, abolished noble titles, ordered the **confiscation of Church lands** and adopted the **Civil Constitution of the Clergy**, and as its principal achievement drafted the **Constitution of 1791**. The Constituent Assembly began its sessions at Versailles, but moved to **Paris** after the **October Days**. It held its final session on 30 September 1791 and was succeeded by the **Legislative Assembly**.

CONSTITUTION OF 1791. The Constitution of 1791 was the first written constitution of France. In its first version, ready for ratification in June 1791, it consisted of seven sections and 208 articles, but the king's flight to **Varennes**, and his denunciation of the proposed constitution as unworkable, brought the addition of two articles relating to royal abdication. The **Constituent Assembly** approved the constitution on 3 September 1791, and **Louis XVI** signed it reluctantly on 13 September. It endured for less than a year, rendered obsolete by the fall of the monarchy after the **uprising of 10 August 1792**.

The Constitution of 1791 preserved monarchy as the form of government for France, but situated **sovereignty** in the nation, not in the person of the king, and made royal authority subservient to the law, to which the king owed obedience. The king would exercise executive power, but as a salaried civil servant of the state, with a civil list of 25 million *livres* per year. Legislative power was to reside in a single-chamber legislature, composed of 745 deputies, the first incarnation of which would be the **Legislative Assembly**. The king was granted only a suspensive veto, not an absolute veto, over legislation proposed by the assembly. He was responsible for foreign policy, served as head of the armed forces, and had authority to name his ministers, although all decrees required the signature of a minister in addition to the king's.

The constitution reformed the electoral system, abandoning the universal manhood suffrage that had prevailed during elections to the **Estates-General**. The citizenry was now divided between **active citizens**, males 25 years of age who paid taxes equivalent to three days' wages, who were granted suffrage, and **passive citizens**, including women and those who paid insufficient taxes, who were granted full civil rights but denied the vote. A new administrative structure was also introduced, with the creation of 83 departments, replacing the provinces of the Old Regime, and local governmental councils at the departmental, district, and municipal levels.

Although Louis XVI signed the constitution, he did so with no enthusiasm and resented its restrictions on royal power and prerogatives. In 1792 he would be accused of violating the constitution and committing treason against the nation, and with the collapse of the constitutional monarchy the Constitution of 1791 became unviable. It would be the dual task of the **National Convention** to declare the Republic and to draft an appropriate constitution for that new form of government. *See also* CONSTITUTION OF 1793.

CONSTITUTION OF 1793. The Constitution of 1793 was the most democratic of the revolutionary constitutions. The **National Convention** created a Constitution Committee in October 1792, composed predominantly of **Girondin** deputies and headed by **Marie-Jean Condorcet**. The trial of **Louis XVI** delayed somewhat the work of the committee, but Condorcet made a report to the National Convention on 15 February 1792. The political struggle within the Convention between Girondins and **Montagnards** doomed that proposal to defeat, and letters poured into **Paris** from the departments throughout the winter and spring, imploring the deputies to overcome their divisions and deliver a constitution to the nation. The expulsion of the Girondin leaders from the Convention after the **uprising of 31 May–2 June 1793** resolved the political stalemate, and in short order a new committee was named, chaired by **Marie-Jean Hérault-Séchelles** and including **Louis-Antoine Saint-Just** and **Georges-August Couthon**. Those deputies remaining in the Convention resolved to debate the constitution each afternoon until agreement was reached, and on 24 June a final document was approved. It was presented to the people, approved in a popular referendum by a vote of 1,784,377 to 11,531, with over four million eligible voters abstaining, and inaugurated in Paris on 10 August 1793, the first anniversary of the fall of the monarchy, in a civic festival choreographed by **Jacques-Louis David**.

The constitution endorsed a republican form of government for France. It confirmed the principle of universal manhood suffrage, which had been introduced in practice in elections in the fall of 1792.

The language of the constitution made clear that the people, rather than the nation, were the source of **sovereignty**, thereby reversing the formula first uttered by **Emmanuel-Joseph Sieyès** and other patriots of the **Estates-General** when they asserted that wherever the National Assembly might meet, there the nation would be found. The constitution drafted by Condorcet's committee had proposed a bicameral legislature, which the Montagnards rejected. The legislature would be a unicameral body, with deputies elected each May to a one-year term. While Condorcet had suggested that an executive council be elected directly by the voters, the Constitution of 1793 called for a 24-member executive committee to be chosen by the deputies themselves from among a list of 84 candidates to be nominated by departmental electoral assemblies. The executive assembly would be responsible to the assembly, not to the voters.

The Constitution of 1793 strengthened the power of the central government at the expense of departmental autonomy. National deputies, for example, were to be elected for every 40,000 inhabitants, with no regard whatsoever for departmental boundaries. Departmental and district administrations were to be elected indirectly, by electoral assemblies, whereas municipal councils would be the product of direct elections. While the Condorcet constitution had included a referendum system, based in the departments, by which voters could force the national assembly to consider a petition or piece of legislation, the Constitution of 1793 made recourse to a popular referendum possible, but very difficult. Instead of institutionalizing referenda, the Montagnards made provision for the exercise of popular sovereignty by strengthening the clause declaring the people's right to insurrection in the **Declaration of the Rights of Man and Citizen**.

Due to the wartime emergency, and the **federalist revolt** in the provinces, the Constitution of 1793 was not immediately implemented, and that situation was formalized in October 1793, when the National Convention decreed that the government would remain "revolutionary until the peace." After the fall of **Maximilien Robespierre**, the **Thermidorians** left the constitution in abeyance, until the **Germinal** and **Prairial riots** of 1795 convinced the deputies of the need for a more conservative document. Although never enacted, the Constitution of 1793 remained an inspiration to the advocates of democracy throughout the 19th century. *See also* CONSTITUTION OF 1791; CONSTITUTION OF 1795.

CONSTITUTION OF 1795. The Constitution of 1795 was the final act of the **National Convention**, drafted in reaction to both the **Constitution of 1793** and the **Terror**. It sought to establish order and respect for the rule of law, and to guard against the danger of dictatorial rule. The new constitution was approved in a popular referendum by a vote of 941,853 to 41,892. As in 1793, more than four million voters abstained. A supplemental decree, which mandated that two-thirds of the members of the new two-chamber legislature must be drawn from the 750 deputies in the National Convention, was approved by a much narrower margin, 205,498 to 108,784.

The constitution began, as had the others, with a **Declaration of the Rights of Man and Citizen**, to which a list of duties was added, and from which the right to insurrection was removed. It called for the creation of a two-chamber legislature, the **Council of Ancients** and the **Council of Five Hundred**. The executive branch was to be composed of five directors, which gave the **Directory** regime its name. These five men were to be selected by the Council of Ancients from a list of 50 nominees drawn from both legislative chambers by the members of the Council of Five Hundred. One director would retire each year, determined by drawing lots initially, and each would exercise chief executive authority for a period of three months on a rotating basis.

France was to remain a republic, but a liberal rather than a democratic republic. All adult males could participate in primary assemblies, but these voted only for electors, for which there were both residency and tax requirements. Electoral assemblies thus numbered only some 30,000 members. Despite that restricted electorate, the Directory regime felt compelled to annul election results on several occasions. France was governed under the Constitution of 1795 until 1799, when **Napoleon Bonaparte** dispensed with it following his **Brumaire** coup.

CORDAY, MARIANNE-CHARLOTTE (1768–1793). Charlotte Corday was the celebrated, or infamous, assassin of **Jean-Paul Marat**. She was born into a Norman family of minor nobility, and was the great-granddaughter of the playwright, Pierre Corneille. Her mother died when she was young, so her father sent Charlotte and her two sisters to be educated at the Abbaye aux Dames in **Caen**. The abbess was Madame de Belzunce and the *coadjutrice* was Madame de Pontécoulant, both of whom had relatives who would figure in Corday's revolutionary experience. Corday made the acquaintance of Colonel Henri de Belzunce, a dashing young aristocrat who fell victim to an angry crowd in Caen in August 1789. Gustave de Pontécoulant would represent Calvados in the **National Convention** in 1792–93, and supported the **Girondins**.

Corday left the Abbaye aux Dames in late 1790, returned briefly to her country home, but returned to Caen in the spring of 1791. She took an apartment near the center of town, and became acquainted with Charles Bougon-Longrais, a departmental administrator in 1792–93. When the proscribed Girondin deputies fled to Caen in June 1793, Corday's acquaintance with Bougon-Longrais brought her into contact with them. She supported their cause and their denunciations of the radical **Montagnards**, and was appalled by the lack of popular support in Caen for the **federalist revolt**. After a particularly dismal public ceremony on 9 July, Corday left Caen for Paris, determined to do her part against the anarchists of the capital. She bought a knife in a shop at the **Palais Royal** and gained an audience with Marat, promising information about the fugitive deputies. She stabbed him on 13 July 1793 while he sat in his bath, making Marat a revolutionary martyr and Corday a traitorous villain. She went to the **guillotine** on 17 July, the day after Marat's funeral, and in death assumed the stature of a royalist martyr.

CORDELIER CLUB. Founded in April 1790, as the Society of the Friends of the Rights of Man and Citizen, the club soon took the name of Cordeliers, after the monastic order in whose building it originally met. The club moved to the hôtel de Genlis, on the place Dauphine in **Paris**, in March 1791 and remained there for the duration of its existence. The Cordeliers counted among their members a number of prominent revolutionaries, including **Jean-Paul Marat, Georges Danton, Camille Desmoulins, Jacques-René Hébert, Louis Legendre, Pierre-Gaspard Chaumette, Antoine-François Momoro**, and **François-Nicolas Vincent**.

The Cordelier club was politically more radical than the **Jacobin club**, and its low membership fee of two *sous* per month allowed **passive citizens** to join. **Women** were also welcome at its meetings, which generally ranged between 300 and 400 in attendance. The club took as its symbol the eye of vigilance, reflective of its self-proclaimed mission to watch over government activities. In July 1791 the Cordeliers took the lead in the campaign for the declaration of a republic, which culminated in the **Champ de Mars** massacre, and the repression that followed temporarily threw the club into disarray. But in August 1792 the club welcomed the **Marseille fédérés** to one of its meetings, and the Cordeliers again played a leading role in the **uprising of 10 August**. Hébert's *Père Duchesne* became a virtual house organ of the Cordeliers in the year that followed, and as the **sans-culotte** movement gained strength in Paris, so too did the Cordelier club.

The Cordeliers again figured in the leadership of the **uprising of 31 May–2 June 1793**, with Hébert and Vincent playing a particularly prominent role. By then the club had also established a network of provincial affiliations, and its influence helped to undermine popular support for the **federalist revolt**. Once again active in the **uprising of 4–5 September 1793**, which brought an extension of the *maximum* to staple goods beyond grain and also made **terror** the order of the day, the power of the club began to decline thereafter. **Maximilien Robespierre** and the **Montagnards** were determined to bring the Paris popular movement under control, turning first against the *enragés* and then against Hébert and a number of his closest supporters. With the execution of Hébert and the others on 24 March 1794, the Cordelier club virtually ceased to exist.

CORSICA. The significance of Corsica in the French Revolution has chiefly to do with **Napoleon Bonaparte**. Had France not conquered Corsica in May 1769, just months before the birth of Napoleon, he could not have claimed French citizenship and risen to the rank of general in the French army nor have been brought into the government as consul in 1799. On 30 November 1789, the **Constituent Assembly** declared Corsica an integral part of France. Corsica had an interesting history of its own during the revolutionary decade, one in which supporters of the French struggled against supporters of England, and a number of other Corsicans played important roles in the events of the Revolution, including **Pascal Paoli**, **Christophe Saliceti**, and **Filippo Michele Buonarroti**.

COUNCIL OF ANCIENTS. The Council of Ancients (*Conseil des Anciens*) was the upper house of the two-chamber legislature created by the **Constitution of 1795**. It numbered 250 deputies, at least 40 years of age, married or widowed, and resident in France for at least 15 years. The deputies were elected to three-year terms, with one-third of the membership renewed each year.

The creation of a two-chamber legislature broke with the Rousseauean conviction, dominant in the Revolution up to that time, that the general will of the people should have a unitary expression. By 1795 the deputies of the **National Convention** had grown more concerned about the danger of dictatorship, which a bicameral legislature would mediate. The Council of Ancients was to be responsible for approving laws proposed by the **Council of Five Hundred**, the lower house. It could not amend those laws, nor propose legislation on its own initiative. But while the Council of Ancients was the upper house, it was not to become a Senate or House of Lords. Its deputies were elected in the same manner, and for the same term, and they enjoyed the same pay and accommodations as their colleagues in the Council of Five Hundred. The two houses were separate but equal, and the revolutionaries were anxious to see that a new **aristocracy** not be allowed to emerge.

It was the prerogative of the Council of Ancients to designate the location where the two houses would convene, and this authority proved to be of some significance on 18 **Brumaire** VIII. But in the three years of their existence, the Ancients never really established a strong identity, and with **Napoleon Bonaparte's** coup, to which they readily acceded, the Council of Ancients ceased to exist.

COUNCIL OF FIVE HUNDRED. The Council of Five Hundred (*Conseil des Cinq-Cents*) was the lower house of the bicameral legislature created by the **Constitution of 1795**. As its name suggests, it was composed of 500 deputies, at least 30 years of age, and as with the **Council of Ancients** they were elected to a three-year term, one-third of the seats to be renewed each year. The Council of Five Hundred had the power to initiate laws, which then had to be approved by the Council of Ancients. The two Councils, and the **Directory** regime more generally, never managed to achieve political stability, as evidenced by the **Fructidor coup** of 1797 and the **Floréal coup** of 1798, which purged **Jacobin** deputies and then royalist deputies in successive elections. But deputies on the left dominated the elections of 1799, and the Council of Five Hundred offered more energetic resistance to **Napoleon Bonaparte's** coup of **Brumaire**, despite the fact that his brother, **Lucien Bonaparte**, presided over the chamber at that moment. The successful coup brought an end to the Council of Five Hundred.

COUNTERREVOLUTION. Almost as soon as the term "revolution" came to assume its modern meaning, very shortly after the fall of the **Bastille**, the fear of counterrevolution became a salient feature of the political landscape in revolutionary France. As soon as the brothers of **Louis XVI**, and then his aunts, fled France, they were suspected of conspiring against the new constitutional regime being shaped by the deputies of the **Constituent Assembly** meeting at **Versailles**. In the weeks following the **October Days**, the *émigrés* who gathered in Coblenz and Turin were widely suspected of corresponding with networks of counterrevolutionaries within France, and violent incidents in **Lyon** seemed to confirm those rumors. The first *camp de* **Jalès**, in 1790, represents the earliest tangible example of counterrevolution on a substantial scale, although the violent confrontation between **Protestants** and Catholics that preceded it in the *bagarre de Nîmes* is also often considered to have been a manifestation of counterrevolution.

   In **Paris** the fear of counterrevolution following the military defeat at Verdun triggered the **September Massacres**, and in spring 1793 the introduction of military recruitment led to rebellion in the **Vendée**, the first widespread counterrevolutionary upheaval in France. Later that summer the **federalist revolts** in **Bordeaux**, **Caen**, Lyon, and **Marseille** took on a counterrevolutionary aspect in their final stages. These uprisings fed the fear of counterrevolution throughout France, but especially in Paris, and gave rise to the **Terror**. The Terror, in turn, produced more recruits to the cause of counterrevolution.

After the fall of **Maximilien Robespierre**, on 9 **Thermidor**, the *jeunesse dorée* grew more bold in their expression of counterrevolutionary sentiments. The violence of the Terror produced a **White Terror** in significant regions of southern France, and the two-thirds decree passed by the **National Convention** elicited an upsurge of counterrevolutionary sentiment quelled only by military action in **Vendémiaire** in 1795. Under the **Directory**, the **Fructidor coup** of 1797 was aimed against royalist supporters suspected of counterrevolutionary sentiments. The fear of counterrevolution did not entirely subside until the rise to power of **Napoleon Bonaparte**, and even into the 19th century the political opposition between left and right most often was seen in terms of revolution versus counterrevolution.

COUTHON, GEORGES-AUGUSTE (1755–1794). Couthon was the son of a notary in Orcet, near Clermont-Ferrand in central France. He studied law in Reims and returned to become an *avocat* in Clermont, where he was known as a lawyer for the poor. Couthon was elected to the 1787 Provincial Assembly, and in 1789 was elected to the Clermont municipal council. He served in 1790 as president of the district tribunal, and in 1791 was elected to the **Legislative Assembly** from the Puy-de-Dôme, which also sent him to the **National Convention** in 1792. Couthon's tendency toward conciliation kept him aloof from the conflict between **Montagnards** and **Girondins**, but he was impressed by the Montagnards during the trial of **Louis XVI** and by May 1793 sat definitively with that group. Couthon joined the **Committee of Public Safety** on 30 May 1793, initially to work on the new constitution and thereafter with responsibility for correspondence. In July 1793 Couthon urged the final abolition of **seigneurial dues** without monetary compensation. In August he was sent on mission to **Lyon**, oversaw the siege of the city, and reinstalled the **Jacobin** municipal council, but balked at applying the full measure of the repression ordered by the Committee of Public Safety. After his return to Paris, he grew close to **Maximilien Robespierre**, with whom he shared a Deist conviction and a commitment to the ideal of a republic of virtue. Couthon played a significant role in the campaigns against the Hébertists and the **Indulgents** in 1794, and in June 1794 delivered the report to the National Convention on a new **Law of Suspects**, which ushered in the final phase of the **Terror**. He was denounced along with Robespierre and **Louis-Antoine Saint-Just** on 9 **Thermidor** and was executed the following day.

CULT OF THE SUPREME BEING. The Cult of the Supreme Being (*Culte de l'Etre Suprême*), which flourished briefly in the spring and early summer of 1794, was intended both to replace Catholicism and to curtail the excesses of the **deChristianization** movement. Its clearest formulation came in a speech before the **National Convention** by **Maximilien Robespierre** on 7 May 1794, in which Robespierre affirmed his belief in the existence of a Supreme Being and the immortality of the soul, and asserted the compatibility between religious and moral ideas and patriotic republicanism. The Convention formally adopted the Cult of the Supreme Being and announced plans for a Festival of the Supreme Being on 8 June 1794. Similar festivals were to be celebrated throughout France, succeeding the **Festivals of Reason** that had already been staged in many towns and cities.

The festival in **Paris** was designed and choreographed by **Jacques-Louis David**, and was perhaps his most successful effort in that regard. The day began with a ceremony in the **Tuileries** gardens, including a speech, or sermon, by Robespierre and a ritual burning of a statue representing Atheism. Those assembled then processed to the **Champ de Mars**, where David had constructed an enormous symbolic mountain. Robespierre led the assembled deputies to the pinnacle of the mountain, watched over by an equally enormous statue of **Hercules**, representing the people. The festival itself was quite popular, and well attended, but many of the deputies were skeptical of Robespierre's intentions and his prominence in the day's events. Similar festivals were indeed held in the provinces, and the Festival of the Supreme Being marks in some sense the apogee of the **Jacobin** project of **regeneration**. But little more than a month later, Robespierre would fall from power and be marched to the **guillotine**, and in the aftermath of **Thermidor** the Cult of the Supreme Being quickly faded from view.

– D –

D'AELDERS, ETTA PALM (1743–?). Etta Palm d'Aelders was born Etta Lubina Derista Aelders in Gronigen, Holland. She married Ferdinand Palm, a Frenchman, and moved to **Paris** in the mid-1770s, after her husband had disappeared. She attended the salon of Sophie **Condorcet**, and in that milieu was exposed to the ferment of ideas on the eve of the Revolution. In the early years of the Revolution she participated actively in the meetings of the **Cercle Social**, and was among the founders of the Confederation of the Friends of Truth, an affiliated club that was among the first to admit **women**. In 1791 d'Aelders published a pamphlet, *Appeal to Frenchwomen Concerning the Regeneration of Morals and the Necessity for Women's Influence in a Free Government*. Along with **Olympe de Gouges** and **Anne Théroigne de Méricourt**, she is considered among the early advocates of women's rights. She was sent on mission to Holland in 1792 by the French government to set up a revolutionary embassy, but came under suspicion the following year and chose to return permanently to Holland at that time. Little is known of her life thereafter.

DAMES DE LA HALLE. The **women** of the central markets (*la halle*, or *les halles*) in **Paris** played a significant role in the political upheavals of the Revolution. The market women initiated the march to **Versailles** during the **October Days** of 1789. Under the Old Regime, it had been customary for the fishwives (*poissardes*) of the central markets to visit the royal palace at Versailles on the occasion of the birth of an heir to the throne. Thus, when food prices, especially for bread, spiked once again in the fall of 1789, the market women turned to that tradition to justify a visit of a different sort. In all of the *journées* of the Revolution that saw political grievances mingled with concern over food shortages, the *dames de la halle* could be expected to participate.

By 1793, however, the price controls introduced by the **National Convention** and supported by the **Jacobin club** had alienated the women of the market, some of whom clashed openly with those women who were members of the **Society of Revolutionary Republican Women**, which met in the church of Saint-Eustache, near *les Halles*. The market women were annoyed, in particular, by a 21 September 1793 decree making mandatory the wearing of a tricolor **cockade**, a decree supported by the club women. In late October the *dames de la halle* violently invaded a meeting of the Society of Revolutionary Republican Women, forcing its adjournment, and subsequently petitioned for its dissolution. This disruption of public order prompted the National Convention to abolish women's clubs.

DANTON, GEORGES-JACQUES (1759–1794). Born in the small town of Arcis-sur-Aube, Danton's grandfather was a **peasant**, his father a local prosecutor. Danton was schooled by the Oratoriens of Troyes, worked his way through law school in **Paris**, and became an *avocat* in Reims in 1784. By 1787 he had moved to Paris, where he bought the position of *avocat aux conseils du roi* and joined the **Freemasons**. Danton was active in the Revolution from the beginning, as an orator at the **Cordelier club** and as a political activist in that district of Paris. In 1791 he was elected *substitut du procureur* of the **Paris Commune**. Danton was forced to flee to England following the **Champ de Mars** massacre, for his role in instigating the petition against the king, and he played a prominent role in the **uprising of 10 August 1792**. In September 1792 he served as minister of justice, during the time of the prison massacres, for which he was widely blamed by the **Girondins** and their followers. Danton was elected to the **National Convention** from Paris, and remained a leader of the popular movement.

One might equally remark his zest for life, his general humanity, his generosity of spirit on the one hand, and on the other, his undeniable venality and sense of self-importance. Danton served briefly on the **Committee of Public Safety** in the spring of 1793, presided over the National Convention from 25 July to 8 August 1793 and then, fatigued, went home to Arcis in October. When he returned to Paris in November he began his campaign for "indulgence," which put him at odds with the **Jacobin** supporters of the **Terror**, including **Maximilien Robespierre**. Arrested in late March 1794, Danton went on trial in April (charged with corruption and treason) along with a small group of supporters and a handful of more disreputable defendants. All were found guilty in what was essentially a political trial and went to the **guillotine** on 5 April 1794.

DAVID, JACQUES-LOUIS (1748–1825). The son of a merchant, David was born in **Paris**, where he trained at the **Academy** of Painting and Sculpture. In 1775 he won the grand prize in painting, and this opened the way for his career by allowing him to study in Rome. He became a leading exponent of the neoclassical style, and even before the Revolution a number of his canvases made a notable impression on the French art world. These included his 1785 painting, *The Oath of the Horatii*, and in 1787 *The Death of Socrates*. The outbreak of the Revolution, however, would propel David to the forefront of French painters.

A number of David's canvases have profoundly influenced our understanding of the Revolution, and central among these is one that he never completed, *The Tennis Court Oath*. The painting was initially commissioned by the **Jacobin club** in 1790, but the club failed to raise sufficient funds. Only in September 1791 did the **Legislative Assembly** vote to foot the bill, but by then David was occupied with other projects. In addition to his painting, he took responsibility for staging many of the great festivals of the Revolution, including the 1790 **Festival of Federation**, the procession that carried the remains of **Voltaire** to the **Panthéon** in 1791, the funeral of **Jean-Paul Marat** in July 1793, the Festival of Unity in August 1793, and the Festival of the Supreme Being in the spring of 1794.

David was elected to the **National Convention** from Paris in 1792. He sat with the **Montagnards** and voted for death in the trial of **Louis XVI** and against the *appel au peuple*. He was an active member of the committee on public instruction, and in 1793 joined the **Committee of General Security**. During this period he painted what is perhaps his most famous canvas, *The Death of Marat*, a masterpiece that rendered one of the most hated men in France a tragic and sympathetic figure in death. David completed two other martyr paintings as well, commemorating the deaths of **Louis-Michel Le Peletier de Saint-Fargeau** and the young **Joseph Bara**.

David was closely associated with **Maximilien Robespierre**, and thus came under suspicion during and after **Thermidor**. Some have suggested that he avoided the **guillotine** only because **Bertrand Barère** warned him to stay away from the National Convention as the plot was unfolding. Still, he was expelled from the Committee of General Security and placed under arrest. He remained in prison until the summer of 1795 and was amnestied in October of that year. David remained aloof from politics thereafter, but he was eventually drawn to the glory and charisma of **Napoleon Bonaparte** and emerged as the official painter of France under the Empire. His most notable canvases of that period were of Napoleon crossing the Alps on horseback and the Coronation of Bonaparte and Josephine. In 1816 David was exiled as a regicide. *See also* CULT OF THE SUPREME BEING.

DECHRISTIANIZATION. It is important to distinguish what might be termed the anti-Church legislation of the first years of the Revolution (for example, the **confiscation of Church lands** in 1789 and the introduction of the **Civil Constitution of the Clergy** in the following year) from the deChristianization campaign that began in late October 1793 and extended through much of the **Terror**. The refusal of most bishops, and roughly 50 percent of the clergy, to swear the **Civil Oath of the Clergy** contributed to anti-religious attitudes, as did the active role played by **refractory priests** in the **Vendée rebellion**.

The beginning of deChristianization is generally dated at 5 October 1793, when the **National Convention** adopted the **revolutionary calendar**, an explicit rejection of the Christian calendar with its Sundays and plethora of saints' days. **Jacques-René Hébert** and his followers were among the most ardent supporters of deChristianization, but the **Jacobin clubs** across France also tended to support the movement. On 6 November 1793 the National Convention recognized the right of all communes to renounce the Catholic faith. Four days later a **Festival of Reason** was celebrated in Notre Dame cathedral, which was now christened a Temple of Reason. On 23 November 1793, the **Paris Commune** closed all of the churches in the capital city.

Such actions occurred elsewhere in France, too, often instigated by particularly zealous **representatives on mission**. **Joseph Fouché**, for example, removed all religious inscriptions from the cemeteries in Nevers, replacing them with the phrase "death is eternal sleep." Local radicals and members of the roving *armées révolutionnaires* defaced Church buildings, knocking off the heads of kings and saints. Devoted revolutionaries now gave their children Roman rather than Christian names, and towns and villages even changed their names to accord with the new dictates.

Maximilien Robespierre never supported the deChristianization campaign, condemning it as aristocratic and immoral as early as 21 November 1793. He shared the belief of **Voltaire** and **Jean-Jacques Rousseau** that the populace needed a god in which to put their faith. To that end he introduced the **Cult of the Supreme Being**, and the celebration of the first Festival of the Supreme Being on 8 June 1794 brought deChristianization to a definitive end, although the campaign had already waned in the previous months. The Catholic Church and refractory priests would face renewed repression under the **Directory**, but nothing quite as severe as that endured in the fall and winter of 1793–94. *See also* CLERGY.

DECLARATION OF THE RIGHTS OF MAN AND CITIZEN. As early as the first weeks of July 1789, the deputies of the newly proclaimed **Constituent Assembly** began to debate the need for a declaration of rights. Those on the left saw such a declaration to be a necessary foundation for a written constitution, while conservatives dismissed the idea of a declaration of abstract and universal rights as inappropriate to a monarchy such as France. Some of the more practical-minded deputies of the **Third Estate** saw the whole project as unduly philosophical and largely irrelevant to the more pressing challenges before them.

Marie-Joseph-Motier Lafayette focused the attention of the deputies on the issue with a speech on 11 July 1789, in which he presented a rationale for a declaration of rights and proposed a draft influenced by advice he had received from Thomas Jefferson. The fall of the **Bastille** on 14 July brought a sense of urgency to the deputies, and the Constitution Committee worked conscientiously on the task over the next five weeks. The committee included deputies from both left and right, among them **Gabriel-Honoré Mirabeau**, **Jean-Joseph Mounier**, **Jérôme-Marie Champion de Cicé**, and **Emmanuel-Joseph Sieyès**. Their work was hastened by news of the **Great Fear** that spread through much of the French countryside in late July, and by the **Night of 4 August**, when liberal deputies pledged to abolish **seigneurial dues** and the Old Regime system of **privilege**.

The Constitution Committee presented the Declaration of the Rights of Man and Citizen (*Déclaration des Droits de l'Homme et du*

Citoyen) to the Constituent Assembly on 26 August 1789, and it was endorsed the following day. It is a short document, comprised of a preamble and 17 articles. The influence of natural law theory and **Enlightenment** philosophy more generally is apparent throughout, as is the specific imprint of writers such as **Jean-Jacques Rousseau**, **Montesquieu**, and John Locke. The Declaration asserted that the purpose of government was the protection of individual rights, rather than the expression of the royal will. It was written in universalist language, implying that these were rights not just for Frenchmen, but for all of humanity. Individual articles proclaimed freedom of religion, freedom of the press, the principle of no taxation without representation, the principle of national **sovereignty**, the principle of legal equality, and the right to private property. The Declaration of the Rights of Man and Citizen has been called the death certificate of the Old Regime and, along with the American Declaration of Independence, the foundation document for human rights in the modern world.

When the document was delivered to **Louis XVI**, the king refused at first to sign it, along with the legislation emanating from the Night of 4 August. Not until after the **October Days**, when the **women** of **Paris** marched to **Versailles**, did Louis XVI affix his signature to the Declaration of the Rights of Man and Citizen. The Declaration was revised in 1793, when the right of resistance to oppression was given prominent expression, and again in 1795, when that right was essentially removed and the ideal of liberty was given fuller expression than the ideal of equality.

DECLARATION OF THE RIGHTS OF WOMAN AND CITIZENESS. In September 1791 **Olympe de Gouges** published the Declaration of the Rights of Woman and Citizeness (*Déclaration des Droits de la Femme et de la Citoyenne*). She addressed her pamphlet to **Marie Antoinette**, with the express hope that the queen would present it to the **Legislative Assembly** for adoption. The final words to her Preamble read, "In consequence, the sex that is superior in beauty as in courage, needed in maternal sufferings, recognizes and declares, in the presence and under the auspices of the Supreme Being, the following rights of woman and the citizeness." The 17 points that followed essentially paralleled the 17 articles of the **Declaration of the Rights of Man and Citizen**.

Perhaps the most interesting part of the Declaration is its Post-script, in which de Gouges characterized marriage as the "tomb of trust and love," and proposed a new social contract between a man and woman that would make wealth communal and recognize the rights of illegitimate children. De Gouges called for education for **women**, and suggested that the key to achieving equality for women was to "join them to all the activities of man." She also called for the marriage of priests, which the revolutionaries would later endorse. While the Legislative Assembly did not adopt the Declaration of the Rights of Woman and Citizeness, and de Gouges went to the **guillotine** as an accused royalist in 1793, it stands as a bold assertion of women's rights and a foundation document for modern feminism.

DELACROIX, JEAN-FRANÇOIS (1753–1794). Delacroix was the son of a surgeon in Pont-Audemer, but preferred to study law himself and became an *avocat* in his birthplace on the eve of the Revolution. In 1790 he was elected *procureur-général-syndic* of the Eure-et-Loir, the same department whose voters would send him to the **Legislative Assembly** in 1791 and the **National Convention** in 1792. Delacroix became active in the **Cordelier club**, where he met **Georges Danton**. He is generally credited with beginning the custom of referring to "left" and "right" to distinguish radical from conservative deputies in the Legislative Assembly. Delacroix accompanied Danton on mission to **Belgium** in early 1793, and like Danton would later be accused of embezzling funds on that mission. He voted for death in the trial of **Louis XVI**, and in February 1794 called for the abolition of **slavery** throughout France's territories. Delacroix was tried and convicted along with Danton and the **Indulgents**.

DEPARTMENTAL ADMINISTRATIONS. On 29 September 1789, Jacques-Guillaume Thouret reported to the **Constituent Assembly** on behalf of its Constitution Committee, presenting a plan for the administrative reorganization of France. The Assembly adopted that portion of the plan calling for the creation of 83 departments on 22 December 1789. Each of the 83 departments, named for elements of nature and geographical features, was to elect an administrative council, composed of 36 members plus a *procureur-général-syndic*. The administrators, predominantly lawyers and landowners, were to serve a two-year term, with half of the council renewed each year. An eight-man directory was elected by the departmental administrators themselves to serve as an executive body.

The responsibilities of the departmental administrations were essentially administrative (e.g., maintaining public order, overseeing the collection of taxes, putting in place new judicial bodies), but through the early years of the Revolution they often played a political role as well. Disputes between rival clubs, or between companies of the **National Guard** and royal regiments, were often referred to departmental administrations. Many of the councils established regular correspondence with their counterparts in neighboring departments. Following the failed uprising of 20 June 1792, a number of departmental administrations sent letters to **Paris** denouncing the actions of the crowd and declaring their support for **Louis XVI**, a gesture that they came to regret. Most significantly, a majority of the departmental administrations protested by letter the proscription of the **Girondin** deputies after the **uprising of 31 May–2 June 1793**, and a smaller number of them led their departments into armed revolt against the **National Convention** in the **federalist revolt** that followed. The National Convention rebuked that assertion of departmental prerogative in the **Law of 14 Frimaire** (4 December 1793), which reduced both the size and the authority of departmental administrations and increased the authority of district administrations, most of which had remained loyal to the **Montagnard** Convention.

DESMOULINS, CAMILLE (1760–1794). Desmoulin's father was a royal magistrate, a lieutenant-general in the *bailliage* of Guise. Camille was sent on scholarship to the *collège* Louis-le-Grand in **Paris**, where he met **Maximilien Robespierre**, and went on to study law in the capital. On the eve of the Revolution he remained resident in Paris, with no particular occupation, and was swept up in the events of 1789. He published his first pamphlet, *La France Libre*, on 12 July 1789, and on that same day, having heard news from **Versailles** of the dismissal of **Jacques Necker**, he mounted a table in the **Palais Royal**, brandishing a green **cockade** (the symbol of hope), and called on the people to rise in insurrection against royal despotism. Two days later the **Bastille** fell.

Desmoulins was among the most incisive and celebrated of the revolutionary journalists in Paris. His first **newspaper** venture, *Les*

Révolutions de France et de Brabant, made its appearance on 28 November 1789 and continued publication until July 1791. As a member of the **Cordelier club**, Desmoulins participated in the petition campaign against the monarchy that culminated in the **Champ de Mars** massacre, and as a result he went into hiding between July and October 1791. When he returned to Paris he joined Robespierre in opposing the calls to war being heard from **Jacques-Pierre Brissot** and his supporters. In early 1792, after quarreling with Brissot over a minor issue, he published a pamphlet entitled *Brissot démasqué* that did much to damage the deputy's reputation.

By July 1792 Desmoulins was publishing decidedly republican ideas in his pamphlets, and he played an important role in organizing the 10 August assault on the **Tuileries** Palace. In September he joined **Georges Danton** as a secretary in the Ministry of Justice, and late that month was elected to the **National Convention** from Paris. He sat with the **Montagnards**, voted for death in the trial of **Louis XVI**, against the *appel au peuple*, and against the indictment of **Jean-Paul Marat**. At Robespierre's instigation in May 1793 he published a pamphlet, *Histoire des Brissotins*, which may have helped to decide the fate of the **Girondin** deputies. Surely Desmoulins believed so—he collapsed in tears when their death sentence was announced in October 1793.

On 5 December 1793 he published the first of six issues of a new newspaper, *Le Vieux Cordelier*. Harkening back to the ideals of the early revolution, the newspaper was both an attack on the radical Hébertists and an apparent critique of the excesses of the **Terror**. Desmoulins was soon expelled from the Cordelier club, and his newspaper was subjected to official censorship. His friendship with Robespierre was strained as well, and while the Incorruptible did protect Desmoulins from expulsion from the **Jacobin club**, he could not, or would not, protect him when he was accused along with Danton and the **Indulgents**. Desmoulins, too, went to the **guillotine** on 5 April 1794. Among the Dantonists, only he and **Pierre Philippeaux** would have their names rehabilitated after **Thermidor**.

DIAMOND NECKLACE AFFAIR. The Diamond Necklace Affair was a confidence game perpetrated in 1785 by Jeanne de La Motte and her husband, which ruined the public reputation of Cardinal

Louis de Rohan and further tainted the public image of **Marie Antoinette**. At the heart of the affair was an exquisite and expensive diamond necklace, a masterpiece produced by the Parisian jewelers Boehmer and Bassange, which had been offered to **Louis XVI** for his queen in 1778, but turned down. Seven years later, Jeanne de la Motte approached Cardinal Rohan, who was eager at the time to regain the favor of the queen, and convinced him that Marie Antoinette desperately desired the necklace, but could not purchase it publicly. Rohan took the bait, and in February 1785 arranged to deliver the necklace to a man he believed to be the queen's valet. The necklace was disassembled and the diamonds sold on the black market, and Rohan was left holding the bag. Both he and Jeanne de la Motte eventually came to trial, and although Marie Antoinette was wholly innocent in the affair, her reputation was besmirched in the public debate that accompanied the trials. Not long before, the queen had purchased the château at Saint-Cloud for her son, and the story of the diamond necklace added to her reputation for frivolous extravagance. The Diamond Necklace Affair is just one of many *causes célèbres* in the last decade of the Old Regime that made private scandal the focus of public attention and in the process called into question the very foundations of Old Regime society.

DIRECTORY. The Directory (*Directoire*) regime was in power from 26 October 1795 until 10 November 1799, succeeding the **National Convention** and giving way to the Consulate following **Napoleon Bonaparte's** coup of 18 **Brumaire**. The regime was defined by the **Constitution of 1795**. To guard against the danger of dictatorship, whether exercised by the legislative or the executive branch, the deputies created a two-chamber legislative structure, consisting of the **Council of Ancients** and the **Council of Five Hundred**, and an executive branch in which five directors, elected by the legislative houses, shared power. There were annual legislative elections, one-third of the deputies being replaced each year, and one director rotated out of power each year, the order to be determined by the drawing of lots.

The Directory never succeeded in achieving political stability. The electorate was narrowed by virtue of the property requirement adopted in the Constitution of 1795, and that electorate was immediately alienated by the Law of Two-thirds, which decreed that two-thirds of the members of the two new councils were to be drawn from the deputies then sitting in the National Convention. Public confidence in the regime was further eroded by the **Fructidor coup** of 1797 and the **Floréal coup** of 1798, in which the directors purged those newly elected deputies whom they considered to be extremists. The legislators initiated their own coup against the directors in **Prairial** 1799, and the regime came to an end, of course, with Napoleon's coup in Brumaire.

The Directory regime was not without accomplishment, however. The finances of the Republic were brought under control, and the tax system was reformed. Significant administrative reform was also introduced. Advances were made in the area of secondary education. These reforms predominantly benefited the **bourgeoisie**, however, while the lot of the poor worsened. The regime also failed to restore peace between the Republic and the Catholic Church, and was plagued by allegations of scandal related to military procurements. Despite its achievements, and its efforts to develop a moderate, liberal parliamentary system, the demise of the Directory regime was lamented by few, and the rise of Napoleon Bonaparte as dictator seemed to be welcomed by most Frenchmen.

DIVORCE LAWS. On 20 September 1792 the **Legislative Assembly** declared marriage to be a purely civil union, and granted both men and **women** the right to initiate divorce. Divorce could be granted for reasons of adultery, for other violations of the marriage contract, for reasons of incompatibility, or on the basis of mutual consent. The **National Convention** issued a decree on 28 December 1793 that streamlined the procedure for obtaining a divorce in family court, and four months later made divorce obtainable by simple presentation of an act of notoriety. Although it remained more difficult for a woman than for a man to prove adultery, women initiated two-thirds of the divorces granted during the subsequent decade.

The **Thermidorians** initiated efforts to curtail legal divorce, and the **Directory** introduced legislation intended to do so, but it was not until September 1797 that a law was actually passed aimed at discouraging recourse to divorce. Under **Napoleon Bonaparte** the Civil Code would severely restrict legal divorce, and shift the legal advantage decisively toward men, but it did not abolish divorce entirely.

This would come with the Restoration, and not until late in the 19th century would the liberal divorce law of 1792 be reclaimed.

DUBOIS-CRANCÉ, EDMOND-LOUIS-ALEXIS (1747–1814). Born in Charleville, Dubois-Crancé's father was a *conseiller du roi* and *commissaire des guerres*. Edmond attended a Jesuit school in Charleville, and at the age of 14 entered the Musketeers. He remained active in the military, moving up through the ranks, until 1789. Dubois-Crancé was elected to the **Estates-General** from the **Third Estate**, joined the **Breton club**, and served on the military and finance committees. In 1791 he assumed an officer's post in the Paris **National Guard**. Elected to the **National Convention** from the Ardennes, he sat with the **Montagnards**, grew close to **Georges Danton**, and voted for death in the trial of **Louis XVI**. Dubois-Crancé presided over the National Convention in late February/early March 1793, but spent much of 1792–93 on mission to the Army of the Alps. He was promoted to brigadier-general in April, and in June urged prompt military action against **Lyon**, then in a state of rebellion. He clashed on this issue with **Robert Lindet** and **Georges Couthon**, was briefly arrested in October 1793, but was soon cleared and released. He went again on mission to the west of France, returning to **Paris** just before 9 **Thermidor**. Still under suspicion himself, he joined those plotting against **Maximilien Robespierre** and Couthon. After Thermidor, Dubois-Crancé served for five months on the **Committee of Public Safety**, and was elected in 1795 to the **Council of Five Hundred**, where he served until 1797. Thereafter, he returned to military duty, served briefly as minister of war in 1799, but opposed the 18 **Brumaire** coup of **Napoleon Bonaparte** and retired to private life.

DUCOS, JEAN-FRANÇOIS (1765–1793). Ducos was the son of a **Bordeaux** merchant, was educated by the Oratoriens of that city, and then placed in a merchant house in Nantes for training in the world of commerce. He found it boring, however, preferring the study of literature and philosophy. In 1789 he was among the founders of the Bordeaux **National Guard**, and in April 1790 joined in the founding of the **Jacobin club** in Bordeaux. Ducos was very close friends with **Pierre Vergniaud**, with whom he was elected to both the **Legislative Assembly** and the **National Convention**, and was the brother-in-law of **Jean-Baptiste Boyer-Fonfrède**, who married Ducos's sister in 1786. Ducos was not very active in the Legislative Assembly, but was well liked by all. In the National Convention he sat with the **Girondins**, but with a certain independence, often seeking conciliation between them and the **Montagnards**. Ducos did not attend the salon of **Manon** and **Jean-Marie Roland**. He supported the abolition of the slave trade, but not of **slavery**, was among the earliest deputies to call for the abolition of the monarchy, and was strongly anti-clerical.

Ducos voted for death in the trial of **Louis XVI**, and against the *appel au peuple*. He refused to support the indictment of **Jean-Paul Marat** in April 1793, and Marat intervened on 2 June 1793 to have Ducos removed from the proposed list of deputies to be proscribed. In the weeks that followed, Ducos ardently defended his proscribed colleagues, calling for the filing of formal charges and insisting on their right to defend themselves before the Convention. He actively participated in the debate over the new constitution, presented on 10 June and adopted two weeks later (*See* CONSTITUTION OF 1793). When **Jean-Pierre Amar** presented his indictment of the Girondin deputies in early October 1793, he added Ducos and Boyer-Fonfrède to the list, and they were immediately arrested. Ducos maintained his good humor in prison, writing songs for the deputies to sing as they awaited trial and their eventual execution.

DUCOS, PIERRE-ROGER (1747–1816). Little is known of the early life of Pierre-Roger Ducos (sometimes known as Roger-Ducos), who was a lawyer in Dax on the eve of the Revolution. He was one of the principal drafters of the *cahier de doléance* for the **Third Estate** of Dax, and served in municipal government in 1789–90. In 1791 he was elected president of the Criminal Tribunal of the Landes, and in 1792 that department elected him to the **National Convention**. He sat with the **Plain** in the Convention, voted for death in the trial of **Louis XVI**, and against the *appel au peuple*, but overall he played no role of consequence in that assembly.

Ducos was elected to the **Council of Ancients** in 1795 from the Pas-de-Calais, and he took a more active role in that body, over which he presided on two occasions. His re-election was annulled, however, by the **Floréal coup** of 1798, and he returned to the Criminal Tribunal in the Landes. Ducos's election to the **Council of Five**

Hundred in the following year was also annulled, but **Paul-François Barras** saved him from provincial obscurity by nominating him as a director. He supported **Emmanuel-Joseph Sieyès** in the **Brumaire** coup, and was rewarded by being named the third consul, after Sieyès and **Napoleon Bonaparte**. He subsequently sat as a member of the Senate, was named to the Legion of Honor in 1804, and a Count of the Empire in 1808. Ducos resumed his seat in the Chamber of Peers during the One Hundred Days, which assured his exile as a regicide in 1816. *See also* DIRECTORY.

DUMOURIEZ, CHARLES-FRANÇOIS (1739–1823). Dumouriez was born into an old, but declining, noble family of Picardy. His father had both a military career and was an *avocat au Parlement*. Charles was educated at the *collège* Louis-le-Grand in **Paris**, and then went on to follow a military career himself. He might best be described as an adventurer, motivated solely by self-interest. By 1761 he was a captain of cavalry. Shortly thereafter he was commissioned to select the site for a new military port on the English Channel, and chose Cherbourg, the construction of which he then oversaw. Dumouriez carried out a number of military/diplomatic missions for the duke of Choiseul, one of Louis XV's chief ministers, in **Corsica**, Poland, and Sweden. He seems to have overstepped himself on the latter mission, prompting the duke of Aiguillon, who replaced Choiseul, to throw Dumouriez in the **Bastille** for six months in 1773.

Dumouriez joined the **Jacobin club** shortly after the Revolution began, and associated with General **Lafayette**, **Gabriel-Honoré Mirabeau**, and **Armand Gensonné**. In March 1792 he was named minister of foreign affairs by **Louis XVI**, in what is often referred to as the **Girondin** ministry, and served briefly as minister of war in June of that year. He was then given a command in the war against Austria, becoming Commander-in-Chief of the Army of the Center after the French defeats at Longwy and Verdun and the departure of Lafayette. Dumouriez's army, supported by General François-Etienne-Christophe Kellerman, scored a decisive and key victory at **Valmy** in September 1792, on the eve of the declaration of the first French Republic. It had long been an ambition of Dumouriez's to invade and liberate **Belgium**, a goal that he now pursued. The French occupied Belgium by December 1792, but when Dumouriez turned his attention to Holland in the following months his fortunes waned. After the defeat of his forces at Neerwinden on 18 March 1793, Dumouriez struck a deal with the Austrians to lead a combined force on Paris in order to restore the monarchy. His treason was a crucial blow to the political fortunes of the Girondins, with whom he had been closely associated. Dumouriez fled France in early April 1793, eventually ending up in England, where he advised Lord Arthur Wellington on the Spanish campaign and the British government on the possibilities of a cross-Channel invasion.

DUPONT DE NEMOURS, PIERRE-SAMUEL (1739–1817). Dupont was born into a **Protestant** family of Normandy, with its roots in Brittany. His father was *horloger du roi* in Rouen. As a youth Dupont was tutored in mathematics, metaphysics, and the military arts, and studied political economy with François Quesnay. He wrote a number of essays in the 1760s on agricultural reform and political economy more generally, and was a supporter of the Physiocrats. He collaborated in the Turgot ministry of 1774, was appointed to the *bureau des finances* of Auch in 1780, and became a *commissaire général des commerces* under **Charles Calonne**. Dupont was the chief negotiator of the 1786 trade treaty with Great Britain.

Dupont served as secretary of the 1787 **Assembly of Notables**, was a member of the **Committee of Thirty** in 1788, and in 1789 was elected to the **Estates-General** by the **Third Estate** of Nemours. Dupont was the most frequent orator in the **Constituent Assembly**, delivering more than a hundred speeches. He served on eight committees, though he resigned from all but the finance committee by July 1790, and he presided over the Assembly in August 1790. Dupont supported **Jacques Necker's** proposal for the creation of a national bank, favored a two-house legislature (but featuring a Senate rather than a House of Peers), opposed the creation of *assignats*, and voted in favor of a royal veto. He was a member of the Club of 1789, and later of the **Feuillants**. After the Constituent Assembly dissolved, Dupont remained in **Paris** and served in the **National Guard**. In that role he went to the **Tuileries Palace** on the night of 10 August 1792 and spoke with **Louis XVI** as he left the palace for the meeting hall of the **Legislative Assembly**. Dupont left Paris after the fall of the monarchy, living quietly on the family estate until his arrest on 20 June 1794. He was saved by **Thermidor**, was elected to the **Council** of **Ancients** from the Loiret in 1795, and in December of that year was elected to the **Institut National**. During this period he made substantial purchases of *biens nationaux* near Nemours to round out the family estate.

Dupont was arrested after the **Fructidor coup** of 1797, escaped with the help of **Germaine de Staël**, and emigrated to the United States with his family in 1799. His son, Victor, had left for the United States before the Revolution, served France as a diplomat during the 1790s, and became a close friend of Thomas Jefferson. Dupont had earlier made the acquaintance of Benjamin Franklin in France. He returned frequently to France over the next 20 years, serving on the Paris Chamber of Commerce under the reign of **Napoleon Bonaparte**, editing the collected works of Anne-Robert-Jacques Turgot, and serving briefly under the restored monarchy of **Louis XVIII**, who rewarded Dupont by naming him a Chevalier of the Legion of Honor in 1815. In that same year he rejoined his family in Delaware, where he died in 1817.

DUPORT, ADRIEN-JEAN-FRANÇOIS (1759–1798). Duport was born into a recently ennobled family. His father was a *conseiller* at the **Parlement of Paris**. Adrien was schooled at the *collège* of the Oratoriens of Juilly, where he met **Marie-Jean Hérault-Séchelles**, and went on to study law. In 1778 he, too, became a *conseiller* at the Parlement of Paris. Duport was well read in the writings of both **Jean-Jacques Rousseau** and **Voltaire**, but was more influenced by the thought of **Montesquieu** and the Physiocrats. In 1784 he founded the Mesmerist society in **Paris**. In 1787 he led the Parlementary opposition to the edicts of **Etienne-Charles Loménie de Brienne**, and demanded that the Edict of Toleration for **Protestants**, issued that year, be extended to **Jews** as well. In 1788 he urged the abolition of *lettres de cachet*, and hosted the meetings of the **Committee of Thirty** at his hôtel in the Marais district of Paris.

In 1789 Duport was elected to the **Estates-General** by the **aristocracy** of Paris, and was among the noble deputies who joined the **Third Estate** in June. In the debate over the **Declaration of the Rights of Man and Citizen**, Duport proposed a more democratic version than that adopted, and played a crucial role in the events of the **Night of 4 August**. Along with **Antoine-Pierre Barnave** and

Alexandre Lameth, Duport was a dominant force in the **Constituent Assembly**, the trio of deputies being referred to by some of their contemporaries as the **Triumvirate**. Duport supported much of the revolutionary program in the early years—the sale of Church lands and the creation of *assignats*; a suspensive, rather than absolute, veto for the king; a broad, rather than narrow, definition of **sovereignty**. But over time he grew fearful of the danger of popular violence and the influence of the crowd. He worked with Lameth and Barnave to strengthen the constitutional monarchy, and in the debate over declaring the ineligibility of Constituent Assembly members for reelection to the **Legislative Assembly**, Duport observed that "the revolution is accomplished, and the danger is to believe that it is not in fact finished."

After the flight to **Varennes**, Duport led the **Feuillant** split from the **Jacobin club**, and continued to advise **Louis XVI** from behind the scenes. During the summer of 1792 he allied with General **Lafayette** and considered the necessity of a military intervention in the capital. In September 1792 he was arrested by order of the **Paris Commune**, and incarcerated in Melun, only to be freed on order of **Georges Danton**. He emigrated to England, returned briefly to France after **Thermidor**, but left again for Switzerland after the **Fructidor coup** of 1797, and died there of tuberculosis.

– E –

EDICT OF TOLERATION. The Edict of Toleration (*Edit de Tolérance*), issued by **Louis XVI** in November 1787, took effect in January 1788. It granted civil rights to French **Protestants** (Calvinists, that is, since the very small number of French Lutherans were not included in this decree) for the first time since 1685, when Louis XIV revoked the Edict of Nantes. The Edict of Toleration did not explicitly grant Protestants political rights, which were recognized only after the call for elections to the **Estates-General**. In towns such as **Nîmes** and **Montauban**, the substantial Protestant minority took a particularly active role in revolutionary politics in 1789 and 1790, leading to a **counterrevolutionary** Catholic backlash and violence in both instances. The extension of religious toleration to Protestants served as a precedent for the eventual extension of such rights to **Jews** by the **Constituent Assembly**.

EDUCATION. There was no comprehensive educational system in France on the eve of the Revolution. Nearly all education was conducted by religious orders in small, local schools. Boys and girls received primary education, but only boys continued on to secondary education, in an array of *collèges* across the country. Religious orders did reserve scholarship spaces for children of the poor in their schools, but by and large the children of the wealthy and the **aristocratic** elite fared better in their access to education, often through private tutors. There were more than 20 universities in France in 1789, the most important of them in **Paris**, but important faculties of law, medicine, theology, and the arts could be found in major provincial cities as well.

There was much debate about education during the Revolution, and many proposals, but relatively little successful reform, in part due to the political upheaval and the vicissitudes of **war**. In December 1789 the **Constituent Assembly** placed education under the responsibility of **departmental administrations**, and in practice many of the schools of the Old Regime continued to operate. By the law of 28 October 1790, educational institutions were exempt from sale as *biens nationaux*, but schoolteachers and university faculty were required to swear the **civil oath of the clergy** in 1791 and this produced serious divisions within the schools and the defection of many teachers. In September 1791 **Charles-Maurice Talleyrand-Périgord** delivered a report on behalf of the Education Committee calling for the complete reorganization of education, but these recommendations were never implemented.

A new Committee of Public Instruction convened under the **Legislative Assembly**, and in April 1792 **Marie-Jean Condorcet** delivered a report on behalf of that committee proposing a comprehensive proposal for national education, including the creation of *lycées*, but the declaration of war against Austria consigned that plan to the dustbin. In August 1792 all religious orders were disbanded, although individual clerics were allowed to continue to teach. The inability of local governments to collect new taxes, however, threw many schools into financial crisis.

The **National Convention** devoted more attention to education than the previous two assemblies. In March 1793 a new law permitted the sale of those *biens nationaux* owned by educational institutions that were not being used for education, the proceeds from which would be used to pay teachers. The law of 30 May 1793 mandated that all towns with a population between 400 and 1,500 should have at least one primary school, and established a minimum salary for teachers at 1,500 *livres*. The **Constitution of 1793**, though never implemented, declared education a civic right. In July 1793 **Maximilien Robespierre** introduced legislation modeled on the reforms first proposed by the martyred deputy, **Louis-Michel Le Peletier de Saint-Fargeau**, calling for universal primary education for boys and girls that would stress practical and patriotic instruction. War and the **Terror** prevented the implementation of this legislation, and it was abandoned after 9 **Thermidor**.

The **Thermidorians** accomplished a great deal in the area of educational reform, reaffirming the principle of universal primary education, allowing the creation of both state and private schools, and adopting general curricula and course syllabi. A law adopted on 25 February 1795 provided a comprehensive plan for national schools, calling for the creation of *écoles centrales* in each department (restricted to boys only), establishing a curriculum, creating scholarships for the poor, and recommending fixed salaries for teachers. The Daunou Law, adopted in October 1795, revised that legislation and called for schools to be funded through the collection of fees, with separate schools to be created for girls. The Ecole Polytechnique was also created in 1795.

Under the **Directory**, efforts were made to improve financial support for education, but without notable success. **Napoleon Bonaparte** would dismantle much of the educational reform of the Revolution and lay the foundation for the modern French educational system.

EGYPTIAN CAMPAIGN. At the end of 1797, only Great Britain remained an active enemy of France. The First Coalition had crumbled in the face of **Napoleon Bonaparte's** triumphant campaigns in Italy, and Napoleon received a hero's welcome in **Paris**. The **Directory** considered a naval expedition against England, or Ireland, but ultimately decided against it. Egypt seemed an attractive alternative. A French presence in Egypt would serve to challenge British naval supremacy in the Mediterranean, and in the future could serve as a staging ground for a French expedition against India, where the French had been defeated by the British in the 1750s. Napoleon offered to lead the campaign, and on 19 May 1798 set sail from **Toulon** with a fleet of more than 400 ships (including 13 ships-of-the-line), some 35,000 troops, and a contingent of more than 150 scientists and other intellectuals.

Napoleon's army easily defeated the Mameluke troops and occupied Cairo, but in August Admiral Horatio Nelson's British fleet attacked the French fleet in Aboukir Bay and virtually destroyed it, leaving Napoleon's forces stranded in Egypt. The French attack on Egypt brought Austria and Russia back into coalition with Great Britain, along with the Ottoman Empire, which claimed Egypt as a possession. In February 1799 Napoleon moved east into Syria with a force of some 10,000 men, where he easily defeated a Turkish army. Another Turkish force was engaged near Aboukir Bay in July 1799, and again the French army triumphed. Without naval support, however, Napoleon could accomplish no grand victory. On 23 August 1799 he turned over command of the army to General Jean-Baptiste Kléber, eluded the British naval blockade, and returned to France. Plague had already raced through the French ranks, and in June 1800 Kléber was assassinated. Not until the fall of 1801 were the remaining 19,000 troops evacuated to France.

The most enduring result of the Egyptian campaign derived from the scholarly part of the expedition. Several notable scientists accompanied Napoleon, including **Gaspard Monge**, the mathematician, and Claude Berthollet, a celebrated chemist. This was the first major contingent of Europeans to visit Egypt, and their task was both to spread the ideas of the **Enlightenment** and to study the remnants of ancient Egyptian civilization. Naturalists, geologists, archaeologists, and historians were among the scholars. They established the Institute of Cairo, discovered the Rosetta Stone (which eventually revealed the secret to Egyptian hieroglyphics), and surveyed the isthmus of Suez to explore the feasibility of a canal. Between 1809 and 1828, a 23-volume *Description de l'Egypte* would be published. This scholarly endeavor is credited with founding the field of Egyptology, but can also be seen as the first manifestation of modern orientalism, placing academic investigation in the service of colonialism.

ÉMIGRÉS. Over the course of the Revolutionary decade, roughly 150,000 *émigrés* left France, some voluntarily due to fear or as a protest of revolutionary reforms, others forced to flee due to political persecution. Approximately 25 percent of those emigrating were members of the **clergy**, 17 percent were members of the **aristocracy**, and the remaining 58 percent were drawn from the **Third Estate**. *Emigrés* left France in waves, generally prompted by political events. A first group of prominent aristocrats, including the Comte d'Artois (brother of **Louis XVI**), left immediately after the fall of the **Bastille**. More aristocrats fled due to the **Great Fear**, and another wave followed the **October Days**. Legislation against **refractory priests** brought a substantial number of *émigrés* among the clergy in 1792. The **September Massacres** late that year inspired another wave of emigration, as did the execution of Louis XVI in January 1793. The **federalist revolt** and its suppression further swelled the number of *émigrés*, and not surprisingly there was consistent emigration during the year of the **Terror**.

The *émigrés* sought many different destinations, and congregated in a number of different places. Several princes of the blood, including Artois and eventually the **Comte de Provence**, gathered in Coblenz, where a small *émigré* army eventually took shape. Turin was an early center of emigration and **counterrevolutionary** intrigue. Perhaps 25,000 *émigrés* fled to England, and a number made the Channel Islands their haven. Spain, Italy, and even Russia each received *émigrés*, as did the United States, where **Pierre-Samuel Dupont de Nemours** and his family would make an important contribution.

Many of those who emigrated did so simply to seek refuge, while others were determined to combat the revolutionary tide from outside France. Particularly in the early years of the Revolution, *émigré* aristocrats played an active role in efforts to support Louis XVI and restore the absolute monarchy. The king was somewhat ambivalent about those efforts, mindful of aristocratic challenges to royal power throughout the last half of the 18th century. But his flight to **Varennes** was a failed effort to join *émigré* forces in Germany, and those forces supported the Austrian army when the two countries went to war in 1792. *Emigré* soldiers participated at the battle of **Valmy**, but the crushing defeat suffered there, followed by the execution of Louis XVI in January 1793, dealt a crippling blow to *émigré* efforts to oppose the Revolution by military force. The disastrous expedition to **Quiberon** was the last serious effort in that regard, although *émigré* soldiers would continue to serve in the armies of Austria, Prussia, Great Britain, Russia, and Spain.

Revolutionary governments adopted shifting policies toward the *émigrés*. In December 1790 the **Constituent Assembly** decreed that any *émigré* holding an official post who failed to return within a month would lose his salary. In July 1791 those *émigrés* who failed to return were to be subject to a tripling of their taxes. But in September 1791, after Louis XVI had accepted the **constitution**, the Constituent Assembly repealed all anti-*émigré* legislation. In the face of continued *émigré* belligerence, however, the **Legislative Assembly** passed new legislation against those who had emigrated, calling in November 1791 for the death penalty against *émigré* conspirators and the sequestration of their property. All *émigré* land was ordered sequestered in February 1792, and was ordered sold as *biens nationaux* in July 1792. In August 1792 the families of *émigrés* were placed under surveillance and forbidden to hold public office, and in October all *émigrés* were banished from France in perpetuity, to be punished by death should they return. The **Thermidorians** would confirm and codify all previous legislation against *émigrés*. The early years of the **Directory** brought a relaxation in the enforcement of that legislation, and the return to France of some *émigrés*, but the **Fructidor coup** of 1797 harshened policy against *émigrés* once again. Only after **Napoleon Bonaparte** came to power were the majority of those who had fled France welcome to return, although many refused to do so until after the Restoration.

Three of the *émigré* princes would rule France between 1814 and 1848. Those aristocrats who had lost their titles were able to reclaim them. And while many *émigrés* lost land during the Revolution, some of it sold at auction, the wealthy aristocrats among them were generally able to reclaim their property. It was principally the small nobility and commoners among the *émigrés* who suffered permanent economic loss.

ENLIGHTENMENT. The Enlightenment was an 18th-century intellectual movement, dominated by French thinkers but not exclusively French, critical of Old Regime social and political institutions, but not overtly revolutionary in its calls for reform. Many of the ideas of the Enlightenment grew out of the Scientific Revolution of the 17th century, but the expansion of the French commercial economy and the accompanying growth of an urban population were also important as impetuses to the social criticism offered by Enlightenment thinkers and to the creation of an educated audience receptive to their ideas.

The term "enlightenment" derives from a French phrase, *le siècle des lumières*, or the *century of lights*. Some have called it the Age of Reason, although that label runs the risk of confusing this period, with its emphasis on inductive reasoning, with the deductive reasoning that characterized 17th-century rationalism, most succinctly expressed by the dictum of René Descartes, "I think therefore I am." For Enlightenment thinkers, knowledge derived not from the human mind alone, but from experiment and observation. In the words of the German philosopher Immanuel Kant, the Enlightenment represented a "daring to know," a willingness to question all conventional knowledge.

Central to Enlightenment thought was a belief in progress and a conviction that human reason was the key to achieving social, political, and economic progress. Enlightenment thinkers ventured boldly into all areas of human knowledge, as exemplified by the *Encyclopédie*, co-edited by Denis Diderot and Jean le Rond d'Alembert. This was a 28-volume project, published between 1751 and 1772, whose purpose was, as Diderot put it, "to collect all the knowledge scattered over the face of the earth, to present its general outlines and structure to the men with whom we live, and to transmit this to those who will come after us...." The *Encyclopédie* included essays from more than 160 writers and represents the single most important publication of the French Enlightenment. Although most of the entries in the *Encyclopédie* were not political, the very premise of the project represented an implicit challenge to both church and crown, and after the initial volumes appeared its publication was banned in France.

Several of the major Enlightenment thinkers, or *philosophes*, had a substantial impact on the social and political ideas of the French revolutionaries. **Baron Charles-Louis de Secondat de Mon-**

tesquieu's *L'Esprit des Lois* had a profound impact on both American and French political theorists. François-Marie Arouet, better known to us as **Voltaire**, ranged widely in his social criticism, but is most noted for his persistent and biting critique of religious intolerance generally, and more specifically the failings of the French Catholic Church. Most important of all was **Jean-Jacques Rousseau**, whose *Discours sur l'origine et les fondements de l'inégalité parmi les hommes* (1755) and *Du Contrat social* (1762) had a profound influence on the political thinking of the revolutionaries. The widespread popularity of Rousseau's novels, most notably *Emile* and *Julie, ou La nouvelle Héloïse*, ensured that his political thought had a much broader currency than would have been the case were he simply a political theorist. It is difficult to exaggerate the influence of Rousseau's writings on **public opinion** in France at the end of the Old Regime. During the Revolution, a bust of Rousseau could be found in virtually every **Jacobin club** meeting hall in France, and the remains of both Rousseau and Voltaire were interred in the **Panthéon** in festivals choreographed by **Jacques-Louis David**.

There has long been debate about whether or not the Enlightenment should be seen as a cause of the French Revolution. Alexis de Tocqueville attributed the inability of the revolutionaries to achieve a stable, constitutional regime to the impractical, abstract theorizing of the *philosophes*, who in his view were out of touch with the fabric of French society. But while the deputies of the various national assemblies during the Revolution were clearly influenced by the ideas of the *philosophes*, the majority of them were men who also had practical experience in the courts, in the royal bureaucracy, or in local government under the Old Regime. It should also be noted that virtually none of the Enlightenment thinkers advocated revolution, and very few, apart from Rousseau and Gabriel Bonnot de Mably, considered participatory democracy to be a workable form of government.

Enlightenment ideas, then, established a context of intellectual ferment, of questioning, of faith in the ideal of progress and in human reason to achieve that progress that made the social and political upheaval of the Revolution possible. The **salons**, the **freemason** lodges, and the provincial **academies** that provided a milieu in which Enlightenment ideas could be discussed also served to create the social networks and institutions that would mobilize the populace after

1789. The *honnête homme* described by so many Enlightenment writers became the political activist of the 1790s, and as those activists sought to remake and **regenerate** French society they naturally turned to the works of the *philosophes* for guidance.

ENRAGÉS. The *enragés*, narrowly defined, were a group of militant activists in the sections of **Paris** in 1792–1793 who advocated direct democracy and progressive social and economic policies. The term "*enragés*," as applied to that group, was coined by the 19th-century historian Jules Michelet. More broadly, the term was applied from 1789 onward in a pejorative sense to any group perceived as radical by opponents of the Revolution.

The *enragés* of 1792–1793 were an unorganized group, led by **Jacques Roux**, **Jean Varlet**, **Jean-Théophile Leclerc**, **Claire Lacombe**, and **Pauline Léon**. They enjoyed some support from the **Cordeliers**, but were not a dominant force in that club. **Maximilien Robespierre** denounced the *enragés* for their alleged complicity in the market riots of February 1793 in Paris, but several among them, most notably Varlet and Leclerc, played a prominent role in the **uprising of 31 May–2 June 1793**, which led to the proscription of the **Girondin** deputies. The *enragés* were not satisfied by the policies pursued by the **Montagnards** in the weeks that followed, however, and on 25 June Jacques Roux delivered an incendiary speech before the **National Convention**, in which he called for additional purges and for aggressive measures to counter food shortages and rising prices. For this, Roux was denounced at the **Jacobin club** and expelled from the Cordeliers. The *enragés* continued to agitate through the summer, however, culminating in the protests of early September 1793, which led to the **Law of Suspects** and the broadening of the *maximum* to include staple goods beyond bread and grain.

At that point, though, the Jacobins moved to control the popular movement in Paris. Roux was arrested and eventually committed suicide. Varlet, Leclerc, and Lacombe also endured persecution and prison, and the *enragés* had disappeared as an effective political group by October 1793. Elements of their progressive program would later be championed, however, by **Jacques-René Hébert** and **Gracchus Babeuf**.

ESPRIT PUBLIC. In the last years of the Old Regime, both critics and defenders of the monarchy regularly appealed to *l'opinion public*, or "**public opinion**," to justify their positions. *L'opinion public* was a suitably ambiguous and amorphous concept in the 1780s, with no clear or tangible representation. After 1789 **sovereignty** shifted from the king to the public, with elections and **popular societies** giving tangible expression to the political views of the citizenry. In this new political order, *l'opinion public* gave way to *esprit public*, or "public spirit," in both official and popular discourse, and the revolutionaries saw a need both to mold and to measure public spirit. In regard to the latter, the government called upon local administrations, and then under the **Terror** the *agents nationaux*, to submit regular reports on *esprit public* in their jurisdictions. Those reports can today be found in the National Archives of France in two separate series of documents devoted to *esprit public* in **Paris** and the provinces. With the rise of **Napoleon Bonaparte** to power, and the accompanying demise of participatory politics, that concern for public spirit gave way to an overriding concern for public order.

ESTATES. Old Regime society was legally divided into three estates, hierarchically arranged. The **First Estate**, the **clergy**, enjoyed that status by virtue of its spiritual function and proximity to God. The **Second Estate**, the **aristocracy**, enjoyed its status by virtue of military service to the king. Many aristocrats, or noblemen, could trace their lineage back to the knights of the Middle Ages, and they passed that status on by blood from generation to generation. The **Third Estate** comprised the remaining 97 percent of the population: urban professionals, **bourgeois**, artisans, workers, **peasants**, and beggars. The first two estates enjoyed many more **privileges**, such as exemption from **taxation**, than the Third Estate, an aspect of the social inequality under the Old Regime that generated increasing resentment on the eve of the Revolution. Each of the three estates elected representatives to the **Estates-General** when it was convened by **Louis XVI** in 1789.

ESTATES-GENERAL. The Estates-General (*Etats Généraux*) was the Old Regime assembly of delegates from the three estates of the kingdom: the **clergy**, or First Estate, the **aristocracy**, or Second Estate, and the commoners, or **Third Estate**. **Louis XVI** called the Estates-General in August 1788, to meet the following spring, because of the financial crisis confronting the monarchy. The Estates-General had not met, however, since 1614, which meant that no one was quite sure what procedures should be followed. Two questions in particular became quite contentious: should the Third Estate be granted additional delegates, to reflect their greater proportion of the population, as some argued? And how should the delegates vote, by head or by order? A considerable pamphlet literature appeared in the final months of 1788, debating these issues, and the **Committee of Thirty** played an active role in urging an affirmative response to each question. At the urging of **Jacques Necker**, the king ordered a "doubling of the Third" by December 1788, but the question of how the delegates would vote remained unresolved until after the Estates-General convened at **Versailles** in May 1789.

The first months of 1789 were devoted to electoral assemblies, organized by estate, at which delegates were chosen. All adult males were eligible to participate. These assemblies also drafted *cahiers de doléances*, to be presented at Versailles by the delegates, relaying the concerns and grievances of the people to their king. This process represented a virtual political mobilization of the nation on 4–5 May 1789. In Versailles, 1,139 delegates gathered: 291 representing the clergy, 270 representing the aristocracy, and 578 representing the Third Estate. An opening speech by Necker went badly, and in the absence of a decree mandating that the vote be by head, the Third Estate collectively refused to verify their credentials or to participate in deliberations. A stalemate persisted for more than a month, until 17 June, when at the instigation of **Emmanuel-Joseph Sieyès** the delegates of the Third Estate declared themselves a National Assembly. Liberal aristocrats and a number of clergy now rallied to the Third Estate, and when the king ordered their meeting hall locked on 20 June some 578 deputies swore the **Tennis Court Oath**. Louis XVI attempted to thwart that initiative on 23 June, by ordering the three estates to resume their separate deliberations, but in the face of determined resistance he accepted unified deliberation and voting by head on 27 June 1789. On 9 July

1789 the delegates to the Estates-General officially declared themselves the **Constituent Assembly**.

– F –

FABRE D'EGLANTINE, PHILIPPE-FRANÇOIS-NAZAIRE (1750–1794). Fabre was the son of a cloth merchant. He was educated at the Doctrinaires in **Toulouse**, but quit the school in 1771 to become an actor. He led a nomadic life until 1789, traveling throughout France, Switzerland, and the Low Countries. In March 1777 he was condemned to hang in Namur for seducing a young woman, but the sentence was commuted to a fine and banishment. His acting career appears to have been successful, and he was a playwright of some note in the 1780s as well.

Fabre traveled to **Paris** in 1789 and became active in the politics of the capital. He joined the **Cordelier club**, where he befriended **Camille Desmoulins**, and served as secretary to **Georges Danton** in the Ministry of Justice. Fabre played an active role in the **uprising on 10 August 1792**. Thereafter he gravitated toward **Jean-Paul Marat**, perhaps to secure his election to the **National Convention**. He sat with the **Montagnards**, and voted for death in the trial of **Louis XVI**. Fabre refused to vote on the indictment of Marat, was attacked by the **Girondins** for allegedly favoring a dictatorship, and in return accused **Margeurite-Elie Guadet** and **Armand Gensonné** of negotiating with the king. Fabre would later testify at the trial of the proscribed Girondin deputies. Fabre is credited with naming the months of the **revolutionary calendar**, but in December 1793 was called to defend his reputation before the **Jacobin club**. He did so successfully, but in subsequently attacking his critics he drew further suspicion to himself, and in January 1794 was expelled from the Cordelier club. As early as July 1793 Fabre suspected manipulation of stock offerings for certain companies, including the *Compagnie des Indes*. Some of the conspirators, including **François Chabot**, tried to bribe Fabre to secure his silence. Failing in that, they tricked him into signing a forged document, which later implicated Fabre in the plot. Although innocent, he went to the **guillotine** in April 1794 with Chabot and the others.

FAUBOURG SAINT-ANTOINE. One of the two celebrated **sans-culotte** neighborhoods of **Paris**, along with the *faubourg* **Saint-Marcel**, the *faubourg* Saint-Antoine was located to the east of the *place de la* **Bastille**. On the eve of the Revolution it retained a partially rural aspect, with gardens and small fields interspersed among the artisanal shops that dominated the neighborhood. Some two-thirds of the inhabitants were recent immigrants to Paris, drawn chiefly by the furniture trade, but employed as well in small pottery and textile shops. There were a few large factories, most notably the **Réveillon** wallpaper factory, which would be the focal point of the first popular uprising of 1789. The *brasserie* of **Joseph Santerre** was also located in the *faubourg* Saint-Antoine.

The *faubourg* established its reputation for militancy on 14 July 1789. Roughly 70 percent of the *vainqueurs* of the Bastille came from the immediate neighborhood, and they sustained their activism throughout the Revolution. One exception to this was the **Champ de Mars** rally, but in the **uprising of 10 August 1792** and the **uprising of 31 May–2 June 1793**, police records and other sources suggest that the citizens of the *faubourg* Saint-Antoine played a leading role.

FAUBOURG SAINT-MARCEL. The *faubourg* Saint-Marcel was the second of the activist neighborhoods in **Paris** during the Revolution. It was located on the left bank of the Seine River, in the southeast section of the city, and included within its boundaries both the Gobelins tapestry works, and the many small tanneries and dyeing shops along the Bièvre rivulette. It was a poorer *quartier* than the *faubourg* **Saint-Antoine**, and was thus the focus of substantial poor relief and police surveillance. It was more densely populated near the Seine, but the southern reaches of the *faubourg* were essentially rural. The peak of political activism for Saint-Marcel came between 1791 and 1793, and its inhabitants responded in particular during times of rising prices. The sections of Saint-Marcel were among the last to abandon **Maximilien Robespierre** on 9 **Thermidor**, and they played a prominent role in the abortive **Germinal** and **Prairial riots** in 1795.

FAUCHET, CLAUDE (1744–1794). Fauchet was born in the small town of Dornes, near Nevers just to the southeast of **Paris**, the son of a prosperous merchant. There were seven children in the family, and

Claude was brought up and educated by the Jesuits of Moulins. He then went on to seminary in Bourges, and after ordination as a priest obtained a position in the parish of St. Roch in Paris. Fauchet was a very eloquent orator, and his sermon before the king at an Easter service in 1783 secured for him an appointment as *prédicateur du roi* at the Abbey of Montfort, in Brittany. In 1786 he pronounced the funeral eulogy for Philippe, Duc d'Orléans, earning more royal favor, but some intemperate remarks in 1788 about the need for kings, rather than tyrants, offended the queen and others at court.

In 1789 Fauchet was an advocate for the cause of the lower **clergy**, and was among the vanquishers of the **Bastille**. He took pride in showing the bullet holes in his soutane, and pronounced the eulogy for those who fell on 14 July 1789, to great popular acclaim. In 1790 he founded a newspaper, *La Bouche de Fer*, and in October of that year joined with **Nicolas Bonneville** to found the **Cercle Social**, whose meetings in the **Palais Royal** were attended by as many as 3,000 people. Fauchet's was among the most democratic voices in Paris in 1790–91. On 4 February 1791 he delivered a sermon in Notre Dame Cathedral in which he described liberty as the true principle of religion and said that Jesus Christ had died in the name of universal democracy.

On 1 April 1791 Fauchet was elected constitutional bishop of Calvados, where his radical views generated considerable controversy. Still, he was elected from Calvados to the **Legislative Assembly** and again to the **National Convention** in 1792. Fauchet presided over the **Jacobin club** in Paris in October 1791, but over time he drew closer in his politics to **Jean-Marie Roland** and the **Girondins**. He was expelled from the Jacobin club in September 1792 after speaking critically of **Jean-Paul Marat**. He opposed the trial of **Louis XVI**, refusing to vote on the question of guilt and then voting for banishment and the *appel au peuple*. In February 1793 Fauchet issued a statement opposing the marriage of priests, and in April voted in favor of the indictment of Marat, both of which alienated the Parisian **sans-culottes**. He somehow avoided proscription on 2 June 1793, but in July was accused by **François Chabot** of complicity with **Charlotte Corday** (Fauchet had accompanied her to the Convention when she first arrived in Paris). Fauchet went to trial in October 1793 with the proscribed Girondin deputies and shared their fate.

FEDERALISM. Federalism was a pejorative term during the Revolution, applied to those who, according to their detractors, wished to undermine the unity and indivisibility of the Republic. Its first use may have been in early 1793, to stigmatize those who called for an *appel au peuple* in the trial of **Louis XVI**. As the year wore on, the **Girondin** deputies were increasingly accused of favoring federalism, because of their criticism of **Paris**, particularly the radical clubbists and **sans-culottes** of the sections, and because some of the Girondin deputies called for a departmental guard to protect the **National Convention** against violent extremists. **Departmental administrations** often protested the undue influence of Paris in the spring of 1793, and reminded the deputies of the Convention that Paris was only one of 83 departments. Such assertions of departmental **sovereignty** further fed the charges of federalism, and when a number of departmental administrations protested the proscription of the Girondin deputies following the **uprising of 31 May–2 June 1793**, the **Montagnards** accused them of supporting a **federalist revolt**. When the **Law of Suspects** was passed in September 1793, to be a partisan of federalism was identified as a targeted offense.

Some historians have recently written of a "radical federalism," or "**Jacobin** federalism." The sectional movement in Paris in the early summer of 1791 has been characterized in those terms, as has the neighborhood club movement in **Lyon** in 1790–1791. Similarly, the effort of the **Marseille** Jacobin club to extend its influence throughout Provence by creating a network of affiliated clubs has been described as "Jacobin federalism." Most historians, however, would emphasize the Jacobins' insistence on a strong central government in contrast to the support for federalism among their moderate opponents.

FEDERALIST REVOLT. The federalist revolt occurred in reaction to the proscription of the **Girondin** deputies from the **National Convention** in June 1793. Almost from its first meeting, the Convention was riven by divisions between the more moderate Girondin deputies and the more radical **Montagnards**. The two factions quarreled over the **September Massacres**, the trial of **Louis XVI**, the **constitution of 1793**, the trial of **Jean-Paul Marat**, and the legitimacy of the **sans-culotte** movement in **Paris** and its influence on national politics. That opposition came to a head in the **uprising of 31 May–2**

June 1793, which led to the proscription of 29 Girondin deputies from the National Convention. Nearly 50 **departmental administrations** protested the proscription of the Girondins, and 13 departments engaged in prolonged resistance to the Montagnard Convention in what has come to be known as the federalist revolt.

The revolt centered around four provincial cities—**Bordeaux**, **Caen**, **Lyon**, and **Marseille**—and in each instance it was departmental administrators who took the leading role. In addition to sending delegations or letters of protest to Paris, they declared themselves in a state of resistance to oppression, withdrew their recognition of the National Convention and all decrees issued by it since 31 May 1793, and called upon their constituents to take up arms and march to the capital to restore the proscribed deputies to office. In several of the cities, rebel authorities arrested **representatives on mission** in the early stages of the revolt. Seven Breton and Norman departments sent delegates to the Central Committee of Resistance to Oppression, meeting in Caen. That assembly sent a small force toward Paris in mid-July, but there was little popular support for the revolt there or elsewhere and the call for a march on Paris failed to mount a serious threat to the capital. The rebel force that embarked from Caen dispersed after a single, rather farcical battle, and none of the other rebel forces ever left the limits of their own departments.

Coupled with the **peasant** rebellion in the **Vendée**, however, the federalist revolt presented the young Republic with the very real danger of civil war. The Montagnards, now in control of the National Convention, responded to that danger in several ways. They attempted to present their version of events in Paris to the rest of the country, sometimes by sending representatives on mission to the federalist cities. They eventually prepared an indictment of the proscribed deputies, some of whom fled Paris and went to support the rebellion in Caen, though it would not be until after the collapse of the revolt, in October 1793, that the Girondin leaders would be brought to trial, convicted, and executed. The Montagnards also redoubled their efforts to complete a new constitution, which was presented to the nation in late June. Finally, the Convention sent armed forces to suppress the rebellion in those areas that continued to resist.

The revolt collapsed quickly in Caen, and by late July a small Parisian army had entered the city. The repression of the revolt in

Normandy, supervised by **Robert Lindet**, was remarkably mild. Those officials who had supported the revolt were dismissed from office, and there were a number of arrests, but very few executions. The revolt also ended quickly in Marseille, where an army commanded by **General Jean-Baptiste-François Carteaux** entered the city on 25 August 1793 after only minor skirmishes. But in Lyon the rebels capitulated only after a two-month siege, in early October, and while there was no violent resistance in Bordeaux, it was late October before national deputies could enter the city in safety. The repression of **federalism** in those three cities was much more violent, marking the first serious episodes of the **Terror**. The National Convention declared that "Lyon is no more" as a punishment for the armed resistance there, renaming the city *Commune-Affranchie*, and the representatives on mission, **Georges Couthon**, **Jean-Marie Collet d'Herbois**, and **Joseph Fouché**, eventually ordered the execution of nearly 1,900 rebels. Approximately 300 people were executed as federalists in both Bordeaux and Marseille.

Although the federalist revolt was nominally a reaction to the proscription of the Girondin deputies, the causes of the revolt ran much deeper. From at least the time of the September Massacres, if not before, political elites in the provinces had grown wary of the militant activism of the Parisian sans-culottes, and resented what they considered the excessive influence of Paris on national politics. Many also resented the interference of representatives on mission in local affairs. In each of the federalist cities, moderate elites had weathered political challenges in 1792–1793 from radical clubbists and advocates of popular democracy. Both the struggle between Girondins and Montagnards in the National Convention, and the federalist revolt that followed, must be seen as part of an ongoing debate over **sovereignty** and how it should be exercised. In that sense, the federalist revolt represents a crucial moment in the French Revolution, when national and local politics came together around the most basic of political questions: who are the sovereign people?

FÉDÉRÉS. The *fédérés* were volunteers, principally **National Guards**, who traveled to **Paris** from the provinces in July 1790 for the first **Festival of Federation**. Two years later, with the country at war, the **Legislative Assembly** once again called *fédérés* to the capital for the celebration of 14 July. **Louis XVI** vetoed that decree, which invited 20,000 volunteers, but many came anyway, most notably from **Marseille** and from the department of Finistère, in Brittany. These *fédérés* played a prominent role in the **uprising of 10 August 1792**. Some of the *fédérés* remained in Paris, some returned home, while many went to join the regular army at the front.

In both of these instances the *fédérés* were seen as a progressive force. After the **September Massacres**, some of the leading **Girondins** suggested that departmental volunteers might be summoned to Paris to protect the **National Convention** against violent anarchists, and they appealed to that earlier tradition. Now, however, **Jacobins** denounced those proposed *fédérés* as potentially leading toward **federalism**, and the term took on a more negative connotation.

FERSEN, AXEL VON (1755–1810). Fersen was a Swedish count, diplomat, and military figure. He fought in the American War of Independence and rose to the rank of colonel in the Royal-Suédois Regiment. Fersen was introduced at the French royal court in 1779 and fell in love with **Marie Antoinette**. The precise nature of their relationship is uncertain, but their friendship persisted throughout the 1780s, despite his frequent absences. When the Revolution began, King Gustavus III appointed Fersen as his secret agent at the French court. Fersen played a crucial role in planning and carrying out the flight to **Varennes**, accompanying the king and queen as far as Bondy disguised as a coachman. He fled to Brussels after the royal family was apprehended, but had a hand in the drafting of the **Brunswick Manifesto** in July 1792, and returned to **Paris** after 10 August 1792 in a failed attempt to rescue the king and queen from the Temple. Fersen was killed by an angry mob in Stockholm in 1810, suspected of having poisoned Crown Prince Christian.

FESTIVAL OF FEDERATION. The first Festival of Federation (*Fête de la Fédération*) was held on 14 July 1790, on the Champ de Mars in **Paris**, to celebrate the anniversary of the fall of the **Bastille**. The first such gatherings occurred spontaneously in the provinces, as **National Guards** in the departments came together in regional centers to pledge their support to national unity and the new regime. **Jean-Sylvain**

Bailly, the mayor of Paris, drew from those celebrations the idea of a truly national federation. This and other revolutionary festivals responded to **Jean-Jacques Rousseau's** call for a civic religion, in which the people would be both participants and spectators. Parisians turned out by the thousands to ready the site for the festival, and **Louis XVI** himself turned a symbolic spade of dirt in preparing the massive amphitheater that would welcome guardsmen from all 83 departments of France. A special throne was erected for the king, **Marie-Joseph-Motier Lafayette** played a prominent role as commander of the Paris National Guard, and **Charles-Maurice Talleyrand-Périgord** presided over a special mass. It was truly a day of national unity and hope. No Festival of Federation would be held the following year, however, due to the king's flight to **Varennes**, and in 1792 the *fédérés* who journeyed to the capital to celebrate the anniversary would play a leading role in the **uprising of 10 August**.

FESTIVAL OF REASON. The Festival of Reason (*Fête de la Raison*) was held in Notre Dame cathedral on 10 November 1793, and is considered to have launched the **deChristianization** campaign that followed. **Antoine-François Momoro** took a principal role in organizing the event and his wife, Sophie, an actress at the opera, played the part of the Goddess of Reason. **Jacques-René Hébert** and **Pierre-Gaspard Chaumette** led a procession from the **National Convention** to Notre Dame, although many of the deputies declined to follow. According to **Louis-Sébastien Mercier**, scantily clad women danced the **Carmagnole** and sang revolutionary songs in Notre Dame. Some have suggested that the excesses of this festival were responsible for turning **Maximilien Robespierre** against the deChristianization movement, leading eventually to the **Cult of the Supreme Being**.

FEUILLANTS. The Feuillants were a political club, composed chiefly of constitutional monarchists, which formed in **Paris** after the king's failed flight to **Varennes** in June 1791. On 16 July the **Jacobin club** voted to support a petition initiated by the **Cordelier club** and the **Cercle Social** calling for charges against **Louis XVI** and the creation of a republic. The next day, the very day of the **Champ de Mars massacre**, more than 260 deputies walked out of the Jacobin club to create a rival society, the Feuillants. They were led by **Antoine-Pierre Barnave**, **Adrien Duport**, and **Alexandre Lameth**, the so-called **Triumvirate**. Many other prominent figures joined the Feuillants as well, including **Emmanuel-Joseph Sieyès**, **Bertrand Barère**, **Marie-Joseph-Motier Lafayette**, and **Charles-Maurice Talleyrand**. These men were committed to the ideals of 1789, but in the current political crisis were more devoted to order than to liberty and equality. The gains of the Revolution, they argued, should be consolidated under the rule of law, and the popular upheaval of the Revolution should come to an end.

The Feuillants took with them the correspondence committee of the Jacobin club, and its **newspaper**, and immediately appealed to the network of clubs in the provinces to join them. More than 400 provincial clubs did so, and in the early going it appeared as if the Feuillants would prevail in their struggle with the Jacobins for political supremacy. But when the **Constituent Assembly** dissolved late that summer, its deputies were legally prohibited from standing for reelection, and the Assembly is where the Feuillants had their strength. Although more than 160 of the newly elected deputies to the **Legislative Assembly** joined the Feuillants, the club's open disdain for popular democracy put it at odds with the political currents of the capital. Under the leadership of **Maximilien Robespierre**, **Jérome Pétion**, and **Jacques-Pierre Brissot** (future rivals, but still allies at this time), the Jacobin club courted the popular movement and redoubled its efforts to secure provincial affiliations. By late fall most of the provincial clubs had returned to the Jacobin fold, while the number of societies affiliated with the Feuillants dropped to barely 80. Clearly the Feuillants had misjudged the political climate. On 10 August 1792 the people of Paris would repudiate their assertion that the day for insurrectionary politics had passed, and the Feuillants, like the monarchy, disappeared from the scene.

FIRST ESTATE. *See* CLERGY.

FLORÉAL COUP. The coup of Floréal VI (May 1798) was the second of the coups of the **Directory** aimed at securing the legislative center by purging extremists from office. But while the coup of **Fructidor** V (August 1797) had been directed against royalists, in this instance the directors acted against the **Jacobin** left. **Paul-François Barras**, **Louis-Marie La Révellière-Lépeaux**, and **Philippe Merlin** took the lead in attempting to influence electoral assemblies through a combination of propaganda and intimidation. The Directory sponsored "secessionary" electoral assemblies in some 25 departments, allowing the government to then choose which slate of candidates it found acceptable. In the end, 106 deputies were *floréalized*, or excluded from office, and 53 seats in the two legislative chambers were left unfilled. The legislature would have its revenge on the directors the following year, in the **Prairial coup**, but the overall result of these transparent attempts to manipulate electoral politics was the undermining of participatory democracy.

FORCED LOAN. The most pressing problem confronting the French monarchy in 1789 was the threat of financial collapse, and this problem would persist throughout the revolutionary decade. A number of measures were taken to address the crisis, including the **confiscation of Church lands**, the creation of *assignats*, and the introduction of new, more rational taxes. In a period of political uncertainty, however, the new taxes were difficult to implement and to collect, and inflation plagued the efficacy of the *assignats* as a new paper currency. At several points, the government therefore resorted to forced loans (*emprunts forcés*) as a means of revenue.

In August 1789 **Etienne-Charles Loménie de Brienne** issued special treasury bills bearing 5 percent interest, and these amounted to a kind of indirect forced loan taken from the state's creditors. On 20 May 1793 the **National Convention** decreed a forced loan on the rich (defined as those with income equal to or exceeding 1,500 *livres*), aimed at raising one billion *livres* for the war effort. Additional forced loans were levied on 22 June and 3 September 1793, with the promise that the sums contributed would be reimbursed after the war was over. The **Directory**, too, resorted to a forced loan to sustain the war, imposing a 600 million *livres* loan in December 1795, to be paid by the wealthiest 25 percent of the citizens of each department. This loan was poorly implemented, however, and yielded only a fraction of the goal. A final forced loan of 100 million *livres* was decreed in August 1799, but this imposition was abandoned after the **Brumaire** coup.

Those wealthy citizens who had already made "patriotic gifts" were exempted from these forced loans. A number of towns and cities had solicited such patriotic gifts, or imposed forced loans of their own, in the early years of the Revolution, usually in the face of food shortages. Some **representatives on mission** also introduced forced loans in particular departments on their own authority, much to the chagrin of local elites, and others played a role in collecting the loans levied by the National Convention, particularly during the **Terror**.

FOUCHÉ, JOSEPH (1759–1820). Fouché, the son of a ship's captain, attended the seminary of the Oratoire in Nantes. It is not clear that he was ever ordained, though he wore clerical garb. He taught at a number of different *collèges* in the 1780s, and in 1788 was appointed to teach physics in Arras, where he met **Maximilien Robespierre** and was rumored to have been engaged briefly to Robespierre's sister, Charlotte. In 1790 Fouché returned to Nantes as principal of a *collège*, and joined the local **Jacobin club**. He antagonized Nantes merchants by expressing his vocal opposition to the **slave** trade, but in 1792 was elected to the **National Convention** from the Loire-Inférieure.

Fouché sat with the **Montagnards** and voted for death in the trial of **Louis XVI**. In March 1793 he was sent on mission to the west of France for recruitment, where he remained until May, undertaking the first efforts to combat the **Vendée** rebels. He went on mission again, to the Côte-d'Or and Aube, in June, and in that region imposed forced contributions on the rich and introduced **deChristianization** measures. In St. Cyr he ordered all priests to either marry or adopt a child within a month, and in Nevers he placed signs at all the cemeteries reading "Death is an eternal sleep." These actions, accompanied by the wholesale dismissal of local officials, aroused considerable opposition. Fouché accompanied **Jean-Marie Collot d'Herbois** to **Lyon** in late October 1793, and must share responsibility for the nearly 1,900 executions ordered in that city following the collapse of the **federalist revolt**. After Collot was recalled to **Paris** in February 1794, however, Fouché moderated his policies, which alienated local radicals and eventually led to his own recall and ejection from the Paris Jacobin club. Though now an enemy of Robespierre, Fouché appears not to have participated in the planning of the **Thermidor** coup, but certainly profited by it.

Fouché then returned to the Jacobin club, became tangentially linked to **Gracchus Babeuf**, and actively opposed the more reactionary **Thermidorians** behind the leadership of **Jean-Lambert Tallien**. But Fouché seems never to have kept enemies, or friends, for long. When citizens of the Allier, where he had been on mission in 1793–94, denounced him, Tallien came to his defense. Fouché was imprisoned all the same, but gained his freedom by the amnesty voted on the last day of the Convention's meetings. He cultivated the patronage of **Paul Barras**, for whom he did some secret police work, and after the **Prairial coup** of 1798 was appointed by Barras and **Emmanuel-Joseph Sieyès** to the post of minister of police. Fouché then approached **Napoleon Bonaparte**, supported his **Brumaire** coup, and continued on as minister of police until 1802, when his opposition to the Concordat and to Napoleon's declaration of himself as first consul for life prompted his dismissal. After election to the Senate, however, Fouché embraced the Empire and returned as Napoleon's minister of police, holding that post until 1810. Even though he came to recognize him for the double-dealer that he was, Napoleon could not do without Fouché's talents, and he survived until the end of the regime. Remarkably, he emerged as minister of police in the early days of **Louis XVIII's** reign, but in 1816 was exiled as a regicide. Having once, as a **representative on mission**, declared the shame associated with being rich, he died with a fortune of 15 million francs.

FOUQUIER-TINVILLE, ANTOINE-QUENTIN (1746–1795). Fouquier-Tinville was the son of a seigneurial landowner, perhaps of minor nobility. He studied law in **Paris**, and in 1774 purchased a position as prosecutor at the **Châtelet** court. Some years later he was forced to sell that post to pay off his debts, and in 1781 took a job as a clerk in the office of the royal police. Fouquier was active in the politics of his section in 1789, and in August 1792 was a supporter of the **sans-culotte** movement. Late in that month he obtained a position on the court newly created to judge the royalists arrested on 10 August, most likely through the influence of his cousin, **Camille Desmoulins**.

Fouquier-Tinville is best known, however, as the prosecutor for the **Revolutionary Tribunal**, created in March 1793. He owed that position, which he would hold until after **Thermidor**, to **Maximilien**

Robespierre and **Georges Danton**, and as public prosecutor he would eventually send both men to the **guillotine**. His manner as prosecutor was dry, to the point, very businesslike. Some would have seen him, no doubt, as cold and unfeeling. Fouquier was denounced and arrested less than a week after Robespierre's fall, but did not come to trial until April 1795. The trial lasted 41 days, and some 400 witnesses were heard. Fouquier defended himself by claiming to have been only "the axe" of the **National Convention**, responsible for enforcing laws over which he had no control. He went to the guillotine, along with nine other members of the Revolutionary Tribunal, insisting that he had nothing for which to reproach himself.

FREEMASONRY. Freemasonry (*franc-maçonnerrie*) migrated to France from Great Britain early in the 18th century, and there were those in France during the 1790s and throughout the 19th century who attributed the upheaval of the Revolution to a conspiracy of Freemasons. There is little evidence to support such an assertion, but it cannot be denied that the spread of Masonic lodges throughout France did contribute to the intellectual and social ferment that led to the Revolution.

By mid-century, Masonic lodges existed in virtually every major town in France. There were two competing national organizations, the Grand Lodge and the Grand Orient. The Grand Master of the Masons was **Louis-Philippe Orléans**, and many other prominent figures who would play a significant role in the Revolution were also Freemasons, including **Marie-Jean Condorcet**, **Georges-Jacques Danton**, **Jacques-Louis David**, **Benjamin Constant**, and **Jean-Pierre-André Amar**. Many more names could be added, but even this short list is a diverse group, and suggests the difficulty in sustaining an argument that the Freemasons had some sort of grand plan that launched the Revolution. In most towns, indeed, there were competing lodges at the end of the Old Regime, with distinctive clienteles, and the competition between rival lodges often foreshadowed a rivalry between competing **popular societies** or conflicting groups during the revolutionary decade. Freemasonry was egalitarian in its ideals, but also hierarchical in its organization, two attributes that would be at odds in the context of the Revolution. Those who joined the lodges, whether liberal or conservative, were universally well educated and drawn from the wealthier classes of society. The sociability of the lodges was therefore important to the political ferment in France both before the Revolution and in its early years. They were as important an element of **Enlightenment** culture as the **salons**. Freemasonry grew dormant in France during the **Terror**, but the organization revived in the latter years of the **Directory** regime.

FRÉRON, LOUIS-STANISLAS (1754–1802). Fréron was the son of Elie Fréron, the famous publicist and adversary of **Voltaire**. Louis was educated at the *collège* Louis-le-Grand in **Paris**, where he knew **Camille Desmoulins** and **Maximilien Robespierre**. After his father died, Fréron renewed the publishing **privilege** of *l'Annexe littéraire*, but the Abbé Royou did all of the work while Fréron led a dissolute life. In 1789, however, he embraced the ideals of the Revolution and in December began publication of a **newspaper**, *L'Orateur du Peuple*, which approached in tone that of **Jean-Paul Marat's** *L'Ami du Peuple*. Fréron was a member of the **Cordelier club**, participated in the 17 July 1791 rally on the **Champ de Mars**, and after the flight to **Varennes** called for the king's head in his newspaper, suggesting that the queen be tied to the tail of a horse and led through the streets of Paris. These intemperate remarks forced him into hiding until after the **uprising of 10 August 1792**.

Not surprisingly, Fréron participated in both the storming of the **Tuileries** Palace and the **September Massacres**. He was then elected to the **National Convention** from Paris. He sat with the **Montagnards** and voted for death in the trial of **Louis XVI**. In March 1793 he was sent on mission for recruitment to the southeast of France with **Paul Barras**. They prolonged their stay into the summer months, and then went on to **Marseille** and **Toulon**, where they ordered harsh repression against those who had participated in the rebellions in those cities and denounced to the **Committee of Public Safety** those deputies on mission who advocated more moderate measures. Both Barras and Fréron were recalled to Paris in January 1794, and Fréron was denounced before the **Jacobin club** by **Jacques-René Hébert**. **Pierre-Joseph Cambon** also stepped forward to accuse the two of embezzling some 800,000 francs, but a local mayor testified that the money had been lost in a swamp in a carriage accident.

Fréron now allied himself with **Jean-Baptiste Carrier** and **Jean-Lambert Tallien** in the conspiracy against Robespierre, and after **Thermidor** he resumed publication of *L'Orateur du Peuple*, which now adopted a reactionary tone. Fréron also became a leader and protector of the *jeunesse dorée* during this period. In September 1795 he was sent again on mission to Marseille, where he lived extravagantly and spent huge sums of public money, shielded from prosecution by his old friend Barras, who had become a director by the time Fréron was recalled to Paris. Fréron was not elected to national office under the **Directory**, but occupied a number of minor posts. After **Brumaire** he became intimately involved with Pauline Bonaparte, and there was even talk of marriage until Fréron's wife and two children reappeared on the scene. Shortly thereafter, **Napoleon Bonaparte** assigned him to a post in **Saint-Domingue**, where he died of yellow fever.

FRUCTIDOR COUP. On 18 Fructidor V (4 September 1797), three of the directors—**Louis-Marie La Révellière-Lépeaux**, **Paul-François Barras**, and Jean-François Reubell—ordered a purge of their two colleagues, **Lazare Carnot** and François Barthélemy, along with 53 right-wing deputies. The three directors enjoyed the support of the army in carrying out this action, in particular that of Generals **Lazare Hoche** and **Napoleon Bonaparte**. The Fructidor coup consolidated the control of republican deputies within the **Council of Ancients** and the **Council of Five Hundred**, and was justified to the public by reports of an alleged royalist plot, probably nonexistent. The political legitimacy of the **Directory** was undermined, however, and would be further damaged by the **Floréal coup** and the **Prairial coup** in successive years.

– G –

GARAT, DOMINIQUE-JOSEPH (1749–1833). Garat was born into an old family of Bayonne, near the Pyrenees. His father was a doctor, but Joseph was brought up by his maternal uncle, an abbot, who encouraged him to attend seminary. Garat left seminary for the *collège* of Guyenne in **Bordeaux**, however, and went on to study law in Bordeaux as well.

He became an *avocat* in the early 1770s, but went to **Paris** to indulge his passion for literature and philosophy. There he met **Marie-Jean Condorcet, Denis Diderot,** Claude-Adrien Helvétius, and others. He was particularly drawn to the ideas of **Montesquieu** and **Jean-Jacques Rousseau**. In 1785 he gained a position teaching ancient history at a *lycée* in Paris.

Garat returned home in 1789 and was elected to the **Estates-General** by the **Third Estate** of Bayonne, as was his older brother. He was present for the swearing of the **Tennis Court Oath**, joined the Club of 1789, and sat on the left of the assembly. In 1791 he returned to teaching, and is credited with coining the term "social science" in a published letter to Condorcet. In 1792 he went to England on diplomatic mission, but returned to France in October to take up the position of minister of justice, to which he had been recommended by Condorcet and **Jacques-Pierre Brissot**. Called upon to investigate the **September Massacres**, he issued a report concluding that while unfortunate, they were a continuation of the **uprising of 10 August 1792** against the monarchy and hence not a criminal act. Following the trial of the king, Garat informed **Louis XVI** of his sentence, and was present on the scaffold at his execution.

In March 1793 Garat succeeded **Jean-Marie Roland** as minister of the interior, a post he would hold until August 1793. He tried to play a mediating role between the **Girondins** and **Montagnards**, but failed in that effort. Garat opposed the creation of the **Commission of Twelve,** but could do nothing to prevent the proscription of the Girondin leaders in June. That summer, during the **federalist revolt**, Garat sent agents into the provinces to gather information about **public opinion** and to spread republican ideals, and appears to have played a role in helping Condorcet elude arrest. He was briefly arrested himself in September 1793, accused of misusing public funds, and remained under surveillance until after **Thermidor**. In 1795 Garat was elected to the **Institut National**, where he became associated with the **Ideologues**, and finding himself once again under suspicion he published his *Mémoire sur la Révolution* as a form of self-justification. He served as ambassador to Naples in 1797, was elected to the **Council of Ancients** from the Seine-et-Oise in 1798, and in 1799 entered the Senate. Garat generally supported **Napoleon Bonaparte**, though he was at times openly critical of his policies. He was named to the Legion of Honor in 1804, and in 1808 was named Count of the Empire. Garat eventually retired to Ustaritz, in the western Pyrenees.

GENSONNÉ, ARMAND (1758–1793). Born in **Bordeaux**, Gensonné was the son of a chief surgeon in the royal army. He was schooled at the *collège* of Guyenne in Bordeaux, and went on to a distinguished career in law, with important ties to the merchant community of Bordeaux. Gensonné was elected to the first municipal council of Bordeaux, joined in the founding of both the **National Guard** and the **Jacobin club** in that city, and in January 1791 was elected judge on the departmental *Tribunal de Cassation*. That summer he was sent on a special mission to the departments of the West to investigate the causes of religious troubles there and to recommend ameliorative measures. He advised a major campaign for public education, leniency for those misled, and severe measures against those nobles and priests who incited the **peasantry** to resist the revolutionary government.

Gensonné was elected to the **Legislative Assembly** from the Gironde, and as a deputy opposed the banishment of **refractory priests**, and supported the declaration of war against Austria. He presided over the assembly in March/April 1792, and in July signed the infamous letter to Joseph Boze, former court painter, that would later be interpreted as a **Girondin** effort to negotiate with **Louis XVI** in order to avert the fall of the monarchy. In September 1792 Gensonné was reelected to the **National Convention**. He sat with the Girondins, but was not close to the **Rolands**. Gensonné voted for death in the trial of Louis XVI, but had a bitter exchange with **Maximilien Robespierre** during the debate over the *appel au peuple*, for which he voted. He also sat on the constitution committee, and joined **Marie-Jean Condorcet** as the principal drafter of the proposal submitted to the Convention in February 1793. He supported the creation of the **Committee of Public Safety**, but opposed the **Revolutionary Tribunal**. He also supported the creation of the **Commission of Twelve**, but did not serve on it.

Gensonné anticipated his proscription on 2 June 1793, and in the midst of the tumult sat at his post drafting an eloquent protest and testament to his constituents. He was arrested by a gendarme whose life he had saved on 10 August 1792, and who now urged Gensonné to flee. He ignored that advice, as well as that of **Joseph Garat** and others that he go into hiding, and was critical of the deputies who fled to **Caen**. At his trial he acknowledged close contact with **General Charles-François Dumouriez**, but refused to respond to the accusation that he was party to his treason. Gensonné marched bravely to the **guillotine** with his fellow Girondins on 31 October 1793.

GERLE, CHRISTOPHE-ANTOINE (1736–1801). Dom Gerle, as he was known, was born in the town of Riom, at the heart of the *Massif Central*, though little is known about his early life or family. He entered the order of the Chartreux in 1761, was tonsured in 1762, and ordained as a priest in 1764. In 1777 he was named prior of Vauclaire, in the Périgord; became prior of an order in Moulins in 1780; and in 1788 became prior of the Chartreuse of Port-Sainte-Marie, in Clermont. Gerle joined the **Freemasons** in 1785. In 1789 he was elected as a substitute delegate to the **Estates-General** by the **clergy** of Rioms, and took his seat in December. He appears in **Jacques-Louis David's** sketch of the **Tennis Court Oath**, though he was not in fact present at that event. In April 1790 Gerle proposed that Catholicism be declared the state religion of France, the only one to be practiced publicly, but he withdrew the proposal when it encountered serious opposition in the **Constituent Assembly**. Gerle swore the **civil oath of the clergy** in December 1790, and shortly thereafter was elected constitutional bishop of the Seine-et-Marne, a post that he declined. Gerle was a member of the **Jacobin club**, which he left temporarily at the time of the **Feuillant** schism. After the Constituent Assembly dissolved, he became involved with Suzanne Labrousse, a kind of prophetess from the Périgord, and then Catherine Théot, who fancied herself the "Mother of God." These associations brought him under suspicion, and he was arrested in May 1794 and forgotten in prison until the **Directory**. Thereafter he lived in **Paris** on his pension, in relative obscurity.

GERMINAL RIOTS. The riots of 12 Germinal III (1 April 1795) were a response both to the food shortages and rising prices of the winter of 1795, and to the political repression directed against **sans-culotte** and **Jacobin** militants by the **Thermidorians**. The **National Convention** abolished the *maximum* in January, and in the months that followed groups of *jeunesse dorée* invaded the meeting halls of **popular societies** and clubs in **Paris** and destroyed the busts of **Jean-Paul Marat**. In the face of growing popular unrest, **Emmanuel-Joseph Sieyès** proposed a law on 1 Germinal, adopted immediately, which established punishments for those who disrupted or attacked the sessions of the National Convention.

The law itself appears to have served as an incitement, for on 12 Germinal as many as 10,000 protesters invaded the hall of the Convention, despite the efforts of the *jeunesse dorée*, posted as guards, to keep them out. The crowd remained in the hall all afternoon, but the protest, virtually a riot, lacked organization or clearly defined goals. Several speakers called for more adequate bread supplies and the **Constitution of 1793**, never implemented, as well as the release of militants who had been arrested since **Thermidor**. Those **Montagnard** deputies who remained in the Convention did not actively support the movement, however, and by early evening the crowd had dispersed. That same night the Convention ordered the deportation of **Bertrand Barère**, **Jacques-Nicolas Billaud-Varenne**, **Jean-Marie Collot-d'Herbois**, and **Marc-Alexis-Guillaume Vadier**. Other Jacobin militants, including **Léonard Bourdon** and **Jean-Pierre-André Amar**, would soon be arrested. The Convention redoubled its efforts to maintain order, but took only halfhearted measures to address the food shortages, which led to the **Prairial riots** barely one month later.

GIRONDINS. The Girondins were one of the two principal factions that emerged in the **National Convention** during the first eight months of its existence, the other being the **Montagnards**. They cannot be called political parties—they lacked the parliamentary discipline or cohesion to justify that label—but they did coalesce into loose groupings, and the struggle between the two factions came to dominate the sessions of the National Convention by the spring of 1793. In the end, the Montagnards triumphed in the **uprising of 31 May–2 June 1793**, which led to the proscription of 29 Girondin deputies from the Convention.

The group first became recognizable in the **Legislative Assembly**, around the leadership of **Jacques-Pierre Brissot**, and included the deputies **Jean-François Ducos**, **Pierre-Victurnien Vergniaud**,

Armand Gensonné, and **Marguerite-Elie Guadet**, all of whom came from **Bordeaux** in the department of the Gironde, which gave the group its future name. In the Legislative Assembly, however, and for some time thereafter, they were more commonly known as Brissotins. Outside of the Assembly, the group included such prominent figures as **Marie-Jean Condorcet**, **Nicolas de Bonneville**, and **Claude Fauchet**, all of whom regularly attended the meetings of the **Cercle Social**. **Jean-Marie Roland**, minister of the interior in 1792, also associated with the Brissotins, as did his wife, **Manon Roland**, who would regularly invite the Girondin leadership to her home for dinners under the National Convention.

The Brissotins in the Legislative Assembly are best known for advocating a preventive war against Prussia and Austria, as a strategy calculated to rally the people to the Revolution and to force **Louis XVI** to reveal his true colors. When the war went badly, the Brissotins became the most vocal critics of the monarchy. Rather than lead the growing popular movement in favor of declaring a Republic, however, Vergniaud, Gensonné, and Guadet chose to negotiate with the king, through an ill-fated approach to the former court painter, Joseph Boze. Vergniaud presided over the Legislative Assembly in early August 1792, and turned away the petition of the **Paris** sections demanding that the king be deposed. Uncomfortable with the street politics of the **sans-culottes**, the Girondins nonetheless profited by the **uprising of 10 August 1792**, which put them in position to dominate the National Convention.

Virtually all of the Brissotins were reelected to the Convention, where they were joined by Condorcet, **Charles-Jean-Marie Barbaroux**, **François-Nicolas Buzot**, **Jean-Baptiste Louvet**, **Jérome Pétion**, **Antoine-Joseph Gorsas**, and **François Bergeoing**. The deputies from the Gironde, all eloquent orators, quickly emerged as the leaders of the group. Fearful of the revolutionary violence of the Paris crowd, they favored constitutional legality. Although initially quiet, they eventually condemned the **September Massacres** and demanded that the perpetrators be brought to justice, identifying **Georges Danton**, **Maximilien Robespierre**, and **Jean-Paul Marat** by name. These were the leaders of the Montagnards, and the champions of the Parisian sans-culottes, and the Girondins came increasingly to be seen as hostile to Paris.

In the trial of Louis XVI, the Girondins favored the *appel au peuple*, denounced by the Montagnards as an effort to save the king. They dominated the constitutional committee, which Condorcet chaired, but could not marshal the votes necessary to pass the constitution that the committee drafted. On other issues, too, the Girondins lost in their struggle with the Montagnards. They opposed the adoption of a **grain *maximum***, yet saw it enacted in May 1793. They opposed the creation of a **Revolutionary Tribunal**, which was established in March. The Girondins had favored the declaration of war in 1792, yet the war continued to go badly, and the defection of General **Charles Dumouriez** to the Austrians in April 1793 dealt a serious blow to their political fortunes, because of his personal association with several of the Girondin leaders.

The political tension within the National Convention, and in Paris, grew throughout the winter months. Girondin deputies complained on many occasions that they were under the threat of assassins' blades, and the sacking of Gorsas's printing press in March seemed to substantiate that allegation. In April they pushed through the impeachment of Marat, for his consistent defense of popular violence, but more specifically for a letter he circulated early that month calling for the dismissal of deputies who had supported the *appel au peuple*. A Parisian jury acquitted Marat, however, and a jubilant crowd escorted him back to the Convention. Next the Girondins created the **Commission of Twelve**, to investigate allegations that the **section assemblies** of Paris were plotting an insurrection against the Convention. This tactic, too, backfired on the Girondins. The arrests of **Jacques-René Hébert** and **Jean Varlet** incited Parisian militants rather than cowing them, and the insurrection that the Girondins feared began on 31 May 1793.

Two days later, 29 Girondin deputies were proscribed from the National Convention. Some of the deputies fled to **Caen**, to support the **federalist revolt**. Those who remained in Paris were brought to trial in October, after the revolt had been quelled, and were executed on 31 October 1793. Others, including Barbaroux, Pétion, and Guadet, were eventually tracked down in the provinces and either committed suicide or died on the **guillotine**. Among the most prominent of the Girondins, only Jean-Baptiste Louvet survived the **Terror** and eventually resumed his place in the National Convention, as did most of the 76 deputies who had been expelled in June 1793 for protesting the proscription of their leaders. But while the **Thermidorians** pursued an agenda in many ways sympathetic to their past ideals, the Girondins could not be said to have reasserted themselves as a group within the National Convention.

GLUCK, CHRISTOPH WILLIBALD (1714–1787). Christoph Gluck was a German classical composer best known for his operas. He gained fame on the opera stage of **Paris** in the 1770s, and his works were the dominant force in French opera during the Revolution. Gluck was born in Bohemia, the son of a forester. He left home as a youth, to avoid following in his father's career footsteps, and went to study music in Prague. He also studied organ in Milan in the 1730s, and spent a number of years in Vienna, where the young **Marie Antoinette** was his student.

During Gluck's years in Paris in the mid-1770s, two camps emerged among Parisian opera followers. One preferred the more serious dramatic works of Gluck, while the other favored the more traditional, light opera of Niccolò Piccinni. Gluck prevailed in the "opera battles," and his operas *Iphigénie en Tauride*, *Iphigénie en Aulide*, *Orphée et Eurydice*, and *Armide* were regularly performed during the Revolution. Gluck's work had a substantial influence on **André Grétry**, the principal French composer of the revolutionary era.

GORSAS, ANTOINE-JOSEPH (1752–1793). Gorsas was the son of a shoemaker in Limoges. He studied at the *collège* of Plessis, in **Paris**, where he met **Pierre Vergniaud**. After finishing school he declined to take orders, as his parents wished (he would remain staunchly anti-clerical during the Revolution), and instead took a position as a clerk on the royal domains at **Versailles**. Gorsas married in 1775 and in 1779 opened a school in Versailles—half military and half civilian in its enrolment—but the principles of liberty that he espoused brought him notoriety and a short visit to the Bicêtre prison in 1788.

On 5 July 1789 Gorsas began publication of *Le Courrier de Versailles à Paris*, which became *Le Courrier de Paris dans les provinces* when he moved to Paris in October, and then *Le Courrier des 83 départements* in October 1791. It was one of the most widely read revolutionary **newspapers**, particularly important for its reporting of events occurring outside Paris. Gorsas published the paper, writing almost everything in it himself, up until 31 May 1793. He was considered among the more radical revolutionaries early on, but in April 1792 **Maximilien Robespierre** denounced him before the **Jacobin club**, and in June, at the time of the first assault on the **Tuileries** Palace, the newspaper took on a decidedly more conservative tone. Gorsas was elected to the **National Convention** from the Seine-et-Oise and sat with the **Girondins**. He voted for banishment in the trial of **Louis XVI** and for the *appel au peuple*. In early March 1793 his printing press was sacked, forcing Gorsas to suspend publication of his paper for more than a week, and this became a subject of harsh recrimination in the debate between Girondins and **Montagnards**.

Gorsas voted in support of the indictment of **Jean-Paul Marat**, and in May was denounced himself by the **Paris Commune**. He was among those deputies proscribed on 2 June 1793, fled to **Caen** to support the rebellion there, and was declared an outlaw on 28 July 1793. He made the mistake of returning to Paris, and was spotted in a reading room in the **Palais Royal**. Since he had already been declared an outlaw, no trial was required, and Gorsas became the first deputy of the Convention to die on the **guillotine**. After **Thermidor** his widow opened a bookstore in Paris and continued to publish pamphlets and brochures with an anti-Jacobin flavor.

GOUGES, MARIE-OLYMPE (1748–1793). Olympe de Gouges, as she is most commonly known, was born in Montauban, where her mother was a small shopkeeper. The identity of her father is less clear—most sources claim that he was a butcher, while a few suggest that Louis XV may have been her father. Finding the truth is complicated by the fact that Olympe quite self-consciously fashioned her own identity as she developed a public persona in adulthood. Sources suggest that she married while young, in Montauban, and had a child, but left her husband in 1770 to pursue a writing career in **Paris**. Her first play, *Mariage inattendu du Chérubin*, was a comedy staged in 1785, but it did not go well. A more serious play, *L'Esclavage des Noirs*, was a flop at the Theater of the Nation in December 1789.

At that point she became active in revolutionary politics and published a number of pamphlets and brochures, always in support of a constitutional monarchy. De Gouges also defended the rights of **women**, most notably in her September 1791 pamphlet, *Déclaration des Droits de la Femme et de la Citoyenne*, which she addressed to **Marie Antoinette**. This was a lengthy piece, seen today as a feminist manifesto, which demanded for women the natural rights that men had denied them in civil society. De Gouges made several attempts to found a women's club in Paris, but without notable success. During the trial of **Louis XVI** she published another pamphlet defending the king, and became a pronounced supporter of the **Girondin** deputies in that period. In the summer of 1793 she addressed one of her more provocative pamphlets directly to **Maximilien Robespierre**, and published another that violently attacked **Jean-Paul Marat**. De Gouges was arrested in late July 1793 as a **federalist** sympathizer, and was tried on 2 November, charged also as a royalist. She went to the **guillotine** the following day. *See also* DECLARATION OF THE RIGHTS OF WOMAN AND CITIZENESS.

GRAIN *MAXIMUM*. The **National Convention** adopted the grain *maximum* on 4 May 1793, following serious market riots in **Paris** in February and March, and weeks of acrimonious debate among the deputies. The law directed **departmental administrations** to establish a *maximum* price for wheat and flour, based on the average price during the first months of the year, and gave them authority to inventory and requisition grain supplies. Generally speaking, **Girondin** deputies opposed the grain *maximum*, favoring free trade, and **Montagnard** deputies supported it, responding to pressure from the **sans-culottes**. The law was unevenly applied, in part due to ambivalence among departmental administrators, and in part due to the disruptions of the **Vendée rebellion** and the **federalist revolt**. The fact that *maximum* prices varied by department also encouraged local authorities to retain control over local grain supplies, thereby interfering with national commerce. **Peasants** tended to resent the grain *maximum*, and many refused to deliver their grain to market, even after the National Convention imposed the death penalty as punishment for hoarders in July 1793. In September 1793, pressured by the *enragés*, the National Convention adopted a more general *maximum* and stiffened its enforcement as part of the legislation of the **Terror**. *See also* BREAD RIOTS.

GRANGENEUVE, JEAN-ANTOINE (1751–1793). Grangeneuve, the son of an *avocat au Parlement* in **Bordeaux**, was among the most illustrious attorneys in that city at the end of the Old Regime. He joined in the founding of the **Jacobin club** in Bordeaux in 1789, and in February 1790 was elected as a substitute *procureur* on the municipal council. In 1791 Grangeneuve was elected to the **Legislative Assembly** from the Gironde, and would be reelected to the **National Convention** the following year. But it was in the Legislative Assembly that he played his most influential role. In November 1791 he demanded that all *émigrés* who refused to return to France be immediately declared traitors, and in January 1792 delivered a formal report on the problem of *émigrés*, focusing in particular on the two brothers of **Louis XVI**. Grangeneuve supported **Jacques Brissot's** call for war against Austria, and was a staunch advocate of free trade. He insisted, in constitutional debates, that the Legislative Assembly and the king were two equal powers, and was among the first of the **Girondins** to call for an end to the monarchy, in July 1792.

Grangeneuve was appalled, however, by the **September Massacres**, and became increasingly moderate and withdrawn thereafter. In the trial of Louis XVI, he voted for imprisonment and for the *appel au peuple*, and in April 1793 voted in support of the indictment of **Jean-Paul Marat**. Grangeneuve was proscribed from the National Convention on 2 June 1793, fled to Bordeaux, and went into hiding. He was declared an outlaw on 28 July 1793, and upon his discovery and arrest in December was executed along with his younger brother, Jean, who had been a leader on the Gironde **departmental administration** during the **federalist revolt**.

GREAT FEAR. The Great Fear (*Grande Peur*) was a sort of rural panic that swept across much of France in the last two weeks of July and the first week of August 1789. The number of beggars and vagrants had grown in rural France in the wake of the poor harvests of 1788, and the convocation of the **Estates-General** and the drafting of *cahiers de doléances* had created a mood of both anticipation and apprehension across the country. In mid-July, news of the dismissal of

Jacques Necker and the fall of the **Bastille** acted like a spark in this very volatile situation.

The Great Fear traveled with astonishing rapidity, following seven currents that covered most of central and south-central France. Each current generated its own variants, but generally speaking the rumor spread that the **aristocracy** had paid brigands to go out into the fields to cut the grain before it had fully ripened, thereby throwing the **peasantry** into even deeper economic crisis and thwarting the popular movement for reform. Rumors of roving bands of brigands often turned out to have been generated by flocks of sheep or cattle, but by the time such false alerts could be put to rest the alarm had raced on to the next town or village. In some instances, peasants attacked the châteaux of local seigneurs, drinking the lord's wine and sometimes seizing and destroying the records of the hated **seigneurial dues**. Considerable property damage resulted, but very few lives were lost in this violence.

The impact of the Great Fear was twofold. Many communities across France created their own **National Guard**, to defend against the rumored bands of brigands, and this mobilization of the citizenry into armed militias also presented a force capable of countering royal troops that might oppose the Revolution. Secondly, as news of the Great Fear reached **Versailles**, the deputies grew concerned, and that concern almost certainly prompted some among them to renounce their seigneurial dues on the **Night of 4 August** and initiate the legislative process that would eventually lead to the abolition of **privilege**.

GRÉGOIRE, HENRI-BAPTISTE (1750–1831). Grégoire was born in a small village in northeastern France, where his father was a tailor and member of the village council. Grégoire went to school in the village, then on to a Jesuit *collège*, before attending the University of Nancy, in 1768, and seminary in Metz beginning in 1772, where he was a student of **Adrien Lamourette**. From that time until the outbreak of the Revolution, he held a variety of posts as a teacher, a vicar, and a *curé*. In 1785, at the inauguration of a synagogue in Lorraine, Grégoire gave a sermon in favor of the emancipation of **Jews** in France, a position that he would advocate throughout the Revolution. In 1789 he was elected to the **Estates-General** as a delegate of the **clergy** of Nancy.

Grégoire was among the most active deputies in the **Constituent Assembly**. He joined the **Breton club**, and later the **Jacobin club**, which he left briefly at the time of the **Feuillant** schism. Grégoire favored the joining of the three orders, and was one of five clergy who went over to the **Third Estate**, though he continued to meet with the clergy as well. He was present for the swearing of the **Tennis Court Oath**, and presided over the famous meeting of the Constituent Assembly on 12 July 1789 that went on for 72 hours while the **Bastille** fell in **Paris**. In August 1789 he argued that the **Declaration of the Rights of Man and Citizen** should include a Declaration of Duties, and called for the name of God to appear at the head of the declaration. Grégoire was among the founders of the **Society of the Friends of Blacks**, and would be influential in the abolition of **slavery** in 1794. He worked tirelessly to improve the lot of the lower clergy, and in late December 1790 was the first to swear the **civil oath of the clergy**, which he ardently defended in the years to come. Following the adjournment of the Constituent Assembly, Grégoire was elected constitutional bishop in the Loir-et-Cher, where he also served on the **departmental administration**.

In 1792 Grégoire was elected from the Loir-et-Cher to the **National Convention**. He was absent during the trial of **Louis XVI**, but opposed the death penalty as a matter of principle. He is perhaps best known in the Convention for his advocacy of French as the universal language of the republic, and his call for legislation abolishing the use of *patois*. He was an opponent of **refractory priests**, but also a vigorous opponent of **deChristianization**. In 1795 he was elected to the **Council of Five Hundred** from the Seine, to the Corps Législatif after **Brumaire**, and to the Senate in 1801. Grégoire opposed the Concordat negotiated by **Napoleon Bonaparte** with the Catholic Church, and refused to support the Empire. Despite this, he was named to the Legion of Honor in 1803, and made a Count of the Empire in 1808. In that latter year he completed his memoirs, in which he praised the accomplishments of the Constituent Assembly while judging more harshly the National Convention. Grégoire had increasingly come to be an advocate of freedom of religion over the course of the Revolution, and at his death remained unreconciled with the Catholic Church.

GRÉTRY, ANDRÉ-ERNEST-MODESTE (1741–1813). Grétry was born in Liège, the son of a violinist. He was a master of the comic opera under the reign of **Louis XVI**, and adapted to the changing cultural politics of the Revolution. Grétry studied first in Liège, and then in Rome, before moving to **Paris** in 1766. En route he stopped in Geneva, where he met **Voltaire**, who would become one of his early patrons, and whose work would inspire his first opera, *Isabelle et Gertrude*. Grétry's first real success was *Le Huron*, completed in 1768. His lyrical style was influenced by the writing of **Jean-Jacques Rousseau** and by the music of **Christoph Gluck**. Grétry's best-known work was *Richard Coeur de Lion* (1784), the refrain from which, "O Richard, o mon Roi," became a rallying song for royalists during the early years of the Revolution. This harmed Grétry's reputation somewhat, but the appearance of *Guillaume Tell* in 1791 and *La Rosière Républicaine* in 1794 (with libretto by **Sylvain Maréchal**) returned him to favor in the public eye. In 1795 he was elected to the **Institut National**, and shortly thereafter became inspector of the new music conservatory. He wrote a number of patriotic pieces during the Revolution, including *Ronde pour la plantation d'un arbre de la Liberté* (1799). In 1802 **Napoleon Bonaparte** named him to the Legion of Honor. He died in 1813 at the hermitage of Rousseau, in Montmorency, which he had bought at the time of the philosopher's death.

GUADET, MARGUERITE-ELIE (1755–1794). Guadet was born in Saint-Emilion and brought up at home until the age of 15, at which point the widow of a rich merchant in **Bordeaux** paid for his education at the *collège* of Guyenne. He eventually inherited 20,000 *livres* from that same widow, and went on to study law in Bordeaux. Guadet left for **Paris** in the mid-1770s, where he worked as personal secretary to a lawyer, and returned to Bordeaux in 1781 to take up a position as *avocat au Parlement*. He enjoyed a good reputation on the eve of the Revolution.

Guadet was among the founders of the **Jacobin club** in Bordeaux, and in July 1790 was elected to the **departmental administration**. In May 1791 he was elected president of the departmental Criminal Tribunal, and later that year was elected to the **Legislative Assembly** from the Gironde. Guadet was a member of the **Society of the**

Friends of Blacks, and a vocal critic of French plantation owners in **Saint-Domingue**. He did not make his first speech in the Assembly until 14 January 1792, but then delivered a stirring call for a declaration of war in defense of the Revolution and the constitution. Guadet was an acerbic speaker, had several barbed exchanges with **Maximilien Robespierre**, and was among the first deputies to condemn **Jean-Paul Marat**, in May 1792. Later that summer, however, he signed the ill-considered letter to Joseph Boze, the former court painter, along with **Armand Gensonné** and **Pierre Vergniaud**, and even went so far as to meet with the king and queen.

This would harm his reputation when the letter was revealed in January 1793, but by then Guadet had emerged, along with **François Buzot**, as a leading spokesperson for the **Girondin** faction in the **National Convention**. He voted for death in the trial of **Louis XVI**, but for the **Mailhe amendment**, and for the *appel au peuple* as well. Guadet took a leading role in the attack on Marat in the spring of 1793, delivering a particularly scathing speech on 12 April that condemned the criminal behavior of Paris militants as well, but in the end declined to vote on the indictment of Marat. In May he proposed that the National Convention be moved to **Bourges**, should the deputies be attacked by the Paris crowd. Guadet was among the deputies proscribed on 2 June. He fled to **Caen**, and then on to Brittany after the collapse of the **federalist revolt**. He eventually took refuge near his home in Saint-Emilion, but was discovered in June 1794 along with Jean-Baptiste Salle and immediately taken to Bordeaux. He died on the **guillotine** along with his father, aunt, and brother.

GUILLOTINE. The guillotine stands as the principal symbol of the **Terror** in the French Revolution. On 20 January 1790, Dr. Joseph-Ignace Guillotin proposed in the **Constituent Assembly** that capital punishment be carried out by decapitation, and the deputies eventually adopted that proposal in legislation approved on 25 September 1791. The machine that was designed to carry out the punishment came to bear Dr. Guillotin's name.

Guillotin's proposal was motivated both by a sense of humanity and a desire for equality. Executions under the Old Regime were often slow and painful. Commoners were either hung, slowly strangling to death, or if their offense was particularly grievous they might be broken on the wheel or drawn and quartered, procedures that could take hours to complete. Only convicted **aristocrats** were entitled to be executed by the sword, a method of decapitation that could sometimes be clumsy and painful itself. Death by guillotine was to be both quick and efficient, and was to be applied to all persons sentenced to die, regardless of rank.

A guillotine was first used on 25 April 1792. The machine itself consisted of a wooden frame, roughly 12 feet in height, at the top of which a diagonal, weighted blade was suspended by a rope, the release of which would allow the blade to descend quickly, severing the head of the victim in one blow. The victim lay face down on a bench, his head and neck placed in a *lunette* directly below the blade. The guillotine was not foolproof. Occasionally the blade failed to sever the neck completely, and the blade had to be raised for a second, or third, descent.

Executions were public, as they had been under the Old Regime, and often drew large crowds. For the execution of **Louis XVI**, the guillotine was erected on the Place de la Révolution, but most executions in **Paris** occurred on the Place du Carrousel. During the Terror, however, it returned to the Place de la Révolution, until June 1794, when the **National Convention** ordered it moved to a less central location. By then, it would seem, the sight of the guillotine had come to offend popular sensibilities.

Initially, though, the guillotine generated considerable curiosity and debate about the moment of death. Was it instantaneous, some asked, or did the head retain consciousness for a split second after being severed from the body? Stories, or myths, soon circulated about the executions of prominent individuals. **Georges Danton** reportedly admonished the executioner to show his head to the crowd, since it was a sight well worth seeing. Those who witnessed the execution of **Charlotte Corday** insisted that her face blushed when the executioner lifted her head to the crowd and then kissed her on the cheek. In the fall of 1793, the **armées révolutionnaires** built ambulatory guillotines that could be rolled from village to village, dispensing revolutionary justice to those who withheld grain from market or sheltered **refractory priests**.

It is an irony that the guillotine, created out of an impulse to make execution more humane, soon came to be viewed with horror, a symbol of cold, efficient, impersonal death, as the machinery of the Terror claimed its thousands of victims. Yet the guillotine remained the means of execution in France until the 1980s, when the government of François Mitterrand finally abolished capital punishment simply by refusing to approve a budget to pay the executioner.

– H –

HÉBERT, JACQUES-RENÉ (1757–1794). Hébert was the son of a master goldsmith in Alençon, in Lower Normandy, but his father died when he was just eight years old, and his childhood was troubled thereafter. He left home after being accused of petty theft, and held a number of odd jobs while traveling about the provinces. The outbreak of the Revolution drew him to **Paris**, and in the fall of 1790 he began publication of *Le Père Duchesne*, which would become one of the most popular, and most maligned, revolutionary **newspapers** of the capital. Hébert was an activist in the **Cordelier club**, signed and circulated the **Champ de Mars** petition calling for an end to the monarchy, was a member of the Insurrectionary Commune in August 1792, and was elected substitute *procureur* of Paris in December of that year.

But it was through his newspaper that Hébert exercised his greatest influence. *Le Père Duchesne* was written in the language of the people, some would say in the language of the gutter, and it became the mouthpiece of the Parisian **sans-culottes**. In 1792–93 Hébert was dogged in his condemnation of the **Girondin** deputies, who ordered his arrest on 24 May 1793. He was released just three days later, however, and the leading Girondins would be proscribed from the **National Convention** less than a week after that. *Le Père Duchesne* now advocated increasingly radical policies, and in September Hébert embraced the economic and social views of **Jacques Roux** and the *enragés*. He pushed for the adoption of the first **Law of Suspects** on 17 September 1793. Hébert had joined the **Jacobin club** in January 1793, but he offended many Jacobins when he accused **Marie Antoinette** of incest with her son in October 1793. He further offended **Maximilien Robespierre** by his atheism and vocal support of **deChristianization**. As political opinion polarized in Paris over the question of the need for continued **Terror**, the **Committee of Public Safety** decided to move first against its critics on the left. Hébert and a number of his supporters in the Cordelier club were arrested on trumped-up charges of conspiring against the Convention and seeking the return of the monarchy. The trial went badly, but Hébert and the others were still found guilty and executed on 24 March 1794, barely a week before **Georges Danton** and the **Indulgents** would meet the same fate.

HÉRAULT-SÉCHELLES, MARIE-JEAN (1759–1794). Born into an old noble family, his father died in battle just before his birth. Schooled by the Oratoriens of Juilly, he also studied law in **Paris**, becoming an *avocat du roi* at the Parlement at the young age of 26. Hérault-Séchelles no doubt benefited from the patronage of **Marie Antoinette** and the Polignac family. He met **Jean-Jacques Rousseau** just before his death. He was present at the fall of the **Bastille**, but as an observer, and was elected to the **Legislative Assembly** from Paris, and to the **National Convention** from the Seine-et-Oise. Described by some as a remarkable orator, his politics were somewhat ambivalent. He supported the **Girondins** in their war policy, but sat with the **Montagnards** in the National Convention. In May 1793 he joined the **Committee of Public Safety** to work on the new constitution. While on mission to the Haute-Savoie some months earlier, however, Hérault-Séchelles had taken a mistress whose husband was an Austrian general. She returned with him to Paris, and this relationship drew suspicion. He further alienated **Maximilien Robespierre** by his support of **deChristianization**, and in December 1793 resigned from the Committee. Three months later he was accused by **Louis-Antoine Saint-Just** of passing diplomatic secrets to foreigners. Hérault-Séchelles went to trial with **Georges Danton** and the **Indulgents**, though he did not share their political views, and was executed with them on 5 April 1794.

HERCULES. On 17 November 1793, the **National Convention** voted in favor of **Jacques-Louis David's** proposal that Hercules be adopted as the principal figure on the official seal of state. For a time, then, Hercules replaced **Marianne** as the symbol of the French Republic. A giant figure of Hercules had first appeared at a festival in **Paris** on 10

August 1793 commemorating the fall of the monarchy. Hercules stood carrying a club, crushing the hydra of **federalism**. David conceived of Hercules as a symbol of popular **sovereignty**, a representation of a virile people defeating the enemies of the Revolution.

The Convention's adoption of Hercules on the seal of state came at the end of a period in which **women** had been increasingly active in Parisian politics, and just weeks after the closing of the **Society of Revolutionary Republican Women**. The symbolic triumph of Hercules over Marianne thus mirrored the exclusion of women from the political arena of the **Jacobin** regime. Hercules can be seen again in an engraving of the June 1794 festival celebrating the **Cult of the Supreme Being**. But with the advent of the **Directory** and the nullification of popular sovereignty, Hercules disappeared from view, as the deputies of the **Council of Five Hundred** adopted increasingly abstract symbols to represent the Republic. In the long run, Marianne would triumph over Hercules, even though women did not gain the vote in France until after World War II.

HOCHE, LOUIS-LAZARE (1768–1797). Lazare Hoche was the son of a military man, and like his father he began work as a stable boy in the royal stables at **Versailles**. He was an autodidact, devouring books on all subjects as a youth. In 1784 he joined the *Gardes Françaises*, from which he was dismissed, along with his regiment, in August 1789. He then joined the **National Guard** in **Paris**, as a sergeant, and as such accompanied the **women** on their march to Versailles on 5–6 October 1789. Hoche achieved rapid promotion through the ranks after war broke out in 1792, performing well at the defense of Thionville and at the sieges of Namur and Maestricht. The latter battle brought him to the attention of **Lazare Carnot**, who was impressed by Hoche's strategy of attacking with massed bayonets. In October 1793 he was named division general of the Army of the Moselle, and shortly thereafter general of the combined armies of the Rhine and Moselle. But in April 1794 Hoche was denounced by a rival, **Jean-Charles Pichegru**, who had the backing of **Louis-Antoine Saint-Just**. Hoche was locked up in the **Conciergerie**, where he would remain until after **Thermidor**.

After his release Hoche was assigned to command the Army of the Cherbourg coast, where he acted as much as an administrator and politician as a general. He pacified the region, long disrupted by the **Vendée rebellion** and the **chouans**, and in January 1795 signed a temporary armistice with François Charette, the most prominent of the Vendéan commanders. In July 1795 Hoche crushed the *émigré* forces that disembarked at **Quiberon**, supported by the British, and in early 1796 he defeated and captured both Charette and Jean-Nicolas Stofflet. That summer he met the Irish patriot Wolfe Tone in Paris, and took the lead in planning an expedition to western Ireland to punish the British for the Quiberon attack. The expedition was delayed, however, by indecisiveness within the **Directory**, and ultimately scuttled by foul weather. In February 1797 Hoche led an army across the Rhine River, and in July declined the post of minister of war, already suffering from the tuberculosis that would kill him two months later near Coblenz. On 1 October 1797 a full military funeral was held on the **Champ de Mars** for the man whom **Napoleon Bonaparte** would describe as the best of the republican generals of the Revolution.

HOSPITALS. Prior to 1789, hospitals in France primarily served the poor and were funded and managed by the Catholic Church. The nationalization of Church lands in November 1789 fundamentally changed that situation, even though hospital properties were in theory exempt from that legislation. Eventually hospitals did lose their income-generating property, and the state took on responsibility for creating a welfare system that would see to the needs of the poor and indigent. Given the economic upheaval of the revolutionary decade, however, the state was never able to achieve its noble aspirations in this area.

By 1793 the situation of most hospitals in France was perilous. Local authorities were responsible for distributing funds to hospitals, but rarely had adequate resources to do so, so that hospital administrators regularly appealed to the national government for emergency support. All Frenchmen were guaranteed free medical care, and hospitals grew even more crowded than they had been under the Old Regime. Hospital budgets were paid almost exclusively in *assignats*, which were wracked by inflation, further undermining the ability of hospitals to fulfill their mission. From 1792 onward, the impact of nearly continuous war increased the overcrowding of hospitals throughout France, but particularly those near the battle fronts or in large cities. Hospital administration was reorganized under the **Directory**, with new funding sources introduced in late 1796. But legislation in January 1797 exempting hospitals from paying debts incurred before 1794 is clear evidence of the continuing financial burden under which they operated.

– I –

IDÉALOGUES. The Idéalogues were a collection of intellectuals in the late **Directory** years committed to the rationalist thought of the **Enlightenment**. They included **Dominique-Joseph Garat**, Antoine Destutt de Tracy, Pierre-Jean Georges Cabanis, and Pierre-Claude-François Daunou. Most had been active politically in the Revolution before turning toward more academic pursuits. Their institutional bases of influence were the Ecole Normale and the **Institut National**. They were committed to applying the social philosophy of the Enlightenment to the development of civic man, but worked as well in the fields of anatomy and science. The term Idéalogue had a pejorative connotation, having been coined by **Napoleon Bonaparte**, who more harshly characterized the group as "vermin," most likely because they had opposed his seizure of power and then his Concordat with the Catholic Church. Other thinkers of the day also tended to belittle the intellectual contribution of the group, however, and their reputation as impractical daydreamers has endured.

IMPARTIALS. The Impartials were one of the first clubs of the Revolution, forming in the early days of the **Estates-General**. **Pierre-Victor Malouet** presided over the club's meetings, guiding it in an aggressive propaganda campaign against the **Jacobin club**. With the declaration of the **Constituent Assembly** in July 1789, the Impartials disappeared, but supporters of the monarchy would continue to be referred to by that term for some time thereafter. Many members of the club would have belonged as well to the **Society of 1789** or, somewhat later, to the **Monarchist club**.

INDULGENTS. The Indulgents were a loosely defined group of deputies that took shape in the **National Convention** toward the end of 1793 around **Georges Danton**. Danton had left **Paris** for a time in October 1793, and when he returned he spoke publicly at the **Cordeliers club** and at the Convention about the need to return to normal life, to repeal some aspects of the **Law of Suspects**, and even to create a committee of clemency. Such views were supported by **Camille Desmoulins**, in the pages of his **newspaper** the *Vieux Cordelier*, by **Pierre Philippeaux** and **Philippe Fabre d'Eglantine**. Politics seemed to be polarizing at this moment between extremists gathered around **Jacques-René Hébert** and the Indulgents who supported Danton's calls for a relaxation of the **Terror**.

On 8 January 1794 **Maximilien Robespierre** denounced both groups in a speech at the **Jacobin club**, referring to them as ultra-revolutionaries and citra-revolutionaries. In the following months, as the *Compagnie des Indes* scandal unraveled, implicating Fabre d'Eglantine, and as the rhetoric of Desmoulins's *Vieux Cordelier* grew harsher, the **Committee of Public Safety** moved against both groups. Hébert and his supporters went to trial first, thereby defusing the **deChristianization** movement, and in late March 1794 the Indulgents were arrested. They were brought to trial with a motley array of defendants, including **François Chabot** and **Marie-Jean Hérault-Séchelles**, all accused of conspiring with foreign enemies, and executed on 5 April 1794.

INSTITUT NATIONAL. The *Institut National des Sciences et des Arts* was created in October 1795 by decree of the **National Convention**. It replaced the old royal **Academies**, which had been suppressed by the Convention in August 1793 at the request of **Henri-Baptiste Grégoire** and **Jacques-Louis David**. The purpose of the Institut National was to advance knowledge in the sciences and arts through the support of research, the publication of new findings, and correspondence with learned societies in other countries. It was to be composed of 144 members, resident in **Paris**, an equal number of associates from the provinces, and 24 affiliates from foreign countries. The **Directory** was to name the first third of the members, who would in turn name the other members.

The Institut National was divided into three sections: the first devoted to mathematics and the physical sciences; a second devoted to the moral and political sciences; and a third devoted to literature and fine arts. A president of the Institut was to be elected every six months, and secretaries for each section were to be elected each year. **Napoleon Bonaparte** reorganized the Institut into four sections in 1803, eliminating in the process the section devoted to the moral and political sciences, which had been a stronghold of the **Idéalogues**.

INVALIDES. The Hôtel des Invalides was a military **hospital** in **Paris** at the end of the Old Regime. On 14 July 1789, roused by the speech of **Camille Desmoulins**, a Parisian crowd marched first to the Invalides in search of arms and then across town to the **Bastille**. The Invalides continued to serve as a hospital for soldiers wounded in battle throughout the Revolution. In the 1840s the remains of **Napoleon Bonaparte** were returned from St. Helena to find their final resting place in the Invalides, which also houses the ashes of **Jean-Claude Rouget de Lisle**, composer of the **Marseillaise**.

ISNARD, HENRI-MAXIMIN (1758–1825). Isnard was the son of a wholesale merchant in Grasse, and eventually inherited his father's commercial and manufacturing business. He was elected to the **Legislative Assembly** from the Var, where he sat on the left and associated with the Brissotins. Isnard urged that **refractory priests** be deported, and in late 1791 spoke eloquently before the Assembly against the plotting of *émigrés*. In 1792 he was elected to the **National Convention**, again from the Var. He voted for death in the trial of **Louis XVI**, and against the *appel au peuple*, but in the months that followed he grew increasingly critical of the dissension within the Convention and the militancy of the **Paris** sections. As president of the Convention, he refused a 25 May demand from the sections for the release of **Jacques Hébert** and **Jean Varlet** with these stern words: "I tell you in the name of the whole of France that if these perpetually recurring insurrections ever lead to harm to the parliament chosen by the nation, Paris will be annihilated, and men will search the banks of the Seine for traces of the city."

Isnard was not included in the proscriptions of 2 June 1793, but at the urging of **Bertrand Barère** he withdrew from the Convention, and when his arrest was ordered on 3 October 1793 went into hiding. He returned to the Convention on 26 February 1795, and the **Committee of Public Safety** approved an indemnity of 150,000 *livres* for the loss of his manufactory, either pillaged or sold during the **Terror**. Isnard was among the most reactionary of the **Thermidorians**. He was sent on mission to the Bouches-du-Rhône in May 1795 to calm troubles, but instead stirred up reprisals against former terrorists. He stood by while a group of **Jacobins** was massacred in the Fort St. Jean in **Marseille**, and in Aix-en-Provence urged on an angry crowd with these words: "If you have no arms, take up sticks; and if you have no sticks, unearth the bones of your buried relatives and use them to strike the terrorists." Isnard was elected to the **Council of Five Hundred**, where he sat until 1797, at which point he returned to the Var and took up a post in the **departmental administration**. He remained active in local politics until 1810, and in 1813 was named a Baron of the Empire. Isnard reportedly grew more religious as he aged, and claimed late in life that he had come to regret his sometimes intemperate rhetoric during the Revolution.

– J –

JACOBIN CLUBS. The Jacobin clubs were the most important of the **popular societies** in France during the Revolution. The first Jacobin club emerged out of the **Breton club**, formed at **Versailles** in April 1789 by delegates to the **Estates-General**. Not long after the **Constituent Assembly** moved to **Paris**, in October 1789, the Jacobin club installed itself in the former monastery of the Jacobins on the rue Saint-Honoré. Its meeting place gave it its popular name. The club's full title was *Société des Amis de la Constitution*, and later *Société des Amis de la Liberté et de l'Egalité*.

At first, the membership in the club was composed almost entirely of deputies in the Constituent Assembly. The purpose of the club was to debate and discuss issues before the Assembly, to support the drafting and acceptance of a constitution, and to correspond with like-minded societies throughout France. Dues for the club were at first quite substantial, and as membership grew it was drawn almost entirely from the ranks of middle-class professionals. By early 1790 there were roughly 1,000 members in the Paris club, and that number more than doubled by June 1791.

Critics of the Jacobin club, including the king himself at the time of the flight to **Varennes**, charged that it was usurping the proper role of the Constituent Assembly, functioning as a shadow parliament and exercising an undue influence on national politics. The **Monarchist clubs** that appeared in late 1790 challenged the Jacobins in those terms, and the resultant controversy and conflict led to a movement of consolidation in provincial towns, with the "mother society" in Paris choosing to affiliate with only one club per town. The network gradually grew, to 426 clubs nationwide in March 1791 and 934 by July 1791, with about half of those formally affiliated with the Paris club. At that time, however, a split occurred as members in Paris disagreed over how to respond to the political crisis caused by the flight to Varennes. Moderate deputies, convinced that a constitutional monarchy should be preserved, broke away to form the **Feuillants**, and at first the new club attracted a majority of the membership. Under the leadership of **Jérome Pétion** and **Maximilien Robespierre**, however, the Jacobins rallied and soon redoubled their membership, both in Paris and the provinces.

Jacobin clubs played an active role in the elections to the **National Convention** and the local elections that followed, with Jacobins achieving political dominance in Paris and some provincial cities, most notably **Lyon** and **Marseille**. In Paris, the **September Massacres** of 1792 prompted many of the **Girondin** deputies to leave the Jacobin club. The proscription of the Girondin leaders in the **uprising of 31 May–2 June 1793** and the ascendancy of the **Montagnards** to power brought the Jacobin clubs to the height of their influence. Jacobin clubs throughout France now functioned as unofficial adjuncts to local authorities. **Representatives on mission** turned to local Jacobins for allies in their efforts to purge **federalist** administrations. Jacobin club members filled the ranks of the **committees of surveillance** and the *armées révolutionnaires*. The clubs themselves were often purged of moderate members in 1793–94, and the membership shifted from professional middle class to more of an artisan/shopkeeper composition.

Given the close association of the Jacobin clubs with the policies of the **Terror**, it is not surprising that their influence waned after **Thermidor**. The shift was not immediate, since a number of Jacobins had in fact participated in the coup against Robespierre, but in the autumn of 1794 the clubs came under attack by the *jeunesse dorée*. The National Convention ordered the closure of the Paris Jacobin club on 12 November 1794. The **White Terror** of early 1795 targeted former Jacobin club members, and the law of 23 August 1795 prohibited all political clubs. There was a clandestine resurgence of Jacobin clubs under the **Directory**, but they operated on the margins of legality and faced the constant threat of suppression.

JALÈS (*CAMP DE*). Jalès is a plain on the southeastern edge of the Massif Central, at the border between the departments of the Gard and the Ardèche, where an assemblage of nobles, **clergy**, and Catholic **peasants** came together in loose camps, or federations, on several occasions in the early years of the Revolution. The first was in August 1790, following the *bagarre de* **Nîmes**, in which Catholics and **Protestants** had clashed. The local **aristocracy**, perhaps in contact with *émigrés* in Turin, appealed to **National Guardsmen** who were disillusioned with the Revolution, and as many as 25,000 may have gathered in the plain below the towering château of Jalès. No battle or confrontation resulted, but a loosely organized leadership did emerge from the camp, and Jalès came to be synonymous with **counterrevolution** in southern France thereafter.

Camps occurred on the plain of Jalès on at least two subsequent occasions, the first in February 1791. Local authorities learned of the plan in advance, however, and easily dispersed the small band that gathered. A third *camp de* Jalès took place in July 1792, after local leaders had contacted *émigré* princes in Coblenz. Once again, local authorities responded, putting a force of some 10,000 volunteers into the field against the assembled royalists. Several hundred rebels were killed, bringing an end to the *camps de* Jalès until the final years of **Napoleon Bonaparte's** empire, when supporters of the monarchy once again gathered there.

JANSENISM. Jansenism was a movement within the French Catholic Church, with its origins in the 17th century. French Jansenists were followers of Cornelius Jansen, a bishop who championed the ideas of Saint Augustine, particularly his emphasis on grace as the key to salvation. Blaise Pascal and Jean Racine were two prominent 17th-century Jansenists. Early in the 18th century, in 1713, Pope Clement condemned the writings of the leading French Jansenist of the time, Pasquier Quesnel, in his papal bull, *Unigenitus*.

Although Jansensists would face persecution in France for the remainder of the century, they were not driven from the kingdom, and from mid-century onward Jansenists constituted a significant percentage of the judges in the **Parlement of Paris**. Not only did the Jansenists challenge the hierarchy of the Catholic Church, by emphasizing its conciliar tradition, they also challenged the absolutist tendencies of the monarchy and defended the Gallican tradition of the French church. Jansenism was thus an important contributing current to French republicanism in the 18th century, and has long been credited as a formative influence on the **Civil Constitution of the Clergy**. Among the revolutionaries, **Henri-Baptiste Grégoire** is the most notable Jansenist.

JAVOGUES, CLAUDE (1759–1796). Javogues was the son of a notary, in a long line of notaries. He attended a Jesuit *collège* in Montbrison, went on to study law at the University of Valence, and returned to Montbrison as an *avocat* in 1785, where he was a bit of a social outcast. Javogues joined the local **National Guard** in 1789, and in 1791 was elected to the Montbrison district administration. The following year he was elected to the **National Convention** from the Rhône-et-Loire. He sat with the **Montagnards**, voted for death in the trial of **Louis XVI**, and against the *appel au peuple*. In April 1793 he spoke in defense of **Jean-Paul Marat**.

In July 1793 Javogues was sent on mission with two other deputies to assist in preparations for the siege of **Lyon**. He preferred to work alone, and over the next six months ordered a tax on the rich in Saint-Etienne, the execution of 64 alleged counterrevolutionaries in Feurs, and severe repression in Montbrison as well. Javogues was twice recalled to **Paris** by the **Committee of Public Safety**, and was denounced before the Convention by **Georges Couthon**, to whom he apologized, thus avoiding formal accusation until April 1795, when a torrent of accusations poured forth from the department of the Loire. Javogues went into hiding, but in September 1796 was implicated in the failed Grenelle conspiracy that followed the arrest of **Gracchus Babeuf** and his supporters. Javogues was tried before a military commission and found guilty of treason, punished more for his past deeds than for the farcical Grenelle uprising. He sang the **Marseillaise** on his way to the firing squad.

JEANBON SAINT-ANDRÉ, ANDRÉ (1749–1813). Jeanbon Saint-André was born into a family of **Protestant** artisans in Montauban. His father was a fuller, and as a youth André joined the merchant marine and became a ship's captain. He returned to Montauban, though, in 1773 to become a minister. When the Revolution began, he joined the **Jacobin club** and was elected to the Montauban municipal council in 1790. Violence between Protestants and Catholics forced him to flee Montauban in May 1790. He was elected to the **National Convention** from the Lot, sat with the **Montagnards**, and voted for death at the king's trial. He served on the **Committee of Public Safety** from June 1793 until July 1794, with principal responsibility for the navy. He pronounced the funeral eulogy for **Jean-Paul Marat**. In March 1795 he was arrested, along with **Robert Lindet**, and accused as a **terrorist**. Both were amnestied later that year. Jeanbon Saint-André served the **Directory** as a diplomat, was imprisoned by the Turks in 1799–1802, subsequently served **Napoleon Bonaparte** as a prefect and was named to the Legion of Honor, and, in 1810, proclaimed a Baron of the Empire. He is featured prominently in the painting of the **Tennis Court Oath** by **Jacques-Louis David**, who was a close friend.

JEUNESSE DORÉE. The *jeunesse dorée*, or "gilded youth," were officially tolerated bands of young thugs, drawn principally from well-to-do families, which were active in most large cities in the period after **Thermidor**. They were essentially reactionary, but played a role somewhat analogous to that of the **sans-culottes** in 1792–1793. In **Paris**, where they had a particularly high public profile, the deputies **Louis-Stanislas Fréron** and **Jean-Lambert Tallien** gave them tacit support.

The Parisian *jeunesse dorée* numbered between 2,000 and 3,000, met frequently at the Café des Chartes in the **Palais Royal**, and targeted former militants for public abuse. They broke the busts of **Jean-Paul Marat** throughout Paris, and mounted a campaign of violent disruption of **Jacobin club** meetings, leading finally to the November 1794 order by the **National Convention** for the closing of the club.

The *jeunesse dorée*, like the sans-culottes before them, also hooted and taunted the deputies from the galleries of the National Convention, pressuring them to bring ex-terrorists like **Jean-Baptiste Carrier**, **Jean-Marie Collot d'Herbois**, and **Jacques-Nicolas Billaud-Varenne** to trial. In cities of the southeast, including **Lyon** and **Marseille**, the *jeunesse dorée* went so far as to resort to murder against their political enemies, and their actions fed the **White Terror** in that region. They were less violent in Paris, but were in the streets during the **Germinal** and **Prairial riots** of 1795, and spearheaded the **Vendémiaire** uprising of October 1795, the suppression of which brought an end to the *jeunesse dorée* movement in the capital.

JEWS. In 1789 there were approximately 40,000 Jews in France. The majority of them were Ashkenazim who lived in the provinces of Alsace and Lorraine along the German border, but there was also a population of nearly 2,300 Sephardic Jews in the city of **Bordeaux**, with others scattered in smaller communities along the southwest coast. As with **Protestants**, Jews did not enjoy official religious tolerance under the Old Regime. In 1788, however, the year following the **Edict of Toleration** for Protestants, a delegation of Jews from Bordeaux traveled to **Versailles** to request similar treatment.

Jews did not achieve civil rights in France until the Revolution. Because they had assimilated more fully into French society, the Sephardim of the southwest were allowed to vote in elections to the **Estates-General** while the Ashkenazim were not. The Jews of the southwest, originally immigrants from Spain and Portugal, were granted full citizenship in January 1790. The **Constituent Assembly** did not grant the same rights to the Yiddish-speaking Ashkenazim until 27 September 1791. In both instances the deputies made clear that Jews were granted civil rights as individuals, not as a group, following the argument first expressed by **Stanislas Clermont-Tonnerre** in late 1789 that "there cannot be a nation within a nation." Jews endured persecution under the **Terror** much as Catholics did, but prospered under the **Thermidorian** regime.

JOURDAN, JEAN-BAPTISTE (1762–1833). Jourdan's father was a surgeon in Limoges, but Jean-Baptiste was orphaned at a young age. He worked briefly as a clerk in a silk shop, but in 1778 joined the

Auxerrois regiment and went to fight in America. Jourdan participated in the battle of Savannah and in the conquest of Grenada. He
returned to France in 1782, was decommissioned in 1784, and returned to Limoges to work as a haberdasher. Early in the Revolution
he became a captain in the **National Guard**, and joined the Limoges
Jacobin club. In 1792 Jourdan assumed command of the Second
Battalion of Haute-Vienne volunteers and performed well at the battles of Jemmapes (November 1792) and Neerwinden (March 1793).
By July 1793 he was a division general, and after the Battle of Hond-
schoote (September 1793), where he performed brilliantly, he was
promoted to General of the Army of the Ardennes. In October 1793
he stopped the Austrians at Wattignies, but when he advised a defensive posture following that victory he was sacked and replaced by
Jean-Charles Pichegru. Jourdan was protected by **Lazare Carnot**,
and within months was back in command of the Army of the Moselle.
His troops scored an impressive series of victories in northern France
and **Belgium** through the spring and summer months of 1794.

Jourdan was relieved of his command once again in 1796 and returned to Limoges. The following year he was elected to the **Council
of Five Hundred** from the Haute-Vienne, but in October 1798 accepted command of the Army of the Danube. After defeat at the hands
of an army commanded by Archduke Charles of Austria in March
1799, Jourdan retired from the army and was elected once again to the
Council of Five Hundred. Jourdan was a spokesperson for the Jacobin
minority in that assembly, and halfheartedly opposed the **Brumaire**
coup. Despite that opposition, **Napoleon Bonaparte** named him ambassador to Turin and then General of the Army of Italy. In May 1804,
Jourdan was named a marshal and accompanied Joseph Bonaparte to
Spain. He was named a Count and Peer of France under the Restoration, but refused to take his seat on the Council of War that was convened to judge Marshal Michel Ney in 1815.

JOURNÉES. There were several important *journées* in the French Revolution, days on which the people rose up in armed demonstrations to
protest government policies or actions and demand change. These include 14 July 1789, the storming of the **Bastille**; the **October Days**,
5–6 October 1789, when the **women** of **Paris** marched to **Versailles**
to protest rising bread prices and return the king to his capital; the **up-**

rising of **10 August 1792**, when the monarchy was toppled; the **uprising of 31 May–2 June 1793**, when the **Girondin** deputies were proscribed from the **National Convention**; and 5–6 September 1793, when the **sans-culottes** demanded an extension of the *maximum* and a declaration of **Terror** as the order of the day. Each of these *journées* could be said to have moved the Revolution forward. Radicals saw them as an expression of popular **sovereignty**, while moderates and conservatives saw in them the threat of popular violence and anarchy. The last *journées* of the Revolution, the **Germinal riots** and **Prairial riots** of 1795, were directed against the **Thermidorians**. Each failed in its objectives and was easily suppressed by authorities now increasingly eager to bring the Revolution to an end and reestablish order and the rule of law. *See also* RÉVEILLON RIOTS.

JULLIEN, MARC-ANTOINE (1744–1821). Jullien's father was a barber-surgeon in a small village in the Dauphiné. Marc-Antoine was self-taught and went on to become a schoolteacher and man of letters. His poetry drew the attention of the abbé Mably, and when he moved to **Paris** in the 1770s he became acquainted with **Marie-Jean Condorcet** and Anne-Robert-Jacques Turgot. Jullien embraced the ideals of 1789, and corresponded with friends back home to encourage them to do the same. Electors in the Drôme responded by choosing him as an alternate deputy to the **Legislative Assembly** and then as a deputy to the **National Convention** in 1792. Jullien joined the **Jacobin club** and sat with the **Montagnards**, voting for death in the trial of **Louis XVI**. In the summer of 1793 he declined to go on mission first to **Nantes** and then to **Bordeaux**, though his son, **Marc-Antoine Jullien fils**, would visit both cities on behalf of the **Committee of Public Safety**. Jullien played no political role under the **Directory**, and refused to support **Napoleon Bonaparte** during the Hundred Days, which spared him exile as a regicide.

JULLIEN, MARC-ANTOINE fils (1775–1848). Routinely referred to during the Revolution as "Jullien de Paris," to distinguish him from his father, "Jullien of the Drôme." His father moved to **Paris** in the 1770s in part to attend to the education of his children, and young Jullien was immersed in the politics of the Revolution from its outset. He regularly attended **Jacobin club** meetings and came to the attention of leading deputies in the **Legislative Assembly**. In May 1792 **Marie-Jean Condorcet** sent him to London as a special intermediary between the **Girondin** leadership and Lord Stanhope. Jullien was barely 17 at the time. Later that year Jullien was sent as a commissioner to the Army of the Pyrenees, stationed in **Toulouse**. During that period he began a personal correspondence with **Maximilien Robespierre**, and in 1793–94 functioned as something of a personal envoy for the Incorruptible in the provinces. Most notably, he traveled to **Nantes** in December 1793 and denounced the excesses of **Jean-Baptiste Carrier**, and then journeyed to **Bordeaux** in April 1794, where he reported critically on the repression being overseen by **Jean-Lambert Tallien** and **Claude Ysabeau**. On a second mission to Bordeaux in May 1794, Jullien brought to justice the last of the Girondin fugitives.

Jullien was imprisoned following **Thermidor**, renounced his loyalty to Robespierre, and was eventually released. He joined the **Panthéon club** in 1795, attracted by the ideas of **Gracchus Babeuf**, but did not participate in the **Conspiracy of Equals**. Jullien was ambivalent about **Napoleon Bonaparte**, though he served his regime for a time in Italy. He withdrew from politics, but continued to publish pamphlets and articles, often on **education**, well into the 19th century. Jullien lived to see the Revolution of 1848 and the declaration of a second French republic.

– K –

KING'S TRIAL. There were many dramatic moments in the French Revolution, but a good argument could be made that none was more pivotal than the trial of **Louis XVI**. The **uprising of 10 August 1792** toppled the monarchy, and the **National Convention** declared France a republic on 22 September 1792, but the fate of the king would not be decided for nearly four more months. When he did come to trial, much more was at stake than the life of a single man.

The **September Massacres** changed the political atmosphere not only in **Paris**, but in the rest of France as well. Even among those who favored a republican government, many now feared the threat of popular violence and the possibility that continued political upheaval might throw the country into anarchy. Some feared the conflict that a trial of the king might bring.

Debate over the fate of the king began in early November. **Louis-Antoine Saint-Just** opened the debate by arguing that Louis XVI was guilty simply by virtue of being king, asserting that no man could reign innocently. **Maximilien Robespierre** disputed the necessity of a trial, claiming that the people of Paris had already found Louis XVI guilty in their insurrection and that, if Louis XVI could be found innocent in a trial, then the Revolution itself must in consequence be guilty. Deputies on the right opposed a trial on the grounds that the king enjoyed inviolability. In the end, those in the middle prevailed and the deputies decided that the National Convention itself would try the king.

A Commission of Twenty-One was formed to gather evidence, and **Robert Lindet** prepared the charges against Louis XVI. The discovery of a hidden safe in the **Tuileries** Palace produced damning, if not conclusive, evidence that the king had conspired with other European monarchs against the revolutionary government. The trial began on 11 December 1792. The king's defense was prepared by **François-Denis Tronchet**, Lamoignon de Malesherbes, and Raymond Desèze, and Louis XVI testified on 25–26 December.

The deputies found Louis XVI guilty by unanimous vote on 15 January 1793. Jean-Baptiste Salle proposed that his sentence be decided by an ***appel au peuple***, a popular referendum, but that motion was defeated by a margin of some 120 votes. The deputies themselves voted on the king's sentence by roll call vote between 16 and 18 January. Most deputies gave lengthy speeches to explain or justify their vote. Of the 721 deputies who voted, 361 voted for death without conditions, and another 26 voted for death with conditions, a slim majority. The sentence was carried out without delay—Louis XVI went to the **guillotine** on 21 January 1793.

The consequences of the king's trial and execution were enormous. By the dignity with which he presented himself both in his testimony and on the scaffold, Louis XVI enhanced his posthumous reputation, earned the respect of many of his enemies and the devotion of his supporters. His execution made virtually inevitable the entry of Great Britain and Spain into war against France. The trial itself raised fundamental issues of **sovereignty** and cemented the division between **Montagnards** and **Girondins** within the National Convention. The opposition between those two groups eventually led to the expulsion of the Girondins, triggering the **federalist revolt**, which along with the deepening war crisis led to the imposition of the **Terror**. It may not have been possible politically to spare Louis XVI, but his execution certainly rendered vulnerable the future of the Republic that his death was intended to secure.

– L –

LACOMBE, CLAIRE (1765–?). Little is known about Lacombe's youth, other than the fact that she was born in Pamiers, near the Spanish border, where her father was a shopkeeper. Claire was an actress of reputation in the years before the Revolution, appearing on stage in **Lyon**, **Paris**, **Marseille**, and **Toulon**. She returned to Paris from Toulon in early 1792, befriended **Pauline Léon**, regularly attended meetings of the **Cordelier club**, and became active in the neighborhood political scene. In July 1792 she spoke before the **Legislative Assembly**, offering to join the war against the tyrants of Europe and calling for the arrest of **Charles Dumouriez**. Lacombe participated in the 10 August 1792 assault on the **Tuileries** Palace, for which she was accorded a civic crown by the Marseille *fédérés*. In the winter of 1792–93 she became engrossed by questions of subsistence and poverty, and in May 1793 joined with Léon to found the **Society of Revolutionary Republican Women**.

The **women's** club played an active role in the **uprising of 31 May–2 June 1793**, and in the summer months Lacombe played a dominant role in the club. She lobbied actively for women's suffrage, and spoke before the **National Convention** on 28 August and 5 September, calling for the dismissal of all **aristocrats** from the army and for a second purge of all moderates from the government. Her remarks drew a denunciation from **François Chabot**, prompting Lacombe to appear once again before the Convention on 7 October 1793 to aggressively assert women's rights. At the end of that month, she was thrashed at the central market by a group of female supporters of the **Jacobins**, and shortly thereafter the National Convention ordered that the Society of Revolutionary Republican Women be shut down. Lacombe went into hiding briefly, reemerged after the trial of **Jacques Hébert**, and was arrested herself on 2 April 1794. She was jailed in the prison of Sainte-Pélagie, where she continued to write, until August 1795. She signed all of her writings "Lacombe, free woman." Lacombe returned to the stage in 1796, but there is no trace of her after 1798.

LAFAYETTE, MARIE-JOSEPH-PAUL-YVES-ROCH-GIBERT DU MOTIER (1757–1834). The Marquis de Lafayette was born into a very rich and old noble family of the Auvergne. His father died two months before his birth, of a wound suffered in battle in the final months of the Seven Years War. At the age of 17, Lafayette married Adrienne de Noailles, then 14, the daughter of an equally prominent and even more fabulously wealthy noble family. Two years later Lafayette set sail for America, in a ship that he bought and outfitted himself, eluding a royal *lettre de cachet* to do so. He had met several Americans, including Benjamin Franklin, in **Paris** and was inspired by their cause. The United States Congress named Lafayette a major-general and he fought alongside George Washington, whom he looked upon as a second father. He distinguished himself in battle, was slightly wounded, and returned briefly to France in 1779, only to return to the United States in March 1780. Following the victory at Yorktown (1781), **Louis XVI** rewarded Lafayette with the rank of *maréchal de camp*.

Lafayette returned to France again in 1785. He attended the 1787 **Assembly of Notables**, and antagonized **Marie Antoinette** by calling for the convocation of the **Estates-General**. He was elected to the Estates-General by the nobility of the Auvergne, and supported the doubling of the **Third Estate** and the unification of orders in June 1789. Lafayette participated in the drafting of the **Declaration of the Rights of Man and Citizen**, and presented the first draft of that document to the **Constituent Assembly** on 13 July 1789. Two days later he was named commander of the Paris **National Guard**, and in that capacity he received Louis XVI at the Hôtel de Ville in Paris on 16 July, along with **Jean Bailly**. Lafayette later ordered the demolition of the **Bastille** on his own authority and sent the keys to George Washington as a symbol of the end to despotism in France. Lafayette was now at the peak of his popularity, but the killings of Louis-Bénigne-François deBertier and Joseph-François Foulon by an angry crowd in July, and the **women's** march to **Versailles** in October, which he failed to control, tarnished his reputation somewhat. Both **Gabriel-Honoré Mirabeau** and **Jean-Paul Marat** were critical of him at this early stage of the Revolution.

In July 1790 Lafayette organized the **Festival of Federation**, well received by the populace of Paris, but less so by the royal court. In late August he expressed his approval of the violent suppression of the **Nancy mutiny**, which had been ordered by his cousin and widely denounced among patriots. The flight to **Varennes** and the **Champ de Mars massacre** were his undoing, however. The king's attempted escape prompted members of the **Cordelier club** to circulate petitions calling for an end to the monarchy, and when a large crowd gathered on the Champ de Mars on 17 July 1791 Lafayette ordered the National Guard to open fire. This bloodshed put the radical movement temporarily on the defensive, and Lafayette joined **Antoine-Pierre Barnave** in founding the **Feuillant club**, a moderate offshoot of the **Jacobin club**. But his actions in July had both alienated the Parisian **sans-culottes** and earned for him the enduring hatred of Marie Antoinette. He resigned his command of the National Guard in October 1791.

Late in 1791 Lafayette took command of the Army of Metz. Patriots in Paris continued to denounce him, though, and after the failed uprising of 20 June 1792 Lafayette published a pamphlet protesting the violence of the crowd and travelled to Paris to condemn the Jacobin club at the rostrum of the **Legislative Assembly**, leaving himself open to charges of having abandoned his command. After the fall of the monarchy on 10 August 1792, he tried to lead his army back to Paris to defend the king, but failed in that effort and left for **Belgium** with a few of his closest officers. There he was arrested by the Prussians, who turned him over to the Austrians. He was imprisoned at Olmütz, where he remained until September 1797, when a special clause in the Treaty of Campoformio secured his release. Lafayette played no public role under the Empire, nor the Restoration, but embraced the July Monarchy in 1830, appearing on the balcony of the Hôtel de Ville with Louis-Philippe, once again the focus of public adulation.

LAKANAL, JOSEPH (1762–1845). Lakanal was the son of a prosperous artisan, an iron-worker, in a small town in southern France.

He appears to have pursued a religious education in Toulouse, was ordained, probably in Bourges, and completed his Doctorate at the University of Angers. On the eve of the Revolution he was a professor of logic in Moulins. In 1791 he was named episcopal vicar to the Constitutional Bishop of Pamiers, in the Ariège, the department that would elect him to the **National Convention** in 1792. While in Pamiers he became a member of the **Jacobin club**, and he would sit with the **Montagnards** in the Convention. Lakanal voted for death in the trial of **Louis XVI**, and against the *appel au peuple*. In March 1793 he discovered a million *livres* in gold and silver in an underground passage at Chantilly, while on mission for recruitment. Lakanal is best known for his role on the Committee of Public Instruction in the Convention. He had a hand in the creation of the Ecole Normale in **Paris** in October 1794, and would oversee its operation along with **Emmanuel-Joseph Sieyès** for some time, and in November 1794 the Convention adopted his report on primary **education**. Lakanal supported the creation of a two-chamber legislature in constitutional debates in 1795, was elected to the **Council of Five Hundred** from the Finistère, and sat as a deputy until 1797. He was also named to the **Institut National** in 1795. In August 1799 the **Directory** sent him to organize the new departments along the Rhine, and at the end of that year he accepted an appointment to the Chair in Classical Languages at the Ecole Centrale of the rue St. Antoine in Paris. Lakanal was exiled as a regicide in 1816. He emigrated to the United States and became president of a university in New Orleans.

LALLY-TOLLENDAL, TROPHIME-GÉRARD (1751–1830). Count Lally-Tollendal was born into an old Parisian family of the **aristocracy**. His father, whom Trophime-Gérard barely knew, served as Viceroy in India and was executed in 1766 after the defeat of French forces by the British. **Voltaire** secured the reversal of that judgment in 1778, and Lally-Tollendal resigned his own military commission in 1785 in order to work for the rehabilitation of his father's name, which came in 1786. Lally-Tollendal was educated at the *collège* d'Harcourt, and in 1773 entered the first company of the Musketeers, on the express order of the king. By 1776 he was a captain of cavalry, and in 1782 was promoted to second captain of the king's regiment of cuirassiers.

In 1789 Lally-Tollendal served as secretary of the assembly of the nobility of **Paris**, and was the third of 10 delegates elected to the **Estates-General** by that assembly. He took a conservative stance at **Versailles**, favoring vote by order and separate deliberations for the three orders, though he ended up among the 47 nobles who joined the **Third Estate** in June. Lally-Tollendal was a supporter of **Jacques Necker**, a member of the close circle of deputies around **Pierre-Victor Malouet**, and among the hundred most active speakers in the **Constituent Assembly**. He supported **Marie-Joseph-Motier Lafayette**'s call for a **Declaration of the Rights of Man**, but also called in late July for punitive measures against those causing troubles in the countryside. His most important speech came on 31 August 1789, in which he proposed a tricameral legislature and an active legislative role for the king, who would also enjoy unlimited veto power. These proposals did not find favor in the Assembly, and on 14 September 1789 Lally-Tollendal withdrew from the constitutional committee.

In early November he resigned his seat, citing health problems, and took refuge in Switzerland. Only later did he cite the **October Days** as a principal factor in his decision to emigrate. He returned to France in 1792 to defend **Louis XVI** from his detractors, was briefly imprisoned following the **uprising of 10 August 1792**, but escaped to England before the **September Massacres**. Lally-Tollendal wrote a series of moderate monarchist pamphlets during the 1790s, including a two-volume defense of French *émigrés* published in 1797. He returned to France after **Brumaire** and lived quietly near **Bordeaux**. Lally-Tollendal later sat on the privy council of **Louis XVIII**, and in 1825 was named a Grand Officer in the Legion of Honor and a Chevalier of Saint-Louis.

LAMARCK, JEAN-BAPTISTE (1744–1829). It is said of Lamarck that he experienced the Revolution from his laboratory, where the work that he did established him as among the most influential of French scientists of the time. He was born into a modest family in a small town in Picardy, attended a Jesuit *collège* in Amiens, and served a short stint in the military until the age of 24. Lamarck then went to **Paris** to further his **education** in medicine and science and became a student of Antoine-Laurent Jussieu. In 1778 he published the three-volume *Flore Française*, which established his reputation.

In 1788 he became conservator of the royal botanical gardens. The Revolution changed the course of his career. When **Joseph Lakanal** created the National Museum of Natural History in June 1793, Lamarck was appointed to the chair for insects and worms. Lamarck was the first to propose a classificatory system for invertebrates (a word that he coined), and also established the field of paleontology. He published voluminously in these areas, and over the course of the following decade laid the foundations for what would become, in the 19th century, Darwinian evolutionary science (though Lamarck's ideas about evolution were quite different from those of Charles Darwin). Lamarck is credited with coining the word "biology" in 1802, and was also among the founding members of the **Institut National** in 1795.

LAMBALLE, MARIE-THÉRÈSE-LOUISE (1749–1792). The Princess de Lamballe was a devoted servant and friend to **Marie Antoinette**. She was born in Turin and married at the age of 17 to the son of the duke of Penthièvre, a dissolute young man who died the following year at the age of 21. In 1774 Lamballe became principal lady-in-waiting to the queen, and in that role became her close friend as well. When the royal family fled toward **Varennes**, in June 1791, the princess embarked from Boulogne for England. When she heard of their capture, she returned to **Paris** to be with the queen. She was present on the night of 10 August 1792, and accompanied the royal family to the Temple. Nine days later she was transferred to La Force prison, which was invaded by the crowd during the **September Massacres**. Lamballe was killed and her head was placed on a pike, to be paraded below the windows of the Temple for the eyes of the queen. She assumed thereafter a prominent place in counterrevolutionary iconography.

LAMETH, ALEXANDRE-THÉODORE (1756–1854). The eldest of the three Lameth brothers, he went by the name Théodore to distinguish him from his younger brother. He also outlived his two younger brothers, and during his long lifetime witnessed five kings, two republics, and two empires in France. His father was in a long line of sword nobility, and his mother was the daughter of the duke de Broglie. The three brothers were either grandsons or nephews to four marshals of France. All three brothers visited the United States and were much influenced by the ideas they encountered there. Their father died in 1761, and the boys relied to some degree on royal patronage for the completion of their **education**.

Théodore entered the navy at age 14, but then joined the army at the time of the American War of Independence. He was a Knight of the Order of Malta. In 1790–91 he sat on the **departmental administration** of the Jura, and in the fall of 1791 was elected to the **Legislative Assembly** from that department. He was one of only seven deputies to vote against the declaration of war against Austria, a war that he saw as a mortal risk for the monarchy. Fearing for the king's safety, he collaborated with **Marie-Joseph-Motier Lafayette** and **Adrien Duport** to prepare an escape for **Louis XVI** to Compiègne, but the king refused to flee a second time. Lameth denounced the **September Massacres**, and then fled France for England, allegedly with the help of **Georges Danton**. He returned to France, however, in December 1792 to assist in a failed effort to rescue Louis XVI, and then remained in obscurity on his property at Pontoise until a final emigration to Switzerland in March 1793. He eventually joined his brothers in Hamburg. Lameth returned to France after **Brumaire**, but with the exception of a brief term in the Chamber of Deputies during the One Hundred Days he played no further political role. *See also ÉMIGRÉS.*

LAMETH, ALEXANDRE-THÉODORE-VICTOR (1760–1829). Alexandre was the youngest, and most influential, of the three Lameth brothers who were active in the Revolution. Like Théodore, he was a member of the Knights of Malta and pursued a career in the army. By 1779 he was a captain in the royal cavalry, and went with Théodore to fight in the American War of Independence in 1782–83. Lameth was promoted to the rank of colonel in 1788, but then retired from the military the next year.

On the eve of the Revolution, Lameth joined the **Society of the Friends of Blacks**, and was a member of the **Society of Thirty**. In 1789 he was elected to the **Estates-General** by the nobility of Péronne, near Amiens. At **Versailles** he sat with the liberal nobility and favored the verification of credentials in common. He was among the 47 nobles who joined the assembly of the **Third Estate** on 25 June. Lameth served on eight different committees and was among the most active orators of the **Constituent Assembly**. On the **Night of 4 August 1789** he enthusiastically embraced the proposals for the abolition of **privilege** (although some biographers have observed that, as the youngest son in the family, he stood to lose very little), and on 3 November moved the abolition of the **parlements**. He was also among the founders of the **Jacobin club**. Indeed, along with **Antoine-Pierre Barnave** and **Adrien Duport**, Lameth was a dominant force in the Jacobin club in 1791–92, so much so that the three came to be referred to as the **Triumvirate**.

Lameth's was a liberal voice, then, in the early years of the Revolution. He favored a suspensive veto for the king, rather than an absolute veto, as a step in the direction of liberty. He spoke critically of **Gabriel-Honoré Mirabeau's** alleged overtures to the court in 1790–91, and voted in favor of the creation of *assignats*. But following the flight to **Varennes**, Lameth tried, along with Barnave and Duport, to steer the Jacobins toward a rapprochement with **Marie-Joseph-Motier Lafayette** (with whom Lameth had fought in America), and when that effort failed the three led the effort to found a rival club, the **Feuillants**. Lameth supported the violent suppression of the demonstration on the **Champ de Mars** in July 1791, and now devoted his efforts to trying to save the monarchy, whose power and authority he had seemingly been determined to curtail up until that point. When the Constituent Assembly dissolved in late 1791, Lameth resumed his military career, as a colonel in the 14th Regiment of dragoons, and also took a seat on the **departmental administration** of **Paris**.

After the monarchy fell, on 10 August 1792, the **Paris Commune** ordered the arrest of Lameth, and he fled France with Lafayette, under whose command he had served on the eastern front. Both were imprisoned by the Austrians at Olmütz, but Lameth was freed in 1795 due to failing health. He then fled to England, where he was not welcomed, before joining his brothers in Hamburg. He returned to France in 1797, but left again after the **Fructidor coup**. Lameth returned definitively after the **Brumaire** coup and served **Napoleon Bonaparte** as a prefect in 1802, a post that he would continue to hold, off and on, into the Restoration. In 1810 Lameth became a Baron of the Empire, was appointed to the Legion of Honor in 1811, and was named a Peer of France in 1815.

LAMETH, CHARLES-MALO-FRANÇOIS (1757–1832). Count Charles Lameth shared the same family history and military career as his brothers. He was wounded at the battle of Yorktown. In 1789 he was elected to the **Estates-General** by the nobility of Arras. Like Alexandre, he sat with the liberal nobility in the **Constituent Assembly**, but did not join the **Third Estate** until after the king's order on 27 June. Charles was somewhat less active in the Assembly than Alexandre, serving on only three committees, but he spoke often. In January 1790 he criticized **Jean-Siffrein Maury** for opposing a luxury tax, and one week later praised **Maximilien Robespierre** for his defense of those less fortunate in society. Lameth supported the creation of *assignats*, and was a consistent opponent of excessive royal power. He took a moderate stance on the issue of **slavery** in the colonies, influenced perhaps by the plantation holdings of his wife's family in **Saint-Domingue**.

As president of the Constituent Assembly after 5 July 1791, Lameth took the lead in organizing those opposed to the resignation of **Louis XVI**, and played a direct role in authorizing the repression of the 17 July demonstration on the **Champ de Mars**. He left the **Jacobin club** shortly thereafter and joined the **Feuillants**. When the Constituent Assembly dissolved, Lameth resumed his military career, but resigned his commission after the **uprising of 10 August 1792**. He emigrated to Hamburg with his wife, and founded a commercial business there. They returned briefly to France in 1797, and again after **Brumaire**. Lameth resumed his military career in 1807 and fought in Spain. In 1809 he was decorated as a Chevalier in the Legion of Honor. Lameth lived to applaud the Revolution of 1830, which he saw as fulfilling the ideals of 1789.

LAMOURETTE, ANTOINE-ADRIEN (1742–1794). Lamourette was a member of the Lazarist Order and Grand Vicar of Arras before 1789. He became a close friend of **Gabriel-Honoré Mirabeau**, swore the **civil oath of the clergy** in late 1790, and in February 1791 was elected Constitutional Bishop of **Lyon**. In late 1791 he was elected to the **Legislative Assembly** from the Rhône-et-Loire. Lamourette was a moderate and pacific individual who made no great impression on the Legislative Assembly until the session of 7 July 1792, following the king's flight to **Varennes**. Alarmed by the dissension within the meeting hall, Lamourette rose and called on his fellow deputies to cease their divisions and swear "to have but a single will, a single sentiment; to swear to unite as a single body of free men. The moment that foreigners see that we are united in our mission, will be the moment that liberty triumphs and that France is saved." Moved by these words, the deputies leapt to their feet and embraced, in what has come to be known as "the kiss of Lamourette." Unfortunately, that spirit of unity did not persist. After the dissolution of the Legislative Assembly, Lamourette returned to Lyon, where he remained during the siege that followed the **federalist revolt**. Thus compromised, he was arrested and taken to **Paris** for trial. Just before his execution, Lamourette retracted the oath he had sworn to the **Civil Constitution of the Clergy**.

LANJUINAIS, JEAN-DENIS (1755–1827). Lanjuinais was born into a **Jansenist** family in Rennes, the son of an *avocat au Parlement*. He was an outstanding student in Rennes, receiving his doctorate in law at the age of 17. The following year he presented himself for a Chair in Law at the University of Rennes, having passed all of the tests and requirements, but was turned down because of his youth. By 1780 he stood among the first rank of *avocats* in Rennes. In 1779 he was elected to the Estates of Brittany, and shortly thereafter published a pamphlet denouncing the aristocratic **privilege** of monopolizing dovecotes. The pamphlet aroused a furor and was suppressed by the Parlement of Rennes, but the lawyers of the city rallied to Lanjuinais's defense. He soon published two more pamphlets critical of aristocratic privilege, was elected by the **Third Estate** to the **Estates-General**, and drafted the *cahier de doléance* for the Third Estate of Rennes.

Lanjuinais was among the most active deputies in the **Constituent Assembly**. He was one of the founders of the **Breton club**, swore the **Tennis Court Oath**, and supported the suppression of **parlements**. As a member of the ecclesiastical committee he played a role in the abolition of monastic orders and contributed to the drafting of the **Civil Constitution of the Clergy**. Although his politics were moderate, Lanjuinais joined the **Jacobin club**, which he left temporarily in 1791 for the **Feuillants**. After the dissolution of the Constituent Assembly, he returned to Rennes as an officer on the municipal council. In late 1792 he was elected to the **National Convention** from the Ille-et-Vilaine. Lanjuinais supported the proposal for the creation of a departmental guard to protect the National Convention, and joined the call for charges against those responsible for the **September Massacres**. On 26 December 1792 he gave a very controversial speech demanding the repeal of the decree that had constituted the Convention as a court to judge **Louis XVI**, and went on to vote for banishment and the *appel au peuple*. Lanjuinais opposed the creation of the **Revolutionary Tribunal**, and in April 1793 voted in favor of the indictment of **Jean-Paul Marat**.

On 2 June 1793 Lanjuinais called for the dissolution of the revolutionary authorities of **Paris**, and as a result was proscribed from the Convention along with the leading **Girondin** deputies. He fled the capital and passed briefly through **Caen**, but did not linger there during the **federalist revolt**. For the next 18 months he hid in his house in Rennes. His wife aided his evasion from justice by divorcing him, but his mother, sister, and brother were all arrested. Lanjuinais returned to the Convention in March 1795 and contributed to the drafting of the **Constitution of 1795**. He was now denounced by **Jean-Lambert Tallien** as a royalist, but defended by **Louis Legendre**, who had been among his accusers in June 1792. Lanjuinais was elected to the **Council of Ancients** in 1795 from 73 departments, but once again chose to represent the Ille-et-Vilaine. He rotated out in 1797, returned to Rennes to teach law, but was named to the Senate after **Brumaire**. Lanjuinais opposed the declaration of **Napoleon Bonaparte** as consul for life, and then the creation of the Empire, but was still named to the Legion of Honor in 1803, made a Count of the Empire in 1808, and elected to the **Institut National** in that same year. Under the Restoration he served in the Chamber of Peers, where he resolutely defended the liberal gains of the Revolution.

LANTHENAS, FRANÇOIS-XAVIER (1754–1799). Lanthenas was the son of a wax merchant in Puy, where he attended *collège* before being apprenticed to a commercial house in **Lyon** in 1770, much against his will. He later traveled to Holland, Germany, and then Italy, where he met **Jean-Marie** and **Manon Roland** in 1777. The Rolands helped get him into medical school, first in **Paris** and then in Reims, where he completed his medical studies in 1784. Lanthenas returned to Puy as a doctor in 1786.

Lanthenas moved to Paris on the eve of the Revolution, still linked to the Rolands. He joined the **Jacobin club** and began writing for the *Patriote français*, edited by **Jacques-Pierre Brissot**. When Roland became minister of the interior after 10 August 1792, Lanthenas obtained a position as a division chief in the ministry, though he was not terribly competent in this job. He was elected to the **National Convention** from the Rhône-et-Loire, sat with the **Girondins**, and came to be referred to by the **Montagnards** as the master of ceremonies for Madame Roland's **salon**. In late November 1792 he was expelled from the Jacobin club along with Roland and **Jean-Baptiste Louvet**. Lanthenas voted for death in the trial of **Louis XVI**, and against the *appel au peuple*. He voted against the indictment of **Jean-Paul Marat**, and although he was associated with the Girondins avoided proscription on 2 June 1793 and spoke out against the **federalist revolt** that followed. He was an admirer of **Thomas Paine**, and the principal translator of his works into French. In 1795 he was elected to the **Council of Five Hundred** from the Ille-et-Vilaine. He rotated out in 1797, took up a minor post in Paris, and hosted the final meetings of the **Society of the Friends of Blacks**, of which he had been a member since 1789. In his last years, Lanthenas also became an advocate of **Theophilanthropy**.

LA RÉVELLIÈRE-LÉPEAUX, LOUIS-MARIE (1753–1824). Born into a bourgeois family of Angers, La Révellière-Lépeaux's father had been a *conseiller du roi* and served as mayor of the small town of Montaigu, in the **Vendée**, for 30 years. Louis-Marie was brought up by a priest, who beat him, leaving him with a bent spine and an intensely anti-clerical attitude. La Révellière-Lépeaux studied law in Angers, became an *avocat au Parlement* in **Paris** in 1775, but did not much like legal work. He married well in 1780, and this allowed him to devote his time to Parisian literary culture. He was elected to the **Estates-General** by the **Third Estate** of Anjou, joined the **Jacobin club** but sat with the centrists, and quit the Jacobins after the **Champ de Mars massacre**. La Révellière-Lépeaux returned to Angers in late 1791 to serve on the **departmental administration**, and organized "patriotic tourneys" in the countryside in an effort to win **peasants** over to the cause of the Revolution.

He was elected to the **National Convention** in 1792, again from Angers, sat with the **Girondins** but voted with the **Montagnards** in the trial of **Louis XVI**. In July 1793 he protested the proscription of the Girondin deputies and went into hiding to escape arrest. Back home, his brother would be executed in 1794 along with a number of other departmental administrators. He returned to the National Convention in March 1795, served briefly on the **Committee of Public Safety**, and helped draft the **Constitution of 1795**. He was elected to the **Council of Ancients** in October 1795 and was among the first directors. As such, La Révellière-Lépeaux carried out the **Fructidor coup** against the royalists in 1797 and supported the **Floréal coup** against the Jacobins in 1798, making him a classical **Directory** politician in this regard. He remained an ardent supporter of **deChristianization** throughout this period, supported the cult of **Theophilanthropy**, and opposed **Napoleon Bonaparte's** rise to power, which ended his own political career.

LA ROCHEFOUCAULD, LOUIS-ALEXANDRE (1743–1792). La Rochefoucauld, the Prince of Marcillac, was born into a noble family that traced its lineage back to the 11th century. His father was a lieutenant-general in the army. Louis, too, was an officer in the army and a Chevalier de St. Louis (1781). He was a friend of General **Lafayette** and Benjamin Franklin, and an admirer of the United States. In 1787–88 La Rochefoucauld sat on both **Assemblies of Notables**. He was a member of the **Society of Thirty** and in 1789 was the second delegate to be elected to the **Estates-General** by the nobility of **Paris**. La Rochefoucauld was among the 47 noble deputies who joined the **Third Estate** in June 1789, and was one of the most active orators in the **Constituent Assembly**, where he sat on nine committees. He saw no need for the king to sanction the constitution, which he argued would stand on its own authority, supported a suspensive veto for the king, and also supported the decrees that emerged from the **Night of 4 August 1789**. He voted for the sale of Church lands, the **Civil Constitution of the Clergy**, and the suppression of monastic orders. The popular disorders of October 1789 caused him alarm, however, leading him to support **Gabriel-Honoré Mirabeau's** proposal for a declaration of martial law.

In July 1791 La Rochefoucauld left the **Jacobin club** for the **Feuillants**. When the Constituent Assembly was dissolved, he was elected to the directory of the **departmental administration** of Paris, where he adopted an increasingly reactionary attitude. He quarreled with **Jérome Pétion**, mayor of Paris, and took a dim view of the militancy of the **sans-culottes**. La Rochefoucauld fled the capital after 10 August 1792, but was recognized by a crowd on the road near Gisors in early September and stoned to death.

LA ROCHEFOUCAULD-LIANCOURT, FRANÇOIS-ALEXAN-DRE-FREDERIC (1747–1827). His father was the Duke of Liancourt, Count of Roucy. François added La Rochefoucauld to his name to honor his cousin (*See* LOUIS-ALEXANDRE LA ROCHEFOU-CAULD), murdered near Gisors in September 1792. François studied at the *collège* La Flèche, served in the king's Musketeers, was named a Chevalier de St. Louis in 1781, and was grand-master of the king's wardrobe, as his father had been before him. He accompanied **Louis XVI** on his 1786 trip to Cherbourg, the king's only trip away from the royal châteaux of the **Paris** basin. La Rochefoucauld-Liancourt frequented a number of the Paris **salons** in the late 1780s, including that of **Marie-Jean Condorcet**. He was a member of the **Society of Thirty**, and was elected to the **Estates-General** by the nobility of Clermont-en-Beauvaisis.

La Rochefoucauld-Liancourt sat with the liberal nobility in the Estates-General, though he did not go over to the **Third Estate** in June 1789. He was among those who insisted that they would need a new mandate from their constituents when the deputies declared themselves a National Assembly later that month. Throughout July he served as an intermediary between the **Constituent Assembly** and Louis XVI, and on 12 July it was he who replied to the king, "No, Sire, it is a revolution," when the king asked, "But, is it then a revolt?" in reference to the brewing insurrection in Paris that would shortly topple the **Bastille**.

At the end of the session of 4 August 1789, La Rochefoucauld-Liancourt proposed a medal to commemorate the sincere union of all three orders, though he would later support the royal veto. After the flight to **Varennes**, in June 1791, he commented that one thing missing from their remarkable revolution was the liberty of the king. He was a member of the Club of 1789, the **Jacobin club**, and then the **Feuillants**. In 1791 he purchased some 200,000 *livres* of ***biens nationaux*** near the family château in the Yvelines, where he had operated a model farm in the years prior to the Revolution. After 10 August 1792, and the murder of his cousin, he resigned his post in the army and fled to England. From 1794 to 1797 he traveled in the United States and Canada. In 1810 he was named a Chevalier of the Legion of Honor, and in 1814 entered the Chamber of Peers.

LA ROCHEJAQUELIN, HENRI DU VERGIER (1772–1794). Henri La Rochejaquelin was born into an old noble family of Anjou. At the age of 13 he joined the cavalry regiment in which his father was an officer. His father emigrated early in the Revolution, and Henri joined the Constitutional Guard of the king. As such, he was present at the **Tuileries** Palace on 10 August 1792, when **Louis XVI** was deposed. La Rochejaquelin returned to his family estate, and in the spring of 1793 joined with his cousin, the Marquis de Lescure, as a leader of the **peasant** insurrection in the **Vendée**. He was present at the battle of Fontenay in May 1793, was leader of the successful assault on Saumur on 9 June 1793, and went on to defeat Generals François-Joseph Westermann and Jean-Antoine Rossignol at Châtillon. Following the defeat of the rebels at Cholet in October 1793, a battle at which Lescure was killed, La Rochejaquelin was named general of the Royal and Catholic Army of the Vendée rebels. He scored several more victories in the next month before defeats at Granville and Angers, and then a serious defeat at Le Mans on 12 December 1793 in which 15,000 rebel troops were lost. La Rochejaquelin's small army then suffered a decisive defeat at Savenay on 25 December. He was killed in an ambush in late January 1794 while in pursuit of a republican soldier. Dead at the age of 21, La Rochejaquelin became a legendary figure among the Vendéen rebels.

LAVOISIER, ANTOINE-LAURENT (1743–1794). Antoine Lavoisier is known to posterity as the father of modern chemistry, but he was also a tax official under the Old Regime and a victim of the **Terror**. He was born into a family of wealthy merchants, although his father was an *avocat* at the **Parlement of Paris**. Lavoisier inherited a large sum of money from his mother, and with this he purchased an office in the Farmers General, in 1769, the income from which allowed him to pursue his experiments and to share his laboratory at the Arsenal with colleagues and young researchers. Both

James Watt and Benjamin Franklin visited his laboratory. Lavoisier was admitted into the French Academy of Science at the age of 25 for his work in chemistry, but he was also interested in agronomy and political economy. In 1775 Lavoisier published a major work, *Opuscules chimiques*, and two years later made public the results of his experiments with oxygen, with Emperor Joseph II of Austria in attendance. His laboratory at the Arsenal, and the **salon** that his wife hosted, were among the intellectual centers of **Paris**.

It was his position as a tax farmer, not his scientific work, that compromised Lavoisier. In 1775 Anne-Robert-Jacques Turgot named Lavoisier a commissioner of gunpowder, responsible for overseeing the collection of excise tax. He introduced measures unpopular in Paris, and would further alienate Parisians in 1787 when he promoted the building of an *octroi* wall around the capital to make more efficient the collection of transit taxes on goods. This wall would be a primary target of insurgents in July 1789. But he also favored reform, and as a member of the Provincial Assembly of the Orléannais he proposed the abolition of the *corvée* and the creation of an old-age fund for the poor. Lavoisier welcomed the Revolution, but played no prominent political role. He did, however, prepare a remarkable statistical report for the **Constituent Assembly**, *Richesse Territoriale du royaume de France*. After 10 August 1792 he thought it prudent to leave Paris. One year later the **Academy** of Science was abolished, and in November 1793 an order was issued for the arrest of all former Farmers-General. Not all would be sent to the **guillotine**, but the memory of the *octroi* wall may have cost Lavoisier his life. There were rumors, too, that he had played a key role in denying admission to the Academy of Science to **Jean-Paul Marat**, an exclusion that the Friend of the People certainly resented. Lavoisier was executed on 8 May 1794. One year later his reputation would be rehabilitated. *See also* TAXATION.

LAW OF 14 FRIMAIRE. The Law of 14 Frimaire (4 December 1793) established the administrative structure of revolutionary government that would rule France for the next eight months. It centralized power in the hands of the **Committee of Public Safety**, formalizing its authority, and brought the machinery of the **Terror** under administrative control. **Representatives on mission** now found their authority more clearly defined, and somewhat restrained, and were henceforth answerable directly to the Committee of Public Safety. In reaction to the **federalist revolt**, in which **departmental administrations** had challenged the authority of the **National Convention**, the Law of 14 Frimaire reduced their size and powers and increased the role of district administrations. The law also mandated the appointment of *agents nationaux*, who were attached to district administrations and expected to report to the Committee of Public Safety every 10 days. Representatives on mission were to oversee purges of local councils, and local elections were suspended. The Law of 14 Frimaire remained the charter of government until the **Thermidorians** countermanded many of its provisions in the decree of 24 August 1794.

LAW OF SUSPECTS. The **National Convention** passed the Law of Suspects on 17 September 1793. It empowered local **committees of surveillance** to draw up lists of suspects and to order their arrest. The law also defined a number of categories of suspect, including enemies of liberty, advocates of tyranny, supporters of **federalism**, those who were denied *certificats de civisme*, those without gainful employ, those *émigrés* who had left France between 1 July 1789 and 8 April 1792, and ex-**aristocrats** who had not shown support for the Revolution. An estimated 70,000 people were arrested as suspects during the year of the **Terror**.

LAW OF 22 PRAIRIAL. The Law of 22 Prairial (10 June 1794) ushered in the final phase of the **Terror**. **Maximilien Robespierre** and **Georges Couthon** took sole responsibility for drafting the legislation, and there is evidence that others on the **Committee of Public Safety** opposed it. The law both streamlined the procedures of the **Revolutionary Tribunal**, in order to alleviate overcrowding in prisons, and broadened the definition of those considered suspects or enemies of the people.

In addition to those identified in the original **Law of Suspects**, the law of 22 Prairial included those who had deceived the people or their representatives, those who circulated false news, those who sought to undermine public morality, and those who opposed republican principles. Nearly anyone who spoke critically of official policy might have been included in these categories, and many national deputies now grew fearful for their own safety. The new law split the Revolutionary Tribunal into four courts, meeting simultaneously; made the death penalty the only option to acquittal; eliminated cross-examination of witnesses; allowed juries to consider "moral" evidence as well as material evidence in reaching a verdict; and declared that once a jury had arrived at a verdict, no further witnesses needed to be heard.

From 10 June 1794 to the end of July, the Revolutionary Tribunal sentenced 1,594 people to death, roughly 500 more than in the previous 14 months of its existence. This acceleration of the Terror, at a time when the threat to public safety from both domestic rebellion and foreign war had subsided, alarmed both the populace and the deputies of the **National Convention**. The coup of 9 **Thermidor**, which toppled Robespierre and Couthon from power, was at least in part a response to the law of 10 Prairial, which was repealed by the Convention five days later.

LE BAS, PHILIPPE-FRANÇOIS-JOSEPH (1764–1794). Philippe Le Bas's father was a notary and steward on the estate of the Prince de Rache. Le Bas studied at the *collège* Montaigne in **Paris**, went on to study law, and became an *avocat* at the **Parlement of Paris** just before the Revolution. He returned home to the Pas-de-Calais at the behest of his father, however, joined the **National Guard** in Saint-Pol, and was a delegate to the 1790 **Festival of Federation**. In 1791 he was elected to the Saint-Pol district administration, and in 1792 was elected to the **National Convention** from the Pas-de-Calais.

In the National Convention he became close to **Maximilien Robespierre**, and in August 1793 married Elisabeth DuPlay, daughter of the family with whom Robespierre lodged in Paris. Le Bas initially had sympathy for **Girondin** positions, but gravitated slowly toward the **Montagnards** through his friendship with Robespierre. He voted for death in the trial of **Louis XVI**, and against the *appel au peuple*. In September 1793 he was elected to the **Committee of General Security**, where he would be one of Robespierre's few allies. In the last months of 1793 he went frequently on mission to the armies with **Louis-Antoine Saint-Just**. He presided over the **Jacobin club** in April 1794, but late that month went again on mission with Saint-Just to the Army of the North. While on mission the two ordered the arrest of all former nobles in the Pas-de-Calais, Nord, Somme, and Aisne, an order that angered **Lazare Carnot**. On 9 **Thermidor**, Le Bas, like **Augustin Robespierre**, demanded to share the fate of Robespierre and Saint-Just. Unlike the others, Le Bas succeeded in killing himself with a pistol shot when the troops of the National Convention arrived at the Hôtel de Ville to arrest them.

LEBRUN-TONDU, PIERRE-MARIE-HENRI (1754–1793). Little is known of Lebrun's family other than the fact that it was of comfortable means. He began his **education** in his natal town of Noyon, to the north of **Paris**, but went on to the *collège* Louis-le-Grand in the capital. He then took orders under the name Abbot Tondu, but soon renounced his monastic vows and went on to lead a varied life — as an employee at the Paris Observatory, as a soldier, and then as a typesetter and journalist in the Dutch Lowlands. In 1787 he participated in the revolt of Liège, and returned to Paris in the early 1790s. There he became a protégé of **Charles Dumouriez** and **Jacques-Pierre Brissot**, whom he first met in Brussels. Through their influence Lebrun obtained a position in the Ministry of Foreign Affairs, rising to the position of minister following the **uprising of 10 August 1792**. After the French victory at **Valmy**, Lebrun advocated and pursued a separate armistice with the Prussians, but failed to achieve it. His close ties to Brissot and Dumouriez made him vulnerable in the struggle between **Girondins** and **Montagnards**, particularly after the April 1793 treason of General Dumouriez. Lebrun was not included among those proscribed on 2 June 1793, but was arrested later that month. He managed to escape in September and fled to Brittany, but was captured on 22 December 1793 and returned to Paris for trial. Lebrun was convicted of complicity with the Girondins and the loss of **Belgium** and went to the **guillotine** on 27 December 1793.

LE CHAPELIER, ISAAC-RENÉ-GUY (1754–1794). Le Chapelier was born into a family with a long legal tradition as *avocats au Parlement*, stretching back into the 17th century. His father was ennobled in 1779. Isaac studied law in Rennes, joined the **Freemasons** in 1775, and in 1780 became a councillor in the Estates of Brittany. In 1788 he petitioned the nobility of Brittany, asking that *annoblis* be eligible to sit as delegates of the **aristocracy** to the **Estates-General**, but with-

Prise des armes aux Invalides, dans la matinée du 14 juillet 1789, in *Tableaux historiques de la Révolution française*. Collection du musée de la Révolution française, Vizille. Inventaire: L.1984-253-14

Taking weapons from the Invalides in the morning of 14 July 1789. Collection of the Museum of the French Revolution, Vizille. Inventory number: L.1984-253-14

Assemblée nationale. Abandon de tous les privilèges. Collection du musée de la Révolution française, Vizille. Inventaire: MRF.1989-67

National Assembly. Relinquishing all privileges. *Collection of the Museum of the French Revolution. Vizille. Inventory number: MRF.1989-67*

Retour de Varennes. Arrivée de Louis Capet à Paris, le 25 juin 1791, in Tableaux historiques de la Révolution française. Collection du musée de la Révolution française, Vizille. Inventaire: L.1984-253-54

Return from Varennes. Arrival of Louis Capet in Paris, 25 June 1791. *Collection of the Museum of the French Revolution, Vizille. Inventory number: L.1984-253-54*

La Séparation de Louis XVI, d'avec sa famille. Collection du musée de la Révolution française, Vizille. Inventaire: MRF.1983-324

The separation of Louis XVI from his family. *Collection of the Museum of the French Revolution, Vizille. Inventory number: MRF.1983-324*

Exécution de Louis XVI. Collection du musée de la Révolution française, Vizille. Inventaire: MRF.1984-477

Execution of Louis XVI. Collection of the Museum of the French Revolution, Vizille. Inventory number: MRF.1984-477

Jugement de Marie-Antoinette d'Autriche. Collection du musée de la Révolution française, Vizille. Inventaire: MRF.1983-323

Trial of Marie-Antoinette of Austria. Collection of the Museum of the French Revolution, Vizille. Inventory number: MRF.1983-323

Intérieur d'un comité révolutionnaire sous le régime de la Terreur. Année 1793 et 1794 in *Tableaux historiques de la Révolution française*. Collection du musée de la Révolution française, Vizille. Inventaire: L.1984-253-103

Inside a revolutionary committee during the Reign of Terror. Years 1793 and 1794. *Collection of the Museum of the French Revolution, Vizille. Inventory number: L.1984-253-103*

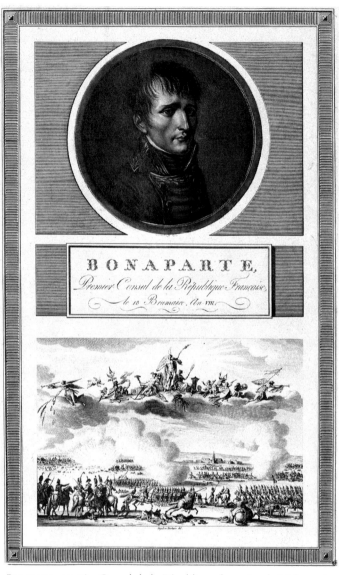

BONAPARTE,

Premier Consul de la République Française, le 18 Brumaire, An VIII.

Bonaparte, premier Consul de la République française, le 18 brumaire, an VIII, in Tableaux historiques de la Révolution française. Collection du musée de la Révolution française, Vizille. Inventaire: L.1984-253-P49

Bonaparte, First Consul of the French Republic, 18th Brumaire, year VIII. *Collection of the Museum of the French Revolution, Vizille. Inventory number: L.1984-253-P49* out success. Le Chapelier was then elected to the Estates-General by the **Third Estate** of Rennes. At **Versailles** he was a founder of the **Breton club** and became known as an early advocate of the unification of the three orders. On 15 June 1789 he supported the call of the **Abbé Sieyès** for the declaration of a National Assembly, and participated in the **Tennis Court Oath**. Le Chapelier was among the most active orators in the **Constituent Assembly**, presided over it twice, and sat on four committees, most notably the constitutional committee. On that committee he favored the separation of powers, the suspensive veto, and the separation of the king from legislative proceedings.

Le Chapelier is best known for two reasons. He presided over the celebrated session of the Constituent Assembly on 4 August 1789, and reported to the king on the measures taken that night, bringing an effective end to **privilege** in France. Consistent with that action was the law that he proposed on 14 June 1791, which came to be known as the Le Chapelier Law. It prohibited the formation of intermediary organizations by workers or any other individuals with shared interests, and would stand as an effective legal deterrent to the formation of labor unions in France until 1884.

In September 1791 Le Chapelier alienated **Maximilien Robespierre** by arguing that clubs and **popular societies**, like the **Jacobin club**, were governed by this law. Following **Louis XVI's** flight to **Varennes**, Le Chapelier had left the Jacobin club for the **Feuillants**, and in the final months of the Constituent Assembly he consistently argued that it was time to bring the Revolution to an end. When the Constituent Assembly dissolved, he returned to legal practice in Rennes. A short trip to London in late 1792 brought him under suspicion of being an *émigré*. He lived discreetly for the next year, but in February 1794 Le Chapelier wrote a letter to the **Committee of Public Safety**, offering to serve as its spy in England. He was arrested in March, on Robespierre's orders, and charged with the reverse, of being in the pay of a foreign power. Le Chapelier was tried and executed in April 1794.

LECLERC, JEAN-THÉOPHILE-VICTOIRE (1771–?). Théophile Leclerc was born in Montbrison, just west of **Lyon**, the fifth and final child of an engineer in the royal Department of Bridges and Highways.

His father took charge of his schooling at home. Leclerc joined the **National Guard** in Clermont-Ferrand in the summer of 1789, but early in 1790 he left for Martinique to join two of his brothers. While there he participated in the island's uprising and in March 1791 was arrested and put back on a ship to France. He landed in Lorient, enlisted in the army, but within a year had been dismissed for once again getting involved in revolutionary agitation. In March 1792 he carried an address from the Lorient **Jacobin club** to **Paris**, where he quickly became active in the militant political movement of the capital. Leclerc was assigned briefly to the Army of the Rhine, fighting at the battle of Jemappes in November 1792, but by February 1793 had been reassigned to the headquarters of the Army of the Alps in **Lyon**.

In Lyon Leclerc immediately reconnected with **Joseph Chalier**, whom he had met the year before in Paris, and became involved in radical politics in Lyon. Chalier soon sent him back to Paris, to seek support for Lyon Jacobins, and in the capital Leclerc became embroiled in the insurrectionary movement against the **Girondin** deputies. On 29 May he was named to the revolutionary committee that prepared the **uprising of 31 May–2 June 1793**, and in the days following the proscription of the Girondins, his was among the most strident voices calling for more arrests and continued insurrection. Leclerc now took his place among the leading *enragés*, and supported **Jacques Roux's** infamous speech of 25 June, which got both of them expelled from the Jacobin club. After the assassination of **Jean-Paul Marat**, Leclerc took over publication of his **newspaper**, *L'Ami du Peuple*, but his rhetoric was so violent that Marat's widow went to the **National Convention** to demand that he be stopped. He did cease publication, in September, after 24 issues had appeared, and in November 1793 married **Pauline Léon**, one of the leaders of the **Society of Revolutionary Republican Women**. By then Leclerc had distanced himself from Jacques Roux and re-enrolled in the army. Léon traveled with him to the Aisne, where his battalion was assigned, and in April 1794 both were arrested. They remained in prison until September, and disappeared without a trace thereafter.

LEGENDRE, ADRIEN-MARIE (1752–1833). Legendre was born in **Paris** and educated at the *collège* Mazarin. He taught mathematics at the Ecole Militaire from 1775 to 1780, and in 1782 won the annual prize from the Berlin Academy for a problem in ballistics. The following year he was admitted to the French **Academy** of Science. Legendre's principal contribution during the Revolution was his work related to the introduction of the **metric system**. He held a variety of minor government posts in the early 1790s, and in 1795–96 sat on the *Agence temporaire des poids et mesures*, which oversaw the introduction of the metric system. In 1795 he was elected to the **Institut National**, and was also appointed to teach at the Ecole Normale. Legendre's most important publication was his *Eléments du Géométrie* (1794), which made several important departures from Euclidean geometry and remained the standard text in the field well into the 19th century. This work was commissioned by the Committee on Public Instruction of the **National Convention**, evidence that there was more going on in 1794 than the **Terror**. In his later years, Legendre made important contributions in the fields of elliptic integrals and number theory.

LEGENDRE, LOUIS (1752–1797). Known to contemporaries as "the butcher of **Paris**," Legendre was the son of a butcher and eventually took up that trade himself, in the Saint-Germain neighborhood. As a youth he worked for 10 years as a cabin boy and then as a sailor. Though without formal **education**, he was a capable speaker with a strong voice. On 14 July 1789 he was on the streets urging people to march to the **Invalides**, and he was among the vanquishers of the **Bastille**. Legendre met and befriended **Georges Danton** through neighborhood politics, helped him to found the **Cordelier club**, and came to be known as Danton's lieutenant. In December 1791 he led a delegation from his neighborhood to the **Legislative Assembly** to demand pikes so that they might defend the city, as the Romans had done against their enemies. Legendre was in the vanguard of the assault on the **Tuileries** Palace on 10 August 1792, and shortly thereafter was elected from Paris to the **National Convention**.

Legendre joined the **Jacobin club**, sat with the **Montagnards**, voted for death in the trial of **Louis XVI**, and opposed the *appel au peuple*. He tried to play the role of conciliator between the Montagnards and **Girondins** in the spring of 1793. He succeeded in removing the name of **Jean-Baptiste Boyer-Fonfrède** from the list of deputies to be proscribed, and after 2 June spoke up to protest the violation of Girondin letters. From 15 June to 15 August 1793, Legendre served on the **Committee of General Security**, and his moderation during this period brought him under suspicion. In January 1794 he would be questioned about his vote on the indictment of **Jean-Paul Marat**, to which he replied that while he had been absent from the Convention on that occasion, for nearly two years he had hidden Marat in his cellar. Legendre's credentials as a Parisian **sans-culotte** could not be easily questioned. In March 1794 he presided over the Jacobin club, just on the eve of the arrest of Danton and the **Indulgents**.

Legendre initially came to the defense of his old friend and mentor, but within two weeks he renounced Danton at the Jacobins, saying that he was now convinced of his guilt. From that point on, Legendre seemed to have lost his spirit and energy. After **Thermidor** he joined the reactionaries in denouncing ex-terrorists. He was elected to the **Council of Ancients** in 1795, but by then was a shell of his former self. Legendre was long remembered, however, for his famous exchange with **Jean-Denis Lanjuinais** on 2 June 1793. When Legendre yelled at Lanjuinais to cede the speaker's rostrum, "Step down or I will fell you," the deputy replied, "First you must decree that I am a cow." Even at a moment of crisis, some revolutionaries maintained their sense of humor.

LEGISLATIVE ASSEMBLY. The Legislative Assembly was the second legislature of the revolutionary decade, convening for its first meetings on 1 October 1791 and holding its final session on 20 September 1792. It consisted of 745 deputies, none of whom had sat in the **Constituent Assembly**, by virtue of the decree of ineligibility proposed by **Maximilien Robespierre**. The deputies were chosen by electoral assemblies in the 83 newly created departments, with the size of departmental delegations determined by three variables: the number of **active citizens** in each department; the direct taxes paid by its inhabitants; and the geographic territory of each department. Very few **clergy** were elected to the Legislative Assembly, and only some two dozen members of the former **aristocracy**. Although the deputies were new to national politics, the majority had experience on **departmental administrations**, in municipal politics, or as local judges. Many had been trained as lawyers, or were substantial landowners.

Three groups of deputies were discernable within the Legislative Assembly. By the last months of 1791, not quite half of them belonged to the moderate **Feuillant** club and took as their principal goal the consolidation of the constitutional monarchy. A smaller group of deputies, perhaps 140 at this same period, belonged to the more radical **Jacobin** club, and they were much more suspicious of **Louis XVI's** commitment to the **Constitution of 1791**. Over time, the numbers in the Jacobin contingent grew, led by **Jacques-Pierre Brissot**, while those adhering to the Feuillants shrank. The remainder of the deputies, never a majority, belonged to neither club.

The main task of the Legislative Assembly was to draft legislation consistent with the Constitution of 1791. The Assembly did not have the power to name ministers, nor could it override a royal veto, which Louis XVI exercised on a number of occasions. Two key issues remained controversial throughout the 12 months of the Legislative Assembly's existence: official policy toward *émigrés* and official policy toward **refractory priests**. Louis XVI vetoed punitive legislation directed against both groups in November 1791. The declaration of war against Austria and Prussia in April 1792, urged by Brissot and welcomed by Louis XVI, for very different reasons, heightened tensions around both issues, and early defeats on the battlefields focused popular resentment on the person of the king.

The Legislative Assembly played no active role in the failed insurrection of 20 June 1792 or the **uprising of 10 August 1792**, which toppled the monarchy. Indeed, under the presidency of **Pierre-Victurnien Vergniaud** in early August, the Assembly turned away a petition from the sections of **Paris** calling for the deposing of Louis XVI, and on 10 August offered refuge to the king and his family. In the weeks that followed, the Legislative Assembly stood in seeming opposition to the more radical **Paris Commune**, but it did pass legislation calling for the election of a **National Convention** by universal manhood suffrage, ushering in the declaration of the First French Republic and the radical phase of the French Revolution.

LÉON, PAULINE (1768–?). Pauline Léon was the daughter of Parisian shopkeepers. Her father was a chocolate maker, and when he died in the 1780s Pauline and her mother took over the operation of the business. Pauline was active in neighborhood politics from the outset of the Revolution. She was in the streets on 14 July 1789, though she appears not to have participated in the march to **Versailles** during the **October Days**. In February 1791 she and a group of **women** publicly broke a bust of General **Lafayette**, and from that date on Léon regularly attended the meetings of the **Cordelier club** as well as those of the Luxembourg section. Léon delivered a dramatic address to the **Constituent Assembly** in March 1791, demanding the right of women to bear arms in defense of the country. That summer she signed the petition initiated by the Cordeliers against the monarchy, and was present with her mother on the **Champ de Mars** on 17 July, near the line of fire. One year later, Léon was again active in the streets during the 10 August 1792 assault on the **Tuileries Palace**.

Along with **Claire Lacombe**, Léon was co-founder of the **Society of Revolutionary Republican Women** in May 1793. The Society played an active role in the agitation in **Paris** against the **Girondin** deputies. Léon herself sat on the insurrectionary assembly that convened in the Bishop's Palace to plan the **uprising of 31 May–2 June 1793**, and on 2 June she spoke before the **National Convention** as president of the Society of Revolutionary Republican Women. Léon and the women's club maintained their activism throughout the summer, shifting over time toward support of the *enragés* and their radical populist agenda. In November 1793 Léon married **Théophile Leclerc**, and after their arrest the following April she disappeared from the political scene.

LE PELETIER DE SAINT-FARGEAU, LOUIS-MICHEL (1760–1793). Michel Le Peletier de Saint-Fargeau was born into an enormously wealthy family. His father was president of the **Parlement of Paris**. Michel received his early **education** at home, from an array of illustrious tutors, went on to study law in **Paris**, and in 1777 became an *avocat du roi* at the **Châtelet** court. In 1779 he joined the Parlement of Paris, rose to the ranks of *conseiller* and *avocat-général* in the mid-1780s, and succeeded his father as *président à mortier* between 1785 and 1790.

Le Peletier was elected to the **Estates-General** by the nobility of Paris in 1789. He sat with the liberal minority, but did not join the **Third Estate** until after 25 June, and was among those who insisted on receiving a new mandate from their constituents when the National Assembly was declared. Le Peletier was among the most active orators in the **Constituent Assembly**. When the Assembly abolished noble titles in June 1790, he shortened his name to Michel Le Peletier. His most notable contribution came on the committee for criminal legislation, where he urged severe restrictions on the death penalty (along with **Maximilien Robespierre**), and introduced legislation to eliminate torture from criminal proceedings.

After the dissolution of the Constituent Assembly, Le Peletier was elected president of the **departmental administration** of the Yonne. One year later, the department sent him as a deputy to the **National Convention**, despite the fact that he urged the electoral assembly to heed the advice of the Paris **Jacobin club** that no priests or ex-nobles be elected. When he returned to Paris, Le Peletier joined the Jacobin club, which he had refused to do back in 1790. In October 1792 he defended complete freedom of the press, in the context of a debate over the **September Massacres**. He sat with the **Montagnards** in the Convention, voted for death in the trial of **Louis XVI**, and against the *appel au peuple*. On 20 January 1793, the eve of the king's execution, Le Peletier was assassinated in the **Palais Royal** by a member of the king's bodyguard, Michel Antonin de Pâris. His final words were, "I die, content, for the liberty of my country." Le Peletier became the first martyr of the Revolution, and the National Convention accorded him the honors of the **Panthéon**. After **Thermidor**, however, the deputies voted that one could not be so honored until 10 years after death, and his remains were moved to the family estate.

LETTRES DE CACHET. *Lettres de cachet* were sealed orders by which the king could order the arrest or imprisonment of anyone without charge or trial. They were widely denounced at the end of the Old Regime as the most egregious example of royal despotism, although they were most often issued at the request of prominent families who wished to discipline unruly members. **Gabriel-Honoré Mirabeau**, for example, was imprisoned in the Château d'If in 1774 by a *lettre de cachet* obtained by his father, and would later denounce them in his *Des Lettres de cachet et des prisons d'état* (1779). **Voltaire**, too, was imprisoned in the **Bastille** by royal *lettre de cachet*, and denounced the abuse in his novel, *L'ingénu*. A great number of the *cahiers de* *doléances* called for the elimination of *lettres de cachet*, and they were abolished by decree of the **Constituent Assembly** in January 1790.

LEVÉE EN MASSE. The **National Convention** decreed the *levée en masse* on 23 August 1793, responding to pressure from the **sans-culottes** of **Paris** and the realization that the volunteer army was dwindling in numbers. The decree stopped short of mandating universal **conscription** into the military, but did amount to a mobilization of the populace in defense of the nation. All unmarried men and widowers without children between the ages of 18 and 25 were called upon to enlist. Married men were encouraged to assist in the manufacture of arms, and **women** were to volunteer in military hospitals or sew uniforms or tents for the soldiers. The army soon grew to 750,000 men, at least 300,000 mobilized by the *levée en masse*.

LIBERTY, EQUALITY, FRATERNITY. Some credit **Maximilien Robespierre** with coining this motto of the French Revolution, while others insist that **Antoine-François Momoro** first put it forward in 1791 and later persuaded **Jean-Nicolas Pache**, then mayor of **Paris**, to inscribe the three words on the facades of all public buildings. Each word evokes an ideal of the Revolution, though in each case much debated throughout the revolutionary decade. Liberty and equality were often paired in **Jacobin club** propaganda, and the ideal of fraternity was closely associated with the 1790 **Festival of Federation**, which brought **National Guards** from throughout the nation to a fraternal celebration in Paris. Critics of the **Terror** denounced it for having trampled on the ideal of liberty, while **Gracchus Babeuf** and his fellow conspirators would later denounce the **Thermidorians** for having allegedly abandoned the ideal of equality.

Each of the three words was associated with particular symbols. Liberty was symbolized in the planting of **liberty trees**, and also in the female figure of **Marianne**. The **phrygian cap** was also a powerful symbol of liberty. Two symbols commonly evoked the ideal of equality—the scales of justice and the equilateral triangle—while the fasces of grain was the most common symbol of fraternity. Alexis de Tocqueville would argue in the 19th century that the French, unaccustomed to the exercise of political liberty under the Old Regime, ultimately sacrificed liberty when **Napoleon Bonaparte** came to power in order to preserve legal equality. Political liberty would remain an elusive ideal for French republicans throughout the 19th and 20th centuries, but the motto "liberty, equality, fraternity" remains still today the best-known symbol of the French Republic, enshrined as it is on all French coins.

LIBERTY TREES. Liberty trees were among the first symbols of the Revolution, and among its most enduring. The earliest reports of the planting of liberty trees date from the autumn of 1789. **Peasants**, hopeful that **seigneurial dues** would be abolished outright following the **Night of 4 August**, rioted in protest in many parts of France, and in the midst of those uprisings often planted, or erected, liberty trees. This symbolic act grew spontaneously out of a traditional peasant custom in the southwest of France, the raising of a maypole at the time of the spring planting. The liberty tree thus borrowed from the maypole the symbolic meaning of fertility, but as a living tree, rather than a dead pole, it also came to connote growth and **regeneration**. The planting of liberty trees became a common feature of revolutionary festivals in 1790, with **National Guards** or municipal officials most often responsible for carrying out the ritual, and played a central role in the **Festival of Federation** on 14 July 1790. By the Year II, the planting of liberty trees was a legislated part of virtually all republican festivals. As a central symbol of the Republic, these trees were to be tall, broad in girth, and long-lived. Oak, linden, fir, ash, and elm were among the varieties most commonly planted. When the symbolism of these trees was expanded to include fraternity, revolutionaries sought to plant trees that were not native to France.

If the planting of liberty trees was a powerful symbol of revolutionary regeneration, it is hardly surprising that the felling of these trees should have emerged as a potent counterrevolutionary symbol. Under the **Terror**, the cutting down of a liberty tree became a capital offense. Eight men died on the **guillotine** in Rouen in September 1793 for having committed that crime. Throughout the 19th century, liberty trees were planted during periods of republican revival, and cut down during times of monarchist restoration. But one can still see in France today liberty trees that were planted in 1790. *See also* LIBERTY, EQUALITY, FRATERNITY.

LINDET, JEAN-BAPTISTE-ROBERT (1746–1825). Robert Lindet is the only member of the "Great" **Committee of Public Safety** to be buried in **Paris**. The son of a prosperous wood merchant in Bernay, in Lower Normandy, Robert studied at the local *collège* and went to study law in Paris. His brother, Thomas, who chose a clerical career, would later join Robert in the **National Convention** and served as Constitutional Bishop of the Eure. Robert Lindet was elected mayor of Bernay in 1790, served on the district council in 1791, and late that year was elected to the **Legislative Assembly** from the Eure, which would also send him to the National Convention. Lindet came to national prominence in November 1792, when he served on, and reported for, the Commission of Twenty-one that drafted the charges against **Louis XVI**. He sat with the **Montagnards**, voting for death in the king's trial, but did not join the **Jacobin club**.

Lindet joined the Committee of Public Safety in April 1793, went on mission that summer to both **Lyon** and **Caen**, where he showed great restraint in his repression of the **federalist revolt**, and devoted considerable energy to matters of food supply and military requisitions. Lindet remained aloof from the political struggles of 1793–94, and was the only member of the Committee to refuse to sign the indictment of **Georges Danton**. Lindet was denounced as a terrorist himself after 9 **Thermidor**, was arrested in May 1795 but amnestied in November. He consistently defended the policies of the Committee of Public Safety, both in speeches and pamphlets, and in 1796 supported the **Conspiracy of Equals** led by **Gracchus Babeuf**. Lindet was acquitted, however, by the High Court of Vendôme, and went on to serve the **Directory** as finance minister. He then refused to support the regime of **Napoleon Bonaparte** and retired to private life.

LOMÉNIE DE BRIENNE, ETIENNE-CHARLES (1727–1794). As the youngest son in a family of the **aristocracy**, Loménie de Brienne chose the traditional route and pursued a career in the Church. He studied theology at the Sorbonne, where his thesis was censured for its liberal views, and was ordained as a priest in 1752. In 1761 Loménie was appointed Bishop of Condom, and two years later was named Archbishop of **Toulouse**. In 1766 he was charged by Louis XV to investigate the decadence of monastic orders, and he produced a very critical report. Twenty-one years later, **Louis XVI** named him his minister of finance, after Loménie had helped to engineer the ousting of his predecessor, **Charles-Alexandre Calonne**. Loménie oversaw the second **Assembly of Notables**, to which he presented a fiscal reform plan not unlike that of Calonne. The aristocrats refused to accept it, however, forcing the convocation of the **Estates-General**. With the treasury teetering on the edge of bankruptcy in August 1788, Loménie decided to suspend certain payments, which led to his own sacking and the recall of **Jacques Necker**.

Loménie was then named Archbishop of Sens and was rewarded for his service to the crown by being named a cardinal in December 1788. In early 1791 he swore the **civil oath of the clergy**, one of the few bishops to do so, and was then elected Constitutional Bishop of the Yonne. In February 1792 **Pope Pius VI** condemned him for swearing the oath, and Loménie resigned his archbishopric and returned his cardinal's cap. He then retired to private life, but came under suspicion early in the **Terror** and was placed under house arrest on 9 November 1793. Three months later he died of apoplexy, in the arms of his brother.

LOUIS XVI (1754–1793). Louis XVI was the grandson of Louis XV. In 1770 he married an Austrian princess, **Marie Antoinette**, and in 1774 was crowned King of France in the cathedral at Reims. The failure of the royal couple to have a child for seven years, accompanied by the frivolous and sometimes scandalous behavior of Marie Antoinette, fed public rumors of the king's impotence and weakness of character. Historical assessment of Louis XVI's effectiveness in the final decade of the Old Regime has diverged widely. Some have praised his efforts at reform, pointing to his appointment of men such as Anne-Robert-Jacques Turgot and **Jacques Necker** to important ministries. But others, while acknowledging his good intentions, characterize him as a man of limited abilities who rarely left the palace at **Versailles** to observe the problems of his kingdom. Whatever one's view of Louis XVI's leadership prior to 1789, there can be little doubt that once the crisis of the Revolution had erupted, he failed to act in a decisive and resolute manner.

The decision to call the **Estates-General** was a bold move, but it unleashed forces that the king had not anticipated. He did not manage well the opening of the meeting, and when the **Third Estate** announced the declaration of a National Assembly, the king moved to obstruct their initiative, first by calling troops to the environs of **Paris** and then by dismissing Necker from office. The fall of the **Bastille** on 14 July 1789 thwarted those efforts and forced the recall of Necker, but the king squandered the good will earned by that decision when he refused to sign both the **Declaration of the Rights of Man and Citizen** and the decrees issued following the **Night of 4 August 1789**. Urged by his advisers to be resolute in the face of the **October Days**, Louis and his family instead returned with the crowd to Paris.

The king's willingness to participate in the **Festival of Federation** on 14 July 1790 seemingly returned him to the good graces of his people. But Louis XVI was uncomfortable in the role of constitutional monarch, and his strong faith made him unwilling at first to accept the **Civil Constitution of the Clergy**. When he fled to **Varennes** with his family on 21 June 1791, he left behind a note expressing dismay at the constraints on his power and denouncing in particular the excessive influence of the **Jacobin club**. Only with reluctance did he sign the **Constitution of 1791** later that summer.

It seems clear that Louis XVI had fled toward the eastern border with the intention of allying with the *émigré* forces gathering in the German states, and in the year following that failed escape, his refusal to deal forcefully with the *émigrés* earned him growing suspicion and denunciation. He was similarly reluctant to support harsh measures against **refractory priests**. Urged on by Marie Antoinette and her advisers, Louis declared war on Austria in April 1792, perhaps hopeful that the other monarchs of Europe might defeat the Revolution where he had failed. The war went badly, of course, but ultimately it brought about the fall of the monarchy, on 10 August 1792, and the declaration of a republic. The discovery of a hidden safe in the **Tuileries** Palace revealed the king's correspondence with the other monarchs and sealed his fate. The dignity with which he carried himself at his trial and at his execution earned for him a respect in death that he had not enjoyed in life. Some 80,000 **National Guards** lined the streets of Paris when he marched to the **guillotine** on 21 January 1793.

LOUIS XVII (1785–1795). Louis-Charles was the second son of **Louis XVI** and **Marie Antoinette** and became dauphin in June 1789 on the death of his older brother. The king took an active role in the **education** of Louis-Charles, who underwent a number of traumatic experiences in his youth, including the **October Days**, the flight to **Varennes**, and the **uprising of 10 August 1792**. In the months after the fall of the monarchy, Louis XVI tutored his young son personally during the family's incarceration in the Temple. After Louis XVI's execution, the comte de **Provence** declared the dauphin Louis XVII, naming himself regent.

Louis XVII's fate became a matter of debate and controversy in the two years following his father's death. In the months leading up to the trial of Marie Antoinette, **Jacques-René Hébert** interviewed the young boy and coerced him into signing a statement alleging an incestuous relationship with his mother, evidence that was introduced at the queen's trial. Louis-Charles was a sickly child by this time—some have asserted that this was due to ill treatment at the hands of his guardian, the shoemaker Simon. Several European monarchies petitioned the French government for the child's exile, but the deputies of the **National Convention** feared that Louis XVII in exile would become a rallying figure for *émigré* royalists, and refused to release him. Louis XVII died of scrofula on 8 June 1795. Myths of his escape inspired a number of pretenders to the throne to step forward in the early 19th century.

LOUIS XVIII. *See* PROVENCE, LOUIS-STANISLAS-XAVIER.

LOUVET, JEAN-BAPTISTE (1760–1797). Louvet's father was a stationer with a shop on the rue Saint-Denis in **Paris**. His **education** was incomplete, but he took an early job as a clerk in a bookstore and there fell in love with literature. In 1790 he published *Aventures du chevalier de Faublas*, a sentimental novel that was a huge success and established his reputation. With the outbreak of the Revolution, Louvet became an activist in the Lombards section of Paris and joined the **Jacobin club**. He turned his writing talent to social and political topics, with a pamphlet defending the **October Days** and a second novel advocating divorce and the marriage of priests. In March 1792 he began to publish *La Sentinelle*, a **Girondin** newspaper with financial backing from **Jean-Marie Roland**. Louvet was elected to the **National Convention** from the Loiret, and on 29 October 1792, delivered a famous speech against **Maximilien Robespierre**, whom he charged with responsibility for the **September Massacres**. This speech established many of the battle lines for the ongoing struggle between Girondin and **Montagnard** deputies.

Louvet voted for the death of **Louis XVI**, but also favored the *appel au peuple* to decide his fate. He was among the 29 deputies proscribed from the National Convention on 2 June 1793. He fled first to **Caen**, then to **Bordeaux**, trying to encourage provincial resistance to Paris. Louvet managed to elude arrest throughout the **Terror**, even though, as a point of honor, he refused to emigrate. After 9 **Thermidor** Louvet returned to the Convention, but did not join other Girondin deputies in their reactionary politics of vengeance. He continued to defend the Republic, both as a deputy to the Convention and then to the **Council of Five Hundred**, and in the pages of his **newspaper**. Louvet's ardent, though moderate, republicanism made him a target for the *jeunesse dorée*, who sacked his bookstore in the **Palais Royal**. He left the Council of Five Hundred in May 1797, fell ill shortly thereafter and died in August. His wife, Lodoiska (she took her name from the heroine in Louvet's first novel whose character she inspired), poisoned herself out of grief, but survived and lived on until 1824.

LYON. Lyon was the second largest city in France in 1789, with approximately 140,000 inhabitants. The city had prospered and grown through most of the 18th century, largely on the basis of its silk industry, but the last quarter of the century brought decline and the 1786 trade treaty with England dealt a serious blow to the Lyonnais economy. An air of malaise and social tension hung over the city as the Revolution began.

There was violence in Lyon in 1789–90, as patriots clashed with royalists over control of the local militia and access to arms. Although there was a substantial merchant class in the city, they were not active politically, leaving control of local administration to the **aristocracy**. The proximity of Lyon to the German and Swiss borders, plus the size of the city and its complicated urban geography, made it a haven for *émigrés* as the Revolution progressed. In contrast to **Marseille**, its sister on the Rhône River, Lyon developed an early reputation for hatching **counterrevolutionary** plots.

The city also generated a vibrant popular movement, however, and a network of **popular societies** appeared in 1790. **Jean-Marie Roland** and **Joseph Chalier** both figured prominently in the revolutionary politics of Lyon in 1790–91. Violence erupted in the city following the **September Massacres** of 1792, and local **Jacobins** gained control of the municipal council in the elections that followed. Lyon moderates mobilized their supporters through **section assemblies** in the spring of 1793 and regained control of the city in late May, just as the **Montagnards** were ousting the **Girondin** leaders from the **National Convention** in **Paris**. At odds with the current in national politics, the Lyonnais threw their support behind the **federalist revolt**. Republican troops laid siege to the city in August, finally defeating the rebels in October 1793.

Declaring that "Lyon is no more," the **Committee of Public Safety** sent **representatives on mission** and a **revolutionary army** from Paris to carry out the punishment of those who had joined the revolt. **Jean-Marie Collot d'Herbois** and **Joseph Fouché** oversaw the imposition of the **Terror** in Lyon. Despite an order that the homes of all wealthy merchants and aristocrats be razed, relatively little destruction of property was carried out, though the city had certainly suffered physical damage during the siege. But between October 1793 and March 1794, nearly 1,900 Lyonnais were executed. So many were condemned to death that the **guillotine** was not equal to the task. Hundreds died by grapeshot fired from cannons. Royalists and moderates would take their revenge in July 1795, under the **White Terror**, killing dozens of Jacobins in a prison massacre.

– M –

MAILHE AMENDMENT. Jean-Baptiste Mailhe was the first deputy to vote in the **National Convention** in the roll-call on the fate of **Louis XVI**. Mailhe, a deputy from **Toulouse**, voted for the death of the king, but proposed that if this should be the will of the majority, the Convention should consider postponing the date of execution, so that the issue might be revisited. This came to be known as the Mailhe amendment, viewed by most as an effort to save the king through a variation of the *appel au peuple*, a motion already defeated. Only 26 deputies voted for the Mailhe amendment, although they included four leaders of the **Girondins**: **François-Nicolas Buzot**, **Pierre-Victurnien Vergniaud**, **Marguerite-Elie Guadet**, and **Jérome Pétion**. Some accused Mailhe of being in the pay of the Spanish, and **Maximilien Robespierre** called him "the most immoral of men." Mailhe laid low during the **Terror**, but was an active **Thermidorian** after the fall of Robespierre.

MALLET DU PAN, JACQUES (1749–1800). Mallet du Pan's father was a **Protestant** pastor in Switzerland, his grandfather a merchant. Jacques studied law and philosophy in Geneva and was drawn to the ideas of the **Enlightenment**. His first work, *Compte-rendu de la défense des citoyens bourgeois de Genève par un natif*, was denounced by the authorities of Geneva and burned, and this brought Mallet to the attention of **Voltaire**. On his visits to Voltaire's estate at Ferney, Mallet encountered Simon-Nicolas-Henri Linguet and began a collaboration with Linguet on his **newspaper**, *Annales Politiques et Littéraires*. When Linguet was imprisoned in the **Bastille** in 1781, Mallet took over publication of the *Annales* until 1788. From 1783 on, he also collaborated with **Charles-Joseph Pancoucke** on the *Mercure de France*, and edited the *Journal Historique et Politique de Genève* as well.

Mallet remained in **Paris** during the early years of the Revolution, working as a political journalist. From the opening of the **Estates-General** he supported the monarchist party, even though in Geneva he had expressed republican ideals. He was particularly close to **Pierre-Victor Malouet** and **Jean-Joseph Mounier**, and was associated with the founding of the **Monarchist club** in Paris. In April 1792 Mallet emigrated to Coblenz, entrusted by **Louis XVI** with a message to the *émigrés*, as well as to the kings of Austria and Prussia, exhorting them not to open hostilities with France except as a last resort. In subsequent years, he served as an agent/informer for the monarchs, traveling to London, Brussels, and Switzerland. In 1793 he published *Considérations sur la nature de la révolution en France*, in which he advocated a constitutional monarchy for France, much to the displeasure of the *émigrés*, who sought the restoration of the absolute monarchy. When France annexed Geneva in April 1798, Mallet was banished. He moved to London, where he published *Le Mercure Bri-*

tannique, modeled on *Le Mercure de France*. He was among the first political journalists to foresee the role that **Napoleon Bonaparte** would play. Mallet du Pan died of tuberculosis in England in 1800.

MALOUET, PIERRE-VICTOR (1740–1814). Malouet was among the most influential of the constitutional monarchists in the early years of the Revolution. He was the son of a notary and *procureur du roi* in Riom, at the heart of the *Massif Central*, but his father was not a wealthy man. Victor would marry the daughter of a rich plantation owner in **Saint-Domingue** in 1770, and this was the source of his personal wealth. He was educated at the *collège* of the Oratoriens at Juilly, and went on to study law in **Paris**. Between 1763 and 1788, Malouet held a variety of posts in royal administration, mostly having to do with the navy and overseas colonies. From 1767 to 1774, he was posted to Saint-Domingue. Out of his reflections on the conditions of black **slaves** emerged a short book, *Mémoire sur l'esclavage des nègres* (1788), in which he drew on John Locke's *Treatise on Civil Government* to justify their status while making a case for improved treatment of slaves. In 1789 he joined the **Massiac Club**, and opposed the **Society of the Friends of Blacks**. Upon returning to Paris in 1774, Malouet frequented the **salons**, making the acquaintance of such luminaries as Denis Diderot, Jean le Rond d'Alembert, and **Marie-Jean Condorcet**. In 1776 he was sent to Guyana for two years, and between 1781 and 1788 served as Naval Intendant in **Toulon**. During those years he came to know **Jacques Necker** well, and advised **Louis XVI** against intervention in the American War of Independence.

In early 1789 Malouet returned to Riom bearing a 14-page model *cahier de doléance*, which circulated widely in the Auvergne. Already at this point Malouet was counseling moderation, fearing the upheaval and anarchy that lay ahead. He was elected by acclamation the first delegate of the **Third Estate** of Riom to the **Estates-General**. Malouet was among the 50 most active orators in the **Constituent Assembly**, but his close association with royal administration, and his advocacy of a bicameral legislature on the English model, made him unpopular with the majority of his colleagues. He signed the **Tennis Court Oath** only with reluctance, and argued that a **Declaration of the Rights of Man and Citizen**, while well suited to the United

States, would not work well in France. Along with **Jean-Joseph Mounier**, Malouet organized a group of deputies on the right of the Assembly to devise a shared political strategy, and in November 1790 he would join with **Stanislas Clermont-Tonnerre** to form the **Impartials**, a group that would eventually become the **Monarchist club**, formed in an effort to counter the influence of the **Jacobin club**. From July 1791 until 10 August 1792, Malouet served in the king's Privy Council. Malouet recognized that his was a minority position within the Constituent Assembly, though he lamented that fact, and as the Assembly dissolved in 1791 he called for an end to the Revolution.

Malouet emigrated to England following the **uprising of 10 August 1792**, but would return to France in 1801 to serve as a commissioner for the Navy. He served **Napoleon Bonaparte** at various posts in naval administration until the emperor dismissed him in 1812 for advising against the Russian campaign. Prior to that, Malouet had been recognized as a Knight of the Legion of Honor (1805), as a Baron of the Empire (1810), and as a Commander of the Legion of Honor (1811).

MARAT, JEAN-PAUL (1743–1793). The "Friend of the People" was born in Switzerland, to a Sardinian father and a French mother who had converted to **Protestantism**. Marat attended *collège* in Neuchâtel, and then went on to study medicine in **Toulouse**, **Bordeaux**, **Paris**, and finally in Scotland, where he earned his diploma in 1774. In that same year he published his first political work, *The Chains of Slavery*, in which he denounced royal and ministerial despotism and argued for the legitimacy of violent insurrection so that the people might escape their **slavery**. The following year he published *A Philosophical Essay on Man*, which drew a sarcastic critique from **Voltaire**.

After practicing medicine in Holland and England, Marat returned to France in 1776 to take a position as doctor to the bodyguards of the Count of Artois. His philosophy having been scorned by Voltaire, he now had his experiments in optical physics rejected by the **Academy** of Science, adding to his feeling of personal resentment. Marat lost his position with Artois in 1784 and led a precarious existence until 1789, when he plunged into the world of politics and revolutionary ideas. In September 1789 he began publication of *L'Ami du Peuple*, the **newspaper** that he would write single-handedly over the next four years. The paper was enormously popular with the people of Paris, because Marat wrote constantly of scandals, schemers, and conspiracies against the common good. He attacked not only the king and his ministers, but also the deputies of the **Constituent Assembly**. After the **October Days**, Marat was forced into hiding and the paper went unpublished for two months, not for the last time. He disappeared again in early 1790. After the flight to **Varennes**, which he had predicted, and his support for the petition against **Louis XVI**, which led to the **Champ de Mars massacre**, Marat fled to England. *L'Ami du Peuple* did not reappear until April 1792, supported now by the **Cordelier club**. Marat helped fuel the popular movement building up to the **uprising of 10 August 1792**, and was widely blamed for causing the **September Massacres**, which he defended in the aftermath, calling for their imitation in the provinces.

Marat was elected to the **National Convention** from Paris. He sat in the highest seats of the Convention, among the **Montagnards**, always wearing distinctive garb and keeping to himself. He voted for death in the trial of Louis XVI, and against the *appel au peuple*. Even the most radical deputies objected to his violent rhetoric, his brutal frankness, his constant tirade against moderates and hidden traitors, but the treason of **Charles Dumouriez** in March 1793 carried his popularity in Paris to its pinnacle. Marat was reviled in the provinces, however, and when he published an appeal to the people of Paris on 12 April to arm themselves against the National Convention, the **Girondin** deputies initiated a decree of accusation against him. On 24 April the **Revolutionary Tribunal** acquitted him and the **sans-culottes** of Paris escorted him triumphantly back to the Convention's meeting hall. Marat now mounted a campaign against the Girondins in his newspaper, contributing to their proscription on 2 June 1793.

Marat had long suffered from a skin disease, contracted years before in England and exacerbated, no doubt, by the weeks and months of hiding in the sewers of Paris. He often took baths to ease the discomfort, and it was in his bath that **Charlotte Corday** stabbed him to death on 13 July 1793. Immortalized in death by the painting of **Jacques-Louis David**, Marat became the second martyr of the Revolution, after **Michel Le Peletier**, soon to be joined by **Joseph Chalier** of **Lyon**. It is impossible to gauge the impact of Corday's deed on the subsequent course of the Revolution.

MARÉCHAL, PIERRE-SYLVAIN (1750–1803). Little is known of the early life of Sylvain Maréchal, but by the early 1780s he had attracted a modest following for his light poetry, published under the pen name of Berger Sylvain, and was employed as a librarian's assistant at the *collège* Mazarin in **Paris**. But in 1784 he scandalized the school by publishing a parody of the Bible, *Livre échappé au Déluge*, and lost his position. Four years later another satirical work, *Almanach des Honnêtes gens*, was burned on order of the **Parlement of Paris**, and Maréchal spent four months in the Saint-Lazare prison.

Maréchal threw himself into Parisian politics after 1789 and quickly fell in with **Camille Desmoulins**, **Georges Danton**, and **Louis-Stanislas Fréron**. When Elysée Loustalot died in September 1790, Maréchal took over the editing of *Les Révolutions de Paris*, published by **Louis-Marie Prudhomme**. Maréchal held egalitarian social ideas, and continued to write independently through the decade. In 1793 he published *Correctif à la Révolution*, which proposed a communitarian ideal, and after **Thermidor** he published *Tableau Historique des événements révolutionnaires*, a catalogue of the crimes of the Revolution, which Maréchal claimed had profited only the **bourgeoisie**. Despite his atheism, he wrote a *Hymne à l'Etre suprême* for **Maximilien Robespierre**, and also collaborated on an opera with **André Grétry**. In 1795 his socialist ideals led Maréchal to join **Gracchus Babeuf's** conspiracy, and he wrote substantial portions of the *Manifesto of Equals*, which stands as his most important contribution to the Revolution. Maréchal was neither arrested nor indicted for his involvement in the conspiracy, however, and lived quietly thereafter. His last literary effort was a *Dictionnaire des athées*.

MARIANNE. Very early in the Revolution, a female figure emerged as the most prominent symbol of liberty, an allusion on the one hand to the virtues of classical antiquity, and on the other to the Christian virtues of Mary, mother of Christ. The fall of the monarchy on 10 August 1792 rendered the old royal symbols nul and void and cleared the way for Liberty to take her place as the central symbol of the Republic. Often she appeared as a goddess-like figure, seated in dignified fashion and garbed in a flowing robe. At other times, as France was at war, she appeared as a more militant figure—dressed in short tunic, often with one breast bared, sporting a **phrygian cap** on her head or atop the spear she carried.

The name "Marianne," coined by those who opposed the Revolution, initially had a pejorative meaning: as Marie-Anne was among the most popular female names in France in the 18th century, to call the Republic Marianne was to characterize it as little better than a **peasant**, or more derisively, as a common whore. But just as with the term "**sans-culotte**," which also had negative connotations, patriots soon adopted Marianne with pride as the sobriquet for the female symbol of the Republic.

Marianne was not unchallenged as a symbol of the Republic. In the midst of the **federalist revolt**, and through the period of the **Terror** that followed, the **Montagnards** proposed **Hercules** as a more virile and powerful symbol than Marianne, and therefore more capable of vanquishing the enemies of the Republic. Hercules did not endure, however, and Marianne reemerged after **Thermidor** as the most prominent Republican symbol. **Napoleon Bonaparte** retained a female symbol when he first came to power as first consul, but dropped Marianne completely with the declaration of the Empire in 1804. Marianne reappeared in 1848, and again in 1870, and remains today the most important symbol of the French republic, portrayed on postage stamps by a series of famous actresses. *See also* LIBERTY, EQUALITY, FRATERNITY.

MARIE ANTOINETTE (1755–1793). Marie Antoinette was the youngest daughter of Emperor Francis I and Empress Maria-Theresa of Austria. She married the young **Louis XVI** in 1770 and became Queen of France at the age of 19. Marie Antoinette was never a popular queen among the French. She was noted for her frivolous tastes from the time of her arrival at **Versailles**, and her fondness for games, for entertainments, and for night life gave rise to rumors and stories, some quite scandalous, which eventually spread beyond court circles to the lower levels of literate society in **Paris**. Marie's lack of appreciation for the niceties of courtly etiquette offended the king's brothers, who joined in spreading calumnies about her. The **Diamond Necklace Affair** of 1785 turned the French public bitterly and permanently against her, even though she was entirely innocent of any indiscretion in this instance.

The rumors and public antipathy toward the queen were fed by stories of the king's impotence and the failure of the royal couple to produce an heir until 1781. The first dauphin died in June 1789, leading to a short period of national sympathy, but reports that Marie had urged Louis XVI to sack **Jacques Necker** in July made her once again the target of public abuse, most notably in the **women's** march to Versailles during the **October Days**. In June 1791 she plotted the flight to **Varennes** with **Axel von Fersen**, and urged the king to declare war in 1792 in the hope that Austrian troops would defeat the revolutionary government. She was separated from Louis XVI and their children not long after the **uprising of 10 August 1792** and incarcerated in the **Conciergerie**, where she remained until October 1793. Marie Antoinette defended herself with pride and dignity at her trial, even when **Jacques Hébert** and **Pierre Chaumette** had the audacity to accuse her of incest with her son. She was convicted of treason and went to the **guillotine** on 16 October, her dignity and scorn for the revolutionaries captured in a final sketch by **Jacques-Louis David**.

MARSEILLE. Marseille, with its population of 120,000 people, was the third largest city in France on the eve of the Revolution, after **Paris** and **Lyon**. Located at the mouth of the Rhône River, it was the most important of France's Mediterranean ports. Commercial trade and shipbuilding were the lifeblood of the city, but there was a growing manufacturing sector in the city as well.

Although there was no **municipal revolution** in Marseille in 1789, the city did witness early protests and the Marseillais were proud of their revolutionary patriotism. In the summer of 1790, protesters seized control of the two "bastilles" of Marseille, the forts of Saint-Jean and Saint-Nicolas. Patriots in Marseille expressed their disappointment with the deputies of the **Constituent Assembly**, who chose to assign the departmental *chef-lieu* to Aix-en-Provence rather than their fair city, a mistake that the local Jacobins would eventually rectify. The **Jacobin club** of Marseille regularly sent expeditions to neighboring towns and villages, garnering for the city a reputation for radicalism. In the summer of 1792 that reputation was confirmed, when **Charles-Jean-Marie Barbaroux** summoned several hundred Marseille **National Guards** to the capital. En route, the soldiers learned a new marching song, destined to become famous as the revolutionary anthem, the *Marseillaise*. The Marseille volunteers also played a key role in the storming of the **Tuileries** Palace on 10 August 1792.

The political scene polarized in Marseille in 1792–93. Elections in the fall of 1792 brought Jacobins to power on the municipal council, while moderates retained control of the **departmental administration**. A number of wealthy merchants and **aristocrats** chose to emigrate in this period. Others began to mobilize their supporters in **section assemblies**, and in spring 1793 the Jacobins were ousted from the municipal council and the club was shut down. After the proscription of the **Girondin** leaders from the **National Convention** on 2 June 1793, the new municipal authorities guided the city toward support of the **federalist revolt**. This rebellion against the national government cost Marseille dearly. Republican troops entered the city in late August 1793, and in the months that followed a series of **representatives on mission** oversaw the imposition of the **Terror** in Marseille. More than 400 people went to the **guillotine** in Marseille, the majority of them convicted of the crime of **federalism**.

The Marseillais never fully succeeded in reclaiming their reputation for revolutionary fervor, as the political polarization that emerged in 1792–93 persisted through the years thereafter. **Thermidor** brought reprisals against local Jacobins who had supported the Terror, and in the aftermath of the **Fructidor coup** in 1797 those Jacobins who survived took their revenge against the local **Thermidorians**. In this the lyrics of the *Marseillaise*, which has endured to this day as the French national anthem, can be said to be quite accurate: revolutionary politics can be both contentious and violent.

MARSEILLAISE. The French national anthem that we know today as the *Marseillaise* was composed in April 1792 by **Claude-Joseph Rouget de Lisle**, a young captain in the army garrisoned in Strasbourg, near the eastern border. The day after the **Legislative Assembly** declared war on Austria, 20 April 1792, the mayor of Strasbourg hosted a dinner party, at which there was much patriotic conversation. Rouget de Lisle returned to his quarters and composed the words and music to what he called *Chant de Guerre de l'Armée du Rhin*. Later that summer the volunteers from **Marseille** made it their marching song en route to **Paris**, and it soon became known in the clubs of the capital as the *Marseillaise*. The **National Convention** made it the official national song by decree on 14 July 1795, but the **Directory** was less enthusiastic about it and it gradually faded from prominence. Not until 1879 was it again embraced as the national anthem of France, and in the years since its revolutionary ardor has at times thrown it out of favor, as during the Vichy period. As recently as the Bicentennial of 1989 there was national debate about the appropriateness of some of the song's more violent lyrics.

MASSIAC CLUB. The Massiac Club formed in August 1789, during the debates over the **Declaration of the Rights of Man and Citizen**, as an adversary to the **Society of the Friends of Blacks**. Supported by the deputies **Alexandre Lameth**, **Antoine-Pierre Barnave**, and **Pierre-Victor Malouet**, the club successfully opposed the granting of citizenship to blacks in the colonies by citing the importance of the slave trade to French commerce in the West Indies. The influence of the club declined, however, after the **Constituent Assembly** disbanded. Shortly after the **National Convention** abolished **slavery**, in February 1794, it also closed down the Massiac Club.

MAURY, JEAN-SIFFREIN (1746–1817). Maury was the son of a shoemaker in the small town of Valréas in the Dauphiné. His grandfather was a **Protestant**, but the family converted to Catholicism in 1685 at the time of the Revocation of the Edict of Nantes. Jean attended *collège* in Valréas and went on to seminary in Avignon. He was ordained as a priest in 1769, and in the following decade established a considerable reputation both within the Church and in the intellectual circles of **Paris**. In 1772 he published a short work, *Réflexions sur les sermons nouveaux de M. Bossuet*, and his 1777 *Essai sur l'éloquence* eventually won him election to the French **Academy**.

In 1789 Maury was elected to the **Estates-General** by the **clergy** of Péronne, near Amiens. Although he served on few committees, he was among the most frequent orators in the **Constituent Assembly**, and was known for his erudition and eloquence. In his speeches he emphasized the importance of history and tradition, and made reference to the English experience in constitutional matters. Maury opposed the unification of the three estates, and argued strongly in favor of an absolute veto for the king. He opposed the sale of Church lands, favored the declaration of Catholicism as the official state religion, and opposed the **Civil Constitution of the Clergy**. Maury believed that 4 August 1789 represented the triumph of license over liberty, and in June 1790 he struggled valiantly against the decree abolishing noble titles.

Maury emigrated following the dissolution of the Constituent Assembly, eventually making his way to Rome, where in 1794 **Pope Pius VI** named him a cardinal. He served as a representative of **Louis XVIII** at the Vatican for some years, but in 1804 he sent a letter of congratulation to **Napoleon Bonaparte**, and in 1806 returned to France. In 1810 Maury was named Archbishop of Paris by Imperial decree, much to the displeasure of the pope, and in 1814 Napoleon named him a Count of the Empire. Maury appealed to both king and pope for a pardon after the fall of Napoleon, but was exiled from France and briefly imprisoned in Rome. He died in a Lazarist monastery in Rome in 1817.

MAXIMUM. The *maximum* is a general term referring to a range of price controls imposed in 1793–94 by the **National Convention**. The common people of France were traditionally suspicious of free trade, as shown by the Flour Wars that erupted in the region around **Paris** in 1775 when Louis XV's minister of finance, Anne-Robert-Jacques Turgot, introduced free trade in grain. The deputies of the National Convention, particularly the **Girondins**, were largely opposed to price controls, but in the face of increasing prices and food shortages, and under intense pressure from the **sans-culottes** of Paris, they passed legislation on 4 May 1793 establishing the first *maximum*, which applied solely to wheat and flour. *Maximum* prices for each were to be established locally, by **departmental administrations**, and the regional variation in prices that resulted stood as an open invitation to smuggling and hoarding. The **federalist revolt** also interfered with enforcement of the first *maximum*.

Economic and political uncertainty brought inflation and a persistent decline in the value of the *assignats*, which reached their lowest mark of 22 percent of face value in late summer 1793. Spurred on by the *enragés*, and by news of the fall of **Toulon** to the British, Parisian sans-culottes took to the streets in massive demonstrations on 4–5

September 1793, and this forced the National Convention to pass a general *maximum* on 29 September. This legislation extended price controls to all grains and many staple goods. The ***armées révolutionnaires*** were dispatched to the countryside, often accompanied by an ambulatory **guillotine**, to requisition grain and enforce the price controls. On 24 February 1794 (6 Ventôse II) the Convention passed a final revision of the *maximum*, introducing greater national uniformity to the price controls and their enforcement. All of these measures taken together, often referred to as the economic **Terror**, did succeed in keeping urban markets reasonably well supplied and in controlling inflation, but they encountered considerable opposition all the same.

After the fall of **Maximilien Robespierre**, the **Thermidorians** dismantled the economic legislation of the **Montagnards** and by December 1794 all price controls had been removed. The value of the *assignats* plummeted once again and prices rose dramatically. The abolition of the *maximum* took a heavy toll among the sans-culottes in the following months, the legendary winter of *nonante cinq*, as thousands died of bitter cold and starvation.

MERCIER, LOUIS-SEBASTIÉN (1740–1814). Mercier was born into an artisanal family—his father was an arms furbisher in **Paris**, his mother the daughter of a mason. Louis-Sébastien studied at the *collège* Quatre-Nations, and spent time at the café Procope as a youth. In the 1760s he moved to **Bordeaux**, where he taught rhetoric. His ambition was to be a writer, however, and he championed prose over poetry among his fellow writers. Mercier was a failed playwright, went to study law in Reims for a time (so that he could sue the theaters that had refused to stage his plays!), but achieved literary success in 1770 with *L'an 2440, rêve s'il en fut jamais*, the most popular utopian novel of the late 18th century in France. 1781 marked the anonymous publication of the first two volumes of his masterpiece, *Tableau de Paris*. His identity as author was soon revealed, however, and Mercier fled to Switzerland when the work was banned by the **Parlement of Paris**. The *Tableau*, eventually to reach 12 volumes, was an eloquent description of Parisian society at the end of the Old Regime in all of its aspects, and was credited by **Jacques-Pierre Brissot** with hastening the onset of the Revolution.

Mercier returned to Paris in 1788, and collaborated briefly with **Jean-Louis Carra** on *Les Annales Patriotiques*. He was an active member of the **Cercle Social**, and contributed to a number of **Girondin** newspapers. In 1792 he was elected from the Seine-et-Oise to the **National Convention**, where he sat with the Girondins, alienated from the **Montagnards**, perhaps, by the fact that he had not been elected from the city that he loved so much. Mercier voted for imprisonment in the trial of **Louis XVI**, and against the *appel au peuple*. In April 1793 he supported the indictment of **Jean-Paul Marat**. Because he signed a letter protesting the proscription of the Girondin deputies, Mercier was himself excluded from the Convention in July, and arrested in October 1793. He remained in prison until the end of the year, resumed his seat in the Convention upon his release, and in 1795 was elected to the **Council of Five Hundred** from the department of the Nord. In that same year he became one of the original members of the **Institut National**, and in 1797 was appointed professor of history at the Ecole Polytechnique. Mercier used those academic posts to attack Copernican science, insisting that the earth was flat and that the sun circled around it. In 1798 he published *Le Nouveau Paris*, six volumes looking back over the Revolution as he had witnessed and experienced it, with interesting observations on the evolution of revolutionary language as well. Mercier detested **Napoleon Bonaparte**, and after 1804 his fondest stated wish was to live to see the fall of the Empire, an ambition that he barely managed to achieve.

MERLIN, PHILIPPE (1754–1838). Born into a family with substantial landholdings in the north of France, Merlin took a degree in law and in 1775 became an *avocat* at the **Parlement** of Flanders. He was elected to the **Estates-General** as a deputy for the **Third Estate** of Douai, and played a substantial role in the drafting of legislation abolishing seigneurial **privilege**. After the **Constituent Assembly**, he became president of the Criminal Tribunal of the Nord, and that department elected him to the **National Convention**. Merlin sat with the **Plain**, but voted with the **Montagnards** in the trial of **Louis XVI**. After 9 **Thermidor**, he served on the **Committee of Public Safety**, ordered the closing of the **Jacobin club** in November 1794, and worked to rehabilitate the ex-**Girondins** in that same year. Merlin advocated the enactment of the **Constitution of 1793** and refused to participate on the committee drafting a new constitution in 1795. Under the **Directory**, Merlin served as minister of justice, minister of police, and director, always taking a centrist, republican position. He was known as a tireless worker and was a celebrated jurist, playing a substantial role in drafting the Napoleonic Code. For that service **Napoleon Bonaparte** recognized Merlin as a Chevalier of the Empire, Count of the Empire, member of the Legion of Honor, and member of the **Institut National**. He was exiled in 1816 as a regicide, and returned to **Paris** from Holland in 1830.

METRIC SYSTEM. In 1790 the **Constituent Assembly** asked the **Academy** of Sciences to name a commission to replace the inconsistent and complicated collection of weights and measures that prevailed under the Old Regime with a more rational decimal system, based in nature. The result was the metric system. **Adrien-Marie Legendre** took a leading role in the project, which took some years to complete. The commission determined, for example, that the common unit of length (what became the meter) should equal one ten-millionth of the quadrant of the circumference of the earth, and so a team set out to measure the quadrant that ran from Dunkirk to Barcelona, passing through **Paris**. The *Agence temporaire des poids et mesures* presented its report to the **National Convention** in April 1795, and the metric system was adopted. The measurement of the meter has been made more precise in the years since, and in most countries of the world (the United States being a notable exception) the metric system is today the standard by which all distances, weights, and liquid volumes are measured.

MIRABEAU, GABRIEL-HONORÉ-RIQUETI (1749–1791). Few men were more influential during the first year of the Revolution than Count Gabriel-Honoré Mirabeau. He was born into a distinguished family of Provence, its noble lineage extending back to the 16th century. His father, Victor the 4th Marquis of Mirabeau, was a physiocrat and celebrated author in his own right. He despised his son, to whom he never gave a penny. Indeed, the Marquis had his son imprisoned on several occasions. Mirabeau was a brilliant but undisciplined student. In 1766 he joined the Berry cavalry regiment and participated in the Corsican campaign. He was presented at **Versailles** in 1771, only to be forbidden from court three years later by a *lettre de cachet*. In 1775 he published *Essai sur le despotisme* in London, a polemic that was probably directed as much at his father as at the monarchy. From 1777 to 1780 he was imprisoned at Vincennes, having been accused of seducing the young wife of the Marquis de Monnier, an offense for which he was sentenced to death. Mirabeau eluded that sentence and went abroad, working for a time as a publicist in Neufchâtel before returning to England, where he met **Jacques Brissot**. While in London he was commissioned by Benjamin Franklin to write *Considérations sur l'ordre de Cincinnatus* (1784), an essay against the idea of creating an American **aristocracy**. Mirabeau returned to France in 1785, but fled again in 1787 after publishing a long pamphlet critical of **Charles-Alexandre Calonne** and the first **Assembly of Notables**. He went to Berlin, where he completed an eight-volume history of the Prussian monarchy.

Mirabeau was intimately involved in the political ferment at the end of the Old Regime. He was a member of the **Society of Thirty** and among the founders of the **Society of the Friends of Blacks**. Mirabeau was rejected by the nobility of Provence in 1789, but waged an active campaign to secure election by the **Third Estate** of Aix-en-Provence as a deputy to the **Estates-General**. He was a dominant figure in the Estates-General from the outset. He urged the deputies of the Third Estate to pursue a stalling strategy, which they did, and worked actively for the declaration of a National Assembly. He swore the **Tennis Court Oath**, and in the Royal session of 23 June he uttered what is perhaps his most famous line. Confronting the royal master of ceremonies, the Marquis de Dreux-Brézé, Mirabeau is reported to have said, "Go tell those who have sent you that we are here by the will of the people, and shall not leave except by the force of bayonets."

Mirabeau served on five committees and was among the most active orators in the **Constituent Assembly**. On 14 July 1789, while Parisians stormed the **Bastille**, Mirabeau attended the funeral of his father, free at last from paternal despotism. In August he reported to the Assembly for the committee that had drafted the **Declaration of the Rights of Man and Citizen**, though he did not fully support its work. He favored an absolute veto for the king, but would lose that debate. On 26 September 1789 he delivered his most celebrated speech, on the subject of the financial crisis, and this established Mirabeau's reputation as the finest orator of the Assembly. The following month he would be accused of engineering the **October Days**, although no evidence was produced to link him to the uprising. On 15 October he drafted a memorandum to **Louis XVI**, urging the king to leave **Paris**, the only way, in his view, to save the monarchy, but the memo never reached the king. Two days later, Mirabeau met for five hours with **Jacques Necker**, but his efforts here similarly produced no positive effect. Cognizant of his activities, on 7 November the Constituent Assembly passed a decree that no deputy could serve as a minister, thereby thwarting Mirabeau's immediate ambitions.

In the spring of 1790 Louis XVI made an approach to Mirabeau through a third party, and by May it appears that Mirabeau was in the pay of the court. He worked within the Assembly to strengthen the authority of the king within the constitutional monarchy, and in the fall of 1790 he made a play to counter the influence of the **Lameth** brothers in the **Jacobin club**, over which he presided in December. In January 1791 he was elected a battalion commander of the **National Guard** in his district, and was also elected to the **departmental administration** of Paris. His influence in the capital seemed to be growing. But in April he died, suddenly and unexpectedly. The nation, in shock, went into mourning, and Mirabeau's remains were interred in the **Panthéon**. Following the **uprising of 10 August 1792**, however, the discovery of Mirabeau's letters in the king's secret safe ruined his reputation, and on 25 November 1793 the **National Convention** ordered that his remains be removed from the Panthéon.

MOMORO, ANTOINE-FRANÇOIS (1756–1794). Antoine Momoro was born into an old Spanish family that had established itself in the Franche-Comté. Little is known about his youth, but by the 1780s he had taken up residence in **Paris** and was employed in a print shop. In 1789 Momoro embraced the ideals of the Revolution and obtained a contract as the official printer for the **Paris Commune**, henceforth touting himself as *Premier Imprimeur de la liberté*. He was among the leaders of the **Cordelier club**, and as such played an active role in the circulation of the petition against the king that led to the

Champ de Mars massacre. Momoro was arrested thereafter and spent much of August 1791 in the **Conciergerie**. He also participated in the **uprising of 10 August 1792**, and in the fall of that year was elected to the Directory of the department of Paris, with particular responsibility for public festivals. As principal organizer of the **Festival of Reason** in the Year II, Momoro cajoled his wife Sophie, a beautiful actress, into playing the role of the Goddess of Reason. Momoro is often credited with coining the revolutionary motto, "**Liberty, Equality, and Fraternity**," because in 1793 he persuaded the mayor of Paris, **Jean-Nicolas Pache**, to inscribe it on the façade of all public buildings, but others credit **Maximilien Robespierre** with inventing the phrase.

Momoro was an advocate of social equality, and in May 1793 published a pamphlet in support of the **grain *maximum***. He was active in the campaign against the **Girondin** deputies that spring, and in the summer of 1793 went on mission to the **Vendée** along with **Charles-Philippe Ronsin**. At a January 1794 meeting of the Cordelier club, Momoro denounced the **Indulgents** as retrograde. Although he was publicly critical of **Jacques-René Hébert** for his timidity, Momoro was accused with the Hébertists of preaching the **agrarian law**, and went to the **guillotine** with Hébert on 24 March 1794.

MONARCHIENS. The Monarchiens were a group of moderate deputies in the **Constituent Assembly** that coalesced in July–August 1789. They favored a bicameral legislature and an absolute veto for the king, in whose person, they argued, ultimate **sovereignty** resided. The most prominent leaders of the group were **Jean-Joseph Mounier**, **Pierre-Victor Malouet**, **Nicolas Bergasse**, and **Stanislas Clermont-Tonnerre**. By September 1789 the Monarchiens counted between 200 and 300 deputies in their ranks and constituted the first organized bloc of deputies in the Assembly. By virtue of their disciplined voting, they controlled the leadership positions in the Constituent Assembly from August through September, though ultimately they did not prevail in the voting on key constitutional issues. Mounier resigned his post following the **October Days**. Malouet and Clermont-Tonnerre played a leading role, in 1790, in the founding of the **Monarchist club** in **Paris**.

MONARCHIST CLUBS. The first Monarchist club, founded in **Paris** in late 1790 by **Stanislas Clermont-Tonnerre** and **Pierre-Victor Malouet**, grew out of the remnants of two earlier clubs, the Club of Viroflay and the *Club des Impartiaux*. The formation of this new club was prompted by a series of legislative initiatives in the **Constituent Assembly** beginning in the late spring of 1790: the vote against declaring Catholicism the official religion of France, the abolition of hereditary nobility, and the adoption of the **Civil Constitution of the Clergy**. Those who joined the Paris Monarchist club viewed each of these initiatives with alarm, and they were equally alarmed by the growing influence of the **Jacobin clubs**. Whereas the stated goal of the **Monarchiens** a year earlier in the Constituent Assembly had been to strengthen the institution of the monarchy in France, for the Monarchist club the simple preservation of the monarchy stood as its most urgent task.

Toward that end, members of the Paris club were urged to support the creation of similar clubs in the provinces. From late 1790 to the end of 1791, at least 35 Monarchist clubs appeared in provincial towns and cities. Some of these formed with the goal of sponsoring slates of candidates in local elections. Some had ties to the *émigré* princes in Turin or Coblenz and were accused of **counterrevolutionary** intentions. Others formed with the explicit objective of securing the elimination of all political clubs, most particularly the Jacobin clubs. In all cases their appearance provoked controversy, and sometimes violence. The Jacobin clubs denounced them and local officials eventually ordered their dissolution. By the end of 1791, the Monarchist clubs had ceased to exist, in Paris and the provinces. The revolutionary ideal of unity would not tolerate an organized opposition, whether loyal or otherwise.

MONGE, GASPARD (1746–1818). Monge was the son of a simple artisan in Beaune, though his father was prosperous enough to send Gaspard to the Oratorien *collège* in Beaune, and then on to the engineering school in Mézières, where Monge would later teach himself. At the age of 20, Monge developed the new field of descriptive geometry, and in 1772 he was appointed professor of mathematics and physics at Mézières, where **Lazare Carnot** and **Jean-Nicolas Pache** would be among his students. Monge was elected to the **Acad-**

emy of Science in 1780, and in 1784 moved to **Paris** to accept a post at the Ecole de la Marine.

Monge took a more public political stance during the Revolution than most French scientists, joining the **Jacobin club** in Paris. In August 1792 he accepted, with some reluctance, an appointment as minister of the Navy. He left the ministry in April 1793 to found what would eventually become the Ecole Polytechnique. At the request of Carnot, Monge contributed to the war effort in 1793–94 in the area of military engineering, and in 1796 he was sent on mission to Italy, where he met and befriended **Napoleon Bonaparte**. Monge became a member of the **Institut National** in this period, and in 1798 was elected to the **Council of Five Hundred**. He left France shortly thereafter, however, to accompany Napoleon on the **Egyptian campaign**, where he nearly died of dysentery. He returned to France in late 1799, was named to the Senate, and was later named to the Legion of Honor and became a Count of the Empire as well. Because of his close relationship with both Napoleon and Carnot, Monge was removed as director of the Ecole Polytechnique in 1815, and when he died in 1818 the school's students were forbidden to attend his funeral.

MONITEUR UNIVERSEL. The *Moniteur Universel* was among the most influential of the daily **newspapers** published in **Paris** during the Revolution. Its first issue appeared on 24 November 1789, edited by **Charles-Joseph Pancoucke**. The newspaper maintained a moderate tone throughout the decade, and was widely respected for its thoroughness and objectivity. In addition to reporting on general news, the *Moniteur Universel* presented a daily account of the debates in the National Assembly. It was named the official newspaper of record under the Consulate and retained that status until 1868. The *Moniteur Universel* remains an important documentary source for historians.

MONTAGNARDS. The Montagnards were the left-wing deputies in the **National Convention** and represented one of the two main political factions within that body, the other being the **Girondins**. The Montagnards first became a recognizable group in the **Legislative Assembly**, where the term was reportedly coined by Joseph-Marie

Lequinio. The deputies of the Mountain (*la Montagne*) were so called because they chose to sit in the highest seats of the meeting hall. The term had a Biblical connotation as well, alluding to the fact that Moses brought the Ten Commandments down from a mountain—so would the revolutionaries deliver to France laws from the Mountain.

Estimates of the number of Montagnard deputies vary from a low of 135 to a high of 270. The term Montagnards is often used inter-changeably with the term Jacobins, but while most Montagnard deputies were members of the **Jacobin club**, there were some notable exceptions, including **Lazare-Nicolas Carnot** and **Robert Lindet**. As compared to other deputies in the National Convention, the Monta-gnards tended to be younger and to have had more political experience during the Revolution, some 40 percent of them as deputies in the Legislative Assembly. The strongest base of support for the Monta-gnards was in **Paris**, particularly among the **sans-culottes**. Twenty-one of the 24 deputies elected from Paris sat with the Montagnards, who also enjoyed electoral support in the departments of the north and the east of France. **Maximilien Robespierre**, **Louis-Antoine Saint-Just**, **Georges-Auguste Couthon**, and **Jacques-Nicolas Billaud-Varenne** were among the leaders of the Montagnards.

The Montagnards clashed with the Girondins over the legitimacy of popular violence, over the definition of **sovereignty** in the young republic, and over the fate of **Louis XVI**. After the expulsion of the leading Girondin deputies following the **uprising of 31 May–2 June 1793**, the Montagnards came to dominate both the National Conven-tion and the **Committee of Public Safety**. The government of the **Terror** can thus be said to have been a Montagnard regime. The fall of Robespierre on 9 **Thermidor** marked an end to Montagnard dom-inance, but not until after the **Prairial riots** of 1795 were the last Montagnard deputies purged from the National Convention. Seven of them, the so-called Prairial martyrs, committed suicide in prison, while many others were exiled. The Montagnards managed only a minor resurgence under the **Directory**, but their example served as the principal inspiration for radical republicanism in France through-out the 19th century.

MONTAUBAN. Montauban was a modest town just north of **Toulouse** with a significant **Protestant** population at the end of the Old

Regime. As in **Nîmes**, local Protestants eagerly embraced the reforms introduced in 1789, and traditional religious divisions in the town tended to underlie political rivalries. Thus, when municipal authorities moved to enact the nationalization of Church lands in the spring of 1790, violence and bloodshed erupted in the town. Hearing of the conflict, authorities in **Bordeaux** sent an expeditionary force of 1,500 **National Guards** to Montauban in May 1790. The Bordeaux guardsmen calmed the tense mood and restored order to the town without even a skirmish, earning praise from the **Constituent Assembly** and gaining for their city a reputation for revolutionary patriotism. Bordeaux would later sully that reputation by its participation in the **federalist revolt**.

MONTESQUIEU, BARON CHARLES-LOUIS DE SECONDAT

(1689–1755). Montesquieu was among the most important of the **Enlightenment** writers in France. He was born into an **aristocratic** family at the château of La Brède just south of **Bordeaux**. Montesquieu trained for the legal profession and, like his father, became president of the **Parlement** of Bordeaux. He sold his office in the parlement in 1726, in order to travel and devote his energy more fully to his writing. His already substantial intellectual reputation gained him election to the *Académie Française* in 1727.

Montesquieu is best known for two of his writings, *The Persian Letters*, published anonymously in 1721, and *The Spirit of the Laws*, published in Geneva in 1748. The first was a work of satire, a thinly disguised critique of French society and the abuses of the monarchy. The second was a more theoretical work, in which Montesquieu described and analyzed various forms of government, concluding in the end that while there was much to be admired in the republican governments of antiquity, a monarchy restrained by aristocratic institutions was the form of government best suited to France. Like **Jean-Jacques Rousseau**, Montesquieu emphasized the ideal of civic virtue. Unlike Rousseau, he called for a separation of powers among the various branches of government. His influence on men such as Thomas Jefferson and Benjamin Franklin can be seen in the system of checks and balances that came to characterize the American system of government. French revolutionaries appreciated Montesquieu for his critique of monarchical absolutism and condemnation of judicial despotism, but were suspicious of his defense of aristocratic **privilege** and his wariness of popular **sovereignty**.

MONTGOLFIER, JOSEPH-MICHEL (1740–1810). Joseph-Michel Montgolfier is celebrated for having developed, along with his brother Etienne, the hot air balloon in France. The first of these balloons, made of taffeta and paper, took flight at Annonay in June 1783. In September of that year, **Louis XVI** and **Marie Antoinette** watched as one of the balloons ascended into the air carrying a sheep, a rooster, and a duck. Two months later the balloon carried its first human passengers. Although the Montgolfiers' balloon was soon surpassed in safety and effectiveness by a hydrogen-powered balloon, designed by Jacques Charles, the brothers were granted noble status and their fame spread throughout the world. During the Revolution, the **National Convention** created a company of hydrogen balloons for surveillance on the battlefield. The word "montgolfier" means hot air balloon in French.

MOUNIER, JEAN-JOSEPH (1758–1806). Mounier is a paradoxical figure. He arrived in **Versailles** in 1789 with a national reputation as a progressive reformer and champion of the **Third Estate**, but within months of the convocation of the **Estates-General** he had joined the ranks of conservatives and stood in opposition to much that that body achieved. Mounier's father was a clothier and small-scale banker in Grenoble, where Jean attended the *collège* Royal-Dauphin. Mounier went on to study law and in 1779 became an *avocat*. Along with his friend, **Antoine-Pierre Barnave**, he took a particular interest in public law and studied the history of French and British institutions. In 1783 he purchased a royal judgeship, which conferred upon him personal nobility.

In June 1788 Mounier attended the assembly of the three orders in Grenoble, along with Barnave, and helped to achieve an understanding between the Second **Estate** and Third Estate. The following month he served as secretary of the assembly at **Vizille**. In February 1789 he published *Nouvelles Observations sur les Etats généraux de France*, in which he attacked the legislative pretensions of the **parlements** and called for a union of the three orders and voting by head. Mounier was elected to the Estates-General by the Third Estate of

Grenoble, and would serve as both secretary and president of the **Constituent Assembly** in 1789.

Mounier's activism in Grenoble assured him a prominent role at Versailles. He immediately joined the **Breton club**, and was vocal in the debate over what to call the National Assembly. He is credited with writing the first three articles of the **Declaration of the Rights of Man and Citizen**, although in the end he felt that the document went too far. In his view, once the king ordered the three estates to meet together on 27 June 1789, the Revolution had been achieved. Mounier expressed his opinions on the proper structure of government in France both from his seat on the constitution committee and in published pamphlets. He sided with those who favored a bicameral legislature, modeled on England or the United States, and supported an absolute veto for the king. When the opposing positions prevailed on these issues, in early September, Mounier resigned from the committee, along with **Nicolas Bergasse** and **Trophime-Gérard Lally-Tollendal**. He presided over the **Constituent Assembly** during the **October Days**, and advised **Louis XVI** to defend the palace with force. In the aftermath of the royal family's return to **Paris**, Mounier resigned his seat and returned to Grenoble.

In late 1789 Mounier published his *Réflexions politiques*, defending his constitutional proposals and advising, among other things, the abolition of all political clubs. In May 1790 he emigrated to Switzerland with his family. Mounier continued to write and publish prolifically over the next decade, advocating a conservative vision of a constitutional monarchy, but he never supported any of the *émigré* efforts to intervene militarily against the revolutionary government. He returned to France in 1801, served **Napoleon Bonaparte** as Prefect of the Ille-et-Vilaine in 1802–04, and in 1805 was named to the Council of State. In 1804 Napoleon named Mounier to the Legion of Honor.

MUNICIPAL REVOLUTIONS. During the spring and summer of 1789, political upheavals occurred in most of the large towns and cities of France, rendering a return to the monarchical absolutism of the Old Regime virtually impossible. The most important of these municipal revolutions occurred in **Paris**, after the fall of the **Bastille** on 14 July. The electoral assembly of the city now declared itself the

Paris Commune, and on 17 July **Louis XVI** visited the capital to accept the key to the city from its new mayor, **Jean-Sylvain Bailly**.

Twenty of the 30 largest towns in France also experienced municipal revolutions. In four of them local patriots created entirely new municipal councils or committees, while in the others newly formed authorities shared power with Old Regime officials. In some cases these events preceded the fall of the Bastille, as in **Marseille**, where the upheaval occurred in February 1789. But in most cities the municipal revolutions were a response to news from Paris and **Versailles** at mid-summer. Not all of the municipal revolutions were violent, but the threat of violence was always present. In addition to the creation of new political bodies, local revolutionaries also generally created bourgeois militias to preserve order, the forerunners of the **National Guard**. The spread of those bourgeois militias was hastened by the panic in the countryside sown by the **Great Fear**, which also contributed to the municipal revolutions. These combined phenomena made it clear to the king and his advisers that revolutionary upheaval was not confined to Paris, nor could the Revolution be undone solely in the capital.

– N –

NANCY MUTINY. The Nancy mutiny of August 1790 marks the most extreme incident of the widespread turmoil affecting royal regiments across France during the first year of the Revolution. In many towns there was tension between royal troops, commanded by **aristocratic** officers, and the newly formed **National Guard** companies, and as **Jacobin clubs** began to appear across the country their members often attempted to find recruits among the royal soldiers. On 6 August 1790 the **Constituent Assembly** outlawed the formation of any sort of club within a military regiment, and this led to the incident in Nancy.

Trouble began when royal officers attempted to confiscate funds from soldiers' committees in the three regiments of Nancy, committees that had been sponsored by local Jacobins. When the soldiers resisted, Swiss officers ordered the public flogging of two of them. Tensions mounted, and serious violence erupted within the garrison by the end of August, despite an order from General **Marie-Joseph-Motier Lafayette** that discipline be restored. On 31 August troops under the command of General François Bouillé advanced on Nancy and subdued the mutinous soldiers. Harsh reprisals followed. Dozens of soldiers were imprisoned, more than 40 were sentenced to the galleys, 22 were hanged, and one was broken on the wheel. All three regiments were transferred elsewhere, and two of them were then disbanded.

In the short term, the severe punishments meted out against the Nancy mutineers restored discipline within the French army. But the lesson of Nancy could not stifle the growing division between officers and enlisted men, nor stem the deteriorating morale within military ranks more generally. Revolutionaries viewed the harsh repression as an appalling vestige of Old Regime despotism.

NATIONAL ASSEMBLY. *See* CONSTITUENT ASSEMBLY, LEGISLATIVE ASSEMBLY, NATIONAL CONVENTION.

NATIONAL CONVENTION. The National Convention was the third national assembly of the Revolution, following the **Constituent Assembly** and the **Legislative Assembly**. It remained in session for more than three years, longer than either of its predecessors, meeting from 20 September 1792 until 26 October 1795. It was called in order to draft a new constitution, a task necessitated by the fall of the monarchy on 10 August 1792. The deputies of the National Convention completed that task, twice. They also declared the first French Republic, conducted the trial of **Louis XVI**, oversaw the military defense of revolutionary France against a coalition of virtually all of the monarchies of Europe, and governed France during the year of the **Terror**.

The 749 deputies of the National Convention were elected by universal manhood suffrage. They were a politically experienced group: 83 had served in the Constituent Assembly, 191 had served in the Legislative Assembly, and more than half had served on local administrative or judicial bodies. Heartened by news of the victory of French forces at **Valmy**, the National Convention declared France a republic on 22 September 1792. In the months that followed, however, the deputies polarized into opposing factions, generally known as **Girondins** and **Montagnards**. Each of these factions (they lacked both the coherence and the discipline that might allow us to call them parties) constituted a minority within the National Convention, the Montagnards somewhat greater in number than the Girondins. Between them sat a less committed and more inchoate body of deputies, known to contemporaries as the **Plain**, or more derisively as the Swamp.

A number of issues divided Girondins from Montagnards: the role of **Paris** in national politics, the legitimacy of popular violence in furthering the revolutionary agenda, the fate of Louis XVI, and the scope of popular **sovereignty**. For the Girondins, the first two issues were crystallized in the **September Massacres**, the responsibility for which they laid squarely on the shoulders of **Maximilien Robespierre**. The Girondins consistently condemned the militancy of Parisian **sans-culottes** and feared their propensity for violence. These same militants whom the Girondins characterized as "anarchists" were championed by Robespierre and the Montagnards as "the people," responsible for leading the assault on the **Tuileries** Palace on 10 August 1792 and toppling the monarchy. When the deputies debated the fate of Louis XVI, Robespierre argued that the people, by their uprising, had already found him guilty. The Girondins not only demanded a trial, but attempted to refer his sentence to a popular referendum, hoping to moderate the radical views of Parisians by the votes of provincial Frenchmen. They failed in that effort and Louis XVI went to the **guillotine** on 21 January 1793. The fate of the king having been decided, the deputies now became mired in stalemate in debates over the proposed constitution and how best to prosecute the war. In all of this, the issue of sovereignty loomed large: did it ultimately lie in the National Convention itself, or with the people of France? And if the latter, how might the people legitimately exercise that sovereignty?

In April 1793 the Girondins turned their energies against one of the most radical exponents of popular sovereignty, **Jean-Paul Marat**. But they failed in their effort to impeach Marat, and his supporters in the clubs and sections of Paris then mounted an assault on the Girondin leaders, forcing the deputies of the National Convention to purge them from their midst in the **uprising of 31 May–2 June 1793**. The Montagnards now controlled the National Convention, and within three weeks drafted a republican constitution. The authority of the Convention was challenged, however, by the **Vendée rebellion** in the West; the **federalist revolt** centered in **Caen**, **Bordeaux**, **Lyon**, and **Marseille**; and the ongoing war with the rest of Europe. Faced with those crises, the deputies placed the responsibility of government in the hands of two committees: the **Committee of Public Safety** and the **Committee of General Security**. Although the new constitution was overwhelmingly approved in a popular referendum, the Convention suspended it until the end of foreign hostilities and placed the country under emergency wartime government. In September 1793 the National Convention passed a general *maximum* and declared **Terror** the order of the day. Some 40,000 people, accused as federalists or **counterrevolutionaries**, were executed in France in that year of the Terror, 1793–1794 (the Year II in the **revolutionary calendar**, adopted by the National Convention in September 1793).

The deputies of the National Convention reasserted themselves on 9 **Thermidor**, toppling Robespierre from power and sending him and a number of his supporters to the guillotine. Although the Committee of Public Safety did not immediately disappear, its powers were gradually reduced. So, too, was the influence of the **Jacobin clubs**, and the **Thermidorians** rescinded much of the social legislation that the Montagnards had introduced over the previous year. Those Girondins who had survived the Terror were eventually returned to office. In August 1795 the National Convention adopted a new constitution, more moderate than the **Constitution of 1793**, with more limits placed upon popular sovereignty. Included in that constitution was a decree ensuring that two-thirds of the deputies of the National Convention would be returned to office in one of the two chambers of the **Directory** regime, a self-serving effort to achieve political stability that was much resented by the electorate.

The three years during which the National Convention ruled France were undeniably the most tumultuous of the French Revolution. It is a period reviled by many for the excesses of the Terror and the imposition of a revolutionary dictatorship, and admired by others for its idealism and noble experiment with participatory democracy. The fact that the National Convention failed to reach its ideals should not obscure its remarkable achievement of holding the French republic together

through three years of war and internal rebellion. *See also* CONSTI-
TUTION OF 1795.

NATIONAL GUARD. The National Guard emerged out of the popular mobilization of 1789. Its first manifestations were informal, as
bourgeois militias were formed in a number of provincial cities in the
winter and spring of 1789 to preserve order. Then in July 1789, as
Louis XVI gathered troops in the vicinity of **Paris**, the electoral assembly of the capital called for the creation of a bourgeois militia of
some 48,000 men. In the weeks following the fall of the **Bastille**,
militias appeared in most provincial towns and cities, both in imitation of Paris and in response to the panic that spread through much of
France during the **Great Fear**.

These bourgeois militias had a dual purpose. First and foremost,
they stood as a counter to the royal army, which had always been controlled by the **aristocracy**. Although aristocrats were not excluded
from these militias, they tended to be dominated by wealthy commoners. Their second function, though, was to defend order and
property against the threat of popular violence. Thus, the National
Guard might act at times in support of revolutionary demands, and at
others in opposition to the revolutionary crowd. For example, the
Paris National Guard put down the demonstration on the **Champ de
Mars** in July 1791, but one year later would lead the insurgents in the
attack on the **Tuileries** on 10 August 1792.

It took some time for these militias to be incorporated into a formal structure. In August 1789 the **Constituent Assembly** decreed
that municipal councils should oversee the creation of local National
Guard companies. National Guard units in the provinces soon initiated contact with one another, and regional *fédérations* of National
Guardsmen began to occur as early as the fall of 1789. These local
federations grew in number the following spring, culminating in the
Festival of Federation in Paris on 14 July 1790. One month prior to
that gathering, the Constituent Assembly decreed that only **active citizens** would henceforth be eligible to join the National Guard, a re-
striction that was deeply offensive to those **passive citizens** who had
taken up arms in support of the Revolution prior to that date.

While Louis XVI presided over the Festival of Federation in 1790,
his flight to **Varennes** barely one year later prompted the Constituent

Assembly to formalize the structure of the National Guard. After the king's return to Paris, some 100,000 National Guards were mobilized for the protection of the fatherland. The National Guard's authority was to be strictly domestic, however, and its mission was to preserve local order and ensure obedience to the law. A decree of 29 September 1791 confirmed the municipal control of National Guard units.

When France went to war in 1792, the importance of the National Guard declined somewhat, as many guardsmen volunteered for the regular army. Guard units became more democratic in 1792–93, after the distinction between active and passive citizens was eliminated. But the creation of *armées révolutionnaires* under the **Terror** rendered nul the revolutionary role that the National Guards had once played. After **Thermidor** the National Guard would once again be called upon to preserve public order, but **Napoleon Bonaparte** suppressed the organization after **Brumaire**.

NATURAL RIGHTS. The idea of natural rights was central to **Enlightenment** thinking, most notably in the writing of **Jean-Jacques Rousseau**. While not all Enlightenment thinkers agreed on the extent of natural rights, or on their origin, virtually all of them grappled with the concept, which became central to the politics of the French Revolution as well, as expressed in the **Declaration of the Rights of Man and Citizen**. Natural rights, it was argued, existed prior to society, deriving either from a creator or from nature itself. Those rights could only be guaranteed, however, by a just and effective government and this was the goal of politics. A theory of natural rights, then, had implications for both a system of justice and for political legitimacy.

French revolutionaries championed three natural rights in particular: the right to life, or security; the right of liberty, without which that first right might quickly vanish; and the right to property. These rights were asserted to be inalienable, that is they both predated human society and could not be taken from those who enjoyed them. These rights were also claimed to be common to all, thereby implying the second term in the French revolutionary motto: **Liberty, Equality, and Fraternity**. The assertion of equal rights directly undermined the Old Regime concept of **privilege**, whereby French subjects enjoyed certain rights (more properly privileges) in accordance with their rank or place in society. Privilege corresponded to corporate identity, to membership in a group, whereas human rights were inherent to all individuals equally, regardless of rank or place in society. Justice must therefore apply equally to all, and be consistent with natural rights.

The principles of equality and of individual liberty implied a political system resting upon a foundation of personal **sovereignty**: the rights to express oneself freely, to control and protect one's body, to enjoy the fruits of one's labors. Men live in society, however, and to secure those personal freedoms and rights, Rousseau asserted the need for a social contract, a contract, were it to be fair and just, which required the consent of the governed. Out of this grew the concept of popular sovereignty and the ideal of democracy, the achievement of which proved to be the central conundrum of the Revolution. How could all participate equally in a country as vast and populous as France? If property were a natural right, were those who did not own property to be considered fully as citizens? How were the ideals, or rights, of liberty and equality to be balanced against each other? And how, in a society in which all were not equal in either talents or education, could one prevent the exercise of liberty from degenerating into license? These were just some of the questions that the assertion and promise of natural rights opened up not only for the French revolutionaries but for all in the modern world who have aspired to their ideals.

NECKER, JACQUES (1732–1804). Jacques Necker was born in Geneva, although the family was English in origin. His father, a professor of law, sent him to **Paris** as apprentice to a Swiss banker, a M. Vernet. In 1762 Vernet left him a considerable sum to invest in his own enterprise, and the Necker bank was soon the leading financial institution in Paris. By 1772 his fortune was made, chiefly through speculation in the grain trade, and Necker turned his talents to writing. His *Essai sur la Législation et le commerce des blés*, published in 1775, was highly critical of the reforms introduced by Anne-Robert-Jacques Turgot, liberalizing the grain trade, and no doubt contributed to Turgot's dismissal. Two years later Necker was named director-general of finances, his Swiss nationality and **Protestant** religion making it impossible to accord him the title of *Contrôleur-Général*. The financial community had so much confidence in

Necker's abilities that he could borrow what was needed to meet royal expenses, and he then set about reorganizing the Treasury. The **salon** hosted by his wife and daughter, the future Madame **Germaine de Staël**, helped to promote his rising star.

Over-confident in his success, perhaps, Necker published a *Compte-Rendu au Roi* in 1781, the first time that the royal budget had been openly published. Necker's report was critical of the waste and excessive spending of the Crown, and itemized the huge pensions being paid to a variety of people at court. It was also fulsome in its praise of English financial institutions. By May 1781 Necker had been forced to resign. Over the coming years he engaged in an ongoing public polemic with his successor, **Charles-Alexandre Calonne**, defending his own financial practices and accounting against the charges of Calonne, and criticizing his policies. He came to be a favorite among the people of Paris, and when Calonne and then **Charles-Etienne Loménie de Brienne** failed to resolve the growing financial crisis, Necker was recalled to office in 1788. He immediately called a second **Assembly of Notables**, mainly to lay the groundwork for the convocation of the **Estates-General**.

Necker enhanced his popularity among the people by endorsing a doubling of the representatives of the **Third Estate**, though he was silent on the question of voting by head. His opening speech to the Estates-General was long and tedious, however, and did little to resolve the political stalemate. Necker's enemies at court, including **Marie Antoinette**, convinced the king to dismiss him on 11 July, and this led to the fall of the **Bastille**. Necker was again recalled to office, but had now lost the confidence of some of the deputies and proved unequal to the task before him. His firm opposition to the creation of *assignats* as a strategy for addressing royal debt made him politically unpopular, and in September 1790 he resigned his post and returned to Switzerland. The death of his wife in 1794 was a crushing blow for Necker, from which he never fully recovered. **Napoleon Bonaparte** met him once, in Geneva, but the future emperor found him ponderous, and could barely tolerate his daughter, de Staël. Necker died a forgotten man on his estate at Coppet in 1804.

NEWSPAPERS. The flourishing of an independent newspaper press was an essential element of the political culture of the French Revolution.

Prior to 1789 the press in France was both restricted and heavily censored. A royal license was required before a newspaper could be published, and few of these were issued. The most prominent national newspaper, the *Gazette de France*, was essentially an official account of events at the court at **Versailles**, with occasional bits of news from abroad. Some 40 newspapers were published in provincial towns and cities, but these were generally collections of announcements and commercial notices. The press of the 18th century scarcely resembled what we know today.

The year 1789 changed all that. The opening of the **Estates-General** sparked an immediate curiosity among the reading public to know what was going on at Versailles. By the end of that year more than 130 new newspapers had appeared in France. Over the course of the revolutionary decade, some 1,300 different titles came and went, more than 500 in **Paris** alone. Some lasted only a few weeks or months, very few spanned the entire decade. Most appeared weekly or bi-weekly, but a few were published daily. The most important newspapers published in Paris enjoyed a national circulation, but provincial papers appeared as well in virtually every major city and town. Newspapers became the most important medium by which the momentous events and ideas of the Revolution were communicated to the people of France. In a period of incredibly rapid change, newspapers both reflected and influenced **public opinion**. Virtually all literate citizens read at least one newspaper, and those who could not read listened to others read them aloud in clubs and cafés, or on street corners.

Among the most important revolutionary newspapers were **Charles Pancoucke's** *Moniteur Universel*, which reported not only on events in the capital but became the official record of debates in the various national assemblies; **Camille Desmoulins**'s *Révolutions de France et de Brabant*; **Jean-Paul Marat's** *L'Ami du Peuple*, one of the most popular of the Paris newspapers; **Louis-Marie Prudhomme**'s *Révolutions de Paris*; **Antoine-Joseph Gorsas**'s *Courrier des Départements*, which reported on news from the provinces; and **Jacques-René Hébert's** *Père Duchesne*, which offended polite readers with its vulgar language, but enjoyed great popularity among the **sans-culottes** of Paris. Many of these newspapers not only reported the news of the day, but also called on their readers to send in their reports and express their views. The revolutionary press was a remarkably free press, but it did not entirely escape government supervision and control. Marat went into hiding on several occasions to elude government persecution for the inflammatory stories printed in *l'Ami du Peuple*. Many of these journalists sought public office, or turned to journalism after launching a political career. Such was the case with **Maximilien Robespierre**, who began to publish *Le Défenseur de la Constitution* following the adjournment of the **Constituent Assembly**, since by law he could not sit in the **Legislative Assembly**.

Newspapers gave expression to and shaped the contentious politics of the French Revolution. They were essential to the vitality of popular politics and to the exercise of participatory democracy. It is scarcely surprising that newspapers declined in number under the **Directory**, or that **Napoleon Bonaparte** would reduce the number of Parisian newspapers to four and subject the press once again to strict government censorship. If the French Revolution marked the birth of modern democracy, though, then certainly the newspapers of revolutionary France inspired our modern press.

NIGHT OF 4 AUGUST 1789. The Night of 4 August is seen as the symbolic end of feudalism and **privilege** in France. Responding to the peasant revolts of the previous weeks, known as the **Great Fear**, a group of liberal noblemen and deputies of the **Third Estate** called an evening session of the **Constituent Assembly** on that date, anticipating that the late hour of the meeting might deter their more conservative colleagues from attending. The plans for the evening had most likely been laid at the **Breton club**.

The session convened shortly after five p.m. The first to speak was the viscount **Louis-Marie de Noailles**, the brother-in-law of **Marie-Joseph-Motier Lafayette**. Noailles called upon his fellow deputies to alleviate the plight of the poor peasants by abolishing their **seigneurial dues**, a gesture that some might have viewed as hollow since, as a younger son, the viscount owned no property of his own. The duke **Armand-Désiré Duplessis-Richelieu Aiguillon** succeeded Noailles at the rostrum and called for an end not only to seigneurial dues, but to all forms of privilege. Inspired or abashed by their noble gesture, other aristocratic deputies followed suit in a virtual orgy of self-sacrifice and altruism. When the session finally adjourned at two in the morning, the remnants of the feudal regime lay in shambles.

To be accurate, feudalism properly speaking had long since ceased to exist in France, as serfdom had disappeared some centuries before. Nor were the noble pronouncements of the Night of 4 August easily converted into legislation in the days thereafter. Some deputies regretted their rash statements, and the more conservative representatives of the **aristocracy** and **clergy** attempted to defend their privileges in debates over the following week. Not until 13 August was a decree finally presented to **Louis XVI**. Personal dues and duties weighing on the **peasantry** were abolished outright, but those that applied to land were deemed a form of property and were to be redeemed through cash payments, oftentimes prohibitively high for the peasantry. The tithes due to the clergy on Church-owned lands were abolished as well. The king, decrying what he termed the despoiling of his clergy and nobility, refused at first to register the decrees. Only on 3 November, after the market **women** had marched to **Versailles** and escorted the royal family back to **Paris** during the **October Days**, did Louis XVI finally sign the decrees into law. Other forms of privilege—noble titles and the guild system, for example—would not be abolished for some time, and seigneurial dues attached to land were not eliminated until July 1793. But the main blow against the siegneurial system and privilege had been struck on the Night of 4 August.

NÎMES. See *BAGARRE DE NÎMES*.

NOAILLES, LOUIS-MARIE (1756–1804). The Vicomte de Noailles was the brother-in-law of **Marie-Joseph-Motier Lafayette**. His family traced its lineage in the nobility back to the 17th century, and his father was a duke and marshal of France who sat on both of the **Assemblies of Notables**. The young Noailles pursued a military career, reaching the rank of colonel in the army, and achieving honor as a Chevalier de Saint-Louis in 1780. Between 1779 and 1781 he fought in the American War of Independence with Lafayette, participating in three sea battles. He returned to France inspired by the liberal ideals that he had encountered in the United States.

Noailles joined a **Freemason** lodge in 1787, and in 1788 became a member of the **Society of Thirty**. He was elected to the **Estates-General** by the nobility of Nemours. Noailles worked to bridge the gap between the Second **Estate** and **Third Estate** at **Versailles**, but did not join the Third until after the king's order on 27 June 1789. He was among the most active orators in the **Constituent Assembly**, but is best known for his pivotal role on the **Night of 4 August**, which led to the abolition of corporate **privilege** and an end to **seigneurial dues**. Thereafter he concerned himself principally with military matters, proposing at one point a system of universal military service. On 19 June 1790 he spoke favorably in regard to the abolition of nobility. The following month he joined the **Jacobin club**, but left for the **Feuillants** after the flight to **Varennes**. The emigration of his brother at that point compromised Noailles's position somewhat, but he remained at his post until the dissolution of the Constituent Assembly in September 1791. He then resumed his military commission, but was so appalled at the lack of discipline and order among the ranks that he resigned in May 1792. Noailles left France, with a legal passport, after the **uprising of 10 August 1792**, and took up residence in the United States, not far from the estate of his old friend, George Washington. Both of his parents were arrested and executed during the **Terror**. Noailles was removed from the list of *émigrés* after 1800, and fought in **Saint-Domingue** with French troops in 1802–03. He was wounded during the evacuation of the island and died in Havana.

NOBILITY. *See* ARISTOCRACY.

NONANTE-CINQ. *Nonante-cinq*, drawn from the northern patois, is the shorthand reference for the winter of 1794–95, the most brutal winter in France since that of 1708–1709. In the aftermath of **Thermidor**, the **National Convention** abolished the *maximum*, and the accompanying poor harvest of 1794 led both to rising prices and grain shortages. The situation was particularly grave in the cities, and in **Paris** the Seine River froze over for the first time in decades. Hundreds died of cold or starvation, leading some to regret the death of **Maximilien Robespierre** and the passing of the **Terror**, with the macabre observation that while blood may have flowed in the gutters there had at least been bread on the table. The hardships of that winter, and the heightened gap between rich and poor, led to the **Germinal** and **Prairial riots** in the spring of 1795.

NOOTKA SOUND DISPUTE. The Nootka Sound dispute began in 1789, with the Spanish seizure of three English ships near Vancouver Island in the Pacific Northwest. The Spanish government then claimed the exclusive right to fish and found colonies in the area, a right that the British also claimed by virtue of the explorations of Captain James Cook. In the diplomatic dispute that followed, with both countries preparing for war, the Spanish sought support from France, appealing to the Family Compact first signed by the two monarchies in 1733 and renewed in 1761. **Louis XVI** was inclined to honor the compact, but the **Constituent Assembly** demurred, making this one of the first incidents to raise the question of whether the initiative in foreign policy lay principally with the king or with the assembly. The deputies, determined to break with the tradition of dynastic diplomacy, ultimately prevailed, and the Spanish were forced to back down.

NOYADES. The *noyades* of Nantes represent one of the most gruesome episodes of the **Terror**. Much of the region to the east and south of Nantes had been afflicted by the **Vendée rebellion** from March 1793 onward, and that summer the city itself was implicated in the **federalist revolt**. In October **Jean-Baptiste Carrier** arrived in Nantes as a **representative on mission**, charged by the **Committee of Public Safety** with pacifying the area and bringing the rebels to justice. Urged on by local radicals, Carrier ordered the execution of more than 3,000 men and **women**. Roughly 1,900 were loaded onto boats and barges by night and drowned in the Loire River. These were the infamous *noyades*. Witnesses later testified that women and priests were among the victims, sometimes stripped naked and tied together in "revolutionary marriages" before meeting their fate in the cold waters of the river. Carrier was recalled to **Paris** in February 1794, though at his own request and not due to reports of the drownings. He survived **Thermidor**, but was eventually denounced and tried for the excesses committed in Nantes. Carrier died on the **guillotine** on 16 December 1794.

– O –

OCTOBER DAYS. The march of Parisian market **women** to **Versailles** on 5 October 1789 marked the second occasion in the Revolution on which an armed intervention by the crowd forced a political accommodation from the monarchy. The prominent role played by women on this occasion also marks it apart from the other major uprisings of the Revolution.

The multifaceted significance of this event grew out of its complicated context. By late September the **Constituent Assembly** was once again at a point of stalemate, having increasingly split into opposing groups in the debate over the proposed constitution. In addition, **Louis XVI** persisted in his refusal to sign either the **Declaration of the Rights of Man and Citizen** or the decrees passed by the deputies following the **Night of 4 August**. The march to Versailles was triggered, however, by two other factors.

On 1 October the royal bodyguards held a banquet in honor of the newly arrived Flanders Regiment. As the king and **Marie Antoinette** looked on, a number of the soldiers tore off their tri-colored **cockades**, symbol of the newly proclaimed unity between **Paris** and the monarchy, threw them on the floor and replaced them with black cockades, symbol of the Austrian monarchy, the queen's family. News of this outrage reached Paris in the following days, just as grain prices were spiking once again. As in July, concern about food combined with political controversy to create a volatile situation.

Women moved from the central markets in Paris to the Hôtel de Ville on the morning of 5 October and decided there to march to Versailles. There was agitation within the Paris **National Guard** to join the women in their march, and while **Marie-Joseph-Motier Lafayette** initially resisted that course of action, late in the afternoon he set out at the head of his troops. By then the women had already reached Versailles, some 12 miles away from Paris, where they met first with deputies in the Constituent Assembly. The king was still away on the hunt, but toward 7:00 in the evening a small delegation of women was escorted to the palace where Louis XVI received them. He assured them of his devotion to his people, and promised that measures would be taken to ensure the provisioning of Paris.

The women outside were completely dissatisfied with these vague assurances, and most of them decided to stay the night at Versailles. By midnight they had been joined by Lafayette and several thousand guardsmen. The crowd grew increasingly restive in the pouring rain, and more were rumored to be en route from Paris. Lafayette, for whom the queen had a particular dislike, informed the king that he could guarantee the safety of the royal family only if they returned to Paris, which the king was reluctant to do. In the early morning hours, however, a portion of the crowd invaded the palace, killing two Swiss guards in the process and threatening to reach the queen's bedchamber. Lafayette and his troops intervened, and in the wake of this terrifying incident the king agreed not only to return to Paris but to sign the legislation that had lain on his desk now for weeks. By 1:00 the next afternoon the royal family was en route to Paris, escorted by Lafayette and the National Guard, and two weeks later the deputies of the Constituent Assembly followed.

The significance of the October Days was threefold. First, they returned the seat of the monarchy to Paris for the first time since Louis XIV had initiated the building of the palace at Versailles in the 17th century. In Paris neither the king nor the successive assemblies would be able to ignore the pressure of the crowd. Second, the events of October forced the king to sign the Declaration of the Rights of Man and Citizen and the decrees abolishing **seigneurial dues**, and to accept the limitations on royal power proposed in the new constitution. Finally, the violence of the October Days ushered in a period of calm and political reaction, as moderate deputies recoiled from the politics of the street. The **Châtelet** court carried out an investigation of those who had allegedly initiated the violence, and some accused **Gabriel-Honoré Mirabeau** of having tried to manipulate the crowd in an effort to install **Louis-Philippe Orléans** on the throne. For a time, at least, the momentum of the Revolution seemed to have been stemmed.

ORLÉANS, LOUIS-PHILIPPE-JOSEPH (1747–1793). Louis-Philippe-Joseph de Bourbon was the son of Louis-Philippe, Duke of Orléans, and the cousin of **Louis XVI**. Upon his father's death in 1785, he inherited his title and his immense wealth. Orléans was tall and good-looking, affable and spirited, but ill-mannered, and was said to be the best horseman in the kingdom. He was also rumored to be the richest man in France, though his gambling and high living left him perpetually in debt. Orléans was not well liked at court, and perhaps because of this traveled widely in England, Holland, Switzerland, and Italy. He owned two properties that would figure prominently in the events of the Revolution: the **Palais Royal** in **Paris**, the very center of revolutionary ferment; and the château at Saint-Cloud, across the Seine River, where **Napoleon Bonaparte** would stage his **Brumaire** coup in 1799. **Marie Antoinette** bought Saint-Cloud from Orléans in 1785 as a gift for the dauphin, a gesture that added to the queen's reputation for extravagance and provided temporary relief for the duke's debts.

Orléans challenged the Bourbon monarchy on several occasions, most notably in 1771–72 when he opposed the reforms of Chancellor René-Nicolas de Maupeou and was sent into exile by Louis XV; and again in 1787 when, as a member of the **Parlement of Paris**, he spoke up at a royal session to question the proposed fiscal reforms of Louis XVI and was once again exiled to the provinces. He was elected to the **Estates-General** by the **aristocracy** of Crépy, but went over to the **Third Estate** on 25 June. On the eve of 14 July his bust was paraded in the streets of Paris along with that of **Jacques Necker**. His popularity was due in large part to the fact that the Palais Royal was such a hub of political ferment. Orléans had constructed an array of boutiques around the square, which he rented out in order to pay off his debts, an act so scandalous and unheard of that at court the square was known as *Palais-Marchand*. As a royal property, the square was exempt from policing, so that it attracted not only commerce, but a steady parade of unsavory characters as well as those eager to hear about the latest calls for reform or the current scandal at court. It was here that **Camille Desmoulins** called on Parisians to march to the **Bastille**. By 1793 the square was known as *Jardin de la Révolution*.

Orléans was accused of having instigated the **October Days** in 1789, and to quiet the rumors **General Lafayette** arranged for him to go to England on a diplomatic mission. Upon his return he reported to the king, and the two seemed to mend their differences, but shortly thereafter, at a Sunday *petit lever*, the ladies at court hissed the duke. He stormed out of the **Tuileries** Palace, and this marked his final break with Louis XVI. Orléans sat on the left in the **Constituent Assembly**, and after the flight to **Varennes** in June 1791 he joined the **Jacobin club**. When nobility was abolished in 1792, Orléans went to the **Paris Commune** to request a new surname. Henceforth he was known as Philippe Egalité.

In September 1792 Egalité was elected as the final deputy from Paris to the **National Convention**. In December **François Buzot** rose in the Convention to challenge the presence of Egalité, demanding that both he and his son be exiled as possible pretenders to the throne. The issue was debated that night at the Jacobin club, where it was denounced as a **Girondin** ploy in their struggle with the **Montagnards**. Nothing came of it at the time, though it may have encouraged Egalité to vote for death in the trial of Louis XVI, a vote that shocked many of the deputies. As **Maximilien Robespierre** observed, Egalité was perhaps the only deputy who could have legitimately recused himself from the vote.

Following the treason of **Charles Dumouriez**, on 27 March 1793, Robespierre called for the exile of all of the Bourbons. When Egalité's son, the Duke of Chartres, fled France on 6 April in the company of Dumouriez, the Convention voted to arrest the entire Bourbon family. They were taken to **Marseille**, where Egalité remained in prison until October 1793. He was returned to Paris for trial when **Jacques-Nicolas Billaud-Varenne** demanded that he be included in the indictment of the proscribed Girondin deputies. Egalité was tried separately from the deputies, though charged with the same crimes. Scornful of the verdict, he said this to the members of the **Revolutionary Tribunal**: "Since you are determined to see me dead, you might at least have found a more plausible pretext, for you will be able to persuade no one that I could be guilty of the charges for which I am convicted." Egalité went to the **guillotine** on 6 November 1793. In 1830 his son would ascend the throne as King Louis-Philippe.

– P –

PACHE, JEAN-NICOLAS (1746–1823). Pache was the son of the concierge at the residence of the Maréchal de Castries, in **Paris**. De Castries liked Jean-Nicolas, made him the tutor of his children, and later secured his appointment as first secretary at the Ministry of the Navy. Pache also served briefly as *contrôleur* in the Maison du Roi, before leaving France for Switzerland on the eve of the Revolution.

Pache returned to Paris in the early 1790s and became active in the politics of the Luxembourg section. In 1792 he found a position in the

Ministry of the Interior, under **Jean-Marie Roland**. Pache impressed everyone as an extraordinarily hard worker and soon moved over to the Ministry of War, under **Joseph Servan**, whom he replaced as minister in October 1792. Up to that point Pache had been close to the **Girondins**, but he gravitated toward the **Montagnards** as he undertook the complete reorganization of the Ministry of War. On the one hand, he centralized purchasing for the army, which alienated the generals (including **Charles Dumouriez**), and on the other he dismissed from the staff many of the Old Regime holdovers, replacing them with militant **sans-culottes** from the Paris sections. When the Girondins secured his dismissal from the ministry in February 1793, the Montagnards backed him as candidate in the Paris mayoral election, which he won handily.

As mayor, Pache's excellent relations with the Paris sections made him a valuable ally to the Montagnards in their struggle with the Girondins. He played no active role in the **uprising of 31 May–2 June 1793**, but may have helped to avert bloodshed, and in the summer months his conscientious efforts were important in preserving the capital from famine. Pache was close to **Jacques Hébert**, but did not go to trial with the Hébertistes, although **Maximilien Robespierre** did arrange his dismissal as mayor in May 1794, perhaps for his own protection. Pache was arrested after **Thermidor**, but amnestied in the final days of the **National Convention**. He then retired quietly in the Ardennes, where he had purchased *biens nationaux* earlier in the Revolution.

PAINE, THOMAS (1737–1809). Thomas Paine was born in Thetford, England, the son of a corset manufacturer. Brought up as a Quaker, Thomas worked for his father as a youth and then became manager of a tobacco plant. In 1759 he married a servant girl, whom he left behind when he sailed for America in 1774 to escape debts. Paine found work in a Philadelphia bookstore and supported the American struggle for independence. In 1776 he published *Common Sense*, which sold more than 100,000 copies in a matter of weeks. Paine befriended George Washington and Benjamin Franklin, and eventually rose to the position of secretary-general in the Pennsylvania Assembly.

Paine first traveled to France in November 1789, having already made the acquaintance of **Jacques Brissot**, **General Lafayette**, and

Marie-Jean Condorcet. He returned to England in 1790 and wrote *The Rights of Man*, a response to **Edmund Burke's** *Reflections on the Revolution in France*. Paine's defense of the French Revolution brought charges of high treason in England, and he made his escape across the Channel to **Paris**. He regularly attended the meetings of the **Cercle Social** during the summer of 1791, and lived at the home of **Nicolas Bonneville**. He collaborated briefly on a **newspaper** with Condorcet. Paine was declared a French citizen on 26 August 1792 (the third anniversary of the **Declaration of the Rights of Man and Citizen**) on the proposal of **Marguerite-Elie Guadet**. The next month he was elected to the **National Convention** from a number of departments, and chose to represent the Pas-de-Calais.

Paine's French was far from fluent, but he sat on the constitutional committee headed up by Condorcet and dominated by **Girondin** deputies. An ardent foe of monarchy, he still wished to spare **Louis XVI**, the man, and voted for imprisonment and eventual banishment during the trial. Although Paine did not sign the formal protest of the proscription of the Girondin leaders, he spoke out in their cause and was proscribed himself on 13 January 1794 and eventually arrested. He wrote *The Age of Reason* during his imprisonment. Paine was released after **Thermidor** and restored to his seat. He spoke in the Convention only once thereafter, to point out the contradiction between the property-based suffrage regime being proposed for the **Constitution of 1795** and the ideals of 1789. No one rose to support him. Paine returned to the United States in 1802.

PALAIS ROYAL. In the 17th century the Palais Royal, originally known as the Palais Cardinal, was the residence of Cardinal Richelieu, who left it to Louis XIII at his death. Louis XIV gave it to his younger brother, the Duke of Orléans, and it passed down on that side of the royal family so that on the eve of the Revolution it was the property of **Louis-Philippe Orléans**, known after 1792 as Philippe Egalité. Orléans was perpetually in debt, which led him to construct a series of arcades and galleries in the Palais Royal in the early 1780s, which he then let out to shopkeepers and café owners. As a royal residence, the Palais Royal was off-limits to the police, and as such it became the center of Parisian libertinage, a haven for gamblers, prostitutes, and their customers. But its many bookshops were also the repository of what has been described as the "literary underground" of the French **Enlightenment**, and its location on the right bank of the Seine in **Paris**, not far from the Louvre and the **Tuileries**, made it a center of both social life and political life in the capital on the eve of the Revolution.

As a center of social and intellectual fermentation, the Palais Royal played a prominent role in the events of the Revolution in Paris. It was here that **Camille Desmoulins** exhorted the crowd on 12 July 1789 to march on the **Bastille** two days later, in protest of the dismissal of **Jacques Necker**. In a hall built to accommodate a circus, **Claude Fauchet** would hold forth to an early meeting of the **Cercle Social** in 1790 on the philosophy of **Jean-Jacques Rousseau**. On 20 January 1793, on the eve of the execution of **Louis XVI**, **Louis-Michel Le Peletier de Saint-Fargeau** was assassinated in a restaurant in the Palais Royal. Less than six months later, **Charlotte Corday** bought a knife in a shop along the arcades of the square, and would later use that knife to stab **Jean-Paul Marat**.

After the execution of Philippe Egalité in November 1793, the square became the property of the state, and was renamed Palais Egalité. Having once been a gathering spot for critics of the Old Regime monarchy, it became during the Revolution a haven for royalist dissenters from the new republican politics. Under the **Directory** the Palais Royal became a zone of contestation, a site for confrontations between gangs of *jeunesse dorée* and those **sans-culottes** who still held on to the militant ideals of the Year II. In 1800, under the Consulate, it housed the meetings of the Tribunat. Today one can still dine in the Grand Véfour, which has occupied its site at the north end of the square since the 1740s.

PALLOY, PIERRE-FRANÇOIS (1755–1835). Palloy is sometimes described as the first capitalist entrepreneur of the French Revolution. An architect by training, Palloy claimed to have been among the *vainqueurs de la* **Bastille**. He was hired after 14 July to oversee the demolition of the royal fortress, a task for which he employed some 500 men. Palloy profited from the opportunity by creating a variety of souvenirs of 14 July 1789: busts, engravings, and miniature models of the fortress, all carved from the stones taken from the Bastille itself. Some of these he presented as ceremonial gifts, to the **Paris Commune** in

February 1790, for example, to the **Constituent Assembly**, and even one to **Louis XVI**, who thanked him for it. Others he sold, to ministers, to **departmental administrations**, and to **Jacobin clubs** throughout France. One of the models of the Bastille can still be seen today in the Carnavelet museum in **Paris**.

PANCOUCKE, CHARLES-JOSEPH (1736–1798). Pancoucke was the son of a Lille bookseller. He moved to **Paris** in 1764 and set up business as a printer/publisher. Pancoucke soon bought *Le Mercure de France* and set up his brother-in-law, Jean-Baptiste Suard, as editor. The circulation of the **newspaper** quickly grew to 15,000 copies, a considerable number for that day. Pancoucke's printing house, which employed 150 workers, produced an enormous number of books and newspapers each year, and published most of the great writers of late 18th-century France. In the late 1770s, he undertook the publication of the Supplement and Index to Denis Diderot's *Encyclopédie*, and later issued a second edition of the entire work.

In November 1789 Pancoucke began publication of *Le Moniteur Universel*, a record of the debates in the National Assembly that would eventually become the official newspaper of the French government. But the Revolution that the works published by Pancoucke could be said to have helped bring about was not kind to him or his enterprise. He stood for election to the **Legislative Assembly** in 1791, but was rebuffed by the voters. His publishing empire suffered as well, particularly due to the inflation brought on by the issuance of *assignats*.

PANTHÉON. Construction of the Panthéon began in 1757, under the reign of Louis XV, on the site of the old abbey church of Sainte-Geneviève in **Paris**. Design of the church was entrusted to Jacques-Germain Soufflot. The towering dome of the new Sainte-Geneviève was inspired by the basilica of the Vatican, while the Corinthian columns forming the porch of the façade were modeled on the Roman Pantheon. The church was very near completion in 1790, when the **Constituent Assembly** renamed it the Panthéon and converted it from its religious function to a civic temple where the remains of great Frenchmen would be interred.

The interior of the building was now redecorated, with new inscriptions and bas-reliefs, resulting in a much more austere effect than that envisioned by Soufflot. Over the next four years, the remains of **Gabriel-Honoré Mirabeau**, **Voltaire**, **Louis-Michel Le Peletier de Saint-Fargeau**, **Jean-Paul Marat**, and **Jean-Jacques Rousseau** were interred in the Panthéon. As the political currents of the Revolution shifted, the remains of first Mirabeau and then Marat would be removed in 1794 and 1795, at which point the **National Convention** decreed that the honors of the Panthéon could not be conferred on an individual until 10 years after his death. In 1801 the Panthéon was restored to Catholic worship by **Napoleon Bonaparte**, and over the course of the 19th century it alternated between religious and civic function. The 1885 funeral rites for Victor Hugo marked its permanent restoration as a civic temple dedicated to the glorification of great French men and women.

PANTHÉON CLUB. The Panthéon club, formally known as the Society of Friends of the Republic, was founded in **Paris** in November 1795 by a printer named Lebois. The club met in the former abbey of Sainte-Geneviève, near the **Panthéon**, from which it drew its name. The politics of the club were initially rather moderate, but it soon attracted a number of former **Montagnards**, including **Jean-Pierre-André Amar**, **Jean-Nicolas Pache**, and **Robert Lindet**, as well as **Gracchus Babeuf** and **Filippo Michele Buonarroti**, who moved the club in the direction of radical republicanism. Membership in the club grew rapidly, and by February 1796 its meetings regularly attracted between 2,000 and 3,000 people. Fearing that the club might challenge public order and its own legitimacy, the **Directory** ordered its dissolution, and on 27 February 1796 **Napoleon Bonaparte**, commanding the Army of the Interior, oversaw the closing of its doors. The leaders of the Panthéon club would subsequently form the core of Babeuf's **Conspiracy of Equals**.

PAOLI, PASCAL (1725–1807). Paoli spent much of his youth in exile in Naples, with his father, who had fought for Corsican independence from Genoa. He returned to **Corsica** in 1755 to renew that struggle for independence, a goal largely achieved by 1769, when the armies of Louis XV arrived to claim the island for France. Paoli went into exile again, this time to London, where he remained for 20 years. The outbreak of revolution in 1789 offered new hope to Paoli and Corsican nationalists. He left London in March 1790, was warmly greeted by the deputies of the **Constituent Assembly** in April, and returned to Corsica, where he became president of the **departmental adminis-tration** and commander of the island's **National Guard**.

Paoli welcomed the constitutional reforms of the early Revolution, but was alienated by the radical agenda of the **Jacobins**, and con-demned the execution of **Louis XVI**. He made overtures to the British, and in April 1793 was dismissed from his posts by the **Na-tional Convention** and summoned to **Paris** to explain his conduct. Instead he led a rebellion against French rule and turned to the British for support of his new campaign for Corsican independence. The French were now replaced by the British, and in the face of increas-ingly reactionary politics on the island, Paoli once again sought exile in London, where he spent his final years.

PARIS. It could be argued, with some exaggeration, that Paris made the French Revolution, and with rather less exaggeration that the Revo-lution restored the primacy of Paris in French national politics. Louis XIV built his palace at **Versailles** in the 17th century precisely to re-move the monarchy from the dangers of popular upheaval, which he had witnessed in Paris as a child during the rebellion known as the Fronde. When the market **women** marched to Versailles during the **October Days** in 1789, they escorted **Louis XVI** and his family back to Paris. Less than three years later, the king would fall victim to the popular upheaval that Louis XIV had so rightly feared.

Paris was far and away the largest city in France in 1789, with a population of more than half a million people (more than three times the size of **Lyon**), and the constant stream of migrants into Paris over the course of the 18th century made it truly a national city. While the Revolution was obviously not a purely Parisian affair, no other city in France could exert as much influence on the current of national politics. The *journées* of the capital city drove the Revolution for-ward: the fall of the **Bastille** on 14 July 1789; the October Days; the assault on the **Tuileries** Palace on 10 August 1792; the **uprising of 31 May–2 June 1793**, which toppled the **Girondins** from power. Parisians were proud of the sacrifices they made on each of those great days in defense of liberty and equality. When we think of the **sans-culottes**, we think first of Paris.

There were **Jacobin clubs** throughout France, but the Paris Jacobin club was the "mother society" and exerted the greatest influence on the **Legislative Assembly** and **National Convention**. The leaders of the **Montagnard** faction in the National Convention were nearly all elected from Paris. The **newspapers** published in Paris carried its influence to every corner of the nation, Parisian volunteers filled the ranks of the republican army, and in the Year II (1793–94) **representatives on mission** emanated from Paris carrying Jacobin ideology to the provinces. In return, the **Terror** brought many of its victims to Paris to be judged before the **Revolutionary Tribunal**. If Versailles had been the stage of the absolute monarchy, then Paris was the stage of the Revolution.

The primacy of Paris did not go unchallenged during the revolutionary decade, however. **Departmental administrators** protested the first, failed uprising against the monarchy on 20 June 1792. Nearly all of France was appalled by the **September Massacres** two months later, and during the first eight months of the National Convention's existence the Girondin deputies consistently denounced Paris militants as anarchists, and called for a departmental guard or the transfer of their meeting place to a neutral city. When the Girondins were purged, a number of departments rebelled against Paris in the **federalist revolt**.

In the end, the sacrifices made by Parisian sans-culottes may have exhausted their ability to sustain the Revolution. Few Parisians rose up to defend **Maximilien Robespierre** on 9 **Thermidor**. The **Conspiracy of Equals** led by **Gracchus Babeuf** was easily suppressed by the **Directory** regime. Still, when **Napoleon Bonaparte** seized power on 18 **Brumaire**, he staged his coup at the château of Saint-Cloud, safely away from the Parisian crowd. Paris remained the center of French politics, though. Napoleon crowned himself emperor not in the cathedral at Reims, where the Bourbon monarchs had been coronated, but in Notre-Dame cathedral at the heart of Paris.

PARIS COMMUNE. The Paris Commune was the municipal government of **Paris**. It took shape spontaneously in the days after the fall of the **Bastille**, was given legal status by the law of 14 December 1789, and given further definition by the law of 21 May 1790. It consisted of 144 delegates, three from each of the 48 sections of Paris.

They were divided into five departments, each responsible for supervising various administrative tasks of the Commune.

The Paris Commune also played an important political role, however. As the authority of the monarchy waned, the issue of where **sovereignty** lay became more and more pressing. Municipal councils throughout France were chosen by direct, rather than indirect, election, and might therefore claim to be the purest expression of the popular will. The Paris Commune, representing the largest city of France, might exercise that claim more aggressively than any other municipal council. In each of the *journées* of the Revolution, the Paris Commune played an important role, but particularly so on 10 August 1792 and again in the **uprising of 31 May–2 June 1793**. In August 1792 the Commune challenged the authority of the **Legislative Assembly**, which played only a passive role in the toppling of the monarchy. When the **Girondins** denounced the undue influence of Paris in the months that followed, the Commune joined the **Jacobin club** in planning the insurrection that ousted them from the **National Convention**.

The Paris Commune continued to champion the cause of the **sans-culottes** through the summer of 1793, but as the **Committee of Public Safety** increased its power and introduced the regime of the **Terror**, the independence of the Commune declined. The trial and execution of **Jacques-René Hébert** and his supporters in March 1794 struck a serious blow against the Commune's influence. **Thermidor** further weakened its power, and the **Constitution of 1795** eliminated its political function completely.

PARLEMENT OF PARIS. The Parlement of Paris was the most important of the 13 **parlements** in France under the Old Regime. These were high courts, not legislative bodies, but they did have a political role to play in the registering of royal edicts. In August 1787 the Parlement of Paris refused to register a new land tax, even in the face of a royal *lit de justice*. **Louis XVI** responded by exiling the members of the parlement to Troyes. Although the *parlementaires* were all members of the **aristocracy**, either by birth or by virtue of the office that they held, they now became heroes to the people for their opposition to monarchical despotism. When the king withdrew the land tax, the people of **Paris** celebrated the return of their Parlement from its brief exile.

Less than one year later, the popularity of the Parlement evaporated when it ruled that the **Estates-General** should meet and deliberate according to its traditional form. By that ruling the Parlement opposed the doubling of the **Third Estate**, as well as the proposal that voting be conducted by head rather than by estate. The Parlement of Paris played little role in the early months of the Revolution.

PARLEMENTS. There were 13 parlements in France at the end of the Old Regime, the most important of which was the **Parlement of Paris**. These were courts of appeal, judicial bodies rather than parliamentary bodies, though they did bear the responsibility of registering royal laws and edicts, thereby exercising a restraint on monarchical despotism. Each parlement consisted of several dozen judges, **aristocrats** who had purchased their offices and therefore enjoyed a certain independence from the crown. In the face of parlementary resistance, the king might issue a *lit de justice* (literally, "bed of justice") to force the judges to register his edict or, that failing, exile the parlement to a small provincial town, as **Louis XVI** did to the Parlement of Paris in 1787. The parlements were suspended in November 1789, and officially abolished by the law of 6 September 1790.

PASSIVE CITIZEN. Passive citizens, as distinct from **active citizens**, were those who enjoyed civil rights but not political rights under the **Constitution of 1791**. **Women** and children were considered passive citizens, as were those adult males who were younger than 25 or who did not pay direct tax equal to three days' wages. Domestic servants, actors, and those without fixed residence were also categorized as passive citizens. The distinction was abolished after the fall of the monarchy on 10 August 1792, when all adult males over 21 years of age were granted the vote. Although a property requirement would once again be introduced in the suffrage system under the **Directory**, the term "passive citizen" fell out of common usage.

PEASANTRY. France was overwhelmingly a peasant society on the eve of the French Revolution. Roughly 85 percent of the population might be considered to have been included in the peasantry, although there were significant gradations among that population. Wealthy peasants were substantial landowners, while poor peasants struggled to survive from year to year. But as attested to by **Arthur Young's** *Travels in France*, the French peasantry was not among the poorest of Europe, and the French Revolution cannot be said to have been initiated by an immiserated peasantry.

Yet, the peasantry played an important part in the initial events of the French Revolution. Peasants bore the brunt of the tax burden under the Old Regime, and they protested this injustice vociferously in the *cahiers de doléances*. They also called for an end to the **seigneurial dues** to which they were subjected, and rebelled against rising bread prices during the summer of 1789. In these ways the peasantry constituted a revolutionary force in the early years of the Revolution, although many peasants supported the **refractory priests** who refused to swear the **civil oath of the clergy**, and in the west of France it was peasants who made up the greatest part of those who rebelled in the **Vendée** against the revolutionary government in 1793. While the peasantry in some parts of France was a potent force in support of the **counterrevolution**, in other regions they benefited from the reforms introduced after 1789, in particular the sale of *biens nationaux*, which ensured that France would remain a nation of small landholders well into the 20th century.

PÈRE DUCHESNE. The name *Père Duchesne* is most readily associated with the radical **newspaper** published by **Jacques-René Hébert** between 1790 and 1794. The origins of the name probably lie in the street theater of **Paris** of the mid-18th century. *Père Duchesne* was taken to be a man of the people, during the Revolution a true **sans-culotte**. Hébert's paper first appeared in September 1790, disappeared briefly at the end of the year, but reappeared in January 1791 and continued publication until Hébert's execution in March 1794. But Hébert's *Père Duchesne* was not the only one—Antoine Lemaire published two newspapers with *Père Duchesne* in the title in the early years of the Revolution, from a more moderate political perspective, and over the course of the decade there were dozens of newspapers that made reference to the celebrated figure on their mastheads.

Hébert's paper was the most popular and influential of these, however. He wrote in the language of the streets, and the eight pages of each issue were laced with vulgarities and obscenities, leading the historian Ferdinand Brunot to characterize Hébert as the "Homer of filth."

Because of this, Hébert offended many of his **bourgeois** readers, but the *Père Duchesne* was explicitly addressed to the sans-culottes, and by 1793 it had come to be seen as an expression of their political views as well. Hébert railed against the **Girondins** as the principal enemies of the Republic, and championed in his newspaper the ideals of direct democracy and the **agrarian law**. The newspaper appeared thrice weekly in 1793, and the government ordered copies sent to soldiers at the front. After the death of **Jean-Paul Marat**, in July 1793, the *Père Duchesne* became the most widely distributed paper in France, with a circulation approaching 50,000. Hébert's execution in March 1794 meant the loss of an important vehicle of communication between the **Montagnards** and their Parisian constituency.

PÉTION, JÉROME (1756–1794). Jérome Pétion's father was an *avocat* and judge at the Présidial court in Chartres, where Jérome attended *collège* along with **Jacques-Pierre Brissot**. Like his father, Jérome pursued a career in law, practicing in Chartres and obtaining a position as subdelegate to the Intendant of Orléans in the 1780s. In 1782 he published *Les Lois civiles et l'administration de la justice* in London, after the book was forbidden by the censors in France. Pétion was elected to the **Estates-General** by the **Third Estate** of Chartres and served on five committees, most importantly the constitution committee.

Pétion's was a forceful voice in the **Constituent Assembly**, over which he presided in December 1790. He was among the most ardent defenders of legislative prerogative, favoring only a suspensive veto for the king and arguing that the legislature should exercise final control over the army. Pétion insisted that the king and his family were citizens like all others, and that all citizens, including the king, were subject to the law. He supported the creation of *assignats*, and argued that all citizens should be eligible to serve in the **National Guard**. Pétion sat on the left in the Constituent Assembly, along with **Maximilien Robespierre**, but while he shared his friend's populist ideas he did not go so far as to advocate universal manhood suffrage. He was a member of both the **Jacobin club** and the **Society of the Friends of Blacks**.

In June 1791 the Constituent Assembly sent Pétion to **Varennes**, along with **Antoine-Pierre Barnave**, to escort **Louis XVI** and his family back to **Paris**. Pétion called for the king to be judged right then, among the few to do so. His popularity in Paris soared—he presided over the Jacobin club in August, and in November succeeded **Jean-Sylvain Bailly** as mayor. Pétion served as mayor until July 1792. In June the Directory of Paris tried to prevent a celebration of the **Tennis Court Oath**, and Pétion refused to issue such an order. The celebration ended in a failed uprising against the monarchy, and as a result the Directory dismissed Pétion on 6 July. One month later, on 3 August, he would stand at the head of a delegation from the sections of Paris to the **Legislative Assembly** demanding that the king be deposed.

After the fall of the monarchy, Pétion was elected to the **National Convention**, and presided over its first meeting. His influence began to decline, however, in the aftermath of the **September Massacres**, when he spoke in support of **François Buzot's** 24 September call for a departmental guard to protect the Convention against Parisian militants. Still, he was overwhelmingly reelected as mayor of the city in October, though he declined to take up the post. Pétion never adopted the anti-Parisian rhetoric of Buzot and others, but his support of the **Girondins** and his unwillingness to be critical of Brissot brought him under attack at the Jacobin club. In early December 1792 he clashed with Robespierre over whether the king should be tried, although ultimately he voted for death at his trial.

Pétion was alarmed by violent protests in Paris in February and March 1793, and spoke critically now of the Paris sections. Though not included in the group of Girondin deputies proscribed on 2 June, he was expelled from the Convention one week later and joined a number of his colleagues in **Caen**. After the collapse of the **federalist revolt** he fled first to Brittany and then to the Gironde, where he hid in the countryside outside **Bordeaux** for nearly a year. In June 1794 he and Buzot killed themselves rather than be caught. Wolves partially devoured their bodies before they were discovered.

PHILIPPEAUX, PIERRE-NICOLAS (1756–1794). Philippeaux was the son of a leather-dresser in a small town outside of **Paris**. Little is known of his **education**, but after marrying in Paris in 1783 he worked as an *avocat* before the Présidial court in Le Mans. In 1790 Philippeaux was elected to the municipal council in Le Mans, and then as a judge on the district tribunal. He founded a **newspaper**, *Le Défenseur de la Liberté*, which appeared from February 1792 to November 1793. Philippeaux was elected to the **National Convention** in September 1792 from the Sarthe. He was a member of both the **Jacobin club** and the **Cordelier club**, and allied himself with the Dantonists. His politics were somewhat equivocal in the Convention. He initially favored the ***appel au peuple*** in the trial of **Louis XVI**, ended up voting against it and for the death penalty, but as a suspended sentence. He supported the creation of the **Revolutionary Tribunal** and opposed the indictment of **Jean-Paul Marat**, although Marat had denounced him in *L'ami du Peuple*.

Philippeaux went on mission to the **Vendée** in the summer of 1793. In September he prevailed in a debate over strategy and tactics, but when his plan proved to be disastrous he was recalled to Paris and subjected to political attack. **Jacques-René Hébert** criticized him at the Jacobin club in December, and even **Georges Danton** seemed to abandon him at this time. In early January he was denied admission to the Jacobin club, and the Cordeliers expelled him as well. **Jean-Baptiste Carrier** denounced him at the Jacobins on 21 February 1794, and in March **Louis-Antoine Saint-Just** included him in his indictment of the **Indulgents**. He went to the **guillotine** with Danton and the others on 5 April 1794.

PHRYGIAN CAPS. Phrygian caps, also known as Liberty caps, are among the most well-known symbols of the Revolution. They were floppy knit woolen caps, typically red in color, with a tri-colored **cockade** often attached to the tip. They appeared at least as early as the first **Festivals of Federation** in the summer of 1790. The name "phrygian" was an allusion to the freed slaves of Roman times, who were given similar caps as a symbol of their liberated status. During the Revolution, the caps came to symbolize freedom from the despotism of the Old Regime, and the newly gained liberty of all French citizens. They appeared frequently on the heads of female figures of Liberty, and became one of the defining aspects of the dress of **sans-culottes**. By 1793 they had became a virtually mandatory element of dress for those attending **sectional assemblies**. A phrygian cap appeared on the medallion of the **Jacobin club**, and they appeared frequently on *assignats* as well. On 20 June 1792, **Louis XVI** was given a phrygian cap to wear by the crowd in the **Tuileries** garden. It fell out of common use after **Thermidor**, but remained a fixture in official iconography well into the **Directory**. *See also* LIBERTY, EQUALITY, FRATERNITY.

PICHEGRU, JEAN-CHARLES (1761–1804). Pichegru was the son of a **peasant** in a village in the Jura. His parish sent him to be a mathematics teacher at the military *collège* at Brienne, but instead Pichegru enlisted in an artillery regiment as a simple soldier. By 1789 he was a sergeant-major. He welcomed the ideals of the Revolution, presiding over the Besançon **Jacobin club** at one point, and in October 1792 joined the Army of the Rhine as a battalion commander. Within 10 months he had risen to the rank of division general, and soon was named to command the Army of the Rhine. Reassigned to the Army of the Nord in February 1794, Pichegru oversaw the conquest of Holland. Early in that campaign he tangled with **Lazare Hoche**, who ended up in prison for a short spell. Pichegru helped to put down the **Germinal riots** in **Paris** in the spring of 1795. He returned to the Army of the Rhine thereafter, and was approached by agents of the Prince of Condé. When the **Directory** regime learned of this, it replaced Pichegru with General Jean-Victor Moreau. In 1797 Pichegru was elected to the **Council of Five Hundred**, even gaining the president's chair with royalist support. But those royalist connections got him proscribed in the **Fructidor coup** of 1797 and deported to Guyana. Pichegru escaped from Guyana in 1798 and traveled to London, where he eventually allied with the **chouan** leader Georges Cadoudal in a conspiracy against **Napoleon Bonaparte**. As part of that plot, Pichegru traveled clandestinely to Paris in 1804, but was arrested and imprisoned in the Temple, where he was found strangled in his cell.

PITT, WILLIAM (1759–1806). William Pitt was prime minister of England throughout the French Revolution, and was viewed by the revolutionaries as one of their greatest enemies. His father was prime minister as well, though of the Whig party, while William Pitt was a liberal Tory. Pitt became a lawyer in 1780, was elected to the House of Commons in 1781, and became chancellor of the exchequer in July 1782, at the age of 22. In December 1783 he became prime minister, a post he would hold until 1801. As prime minister he signed the 1786 trade treaty with France, so disastrous to French textile interests and beneficial to the British economy.

Pitt was initially unconcerned by the Revolution, but after the French advances into **Belgium** and the Lowlands in 1793 he began to subsidize aggressively the armies of the coalition against France (Prussia, Austria, Russia, and Spain) and also paid agents sent to France to undermine the revolutionary government. The Jacobins railed constantly against "Pitt's gold" as the source of every **counterrevolutionary** plot. After the execution of **Louis XVI**, Pitt ordered the French ambassador to England expelled, and declared a "war of extermination" against the regicide republic. The French government in turn labeled Pitt an "enemy of humanity."

Pitt resigned as prime minister in 1801, after a dispute with George III over the Irish situation, but returned to the post in 1804. His efforts were crucial to the formation of the Third Coalition against France. Although he died shortly after the battle of Austerlitz, a triumph for **Napoleon Bonaparte**, the war against France would endure until the Emperor was defeated at Waterloo.

PLACE DE LA RÉVOLUTION. The *Place de la Révolution*, known under the Old Regime as *Place Louis XV*, was designed by Jacques-Ange Gabriel and completed in 1772. It sits between the Champs Elysées and the **Tuileries** gardens in **Paris**. An equestrian statue of Louis XV, which stood at its center, was toppled following the **uprising of 10 August 1792**, to be replaced by an enormous statue of a female Liberty, which **Napoleon Bonaparte** ordered demolished in 1800. **Louis XVI** was executed on the square on 21 January 1793, and the square was renamed *Place de la Révolution* during the Year II. From 11 May 1793 until 8 June 1794, the **guillotine** stood permanently on the square. It was then moved to a more obscure location, but returned to the *Place de la Révolution* for the execution of **Maximilien Robespierre**. The square also hosted an elaborate revolutionary festival on the first anniversary of the fall of the monarchy, 10 August 1793. Napoleon renamed the square *Place de la Concorde*, which remains its name today.

PLAIN. The Plain, also known as the Marsh or Swamp (le Marais), refers to that group of deputies in the **National Convention** who held themselves aloof between the opposing factions of **Girondins** and **Montagnards**. They numbered roughly 250 deputies, giving them the capacity to sway the balance of power within the Convention, a capacity they seldom chose to exercise. Their moderate to conservative political views gave them a natural affinity for the Girondins, but some among them were skeptical of Girondin ambitions for power, and on 2 June 1793 enough deputies in the Plain supported the Montagnards to secure the proscription of the Girondin leaders. In the months that followed, most members of the Plain sustained their noncommittal politics, but a minority went on mission into the departments and participated in the government of the **Terror**. Many of those deputies associated with the Plain appeared later in the ranks of the **Thermidorians**.

POPE PIUS VI (1717–1799). Born Giovangelo Braschi, Pius VI held a position in the Papal Curia from 1740, was named a cardinal in 1773, and succeeded Clement XIV as pope on 15 February 1775. His election was greeted with enthusiasm. Having failed in his overtures to Emperor Joseph II in 1782, who was then imposing reforms on the Austrian church, Pius VI adopted a policy of reserve and restraint when the **Constituent Assembly** passed the **Civil Constitution of the Clergy** in July 1790. **Louis XVI** signed the legislation one month later, only to see it condemned by Pius VI in his papal brief of March 1791.

Pope Pius VI was similarly indecisive when the French annexed Avignon and the Comtat Venaissin (papal territories within French borders) in September 1791. He finally recognized the French Republic in 1796, in the Papal Bull *Pastoralis sollicitudo*, only to see the Papal States and then Rome itself invaded by French troops in 1797 and 1798. Pius VI was taken prisoner in the latter invasion and died in Valence while still in French hands. His successor, Pius VII, would negotiate the Concordat with **Napoleon Bonaparte** in 1801, restoring good relations between the French state and the Catholic Church.

POPULAR SOCIETIES. Popular societies, or *sociétés populaires*, are often taken to be synonymous with **Jacobin clubs**, but while the two overlap they were distinct entities. The Jacobin clubs were among the first popular societies, but the Jacobins soon achieved such a level of power and influence, through their national network and political orthodoxy, that they quickly overshadowed the other political clubs. Most provincial towns, and **Paris** as well, saw the appearance of several popular societies in 1789 and 1790. In **Lyon**, by 1790, each section had its own neighborhood club. In Aix-en-Provence there were two revolutionary clubs, the Jacobins and the *Antipolitiques*, as well as a **Monarchist club**, which called itself the *Amis de la Paix*. **Women**'s clubs appeared in Paris and a number of provincial cities as well.

As the Jacobin club of Paris (the "mother society") began to develop a network of affiliated clubs in 1790, the *Club Monarchique* in Paris attempted to develop its own network of Monarchist clubs. The confrontation between the two, often violent, generated a national debate about the legitimacy of these popular societies. The Paris Jacobins insisted that there could be only one affiliated club per town, and this often led to the merging of the two or more radical clubs, lest the general will, of which **Jean-Jacques Rousseau** wrote, be undermined. By the spring of 1791, the Monarchist clubs had ceased to exist, and in September 1791 **Isaac-René Le Chapelier** proposed legislation aimed at abolishing political clubs entirely. By then, however, the Jacobin club network was so firmly entrenched that the new law had little impact.

The origins of the popular societies lay in the literary societies and **confraternities** of the Old Regime. Consistent with those roots, the societies had varied functions in the early years of the Revolution. Many operated as debating societies, in which news from Paris and speeches by deputies in the **Constituent Assembly** would be read and discussed. Some saw the proper role of the popular societies as essentially didactic—they would be an arena in which "subjects" could learn to be "citizens" under the new political regime. Others foresaw a more activist role for the clubs, envisioning them as lobbying groups or pressure groups whose principal role was to shape and express the general will, rather than to educate the people. By 1792 many of the popular societies had formed correspondence committees and became active in electoral campaigns. None was more active, or successful, than the Jacobins, who came to dominate the political scene in 1793 and whose political ideology, and insistence on orthodoxy, must bear chief responsibility for the policies of the **Terror**. But one must give much credit to popular societies, as well, for the political vitality of the Revolution.

POPULAR SOVEREIGNTY. *See* SOVEREIGNTY.

PRAIRIAL COUP. The coup of 30 Prairial VII (18 June 1799) was the third under the **Directory**, each of which served to undermine public confidence in the political legitimacy of the regime. Unlike the preceding coups of **Floréal** and **Fructidor**, in which the directors purged unacceptable candidates recently elected to legislative office, in 1799 the deputies of the **Council of Ancients** and the **Council of Five Hundred** took the initiative themselves and forced the resignation of two directors, **Louis-Marie La Révellière-Lépeaux** and **Philippe Merlin**. They were replaced by **Pierre-Roger Ducos** and General Jean-François Moulin. The Prairial coup strengthened the position of **Emmanuel-Joseph Sieyès** among the five directors, and paved the way for the seizure of power by **Napoleon Bonaparte** later that year.

PRAIRIAL RIOTS. The Prairial riots (20–23 May 1795) mark the final uprising of the **sans-culotte** movement in **Paris** during the Revolution. In the wake of the **Germinal riots**, the **National Convention** had taken additional measures to preserve order and suppress the popular movement, but continued inflation and food shortages led to protest not only in the capital but in provincial cities as well. The attempted uprising of 1 Prairial was planned by arrested militants being held in the Plessis prison. Unlike the Germinal riots, this was an armed uprising, composed chiefly of militants from the *faubourg Saint-Antoine*. The crowd mobilized early in the morning, and invaded the Convention at mid-afternoon, overwhelming the guards and streaming over the barriers outside the doors into the hall. In the mêlée that ensued, the deputy Jean-Bertrand Féraud was killed and beheaded, and his head paraded on a pike before the speaker's rostrum.

As in Germinal, the insurgents called for bread and the **Constitution of 1793**. On this occasion, however, perhaps intimidated by the violence, certain **Montagnard** deputies responded to the demands of the crowd and passed legislation that evening ordering the release of militants arrested since **Thermidor**, the resumption of house searches directed against suspected hoarders, and a return to the permanence of **sectional assemblies**. As early as 2 Prairial, the government mobilized **National Guard** battalions from the more conservative sections in the west of Paris, and by 3 Prairial they had succeeded in subduing the insurgents from the eastern and southeastern neighborhoods. A number of Montagnard deputies were arrested, including seven who became known as the Prairial martyrs: **Charles-Gilbert Romme**, Jean-Michel Du Roy, Philippe Rühl, Claude-Alexandre Goujon, François-Joseph Duquesnoy, Pierre-Amable Soubrany, and Pierre Bourbotte. Du Roy and Bourbotte died on the **guillotine**, while the others committed suicide, several with a shared knife. In the weeks that followed the riots, there were dozens of arrests among the militants of the sections, more than 20 of whom would also be sentenced to death. This repression marked the final triumph of the **Thermidorians** over the last major insurrection in Paris, although **Gracchus Babeuf** and the **Conspiracy of Equals** would draw inspiration from the aspirations of the Prairial martyrs.

PRIEUR, PIERRE-LOUIS (1756–1827). Little is known of Prieur's family background except that before the Revolution he worked as an *avocat* in Chalons-sur-Marne, where he was elected as a deputy of the **Third Estate** to the **Estates-General**. His career in that assembly was unremarkable. He returned to the Marne in late 1791 as a departmental administrator, and was elected to the **National Convention**, again from the Marne, in 1792. Prieur was a member of the **Jacobin club**, voted for death in the trial of **Louis XVI**, and in July 1793 was elected to the **Committee of Public Safety**. He was frequently on mission in 1793, first for military recruitment in the West, then to combat the **federalist revolt** in Brittany and later the **Vendée uprising**. He replaced **Jean-Baptiste Carrier** in Nantes, which indirectly associated him with the **terrorist** excesses carried out in that city. For this he came under attack in 1795, having been removed from the Committee of Public Safety after 9 **Thermidor**. He joined the protesters who invaded the National Convention in the **Germinal uprising**, and was forced into hiding after the **Prairial uprising** in 1795. Under the **Directory** he resumed his legal career, was exiled in 1816 as a regicide, and died in Brussels in poverty. Prieur's portrait, painted by his friend **Jacques-Louis David**, hangs today in the Besançon museum.

PRIEUR-DUVERNOIS, CLAUDE-ANTOINE (1763–1832). Prieur's father was a royal tax collector, but he was orphaned at age four and brought up by an aunt. In 1779 he entered the military engineering school at Mézières, where **Gaspard Monge** was among his professors. He graduated with the rank of sub-lieutenant, and moved around to various garrison towns in the 1780s. In 1791 Prieur was elected to the **Legislative Assembly** from the Côte-d'Or, and then to the **National Convention**. He sat with the **Montagnards**, voted for death in the trial of **Louis XVI**, but did not attend the **Jacobin club**. In June–July 1793, while on mission in Normandy, he was held hostage by the federalist rebels in **Caen**, along with **Gilbert Romme**. More of a technician than a politician, Prieur is known as the "second organizer of victory" for his role on the **Committee of Public Safety** overseeing military preparations with **Lazare Carnot**, who was also a student of Monge. After leaving the Great Committee in October 1794, he served on the Committee of Public Instruction, helping to create what would become the Ecole Polytechnique. Prieur was elected to the **Council of Five Hundred** in 1795, serving there until 1798, and retired from public life after the **Brumaire** coup. In 1808 he was named a Count of the Empire.

PRIVILEGE. Old Regime France was a society of privilege. We tend to think of the first two estates, the **clergy** and **aristocracy**, as the privileged orders of the old Regime, and they did indeed tend to enjoy more privileges than members of the **Third Estate**, some of them honorific and some more real, as in their exemption from the payment of most taxes. But many other people enjoyed privileges as well by virtue of belonging to one corporate body or another. Those provinces that were *pays d'état*, for example Brittany, were exempt from paying certain taxes. Those who lived in chartered towns or cities enjoyed certain privileges. Members of guilds were granted the privilege of practicing their trade and generally exercised a virtual monopoly in that trade. Those who held royal office, often purchased, enjoyed the privileges associated with that office.

The **Declaration of the Rights of Man and Citizen** represented an implicit renunciation of privilege, by asserting that all men shared equally a common body of rights. The **Night of 4 August** brought an explicit attack on **seigneurial dues** and other vestiges of feudal privilege, and over the next two years the **Constituent Assembly** issued a series of decrees eliminating privileges in all spheres of public life.

The abolition of privilege was given definitive expression in the preamble to the **Constitution of 1791**.

PROTESTANTS. There were approximately 700,000 Protestants in France on the eve of the French Revolution. The Huguenots, as they were called, had been denied civil status and the right to practice their religion openly since Louis XIV's revocation of the Edict of Nantes in 1685. **Louis XVI** issued an Edict of Toleration in November 1787, which granted Protestants the right to worship openly and to register births, marriages, and deaths in their own churches. While the situation of Protestants in France was much improved by that edict, many questions remained in regard to their civil status. In 1788, for example, Protestants petitioned the king to ask if they would be eligible to sit in the **Estates-General**. The crown ruled in the affirmative, and **Jean-Paul Rabaut Saint-Etienne**, a Protestant pastor, was among those elected as a deputy for the **Third Estate**. It was not until 24 December 1789, however, that the **Constituent Assembly** ruled that Protestants were eligible to hold public office.

Most Protestants responded with enthusiasm to the reforms introduced by the Revolution, but in some parts of France political rivalries reawakened religious tensions and there was violence between Protestants and Catholics. The most serious such confrontation was the *Bagarre de* **Nîmes** in late spring 1790, but there was violence, too, in **Montauban** that summer. In the town of **Caen**, which had a sizable Protestant population, there was no religious violence, but Samuel Chatry declined his election as mayor in 1791 for fear that his Protestant faith would be a source of public controversy. A number of Protestants did accept public office during the Revolution, however, including Rabaut Saint-Etienne and **André Jeanbon Saint-André**, who served in 1793 on the **Committee of Public Safety**.

PROVENCE, LOUIS-STANISLAS-XAVIER (1755–1824). The Comte de Provence was the younger brother of **Louis XVI**, heir to the French throne until the birth of the dauphin in 1781. Although gravely disappointed, Provence devoted himself thereafter to his interest in the arts and literature, while residing at the Palace of Luxembourg in **Paris**. From behind the scenes, however, he played a role in the falls of Anne-Robert-Jacques Turgot, **Jacques Necker**,

Charles-Alexandre Calonne, and Etienne-Charles Loménie de Brienne, thereby helping to stymie all efforts at reform in the late Old Regime. At the Assembly of Notables, in 1787, when the opportunity arrived to engage politics and affairs of state on a public stage, Provence was upstaged by his cousin, the Duke of Orléans.

Provence was opposed to the Revolution from the outset, and compromised himself in the Favras Affair of 1789, in which he hoped to use the Marquis de Favras in a scheme that would have made Provence regent of France. He emigrated to Holland at the same time as Louis XVI's failed flight to Varennes, and soon installed himself among the *émigrés* in Coblenz. From there he engineered the August 1791 Declaration of Pillnitz, by which Austria and Prussia pledged intervention in France to defend the monarchy. In September 1792 Provence entered France at the head of an *émigré* army of 14,000, commanded by the Duke of Brunswick, but it was defeated at Valmy.

After the execution of Louis XVI, Provence declared himself Regent of France, and when the young Louis XVII died in June 1795 he declared himself king. It would be nearly 20 years, however, until Napoleon Bonaparte's defeat at Waterloo, before Provence would ascend the throne as Louis XVIII. Between 1795 and 1814 he supported all sorts of intrigues—the Vendée rebels, the Quiberon landing, the scheming of Georges Cadoudal and Jean-Charles Pichegru—but all were failures. Louis XVIII ruled France until 1824.

PRUDHOMME, LOUIS-MARIE (1752–1830). Louis-Marie Prudhomme was born in Lyon, where he worked as a clerk and binder in the book trade. He moved to Paris in 1787, opened his own bookshop, and claimed to have published as many as 1,500 pamphlets on the eve of the Revolution. In July 1789 he began publication of the *Révolutions de Paris*, a weekly newspaper that quickly achieved a substantial circulation and became one of the most influential of the revolutionary papers. Prudhomme left much of the writing to others, but clearly exercised an active editorial hand throughout the years of its publication. The newspaper gained the support of the Cordelier club, but by 1793 Prudhomme's political views had moderated and he came under suspicion as a supporter of the Girondins. Later he was attacked for abuses allegedly committed while on mission in the provinces with Jacques-Nicolas Billaud-Varenne.

As the political climate grew more precarious under the **Terror**, Prudhomme suspended publication of *Les Révolutions de Paris* in February 1794. He withdrew from politics for some time, but in 1797 published *L'Histoire générale et impartiale des erreurs, des fautes et des crimes commis pendant la Révolution*, a six-volume work that was suppressed by the **Directory** regime. Prudhomme became director of **hospitals** in Paris for a brief time in 1799, but soon resumed his career as printer and bookseller. He did not support the Empire of **Napoleon Bonaparte**, and despite his republican views of the 1790s welcomed the Restoration in 1814.

PUBLIC OPINION. In the theoretical conceptualization of absolutist monarchy, most eloquently promulgated in the 17th century by Bishop Jacques-Bénigne Bossuet, the king was the only public person in the realm. All others were private individuals, possessed of varying **privileges** in accordance with their place or rank. The king might consult their views from time to time, but in the end it was his opinion that mattered and all were subject to his absolute power.

Most historians would argue today that royal power was never as absolute as Bossuet would have had it, but it is also clear that over the course of the 18th century royal authority came increasingly to be challenged, and in that process both critics of the monarchy and eventually the monarch himself began to appeal to public opinion. For example, members of the **Parlement of Paris** sometimes wrote remonstrances, in which they took issue with royal edicts, and from the 1750s onward those remonstrances tended to be published with greater frequency. In similar fashion, lawyers involved in the *causes célèbres* of the late Old Regime often published their briefs, written in narrative form, in an effort to carry their case from the seclusion of the courtroom to the more open tribunal of public opinion. In the early 1780s **Jacques Necker** published an account of his stewardship of the royal treasury, defending his actions to the public. After 1787, faced with an intransigent **Assembly of Notables**, **Louis XVI** himself appealed to public opinion through his ministers. In all of these ways, public opinion came gradually to constitute an important, though intangible, political force.

The culmination of this came with the convocation of the **Estates-General** and the accompanying call, by the king, for the drafting of *cahiers de doléances*. The public had now been empowered by royal edict. **Sovereignty** quickly shifted, in 1789, from the person of the king to the collective public, to the nation. It would be the task of the revolutionaries thereafter to give public opinion more tangible definition and expression, through elections, legislative assemblies, and political clubs. To borrow Keith Baker's apt phrase, the public power of the sovereign had become the sovereign power of the public. *See also ESPRIT PUBLIC.*

PUISAYE, JOSEPH-GENEVIÈVE (1755–1827). Count Joseph Puisaye was the son of a marquis, an officer in the royal army. His parents sent him to *collège* in Laval, and then Sens, and hoped for a calling in the Church for their son, but he chose to pursue a military career instead. When he retired in 1787, Puisaye held the rank of lieutenant-colonel in the Swiss One Hundreds. Puisaye was elected to the **Estates-General** by the nobility of the *bailliage* of Perche. He protested the abolition of noble titles, but otherwise made little impression in the **Constituent Assembly**. Puisaye rejoined the army in late 1791, as a *maréchal de camp*, and in 1793 was named chief of staff to General Félix Wimpffen in the Army of the Coast of Cherbourg.

In June 1793 General Wimpffen lent his support to the **federalist** rebels in **Caen**, and Puisaye took charge of the vanguard dispatched to Evreux in early July. After those troops were routed at Pacy-sur-Eure on 13 July 1793, Puisaye fled to Brittany where, with financial support from England and the Comte d'Artois, he took up a leadership position among the *chouan* rebels. In July 1795 he collaborated with agents of **William Pitt** to plan the **Quiberon** expedition, which proved to be an utter debacle. His military reputation now ruined, Puisaye left France in 1797 for England and then Canada, where he attempted to found a *chouan* colony. That project faltered as well, and Puisaye returned to England, where he wrote his memoirs and lived out his life in quiet seclusion.

– Q –

QUIBERON. On 27 June 1795, some 3,000 *émigré* troops disembarked on the Quiberon peninsula in southwest Brittany, under the command of General **Joseph Puisaye**. The expedition was supported by the British government, which hoped to open a second front in its war with the French Republic by linking up with the remnants of the **Vendée rebellion** and the persistent *chouan* uprisings in the West of France. The expeditionary force was amply supplied, but their numbers were fewer than originally planned. Moreover, Puisaye disagreed with other **aristocratic** officers among the *émigrés*, many of whom were less than enthusiastic about active collaboration with the **peasant** *chouans*. Thousands of *chouans* did in fact flock to the disembarkation point, but a superior republican force, under the command of General **Louis-Lazare Hoche**, easily routed the disorganized rebel forces in mid-July. Hoche treated the *chouans* leniently, but over 600 of the captured *émigrés* were shot in Vannes, in accordance with a law stating that the mere presence of an *émigré* on French soil bearing arms was an offense punishable by death. The debacle at Quiberon ruined the military reputation of General Puisaye, alienated French royalists from the British government, which they felt had betrayed them, and greatly enhanced the reputation of Lazare Hoche.

– R –

RABAUT SAINT-ETIENNE, JEAN-PAUL (1743–1793). Rabaut's father was a **Protestant** minister, who sent all three of his sons to Lausanne for **education** in order to escape religious persecution. In 1785 Jean-Paul traveled to **Paris** to petition for civil status for Protestants, which **Louis XVI** would grant in 1787. His stay in Paris made clear to Rabaut the seriousness of the national crisis, and he published several pamphlets calling for an enhanced role for the **Estates-General**. Despite opposition from local **clergy**, he was elected to the Estates-General by the **Third Estate** of Nîmes. He was a steady advocate of freedom of religion, supported the creation of a constitutional monarchy, and favored a single-chamber legislature. In June 1790, shortly after his election as president of the **Constituent Assembly**, religious violence erupted in the *bagarre de* **Nîmes**. Rabaut was troubled by the flight to **Varennes**, but refused to blame the king, perhaps out of loyalty to Louis for his willingness to grant Protestants civil status. The events of 1792 disabused him of that loyalty, however, and while he voted for a suspended sentence he also spoke against the king at his trial. Rabaut sat with the **Girondins** in the **National Convention**, served on the **Commission of Twelve** in May 1793, and was proscribed on 2 June. He fled Paris, encouraged rebellion in Nîmes, was declared a traitor in July, and was executed immediately upon arrest in early December 1793. In October 1795 the National Convention decreed his posthumous rehabilitation.

REFRACTORY PRIESTS. Those priests who refused to swear the **Civil Oath** mandated by the **Civil Constitution of the Clergy** were known as refractory priests, or *réfractaires*. Approximately 50 percent of the parish priests across France fell into this category. Initially the **Constituent Assembly** ruled that refractory priests might continue to hold religious services, but over time they came to be increasingly persecuted. In June 1791 they were deprived of their pensions. In November 1791, due to a growing number of public disruptions, refractory priests were forbidden to hold services in churches and placed under municipal surveillance. In May 1792 the **Legislative Assembly** decreed that refractory priests could be deported at the request of 20 **active citizens**. Harsher laws were passed in 1793: in April the **National Convention** decreed that refractory priests might be deported at the request of only six citizens, and in August it ordered that all refractory priests be deported. Over the course of the Revolution, as many as 30,000 priests left France, either voluntarily or by deportation.

Refractory priests suffered violence as well as deportation. The **September Massacres** claimed the lives of 225 priests, and there were numerous refractory priests among the *noyades* of Nantes. Donald Greer estimated that 6.5 percent (roughly 2,600) of the victims of the **Terror** were clergy, most of them no doubt refractory priests. Persecution of the clergy diminished after **Thermidor**, and in August 1797 all repressive legislation against the refractory clergy was repealed. That amnesty lasted less than a month, however, before the old laws were reinstituted and a new wave of persecution began, lasting until the Concordat of 1801.

REGENERATION. The idea of regeneration was present from the very beginning of the Revolution. Many of the pamphlets published in 1789 asserted the need for regeneration in the face of the national crisis, and even **Louis XVI** spoke of the **Estates-General** as charged with the task of national regeneration. The **liberty tree** was a potent symbol of that very thing. The **Declaration of the Rights of Man and Citizen** might be seen as the first tangible expression of the ideal of regeneration, and the first celebration of the fall of the **Bastille**, the **Festival of Federation** in July 1790, was seen by many revolutionaries as marking the dawn of a new age.

Education was to be a principal means by which that regeneration might be achieved. The **Legislative Assembly** created a Committee of Public Instruction, on which **Marie-Jean Condorcet** played a leading role. Condorcet was among the earliest advocates of the declaration of a republic, but he realized that most French men and **women** (for he was among the few revolutionaries who called for full citizenship for women) were not yet prepared to assume the responsibilities that went along with the liberties of republican government.

As the Revolution progressed, the **Jacobin clubs** increasingly called for both civic and cultural regeneration. But whereas Condorcet may have believed that republicanism could be cultivated through voluntary education, the Jacobins tended to embrace **Jean-Jacques Rousseau's** admonition that man must be forced to be free, and advocated a more aggressive approach to regeneration. The revolutionary martyr, **Louis-Michel Le Peletier de Saint-Fargeau**, proposed a system of compulsory education that exerted much influence after his death, though it was never implemented. The deputies of the **National Convention** did introduce a number of measures, however, consistent with the ideal of regeneration: the **revolutionary calendar**, the **Festival of Reason**, the introduction of republican names for public places and newborn children, and the **Festival of the Supreme Being**.

Thermidor marked a rejection of the more coercive Jacobin approach to regeneration, but the idea did not disappear. **Henri-Baptiste Grégoire**, in particular, continued to advocate the importance of education to this endeavor under the **Directory**. So long as there were **counterrevolutionary** threats to the republic, there would be calls for regeneration to meet them, but the ideal of a revolutionary "new man" did indeed fade from view with the fall of **Maximilien Robespierre**.

REPRESENTATIVES ON MISSION. The **National Convention** dispatched deputies on special missions out to the provinces as early as the fall of 1792, but the first wave of representatives on mission was sent out in March 1793, principally to assist in the recruitment of men into the army. At that time the Convention divided the country into 41 sections and sent two deputies to each, typically one from the area and another who was a stranger to the locale. Those sent out in the spring tended to be drawn from the ranks of the **Montagnards**, and after the proscription of the **Girondin** leaders on 2 June 1793, that was almost exclusively the case until after 9 **Thermidor**, when former Girondins and deputies from the **Plain** more often went out on mission.

Initially the National Convention established no clear limit to the authority of the representatives on mission, and the tendency of some to intervene quite actively in local affairs prompted **departmental administrators** in some areas to denounce them as virtual proconsuls. Following the **uprising of 31 May–2 June 1793**, representatives on mission were harassed, even taken hostage, in a number of provincial cities, and one of their principal tasks now became the suppression of the **federalist revolt**. After the revolt collapsed, representatives on mission oversaw the purging of local administrative bodies. Local **Jacobin clubs** were an essential ally to the deputies in that task, though eventually the representatives on mission often carried out a purge of the clubs themselves. By the **Law of 14 Frimaire** the National Convention limited and defined more explicitly the powers of the representatives on mission. Under the regime of the **Terror**, however, some representatives continued to abuse their authority.

It is indeed those abusive representatives on mission who have received the most prominent treatment by historians. The excesses of **Jean-Baptiste Carrier** in Nantes, of **Jean-Marie Collot d'Herbois** in **Lyon**, of **Claude Javogues** in the department of the Loire, of **Joseph Fouché** in Burgundy are well chronicled. But there is a host of other representatives on mission who carried out their duties more responsibly and with greater restraint, men such as **Robert Lindet**, **Charles-Gilbert Romme**, **Georges-August Couthon**, and **Claude-Alexandre Ysabeau**. Although figuring less prominently in histories of the Revolution, their missions are amply documented by the letters and reports that they submitted to the **Committee of Public Safety**, which was responsible for making appointments of representatives on mission from June 1793 forward. Beyond their role in recruitment and repression, the representatives on mission made a major contribution to the revolutionary agenda of **regeneration** by carrying Jacobin ideals out from **Paris** to the provinces.

RÉVEILLON RIOTS. The Réveillon riots of 27–28 April 1789 are generally considered to be the first popular insurrection of the Revolution in **Paris**. Jean-Baptiste Réveillon was a wealthy wallpaper manufacturer in the *faubourg* **Saint-Antoine**. He had been decorated for his contributions to industry, was generous to his workers, and an elector for his district. On 23 April he gave a speech at his electoral assembly in which he lamented the increasing costs of production, in particular the high cost of labor. Similar remarks were reportedly made by a gunpowder manufacturer named Henriot at another assembly, and in a period of rising food prices and economic uncertainty the rumor soon spread through the *faubourg* that the two employers were in collusion to force wages down.

Trouble began on the afternoon of 27 April, a day off for workers, when a large crowd gathered near the **Bastille** and hanged Réveillon and Henriot in effigy. The crowd, which soon numbered 3,000, paraded through the neighborhood to Réveillon's mansion, but finding it heavily guarded moved on to sack Henriot's house. Police dispersed the crowd that evening without casualty, but it re-formed the next day in even greater numbers and returned to sack Réveillon's mansion. Police opened fire on those massed in the street, killing at least 25, with many more wounded. Exemplary justice soon followed. The very next day, 29 April, two rioters were hung on the *place de Grève*, and more executions and lengthy sentences to the galleys were handed down later. Coming as they did on the very eve of the first session of the **Estates-General**, the Réveillon riots almost certainly made an impression on the delegates, and can be seen as the first of the great *journées* of the Revolution. It should be noted, however, that unlike the major uprisings to follow, these were carried out almost exclusively by wage earners.

REVOLUTIONARY CALENDAR. The introduction of a revolutionary calendar in the fall of 1793 can be seen as an element of the **deChristianization** campaign and more generally as consistent with the ideal of **regeneration**. The **National Convention** endorsed the idea of a new calendar shortly after the declaration of the Republic on 22 September 1792. The task was assigned to the Committee of Public Instruction, chaired by **Charles-Gilbert Romme**. Romme drafted a version of the calendar while held hostage in the Château of **Caen** during the **federalist revolt**, and the Convention adopted the new calendar on 5 October 1793. The first day of the republican calendar, 1 vendémiaire I, corresponded to 22 September 1792.

The names of the months in the revolutionary calendar were devised by the poet **Philippe Fabre d'Eglantine**. They were meant to evoke elements of nature. Thus, vendémiaire was the month of the wine harvest, **brumaire** the month of fog, floréal the month of flowering, and **thermidor** the month of heat. Each month was divided into three *décadis* of 10 days each, in keeping with the **metric system**, and at the end of the year five extra days were known as *sans-culottides*. The revolutionary calendar was not popular among the common people, who regretted that the usual four Sundays of the month had been reduced to three days of rest. The calendar was never exported beyond French borders, even as revolutionary armies expanded French territory, but all official documents bore the new dates until after **Napoleon Bonaparte** came to power. The dates of the Gregorian calendar once again began to appear alongside the revolutionary dates in late 1802, and in January 1806 the revolutionary calendar was formally abolished.

REVOLUTIONARY TRIBUNAL. The Revolutionary Tribunal in **Paris** was created in March 1793 on the proposal of the deputy **Jean-Baptiste Carrier**, who would one day be sentenced to death by the tribunal he had helped bring into being. It was a time of crisis for the young French Republic, with military setbacks in **Belgium**, the treason of **General Charles-François Dumouriez**, and the first signs of rebellion in the **Vendée**. Crimes of treason or **counterrevolution** were to be judged by the Revolutionary Tribunal, which consisted of five judges, a jury of 12 men, and a public prosecutor. On 5 September 1793 the Revolutionary Tribunal was expanded so that four courts might operate concurrently.

From April 1793 until **Thermidor**, **Antoine-Quentin Fouquier-Tinville** served as public prosecutor. Over time the procedures of the

Revolutionary Tribunal grew increasingly streamlined. During the trial of the **Girondins**, the **National Convention** decreed that juries might restrict the proceedings to three days if they were convinced of the guilt of the accused. The **Law of 22 Prairial** (10 June 1794) eliminated defense counsels and cross-examination, decreed that moral evidence as well as material evidence might justify a conviction, and restricted juries to two possible verdicts: acquittal or death. This law ushered in the most active period of the Revolutionary Tribunal's existence, the final two months of the **Terror**.

Fouquier-Tinville presided over the trials of the most celebrated victims of the Terror: **Charlotte Corday**, the Girondin leaders, **Marie Antoinette**, **Louis-Philippe Orléans**, **Jacques-René Hébert**, **Georges-Jacques Danton**, and **Jean-Sylvain Bailly**. There were other revolutionary tribunals in the provinces—they appeared in areas of revolt or rebellion, such as **Lyon**, **Marseille**, **Bordeaux**, and the Vendée—but none rivaled the impact of the Revolutionary Tribunal in Paris. Between March 1793 and May 1795, when it was abolished, its judges sentenced more than 2,700 people to death. Among its final victims was Fouquier-Tinville himself.

RÉVOLUTIONS DE PARIS. *Révolutions de Paris* is the name of the **newspaper** published by **Louis-Marie Prudhomme** from July 1789 until February 1794. It was perhaps the most influential of the papers in **Paris**, estimated by **Camille Desmoulins** to have had as many as 250,000 subscribers. The paper was published weekly, consistently 48 pages in length, making it one of the most substantial Paris papers as well. Although Prudhomme's editorial hand is evident throughout its run, a number of other prominent revolutionaries wrote for the newspaper, including Elisée Loustalot, **Philippe Fabre d'Eglantine**, **Pierre-Gaspard Chaumette**, and **Pierre-Sylvain Maréchal**. The paper was initially composed in diary form, a narrative account of the events of the past week. Over time it introduced regular features, such as reports from the **Constituent Assembly**, foreign news, and engravings of dramatic events. Its editorial policy was radical, consistent with its loose affiliation with the **Cordelier club**, but Prudhomme eschewed the inflammatory style of other radical newspapers, such as **Jean-Paul Marat's** *L'Ami du Peuple*, or **Jacques-René Hébert's** *Père Duchesne*, preferring instead an objective tone, bolstered by as much evidence and factual material as could be amassed. When freedom of the press began to be curtailed under the **Terror**, Prudhomme chose to suspend publication of the newspaper voluntarily.

ROBESPIERRE, AUGUSTIN-BON-JOSEPH (1763–1794). Augustin and his older brother, **Maximilien**, were both brought up in Arras by their maternal grandfather, following the death of their mother and their father's desertion of the family. Augustin followed Maximilien to the *collège* Louis-le-Grand in **Paris**, where he eventually studied law and emerged as an *avocat*. Having returned to Arras to practice law, he became active in local politics, joined the local **Jacobin club** (over which he would later preside), and was elected to the post of municipal *procureur*. In 1791 he was elected to the **departmental administration** of the Pas-de-Calais, and in the following year was elected from Paris to the **National Convention**. He voted for death in the trial of **Louis XVI**, and opposed the indictment of **Jean-Paul Marat**. In July 1793 Augustin was sent on mission to the Army of Italy, and was present at the siege of **Toulon** later that fall. So impressed was he by a young artillery officer by the name of **Napoleon Bonaparte**, that he wrote a letter to his brother in praise of his talents. Robespierre stopped in the Haute-Saône on his way back to Paris, and while there ordered the release of a number of local officials, previously arrested by the deputy André-Antoine Bernard. For this he earned the enmity of Bernard, and the eternal gratitude of the local people.

Once back in Paris, Augustin commented at the Jacobin club that the tenor of political debate had deteriorated in his absence, and in particular spoke critically of the **deChristianization** campaign. On 9 **Thermidor** he insisted on sharing the fate of his brother, though he might well have otherwise been spared. When troops arrived at the Hôtel de Ville that evening, he attempted suicide by jumping from an upper-story window. He was taken to the **guillotine** the following day, bloody and still unconscious.

ROBESPIERRE, MAXIMILIEN-FRANÇOIS-ISIDOIRE (1758–1794). Maximilien was the first of five children, born in Arras into a long line of *avocats* and small merchants on his father's side of the family. His mother died during childbirth in 1764, and his father, an *avocat*, abandoned the family shortly thereafter, leaving the children to be brought up by their maternal grandparents. Maximilien took a paternal interest in his younger brother and sisters, but little is known of their childhood. Robespierre attended the school of the Oratoriens in Arras for some years, and then went on to the *collège* Louis-le-Grand in **Paris** as a scholarship student. Among his fellow students was **Camille Desmoulins**. He earned his law degree in 1780, and returned to Arras to take up a career as an *avocat*.

Robespierre enjoyed considerable success in his early career, taking on several prominent cases, and entered both the local **Academy** and the Rosati literary society, where he met **Lazare Carnot**.

In 1789 he was elected by the **Third Estate** of Artois to the **Estates-General**. Robespierre joined the **Jacobin club** and sat with the "democrats" in the Assembly, but he was not a major force in the **Constituent Assembly** (some complained that he was an ineffective orator). One sees in his speeches, however, the same disciplined and principled political thought that would characterize him throughout the Revolution. His most notable contribution in the Constituent Assembly was his successful proposal that deputies be declared ineligible for re-election to the **Legislative Assembly**. He remained in Paris during the following year, moving in with the Duplay family on the rue St. Honoré in the summer of 1791. He emerged as a leader in the Jacobin club following the split with the **Feuillants**, and maintained his public prominence through the club, his **newspaper** (*Le Défenseur de la Constitution*), and his participation in Parisian municipal politics.

Robespierre was very popular among the Parisian **sans-culottes**, whose cause he championed before and after the **uprising of 10 August 1792**. Robespierre characterized the toppling of the monarchy as a victory of the people, and called for an end to the distinction between **active** and **passive citizens**. He was elected to the **National Convention** from the city of Paris. Denounced by **Jean-Baptiste Louvet** as responsible for the **September Massacres**, along with **Jean-Paul Marat** and **Georges Danton**, Robespierre became the principal focus of **Girondin** attacks. In the trial of **Louis XVI**, Robespierre first argued that no trial was necessary, the king having already been found guilty of treason by the insurrectionary people, and then led the charge for a verdict of guilt and a sentence of death. As divisions deepened within the National Convention, Robespierre emerged as the most prominent leader of the **Montagnards**. In May he exhorted the militants of the Paris sections, from the rostrum of the Jacobin club, to rise up against the Girondin leaders, who viewed with suspicion the influence of Paris on national politics. As in August 1792, Robespierre remained aloof from the actual upheaval of late May and early June, which resulted in the proscription of 29 Girondin deputies.

Elected to the **Committee of Public Safety** in late July 1793, he concerned himself with all of the affairs of the Committee—the war effort, the revolts in the provinces, correspondence, the situation in Paris. He became spokesperson for the Committee before the National Convention, a role that contributed to his reputation as the dominant figure in the executive branch. He gave particularly notable speeches before the National Convention in December 1793 (*On the Principles of Revolutionary Government*) and in February 1794 (*On the Principles of Political Morality*). Both speeches show very clearly the influence of **Jean-Jacques Rousseau** on the political thought of Robespierre. In the spring of 1794 he called for the creation of a **Cult of the Supreme Being**, in order to curb the **deChristianization** movement, and in its first national festival on 7 May 1794 (choreographed by **Jacques-Louis David**) played a role that seemed to suggest an ambition to be the High Priest of that cult, a step that alienated many of the deputies in the National Convention.

Robespierre was the target of two alleged assassination attempts in the spring of 1794. This led to a harshening of the **Terror**, by the new **Law of 22 Prairial**, at a time when the threat to the Republic from civil war and external enemies had substantially diminished. Physically and mentally exhausted by the strains of revolutionary politics, Robespierre withdrew from his duties in June, appearing only rarely in public. When he returned to the club and the Convention, he spoke of a need to redouble revolutionary vigilance, but he seemed to have lost some of his verve and self-confidence. Led by **Joseph Fouché** and **Jean-Lambert Tallien**, his enemies on both left and right now rallied against him. In his final speech, on 8 **Thermidor** at the Jacobin club, Robespierre denounced those conspiring against him, or against the Revolution, but his vague accusations simply impelled more fearful deputies to join the conspiracy. By this point, indeed, Robespierre seemed resigned to his own fate. On 9 Thermidor the deputies refused to allow him or his supporters to speak. Robespierre was arrested along with **Georges Couthon** and **Louis-Antoine Saint-Just**, his most trusted and loyal supporters in recent months. They took refuge that night in the Hôtel de Ville, but the sans-culottes of Paris failed to rally in sufficient numbers to their defense, either out of exhaustion from four years of revolution, or because so many of them had by then been incorporated into the revolutionary government that had now officially declared Robespierre to be an outlaw. In the mêlée that evening, Robespierre blew off a portion of his jaw and lay in agony all night on a table until being taken to the **guillotine** the following morning, along with Saint-Just, Couthon, and his brother **Augustin**, among others. Another 86 supporters of Robespierre, known to friend and foe alike as the *Incorruptible*, would follow in the next few days, bringing to an end the **Terror** and the revolutionary government of the Year II.

ROLAND, JEAN-MARIE (1734–1793). Jean-Marie Roland was born in Villefranche, in the Beaujolais. His father was a *bailliage* magistrate, while his mother came from an impoverished noble family. Four of his brothers were priests, but Roland chose a career in the royal bureaucracy. He obtained a minor post in the administration of manufactures in 1755, became an inspector in 1766, and in 1784 was named general inspector of manufactures in **Lyon**. Roland also had an interest in scientific research and traveled widely in Europe. He wrote extensively about industry and manufacturing, most notably a three-volume *Encyclopédie méthodique* that was published by **Charles-Joseph Pancoucke** in the 1780s. In 1780 he married Manon Philipon, daughter of a Parisian engraver. The Rolands moved back and forth between the provinces and **Paris** in the 1780s, and Jean-Marie joined the **Freemasons** and became acquainted with intellectual circles in the capital. Roland was drawn to the ideas of **Adam Smith**, but in 1786 condemned the commercial treaty between France and England.

Roland was elected as a *notable* to the Lyon municipal council in February 1790, and then as an officer in November. He played a key role in mobilizing the neighborhood club movement in Lyon during the first years of the Revolution, and in this endeavor allied himself, if only briefly, with **Joseph Chalier**. In February 1791 the city sent

Roland to Paris, to report to the **Constituent Assembly** on the critical state of the silk industry and to seek relief for Lyon's debt. While in Paris, Roland frequented the **Cercle Social**, where he strengthened his relationship with **Jacques-Pierre Brissot** and met a number of other prominent political figures. During this visit of some seven months, **Manon Roland** opened her first **salon**, which also served to broaden her husband's circle of acquaintances in the capital. The Rolands returned to Lyon at year's end, but as the inspectorate of manufactures had been abolished they did not stay long, preferring to establish residency in Paris. Roland now joined the **Jacobin club**, and in March 1792 was named minister of the interior, in part due to his contacts with Brissot and his circle, in part due to his past experience.

Roland's first term as minister was short-lived. With the war effort going badly, the Brissotins chose to present **Louis XVI** with a set of ultimatums, delivered to the king in a letter from Roland, probably drafted by Manon, who had long edited most of her husband's writing. The king could accept some, but not all, of the demands, and chose to sack Roland and two other ministers, leading to the failed uprising of 20 June 1792. After the fall of the monarchy on 10 August, Roland returned as minister of the interior with a good deal more power and independence. He soon alienated Parisian **sans-culottes**, however, on two scores. First, as minister he was responsible for the inventory of the king's apartments in the months leading up to his trial. Although credited for the discovery of the secret safe in the **Tuileries** Palace, Roland allowed the papers found in it to be inventoried without supervision, and this was attacked in the press. Some property was also stolen from one of the king's warehouses, which also drew suspicion. Second, Roland became embroiled in the controversy over the **September Massacres**. He initially characterized the prison killings as a regrettable but necessary measure. But in October he used funds from the newly created *bureau de l'esprit public* to print and distribute 10,000 copies of **Jean-Baptiste Louvet's** speech denouncing **Maximilien Robespierre** as having planned the massacres. Roland used those same funds to subsidize Louvet's **newspaper**, one of the principal organs of the **Girondin** deputies. In addition to all this, Manon Roland's salon was now widely perceived as a virtual headquarters for the Girondin faction.

Roland, an aging man, could not endure the mounting public attacks against him, and shortly after the execution of Louis XVI he resigned his ministry. He was not allowed to leave the capital, and as the Girondins came under attack in May, Roland was denounced as well. Now Manon did manage to secure her husband's escape, just before the proscription of the Girondin deputies on 2 June. He hid for a time in Montmorency, then fled to Rouen. When he learned of Manon's execution on 8 November 1793 he went out into the countryside and killed himself with his cane sword.

ROLAND, MANON (1754–1793). Born Jeanne-Marie Philipon, Manon Roland was the daughter of a Parisian engraver with a shop on the Place Dauphine. The family was comfortable financially, and Manon was well-educated, reading widely in the classics, from Plutarch to Montaigne and **Rousseau**. Her mother died when she was just 11. In the 1770s Manon carried on a lengthy courtship with **Jean-Marie Roland**, a man 20 years her senior, whom she married in 1780. Both families were somewhat uncomfortable with this match, but in Roland Manon had found a man who would accept, indeed encourage, her intellectual interests. She became intimately involved in his work, editing much of his writing and supporting his political ambitions.

When the Rolands moved near **Lyon** in 1784, Manon began her regular social/intellectual gatherings. **François-Xavier Lanthenas**, a young doctor whom they had met in Italy, was frequently in attendance, and he would in turn introduce the Rolands to his political contacts in **Paris** once the Revolution began. Early in the Revolution, Manon contributed a number of articles, published anonymously, to the **newspaper** edited by **Jacques-Pierre Brissot.** Manon opened her first **salon** in Paris in 1791, and **François Buzot**, **Jean-Baptiste Louvet**, **Charles Barbaroux**, Jean-Baptiste Salle, and **Margeurite-Elie Guadet** were soon regular in their attendance. By 1792 she was hosting twice-weekly dinners, followed by political discussion and debate. Manon tended to remain aloof from those discussions, but was very much the intellectual equal of the men who gathered in her living room and exerted a quiet influence on their ideas. When the **Montagnards** attacked Jean-Marie Roland and other **Girondin** leaders for their anti-Parisian rhetoric in the fall of 1792, Manon became a target as well, so much so that she felt compelled to defend herself before the **National Convention** on 7 December 1792. She spoke so eloquently that the deputies voted her the honors of the day.

On the day that Jean-Marie Roland resigned as minister of the interior, Manon informed her husband that she loved another, although it was not until the 1860s that the identity of her lover, François Buzot, became public knowledge. She remained devoted to her husband, however, and secured his escape from Paris in May 1793 as political tensions mounted. Manon was arrested on 31 May, by order of the **Paris Commune**, not the National Convention. She was released in late June, after protesting her illegal arrest, but was reimprisoned almost immediately. During her imprisonment she managed to maintain a secret correspondence with Roland, Buzot, and Brissot, and she also completed her memoirs, which show not only the influence of Jean-Jacques Rousseau on her thought, but also her integral involvement in the politics of the Revolution. Manon Roland defended herself with eloquence and dignity at her trial in November 1793, and as she stood at the foot of the **guillotine**, looking across the square at the statue of **Marianne**, uttered her famous last words, "Liberty, what crimes are committed in thy name."

ROMME, CHARLES-GILBERT (1750–1795). Romme was the son of a *procureur* in Riom, in the heart of the *Massif Central*. The family was not wealthy, and Charles attended school at the local Oratorien *collège* before going on to medical school in **Paris**. In 1779 he went to St. Petersburg, where he spent five years as the tutor for the son of Prince Stroganov, whom he had met in Paris during his studies. Romme traveled widely in Russia with his protégé, was presented at court, and in 1786 returned to Riom with young Stroganov in tow. The two spent two years in Switzerland before moving to Paris in 1789. Romme immersed himself in politics, taking his charge to club meetings, to section meetings, and to sessions of the **Constituent Assembly**. In 1790 Romme helped to found a club, *Les Amis de la Loi*, which met at the home of **Anne Théroigne de Méricourt** and took as one of its goals equality of the sexes. Both he and Stroganov also joined the **Jacobin club**, which prompted the Prince to summon his son back to Russia.

Romme then returned to Riom, bought some *biens nationaux*, and became president of the local Jacobin club. In late 1791 he was elected to the **Legislative Assembly** from the Puy-de-Dôme. Romme was quite active as a deputy, serving on the committee of public instruction and also taking an interest in matters of food supply. He was reelected in 1792 to the **National Convention**, where he sat with the **Montagnards**. He voted for death in the trial of **Louis XVI** and against the *appel au peuple*. In April 1793 he was sent on mission to the Army of the Coast of Cherbourg, with **Claude-Antoine Prieur**, and both were taken hostage in **Caen** at the beginning of the **federalist revolt**. During their two months of confinement, Romme drafted a proposal for the **revolutionary calendar** that would be adopted later that fall.

Romme presided over the Convention in November 1793, and it was he who proposed that the remains of **Jean-Paul Marat** be interred in the **Panthéon**. Although an atheist, Romme did not support **deChristianization**, nor did he regret the fall of **Maximilien Robespierre**. But he soon grew concerned by the reactionary tendencies of the **Thermidorians**, and was troubled by the spectacle of growing poverty and misery at a time when speculators were growing rich on the black market. During the **Prairial riots** of 1795, he called for the release of those who had been arrested during the **Germinal riots**, and demanded regulations prescribing the baking of a single type of bread. Romme also called for the reestablishment of **sectional assemblies** *en permanence*, a practice suspended since 1793, and suggested that houses be searched in order to find food for the poor. When the reaction came in the Convention, **Jean-Lambert Tallien** denounced Romme, and he and six others were taken from their seats to the **Committee of General Security** and then to the château du Taureau on the Finistère coast. Romme was soon brought back to Paris for trial, along with the other "martyrs of Prairial," charged with conspiring against the Convention and the Republic. All were convicted, and five of them, including Romme, stabbed themselves to death rather than go to the **guillotine**. Jules Michelet compared Romme's death to that of Socrates.

RONSIN, CHARLES-PHILIPPE (1751–1794). Ronsin was born in Soissons, northeast of **Paris**, the son of a master barrelmaker. At the age of 17 he joined the army, which he quit after four years, having attained the rank of corporal. Ronsin now turned his energy to the world of art and letters. He wrote a number of plays in the 1780s, and made the acquaintance of **Jacques-Louis David**. In 1789 he held the rank of captain in the **National Guard** in the Saint-Roch district of Paris. Over the next three years, he produced a number of patriotic plays in the capital, and relocated to the Left Bank, where he became an activist in the **Cordelier club**.

In November 1792 **Jean-Nicolas Pache** named Ronsin a commissioner to the army commanded by **Charles-François Dumouriez**. Ronsin managed to alienate military suppliers, but retained the confidence of Pache, and in April 1793 was named deputy to Pache's successor as minister of war, **Jean-Baptiste Bouchotte**. Bouchotte assigned Ronsin to the **Vendée** war zone, again responsible for overseeing military procurement, and it was in that theater that he would make his reputation. Due to his connections at the ministry, and among the Cordeliers, Ronsin jumped in rank in a single week from captain to general, and soon found himself in command of the Paris *armée révolutionnaire* assigned to the Vendée. There were those who resented Ronsin's rapid advancement, however, given his modest military talents, and his propensity for intemperate words eventually landed him in trouble. Caught in the political crossfire between the Hébertists and **Indulgents** in late 1793, Ronsin was arrested along with **François-Nicolas Vincent**. Both were released in February 1794, due to pressure from the Cordeliers, only to be arrested again the following month, Ronsin now accused of leading a vast military conspiracy against the government. He marched to the **guillotine**, alongside **Jacques-René Hébert**, on 24 March 1794.

ROUGET DE LISLE, CLAUDE-JOSEPH (1760–1836). Rouget de Lisle was the son of an *avocat au bailliage* in Lons-le-Saunier. He attended the Ecole Militaire in **Paris** for six years, and then the military engineering school at Mézières. Rouget de Lisle was promoted to the rank of captain in 1791, and in 1792 was garrisoned in Strasbourg. On 21 April, the day after the **Legislative Assembly** declared war on Austria, he was invited to dinner at the mayor's house. Stirred by the patriotic conversation at the table, he went home that night and composed the words and music to what he called *Chant de Guerre de l'Armée du Rhin*, destined to become *La Marseillaise* after volunteers from **Marseille** took it up as their marching song en route to

Paris that summer. Those Marseille volunteers would lead the charge against the **Tuileries** Palace in the **uprising of 10 August 1792**.

Rouget de Lisle, however, did not support the toppling of the monarchy. He was suspended from his post on 25 August 1792, reenlisted as a volunteer in October 1792, but again came under suspicion and was arrested in August 1793. After spending a year in prison, he was released after **Thermidor** and composed *Le Chant du 9 Thermidor*. He returned to the army, was wounded at **Quiberon**, and finally resigned his commission in March 1796. Rouget de Lisle returned to Paris and lived in relative poverty, composing hymns, writing poetry and opera librettos, including three for **André Grétry**. King Louis-Philippe granted him a modest pension under the July Monarchy.

ROUSSEAU, JEAN-JACQUES (1712–1778). Among all of the *philosophes* of the **Enlightenment**, none is credited, or blamed, more for his influence on the French Revolution than Jean-Jacques Rousseau. **Louis-Sébastien Mercier** wrote a book that asserted, in its title, that Rousseau was "*l'un des premiers auteurs de la Révolution.*" **Jean-Paul Marat** allegedly read sections of the *Contrat social* (1762) to large crowds gathered on **Paris** street corners. The **Constituent Assembly** installed a bust of Rousseau in its meeting hall, and the **Declaration of the Rights of Man and Citizen** bears the mark of Rousseau's political theory, most strikingly in its assertion that law was the product of the general will. **Maximilien Robespierre's** ideal of republican virtue sprang directly from Rousseau's thought, borrowed most obviously from a passage near the end of the *Discours sur l'origine et les fondements de l'inégalité parmi les hommes* (1755). The excesses of the **Terror** are often attributed to the concept of the general will, to Rousseau's insistence on transparency in public affairs, and to his observation that men who had lived under despotism might need to be "forced to be free." Yet Rousseau never advocated revolution, nor violence in the pursuit of political change. It was the power of his critique of Old Regime society, including monarchical despotism, and his advocacy of popular **sovereignty**, at least in the abstract (one biographer has called him a "dreamer of democracy"), that made Rousseau such a potent influence on the French revolutionaries.

Rousseau was born in the Swiss city of Geneva, the son of a watchmaker. His mother died within days of Jean-Jacques's birth, leaving him in the care of a father who instilled in his son a love of books, but did not provide him with a sound **education**. In 1722 Rousseau's father was forced into exile after a quarrel, and Jean-Jacques went to live with an uncle, and would leave Geneva himself six years later. Rousseau idealized Geneva in his later writings, and longed to return, though he never succeeded. In subsequent years Rousseau worked as an apprentice, a servant, a music teacher, and a tutor, experiences which left in him the conviction that to be dependent on another person was among the greatest afflictions of the human condition.

Rousseau met Denis Diderot in **Paris** in the 1740s, and contributed several essays on music to the *Encyclopédie*. Diderot encouraged his friend to enter the 1749 essay contest sponsored by the Dijon **Academy**. Rousseau's *Discourse on the Arts and Sciences*, which won first prize, argued that progress in the arts had led to the moral corruption of man. Six years later Rousseau entered the Dijon contest again, and that second *Discourse on the Origins of Inequality* continued the themes of the first, arguing that society had corrupted the natural goodness of man and deprived him of his freedom. This was a scathing indictment of 18th-century European society, but Rousseau was not entirely pessimistic. Since man had created society—it was not a "natural" creation, as Plato and Aristotle had argued—man could also reform, or **regenerate**, society.

Rousseau presented an abstract formula for the creation of such a regenerated society in the *Social Contract*. The false social contract, imposed by the strong on the weak, could be replaced, Rousseau argued, by a true social contract that would replace natural liberty with moral, or civil, liberty, and replace natural inequality with moral, or civil, equality. This would be difficult to achieve—Rousseau was not optimistic about the prospects for it. Given the existing corrupt state of society, initially the good service of a "Legislator" might be required, someone who, like Lycurgus or John Calvin, could rise above that corruption to introduce a legitimate social contract. Thereafter the "general will' (not the rule of the majority, necessarily, but in a more abstract sense the voice of the people, thinking of the common good) would ensure that government worked for the good of the nation and not for individual interests.

Some have argued that the *Social Contract* was not widely read in the decades leading up to the Revolution, attempting to minimize

Rousseau's impact in 1789, but one also finds his political ideas in his novels, *Julie, ou la Nouvelle Héloïse* and *Emile*, and these were enormously popular. One finds his ideas, and concepts, not only in the radical pamphlets of the Revolution, but in moderate and even monarchist writings as well. That his bust presided over every **Jacobin club** in France is evidence of the pervasiveness of his influence in the 1790s, and the transfer of his remains to the **Panthéon** in 1794 demonstrates the esteem of the deputies of the **National Convention** for his political thought.

ROUX, JACQUES (1752–1794). Jacques Roux's father was an infantry lieutenant, but sent his son to the Lazarist seminary in Angoulême, where Jacques was ordained as a priest and later taught. In 1785 he took a position as vicar in Saintes, and in 1789 took a new position as *curé* in the village of Saint-Thomas de Conac. The following April trouble erupted in the village and the **peasants** pillaged and burned two châteaux. Roux was accused of having preached that the earth belonged equally to all, thereby inciting the peasants, and while he escaped judicial proceedings, he did not escape suspension by the bishop. He then took an assumed name and moved to **Paris**. In January 1791 Roux swore the **civil oath of the clergy** and became vicar at the church of Saint-Nicolas-des-Champs in the Gravilliers section. He joined the **Cordelier club** and began the political activism and radical preaching that would garner for him the nickname of the "Red Priest."

After 10 August 1792, Roux's section named him to the General Council of the **Paris Commune**, and in January 1793 he was assigned to accompany **Louis XVI** to the scaffold. Roux behaved in an insulting manner to the king during the procession across the city. During the hard winter months that followed, Roux called for a tax on the rich and price controls. Surrounded by the *enragés*, and supported by the **Society of Revolutionary Republican Women**, Roux preached the **agrarian law**. On 25 June 1793 he appeared before the **National Convention** to read his celebrated *Manifeste des Enragés*, an address so radical and incendiary that **Maximilien Robespierre** denounced him at the **Jacobin club**, and the Cordeliers expelled him. After the death of **Jean-Paul Marat** he published a **newspaper**, *l'Ombre de Marat*, that Simone Evrard soon denounced. Under pressure from the

Jacobin club, the Commune arrested Roux on 22 August 1793. He languished in prison, forgotten, for some months. Not until February 1794 was he brought to trial before the **Revolutionary Tribunal**. Sensing his fate, Roux stabbed himself on 4 February, and then again, fatally, on 10 February in the infirmary. Five months later, remembering the persecution of their hero, the **sans-culottes** of the Gravilliers section joined the troops of the Convention as they marched to arrest Robespierre following the **Thermidor** coup.

– S –

SADE, DONATIEN-ALPHONSE-FRANÇOIS (1740–1814). The Marquis de Sade was born into a wealthy, aristocratic family. He studied at the *collège* Harcourt in **Paris** and then entered the army, rose to the rank of captain in the cavalry, and fought in the Seven Years War. In 1763 he married Renée Pélagie de Montreuil, and five months later was imprisoned for excesses committed in a house of prostitution. He was arrested again in 1768, for several months, and in 1772 was pursued for having given aphrodisiac candies to prostitutes. In 1778, at the de Sade family estate, he was accused of sexual improprieties with young girls, and his mother-in-law secured a *lettre de cachet*. He was imprisoned first at Vincennes, before being transferred to the **Bastille** in 1784, where he remained until 4 July 1789. During those 11 years of incarceration he wrote *Justine*, *Aline et Valcourt*, and *Les Cent Vingt Journées de Sodome*.

Over the course of the revolutionary decade, there is a striking concurrence between the periods of political liberty for the populace in general, and the periods of Sade's personal freedom; and likewise between periods of political repression and the periods of Sade's confinement. In July 1789 he was transferred to the asylum at Charenton, and then released on 2 April 1790, when all *lettres de cachet* were nullified. He then published *Justine*, wrote a few plays (one of which would be produced at the Comédie Française), and became active in Parisian politics. Indeed, he became secretary and then president of the Piques section, and used his influence to safeguard his in-laws early in the **Terror**. But in December 1793 Sade was arrested as a former noble, and returned to prison. As the Terror came to an end following **Thermidor**, Sade was once again released. He now published an expanded edition of *Justine*, wrote *Philosophie dans le Boudoir*, and in 1797 published *l'Histoire de Juliette*. His works sold well through the period of the **Directory**. On 6 March 1801, however, **Napoleon Bonaparte** ordered his arrest, and in 1803 he was returned to Charenton, where he organized theatrical presentations among the patients, their plays attended by Parisian socialites. He died in 1814, having spent 28 of his 74 years in prison. Sade was long forgotten, or reviled, but in the early 20th century Guillaume Apollinaire would play a crucial role in establishing his literary reputation, which is substantial.

SAINT-DOMINGUE. Saint-Domingue was the most important French colony in the West Indies, located on the western third of the island of Hispaniola. In the debate in the **Constituent Assembly** over the issue of **slavery**, the planters of Saint-Domingue supported the **Massiac Club**, which opposed the calls for emancipation issuing forth from the **Society of the Friends of Blacks**. The failure to abolish slavery in the colony led to rebellion in 1791 and the creation of the first independent black state in the western hemisphere, led by **François-Dominique Toussaint-Louverture**. French armies attempted to regain the colony under **Napoleon Bonaparte**, but ultimately failed in that effort. Saint-Domingue retained its independence and is known today as Haiti, among the poorest of Caribbean nations.

SAINT-JUST, LOUIS-ANTOINE (1767–1794). Saint-Just was the son of a soldier, who earned the Cross of Saint-Louis for his battlefield valor and was ennobled for his military service. His father died in 1776. Saint-Just's mother came from a comfortable **bourgeois** family. He quarreled with his mother in 1786 and left home for **Paris**, allegedly having stolen the family silver to finance his trip. His mother obtained a *lettre de cachet* against her son, and he spent six months in prison. Schooled at the Oratoriens in Soissons, Saint-Just was a talented, though rebellious, student. He went on to study law in Reims.

In 1789 Saint-Just returned to Blérancourt, his father's hometown, where he moved freely among artisans and workers, an experience that seems to have profoundly affected his later political views. He became active in local politics, rose to the rank of lieutenant-colonel in the **National Guard**, and in 1792 was elected to the **National Convention** (its youngest member) from the Aisne. Saint-Just made his mark on the national political scene with his maiden speech in the National Convention, on 13 November 1792, boldly asserting in the debate over whether or not to try **Louis XVI** that, "No man can reign innocently. The folly is all too evident. Every king is a rebel and a usurper. . . ."

Saint-Just joined the Paris **Jacobin club** and became a close political ally of **Maximilien Robespierre**. He entered the **Committee of Public Safety** in late May 1793, assigned to draft a new constitution, and in July wrote the preliminary report on the proscribed **Girondin** deputies. He was frequently on mission in 1793–94 to the armies and departments of the north and northeast. Saint-Just was a political idealist, and as such was also inflexible. He is associated with the **Ventôse Decrees** of the Year II, which, though never implemented, were the most egalitarian social legislation of the Revolution. In that same month he asserted in a speech before the Convention that "happiness is a new idea in Europe." Saint-Just was denounced with Robespierre on 9 **Thermidor**, and accompanied him to the scaffold the following day.

SALICETI, CHRISTOPHE (1757–1809). Saliceti was born into an old Italian family, expatriated from the duchy of Plaisance to **Corsica** during a period of warfare in the 14th century. Christophe attended a Jesuit *collège* in Corsica, and then went on to study law in Pisa, returning to Corsica to practice. He took principal responsibility for drafting the *cahier de doléance* for the **Third Estate** of Corsica, and was elected by the Third Estate as a deputy to the **Estates-General**. Saliceti was influential in repatriating **Pascal Paoli** to Corsica from his London exile and in securing his appointment as commander of the Corsican **National Guard**. After the dissolution of the **Constituent Assembly**, Saliceti returned to a position in the **departmental administration** of Corsica.

In 1792 Saliceti was elected to the **National Convention**, where he sat with the **Montagnards**. He voted for death in the trial of **Louis XVI**, and against the *appel au peuple*. Saliceti was frequently on mission for the Convention. He went first to Corsica in April 1793 to meet with Paoli, who was in rebellion against France by that time, but gained nothing for the effort. He then joined up with General **Jean-Baptiste Carteaux's** army, en route to occupy **Marseille**, and from there went on to **Toulon**, where he gave **Napoleon Bonaparte** his first artillery command. Saliceti allied himself in Toulon with **Augustin Robespierre**, in opposition to the excessive repression being imposed by **Paul-François Barras** and **Louis-Stanislas Fréron**.

In March 1794 Saliceti was attached to the Army of Italy, where he remained until November 1794. At that point he and **Jeanbon Saint-André** were assigned by the Convention to prepare a secret expedition against Corsica, an enterprise that ended in failure. Suspected as a Montagnard sympathizer after **Thermidor**, Saliceti was back in good graces by late 1795, and the **Directory** sent him once again as a commissioner to the Army of Italy, principally to keep an eye on Napoleon. In 1797 he was elected to the **Council of Five Hundred** from the new department of Golo, and after **Brumaire** he rallied to Napoleon. In January 1806 Saliceti became minister of police in Naples, first under Joseph Bonaparte and then Joachim Murat. Neither Joseph nor Murat much liked Saliceti, but he was popular among the Italians. Napoleon had great respect for his abilities and fortitude, and insisted that he remain at his post. In 1803 he was named to the Legion of Honor.

SALONS. Salons played an important role in the social and intellectual life of **Paris** from the last decades of the Old Regime up into the middle years of the Revolution. They were an outgrowth of court society, but operated independently from it, and as such fostered the unfettered exchange of ideas that was so characteristic of the French **Enlightenment**. The salons were nearly all hosted by **women**, and thus were a social milieu in which women and men interacted, as well as being a milieu in which **aristocrats** and commoners might interact. Individual salons had their own clientele and character, though discussions in all tended to focus on literary topics and current events. The discussions were lively, but polite, conversations more than arguments, but free from the gaze of censors or the court, those conversations could range as widely as those participating liked.

The salons met regularly, generally once a week, and one attended only by invitation. Some of the salons were quite celebrated and enjoyed a public reputation, such as those of Madame Marie-Thérèse Geoffrin, Madame Stéphanie de Genlis, and Madame Julie de Lespinasse. They were not only sites for the exchange of ideas, but exercised a tangible influence in the Parisian world of letters. Madame Marie du Deffand, for example, helped to secure Jean Le Rond d'Alembert's election to the *Académie Française*. The salons not only played an important role in shaping **public opinion** on the eve of the Revolution, they could also provide an indirect contact between Parisian society and courtly circles. Thus, the wife of **Jacques Necker** was hostess to a regular salon where matters of finance and politics were discussed.

A few of the salons bridged the divide between the Old Regime and the Revolution, including that of Madame Necker and the salons of Madame **Pancoucke** and Madame **Condorcet**. In 1792–1793, **Manon Roland** hosted weekly dinner parties that a number of the leading **Girondins** attended regularly, and **Germaine de Staël** hosted an influential salon in the early years of the **Directory**. The central role played by salons in the 1780s, however, was assumed by **popular societies** and **section assemblies** in the more open political atmosphere of the 1790s.

SANS-CULOTTES. The image of the sans-culottes has evolved considerably over the two centuries since the French Revolution. For those sympathetic to the ideals of 1789, the term conjured up images of the *menu peuple*, the little people who took to the streets of **Paris** during the great *journées* of the Revolution. For Hippolyte Taine, a historian writing late in the 19th century, the sans-culottes were nothing more than the mob or the rabble. In the 20th century, social historians such as George Rudé and Albert Soboul put a face on the sans-culottes, whom they described as a sort of proto-proletariat composed of artisans and small shopkeepers, the vanguard of the Revolution in Marxist terms. With the demise of the Marxist interpretation of the Revolution over the past two decades, a new image of the sans-culotte has emerged, one that emphasizes political and cultural aspects more than class or social origins.

The literal meaning of the term is a reference to the long trousers worn by artisans and shopkeepers, in contrast to the knickers (*culottes*) more commonly worn by the **aristocracy** and wealthy **bour-**

geoisie. The classic representation of the sans-culotte during the Revolution was the **Père Duchesne**, the rustic artisan and family man, man of the people, always ready to speak his mind in sometimes vulgar language, whom **Jacques-René Hébert** took as the title for his popular **newspaper**. Many of the sans-culottes would have been among the **passive citizens** prior to September 1792, those excluded from electoral politics whom **Maximilien Robespierre** championed as "the people" following the collapse of the monarchy. But we know today that the sans-culottes also included rather more substantial shopkeepers or manufacturers, some of them even wealthy.

While the social definition of the sans-culottes has thus grown a bit fuzzy, the term is still clearly associated with popular politics in the Revolution, particularly in Paris. Without the sans-culottes there would have been no fall of the **Bastille**, no assault on the **Tuileries** Palace, no **uprising of 31 May–2 June 1793**. The **Montagnards** were willing to ally themselves with the sans-culottes, and their sometimes violent demonstrations, whereas the **Girondins** grew increasingly uncomfortable with the politics of the street. The apogee of sans-culotte influence may have come in September 1793, when demonstrations in Paris forced the adoption of the general *maximum* and the addition of **Jacques-Nicolas Billaud-Varenne** and **Jean-Marie Collot d'Herbois** to the **Committee of Public Safety**. Shortly thereafter, however, the Montagnards moved to control the popular movement, with the trial of the *enragés*, and the sans-culottes would never again constitute a truly potent political force. They could not be mobilized to defend Robespierre on 9 **Thermidor**, and the inability of **Gracchus Babeuf** to organize the sans-culottes was a crucial reason for the failure of the **Conspiracy of Equals**. The ultimate failure of the sans-culottes, as well as the ambiguity of their social definition, have both, no doubt, contributed to the enduring power of their image in the revolutionary mythology of 1789.

SANSON, CHARLES-HENRI (1739–1806). Charles-Henri Sanson succeeded his father, Charles-Jean-Baptiste Sanson, as royal executioner in 1778. Charles-Henri was the fourth Sanson to hold the position, his ancestor, Charles, having been appointed royal executioner by Louis XIV in 1688. Despite the fact that Sanson played a central role in the drama of the Revolution, overseeing the executions of

Louis XVI, Charlotte Corday, Marie Antoinette, Georges Danton, and Maximilien Robespierre, little is known of his personal life and no known portraits of the man survive. He resigned his position in August 1795 and was replaced by his son, Henri. Henri, in turn, would be succeeded by his son, Henri-Clément, but he would be the last of the Sansons to serve as executioner. He was dismissed in 1847, after having pawned the **guillotine** to pay off a debt.

SANTERRE, JOSEPH (1752–1809). Santerre was the son of a well-to-do brewer in Cambrai who relocated to the *faubourg* Saint-Marcel in **Paris**. By 1772 Joseph Santerre was the owner of a *brasserie* in the *faubourg* **Saint-Antoine**, the very center of **sans-culotte** activism during the Revolution. Santerre was a wealthy **bourgeois** with **aristocratic** tastes—he loved horse racing, for example, and fancied himself the second-best horseman in the kingdom, after **Louis-Philippe Orléans**. But he was also popular among the common folk of the quartier, to whom he was generous with handouts during hard times. In early July 1789 Santerre was elected battalion chief of the **National Guard** in his neighborhood. He participated in the taking of the **Bastille**, as well as the march to **Versailles** during the **October Days**. The 20 June 1792 uprising was planned (though badly) in his *brasserie*, and in the **uprising of 10 August 1792** he served as the commanding general of the Paris National Guard. On 21 January 1793 Santerre commanded the military escort that conducted **Louis XVI** to the **guillotine**, and it was he who ordered the drum roll that drowned out the king's final words.

Thinking himself destined to be a military commander, Santerre requested assignment to the **Vendée** in May 1793. The campaigns he commanded went badly, however, and he was recalled to Paris and eventually imprisoned, where he remained until after **Thermidor**. While he was in prison his wife bankrupted the *brasserie* and left him. Under the **Directory**, Santerre obtained a contract to purchase horses abroad for the army, and by that means, as well as speculation in *biens nationaux*, he rebuilt his fortune. In 1804, however, he made an ill-considered purchase of a château in Normandy and lost his fortune once again. He died five years later in relative poverty.

SECOND ESTATE. *See* ARISTOCRACY.

SECTION ASSEMBLIES. As part of the administrative reorganization of France in 1789, major towns and cities were divided into sections for electoral purposes. The **Constituent Assembly** left it to local authorities to determine the size and number of sections, which
therefore varied across the country. **Caen**, for example, with a population near 32,000, was divided into five sections, while **Marseille**,
with 76,000 inhabitants, was divided into 24 sections; **Bordeaux**,
with 83,000 inhabitants, was divided into 28 sections; and **Lyon**, with
139,000 inhabitants, was divided into 32 sections. **Paris**, the largest
city in France at 525,000, was divided into 48 sections.

Section assemblies met just once a year for electoral purposes, but
when the **Legislative Assembly** declared *la patrie en danger* in July
1792 it also granted the sections of Paris the right to meet *en per-
manance*, and many sections of the capital were soon meeting on a
daily basis. A number of provincial cities followed suit, and for the
next year section assemblies became the principal arena for direct democracy and **sans-culotte** militancy. In both Lyon and Marseille,
however, local moderates used section assemblies to challenge the
political power of the more radical **Jacobin clubs** in 1793, and those
sectional movements succeeded temporarily in ousting municipal
councils dominated by Jacobins.

Section assemblies in Paris played an important role in the **uprising of 10 August 1792**, and in the campaign that ultimately led to the
proscription of the **Girondin** deputies. In September 1793 the **National Convention** authorized a modest stipend to be paid to the poor
in Paris for attending up to two section assemblies per week. Ironi-
cally, this measure contributed to the bureaucratization of the popular movement in Paris, as section assemblies began to lose their vitality. The persecution that fall of the *enragés*, who had been activists
in section assemblies, contributed to that trend. Section assemblies,
once the cradle of Parisian radicalism, failed to rise up in support of
Maximilien Robespierre on 9 **Thermidor**, and in the wake of the
Germinal and **Prairial riots** of 1795 the Convention ordered the disarming of section militants. In October 1795 the Convention finally
abolished the section assemblies.

SEIGNEURIAL DUES. Peasants throughout France still owed in the
1780s an array of seigneurial dues (*droits féodaux*), or duties, to their

lords. These lords were often, though not always, members of the **aristocracy**. Seigneurial dues included the *cens* (a cash payment), the *champart* (a portion of the harvest), the *lods et ventes* (a kind of inheritance tax), as well as the obligation to bake bread in the lord's oven or mill grain in his mill (the *banalités*), and the obligation to labor for a certain number of days each year on the lord's land (the *corvée*). These dues tended to be more common in the north (where as the saying went, there was no land without lord) than in the south (where it was said that there was no lord without legal title), and weighed more heavily on the peasants in some provinces, such as Burgundy, than in others.

All across France, however, peasants complained bitterly about seigneurial dues in the ***cahiers de doléances*** that they prepared in advance of the meeting of the **Estates-General** in 1789. During the **Great Fear** that summer, peasants invaded the châteaux of their seigneurial lords in many parts of the country and destroyed the deeds that documented the hated dues, which they henceforth ceased to pay or perform. Responding to that wave of violence, a number of liberal aristocrats stood up in the **Constituent Assembly** on the **night of 4 August** and renounced their seigneurial dues, along with a host of other **privileges**. The Assembly subsequently drafted legislation abolishing seigneurial dues, which **Louis XVI** reluctantly signed after the **October Days**. Since they viewed those dues as a form of property, however, they were to be suspended only after the peasants paid compensation to seigneurial landowners. Although most peasants refused to make such payments, the system was not abolished outright until the summer of 1793. It is in connection with this abolition of seigneurial dues that the Revolution has sometimes been said to have abolished feudalism.

SEPTEMBER MASSACRES. Between 2 and 6 September 1792, as Prussian troops advanced on **Paris**, militant **sans-culottes** invaded a number of prisons in the capital and massacred more than a thousand prisoners. Less than one month earlier, the monarchy had fallen in the **uprising of 10 August**, and some would later argue that the September Massacres were an extension of that *journée*, a necessary blow against the enemies of the Revolution. At times the killing took on the appearance of summary justice, preceded as it was by trials in the streets or courtyards of the prisons. But more often, popular vengeance was visited indiscriminately on those whom the militants, including **National Guardsmen** and *fédérés* from the provinces, found in the prisons. The mood of panic in the country fostered violence in some provincial cities as well, but none on the scale of what occurred in Paris.

The initial reaction to the massacres was one of stunned acceptance. Many deputies adopted the attitude of **Jean-Marie Roland**, then minister of the interior, who described the massacres as a regrettable but necessary measure, "over which perhaps a veil must be drawn." But on 16 September 1793, **Pierre-Victurnien Vergniaud** demanded that those responsible for the massacres be brought to justice, and pointed an accusatory finger toward the **Paris Commune**, suggesting that he and other **Girondin** deputies had been targets for assassination. Near the end of October, **Jean-Baptiste Louvet** escalated the rhetorical attack, explicitly accusing **Maximilien Robespierre** of having instigated the violence and suggesting that **Georges Danton** and **Jean-Paul Marat** had conspired with him in a plot to install themselves as a **Triumvirate** in power.

From this point forward, the issue of the September Massacres, and popular violence more generally, became a focal element in the struggle between the Girondins and **Montagnards** within the **National Convention**. The Girondins denounced the perpetrators as bloodthirsty anarchists, and Marat, who defended the massacres in his **newspaper** and called for more heads to roll, came in for particular opprobrium. The Montagnards did not go so far as to defend the massacres, but did describe them as a regrettable instance of popular justice. To attack the September Massacres, in the view of the Montagnards and **Jacobins**, was to deny popular **sovereignty**, while to defend the perpetrators of the violence, in the view of the Girondins, was to deny the rule of law. In the end, the stance of the Girondins alienated them from the Parisian populace and led to their proscription from office. None of those responsible for the prison massacres was ever brought to trial. But they became a political issue once again after **Thermidor**, and those who had defended the killings back in 1792 now found themselves denounced as **terrorists**.

SERVAN, JOSEPH-MARIE (1741–1808). Son of a minor nobleman, Servan entered the Dauphiné infantry as an ensign in 1762 and moved quickly up through the ranks. A man of literary talent as well, he contributed articles on the military to the *Encyclopédie* and in 1781 published a small book entitled *Le Soldat Citoyen*, which gained for him a certain celebrity. During the first two years of the Revolution, Servan was on leave in **Paris**, and moved in the circles of **Jacques-Pierre Brissot** and **Gabriel-Honoré Mirabeau**. In November 1791 he became lieutenant-colonel of the Vermandois Infantry, and by 1792 had been promoted to *maréchal de camp*. Servan was appointed minister of war in the **Girondin** ministry in May 1792, at the suggestion of **Jean-Marie Roland**, only to be dismissed along with Roland and Etienne Clavière on 12 June. It was Servan who ordered the transfer to Paris of 20,000 *fédérés* that summer, against the wishes of **Louis XVI**. He returned as minister of war after the **uprising of 10 August 1792**, remaining in that post only until 30 September, when he took command of the Army of the Pyrenees. Servan lost that post, too, accused in July 1793 of being a Girondin sympathizer. He remained in prison until January 1795, represented the **National Convention** as a plenipotentiary minister to Spain in July 1795, and was recommissioned as a general under the **Directory**. Servan served **Napoleon Bonaparte** in the early 1800s in campaigns against brigands within France, and retired in 1807, having been decorated with the Cross of the Legion of Honor.

SIEYÈS, EMMANUEL-JOSEPH (1748–1836). Few men played as substantial a role in French politics throughout the revolutionary decade as the Abbé Sieyès. His father was a *contrôleur des actes* and *directeur de la poste aux lettres*, and his mother was the daughter of a local notary. Sieyès attended religious school in Draguignan and went on to the Seminary of Saint-Sulpice in **Paris**. In 1780 he was appointed canon and vicar-general of the Cathedral at Chartres, where he met the future mayor of Paris, **Jérome Pétion**. In 1787 he represented the **clergy** in the provincial assembly at Orléans. His pamphlet, *What is the Third Estate?*, published in early 1789, was among the most influential pre-revolutionary pamphlets, offering a virtual script for the events leading up to the declaration of a National Assembly. Although he reserved his most pointed barbs for the **aristocracy**, the notoriety of the pamphlet alienated his fellow clergymen to the point that he could not be elected to the **Estates-General** from any of the assemblies of the **First Estate**. His membership on the **Committee of Thirty** made him well-known in Paris, however, and Sieyès was elected from that city as its final delegate for the **Third Estate**.

In the Estates-General he played an active role in the declaration of the National Assembly and in the swearing of the **Tennis Court Oath**, and participated in the drafting of the **Declaration of the Rights of Man and Citizen**. But he faded from public view after 1789. Upon the dissolution of the **Constituent Assembly**, Sieyès obtained a seat on the departmental directory of the Seine, a post from which he resigned late in 1791, somewhat discredited politically. In 1792 he was elected to the **National Convention** from the Sarthe. He voted for the death of **Louis XVI**, but remained aloof from political factions. At the moment of the **Girondins'** proscription, in June 1793, Sieyès remained publicly silent, leading **Maximilien Robespierre** to label him "the mole of the Revolution," because he was always busy "in the underground passages of the assembly."

Sieyès returned to the political forefront, however, after 9 **Thermidor**, serving a term on the **Committee of Public Safety**, urging the reintegration into the National Convention of the proscribed Girondin deputies and sympathizers, and actively participating in both foreign affairs and the debate over the **Constitution of 1795**. He was elected to the **Council of Five Hundred** in 1795 and named ambassador to Berlin in May 1798. Sieyès was elected director in May 1799, and played a key role in the coup of 18 **Brumaire** that brought **Napoleon Bonaparte** to power. He subsequently served as consul along with Napoleon and **Pierre Roger-Ducos**. In 1799 he was elected to the Senate, over which he later presided, and in 1808 was named a Count of the Empire. Sieyès went into self-imposed exile to Brussels in 1815, but returned to Paris in 1830. *See also* DIRECTORY.

SLAVERY. The institution of slavery, and the slave trade, were integral to the growth of the French economy in the 18th century. The Atlantic port cities of **Bordeaux**, La Rochelle, and Nantes all participated in the traffic of black slaves and profited enormously from it. A number of **Enlightenment** figures, including **Montesquieu**, **Voltaire**, and **Jean-Jacques Rousseau**, wrote eloquently against slavery, but this produced no public opposition to the practice until 1788, when the **Society of the Friends of Blacks** was formed in **Paris**. Many prominent deputies to the **Estates-General** joined the club, which called for the abolition of the slave trade, though not for an end to slavery itself. French planters formed a rival group, the **Massiac Club**, to lobby for the continuation of the slave trade. With the adoption of the **Declaration of the Rights of Man and Citizen**, the legitimacy of slavery grew more tenuous, at least in theory.

The **Constituent Assembly** proved incapable of confronting the issue, however, managing only to abolish slavery within France, a rather meaningless gesture since the relatively few blacks on French soil had nearly all been granted their freedom on arrival. The failure of the Constituent Assembly to abolish the slave trade, or slavery in French colonies, led to the 1791 slave uprising in **Saint-Domingue**. Not until February 1794, under the ascendancy of the **Montagnards**, did the **National Convention** vote to abolish slavery outright. The new laws were not aggressively enforced, however, and in 1802 **Napoleon Bonaparte** restored both slavery and the slave trade. Both would survive until the Revolution of 1848.

SMITH, ADAM (1723–1790). Adam Smith was a Scottish economist and moral philosopher. Smith visited **Paris** in 1766 and at that time was introduced to a number of **Enlightenment** thinkers from the French school of economists collectively known as the physiocrats. Smith's ideas about the market economy were thus well-known in France on the eve of the Revolution, and clearly influenced those who advocated free trade after 1789, particularly among the **Girondins**. It is also noteworthy that the agents/observers sent out into the provinces in the summer of 1793 by Minister of the Interior **Dominique-Joseph Garat** were given copies of Smith's *The Wealth of Nations* (1776) to guide them in their work.

SOCIETY OF 1789. The Society of 1789 was a moderate political club in **Paris**, formed in April 1790 to counter the growing influence of the **Jacobin club**. Its leading figures included **Marie-Joseph-Motier Lafayette**, **Emmanuel-Joseph Sieyès**, **Gabriel-Honoré Mirabeau**, and **Jean-Sylvain Bailly**. They were constitutional monarchists, interested in consolidating the gains of 1789 and in strengthening the monarchy. The Society's membership was drawn from among the wealthy, and it met in an upper balcony overlooking the park of the **Palais Royal**. As the political currents of the Revolution shifted in 1791, some of the members of the Society of 1789 turned toward the Jacobins, while others gravitated toward the **Feuillants**, as the Society itself disappeared from the scene.

SOCIETY OF THE FRIENDS OF BLACKS. The Society of the Friends of Blacks (*Société des Amis des Noirs*) was founded in February 1788, inspired initially by the ideas expressed in the American Declaration of Independence, but also by the creation of a similar society in London. **Jacques-Pierre Brissot** and **Marie-Jean Condorcet** were among the founders of the Society, which included in its early membership **Nicolas Bergasse**, **Marie-Joseph-Motier Lafayette**, and **Gabriel-Honoré Mirabeau**. Many **Enlightenment** thinkers had written critically of the institution of **slavery**, including Montesquieu, **Jean-Jacques Rousseau**, **Voltaire**, and the Abbé Raynal, but those philosophical critiques had inspired no call to action until 1788. The Society of the Friends of Blacks was a small group initially, drawn principally from elite circles and the world of **freemasonry**. Their publications called for the abolition of the slave trade, but not slavery itself, which they thought would naturally follow later.

The Revolution brought an expansion in the membership of the Society, but also cleavages. Bergasse, the **Lameth** brothers, and **Adrien Duport** left the Society because of the dominance of Brissot, but **Henri-Baptiste Grégoire**, **François Buzot**, and **Jérome Pétion** soon joined, and the adoption of the **Declaration of the Rights of Man and Citizen** brought an added urgency to the issue of slavery. To abolish the slave trade, however, would threaten the economic interests of merchants in the port cities of **Bordeaux** and Nantes, as well as those of French planters in **Saint-Dominguc**. A rival society, the **Massiac Club**, formed in 1789 to defend those interests and oppose the abolition of the slave trade. No progress was made by the **Constituent Assembly**, and in August 1791 a massive slave revolt in Saint-Domingue made the issue both more pressing and more contentious.

After elections to the **Legislative Assembly**, a number of **Girondin** deputies joined the Society of the Friends of Blacks, including

Pierre-Victurnien Vergniaud, **Armand Gensonné**, **Marguerite-Elie Guadet**, and **Jean-François Ducos**. Despite the fact that they represented Bordeaux, these men spoke eloquently in opposition to the slave trade, and the influence of the Girondins in the Legislative Assembly and then in the **National Convention** in its early months kept the issue in public view. The Society continued to advocate the abolition of the slave trade, not slavery itself, but no action was taken until February 1794, months after the proscription of the Girondins, when the National Convention voted to abolish slavery outright. By then the Society of the Friends of Blacks had ceased to meet, crippled by the loss of its Girondin leadership. The laws abolishing slavery were never aggressively enforced under the **Directory**, and in May 1802 **Napoleon Bonaparte** repealed them and restored both slavery and the slave trade in French colonial territories.

SOCIETY OF REVOLUTIONARY REPUBLICAN WOMEN. The Society of Revolutionary Republican Women (*Société des Citoyennes Républicaines Révolutionaires*) took shape in the winter and spring of 1793, after the **Jacobin club** denied the use of their meeting hall to a group of **women** concerned about rising food prices. The **Paris Commune** granted formal recognition to the new women's club in May. Its founding members had been active in **section assemblies** over the past year, and some, like **Pauline Léon**, had regularly attended meetings of the **Cordelier club**. Alongside Pauline Léon, **Claire Lacombe** took an active leadership role in the new club.

Both Léon and Lacombe had participated in past *journées* in **Paris**, and members of the Society of Revolutionary Republican Women joined in the agitation leading up to the **uprising of 31 May–2 June 1793**. As many as 100 women sat in the insurrectionary assembly that met in the Eveché palace in May, and club members harassed **Girondin** deputies at public speeches and were posted at the doors to the **National Convention** meeting hall when the uprising began. Women in the club were sympathetic to the *enragé* movement, and both Léon and Lacombe had personal ties to one of the *enragé* leaders, **Jean-Théophile Leclerc**, although they did not support **Jacques Roux's** controversial speech to the National Convention on 25 June 1793. But as the political and economic situation worsened that summer, the Society of Revolutionary Republican Women joined the *enragés* in their demands for an extension of the **maximum** and for a declaration of **Terror** as the order of the day. Those demands were largely achieved in September 1793, after which point the **Montagnards** turned against both groups. The National Convention did adopt a law proposed by the women's club, mandating that all women wear the tricolor **cockade**. But when the *dames de la halle* denounced that decree and attacked a meeting of the Society of Revolutionary Republican Women in late October, the Convention moved quickly to close its meeting hall and the club ceased to function. Leading Jacobins, most notably **Jean-Pierre-André Amar** and **Pierre-Gaspard Chaumette**, took advantage of the occasion to remind women that their natural place was in the home.

SOVEREIGNTY. The issue of sovereignty was of central importance in the French Revolution. Sovereignty resided in the person of the king under the Old Regime, but the convocation of the **Estates-General** initiated a transformation of that reality. In the **Tennis Court Oath**, the deputies asserted that sovereignty resided in the nation, of which the king was only one part. The "nation" itself was an abstract category, and in their debates over a proposed constitution, the deputies of the **Constituent Assembly** began to give clearer definition to what sovereignty might mean under the constitutional monarchy. They divided the populace of France into two categories, **active citizens** and **passive citizens**, with only the former accorded the full rights of sovereignty. Only active citizens would have the right to vote in elections.

Voting was not the only means by which sovereignty might be exercised, however. More than 80,000 Parisians took to the streets on 14 July 1789 and viewed the storming of the **Bastille** as an expression of their sovereignty. By the end of that year, political clubs had begun to appear, most notably the **Jacobin club**. Their critics argued that they should not be allowed to exist, since they represented a usurpation of the sovereignty that legitimately resided in the National Assembly alone. As people began to lose trust in their elected representatives, certainly by the time of the king's flight to **Varennes** in June 1791, they began to reclaim their sovereignty. **Maximilien Robespierre** argued that the toppling of the monarchy in August 1792 was a victory for the people, and in the wake of that event the distinction between active and passive citizens was abolished. All adult males were now eligible to vote. **Women**, though they had played a part in the **uprising of 10 August**, were still excluded from the sovereign people.

The divisions within the **National Convention** reflected disagreement over the issue of sovereignty. The **Girondins**, by and large, were skeptical of the notion of popular sovereignty, and particularly of the assertion that **Paris** somehow embodied it. The **Montagnards** were more willing to embrace the ideal of popular sovereignty, although they, too, were wary of the danger that popular politics might degenerate into popular violence. Sovereignty was also contested at the local level during this period. Jacobins in both **Lyon** and **Marseille** presented organized slates of candidates for municipal office in the elections of 1792, a tactic denounced by moderates as a violation of the people's sovereignty. At both the local and the national levels, radicals argued that the electorate did not transfer their sovereignty to their elected officials, but retained the right to recall them at any time.

The **Constitution of 1793** incorporated the most liberal definition of sovereignty of any of the constitutions of the Revolution—universal manhood suffrage—but it was never implemented in practice, and there were no elections until 1795. By that time, a new constitution had once again reduced the electorate to those adult males who owned substantial property. Under the **Directory**, sovereignty would similarly be confined to the propertied elite. **Napoleon Bonaparte** restored universal manhood suffrage, but the opportunity for the voters to exercise their sovereignty was restricted to the occasional plebiscite.

STAËL, ANNE-LOUISE-GERMAINE (1766–1817). Germaine de Staël was the daughter of **Jacques Necker**. She met many of the literary and philosophical luminaries of the day at her mother's **salon**, and was a cultivated and well-educated young woman herself. In 1786 she married the Baron de Staël, the Swedish ambassador to the French court. Two years later, her first work was published, a short book entitled *Lettres sur les ouvrages et le caractère de Jean-Jacques Rousseau*. Many more would follow, but this early interest in **Rousseau** would inspire her particular synthesis of the rationalism of the **Enlightenment** and the emerging Romantic spirit of the time.

Staël was swept up in the excitement of the Revolution, always supportive of her father's affairs and initiatives. She was distressed at Necker's resignation in 1790, and grew quite wary after the **September Massacres** in 1792, leaving first for the family estate outside Geneva, and then for a year living among *émigrés* in London. Staël returned to **Paris** after **Thermidor** and established a salon on the rue du Bac. She soon became the lover of **Benjamin Constant**, and her salon became a gathering place for political liberals. In 1796 she published *De l'Influence des passions sur le bonheur des individus*, a pre-Romantic work. Both Staël and Constant were critical of **Napoleon Bonaparte's** usurpation of power, and the infringement of civil liberties that his regime embodied. Both were in turn persecuted by Napoleon. He forbade Staël from entering Paris after the 1802 publication of *Delphine*, and in 1803 forcibly exiled her from France on the pretext that she had something to do with the publication of her father's book, *Dernières vues de politique et de finance*.

In 1807 the publication of *Corinne* placed Staël at the very center of the Romantic movement. Her 1813 work, *De l'Allemagne*, is considered by some to be the equal of **Voltaire's** *Lettres sur les Anglais* and Alexis de Tocqueville's *Democracy in America* for its ability to capture the national spirit of a people. Staël's final work, *Considérations sur les principaux événements de la Révolution française*, was published posthumously. Her legacy, an important one, is as a pioneer of the psychological novel, a literary theorist, and one of the earliest advocates of political liberalism. *See also* ROUSSEAU, JEAN-JACQUES.

SWISS GUARDS. The Swiss Guards were first created by order of Charles IX in 1573, were organized as a military regiment under the reign of Louis XIII, and served henceforth in the royal household as personal guards of the king. Two Swiss guards were killed during the **October Days**, when the **women** of **Paris** invaded the palace at **Versailles**. They defended the **Tuileries** Palace valiantly during the **uprising of 10 August 1792**, but perished almost to a man at the hands of the angry crowd after **Louis XVI** ordered them to lay down their arms. The Swiss Guards were bitterly reviled by the populace, having come to be seen as a symbol of royal despotism.

– T –

TALLEYRAND-PÉRIGORD, CHARLES-MAURICE (1754–1838).

Charles-Maurice Talleyrand was the eldest son in an old noble family of the Périgord, in southwestern France. Denied a military career by his physical disability (he was lame), he studied instead for a life in the Church. Talleyrand attended Saint-Sulpice seminary in **Paris**, obtained an administrative appointment in 1780, and was named bishop of Autun in 1788.

Talleyrand was drawn more to **Enlightenment** philosophy than to Catholic theology, and in 1789 joined the ranks of the liberal **aristocracy** in the **Estates-General**. Along with **Armand-Désiré Duplessis-Richelieu Aiguillon** and Alexandre-Frédéric Liancourt, he favored the abolition of **privilege**, and in November 1789 was the first to propose that Church lands be confiscated as *biens nationaux* in order to eliminate the royal debt. Talleyrand swore the **civil oath of the clergy**, celebrated mass at the **Champ de Mars** for the **Festival of Federation** on 14 July 1790, and consecrated the first constitutional bishops. After being condemned by **Pope Pius VI**, Talleyrand left the Church and pursued a diplomatic career.

Talleyrand traveled to London in February 1792, sent as a diplomatic envoy by the **Legislative Assembly** to secure British neutrality in France's war with Austria and Prussia. After the discovery of **Louis XVI's** secret papers, in November 1792, Talleyrand was denounced by the **National Convention**. He fled to the United States in 1794, where he remained for two years, until his name was removed from the list of *émigrés*. Under the **Directory**, Talleyrand was named minister of foreign affairs, due in part to the influence of **Germaine de Staël**. He supported the coup of 18 **Brumaire** and served **Napoleon Bonaparte** as foreign minister through much of the Empire. In the end, however, he abandoned Napoleon and sold his services to the Austrians and Bourbons. Napoleon is reported to have once told **Joseph Fouché** that he regretted not having killed Talleyrand long before.

Talleyrand represented France at the Congress of Vienna in 1814, but supported the Orléans branch of the royal family thereafter. At the end of his life he reconciled with the Catholic Church and received the final sacraments due a bishop, despite the fact that he had fathered a number of children, most notably the painter Eugène Delacroix.

TALLIEN, JEAN-LAMBERT (1767–1820). Tallien was born in **Paris**, where his father was *maître d'hôtel* for the Marquis of Bercy. Tallien attended the *collège* of Cardinal Lemoine and went on to study law. He worked briefly in the 1780s as clerk to a prosecutor, and then as personal secretary to the **Lameth** brothers. Swept up in the revolutionary politics of Paris in 1789, he obtained a job as a typesetter in the printing shop of the *Moniteur Universel*, which put him close to the action at **Versailles**. Tallien joined the Paris **Jacobin club**, and in August 1791 began publishing a **newspaper**, *L'Ami du Citoyen*, which he modeled on the more famous newspaper of **Jean-Paul Marat**. He participated in the **uprising of 10 August 1792**, and became secretary of the **Paris Commune** thereafter. But both Marat and **Maximilien Robespierre** viewed him as something of an opportunist, which forced him to seek election to the **National Convention** from the Seine-et-Oise. In the Convention he sat with the **Montagnards**, voted for death in the trial of **Louis XVI**, and played an active role in the May 1793 uprising against the **Girondin** deputies.

Tallien was sent on mission to **Bordeaux** in October 1793, where he supported **deChristianization** and organized a **Festival of Reason**. Despite this, he was accused of political moderation and recalled to Paris, where he played a central role in the conspiracy against Robespierre. Tallien served on the **Committee of Public Safety** after 9 **Thermidor**, principally charged with matters of commerce and food supply. In the spring of 1795 he dealt harshly with both the insurgents of the **Prairial riots** and the *émigré* rebels of **Quiberon**. Tallien was elected to the **Council of Five Hundred** in 1795, but was increasingly viewed with hostility by those on both the left and the right. He accompanied **Napoleon Bonaparte** on the **Egyptian campaign** in 1798, where he endured the double misfortune of being captured by the British and contracting yellow fever. He never fully recovered from his illness, though it spared him exile as a regicide in 1816.

TALMA, FRANÇOIS-JOSEPH (1763–1826). Talma was the most celebrated actor on the **Paris** stage during the Revolution. His father was a valet, and François accompanied him to his various posts throughout his youth, most of them in Flanders and England. His acting abilities first became apparent at the *collège* of Clermont, and in 1786 he enrolled in the *école royale dramatique*. Talma joined the

Comédie Française in 1787, and became a *sociétaire* in 1789. His first triumph on stage came in November 1789, in **Marie-Joseph Chénier's** *Charles IX*.

Talma was impassioned by the ideas of the Revolution, which gave him the opportunity to realize one of his earlier dreams, to dress in period costume on stage, appropriate to the roles in historical dramas. He visited museums to study details, and worked with **Jacques-Louis David** on the design of costumes. In April 1791 the Comédie Française split, and Talma led the dissidents to found the *Théâtre français de la rue de Richelieu*, which became the *Théâtre de la République* in 1792, occupying the site where the Comédie Française stands today. Talma's marriage in 1790 to Julie Carreau was viewed by some as scandalous, as she was a former dancer at the Opera. She operated a **salon** on the rue Chantereine that was much frequented by **Pierre-Victurnien Vergniaud** and some of the other **Girondins**, and Vergniaud became a dévoté of Talma as well. Talma played in both *Othello* and *Hamlet* during the Revolution, his leading role in the latter making a particular impression on **Germaine de Staël**. He survived the politically treacherous waters of the **Terror**, and then those of **Thermidor**, and eventually became both the favorite actor and good friend of **Napoleon Bonaparte**.

TARGET, GUY-JEAN-BAPTISTE (1733–1807). Target was an *avocat* at the **Parlement of Paris** from 1752, and a member of the Académie Française from 1780. He made a public name for himself under the Old Regime by publicly protesting the Maupeou reforms in 1771, and by defending Cardinal Rohan in the 1785 **Diamond Necklace Affair**. Target was elected to the **Estates-General** by the **Third Estate** of **Paris**. He served on the constitutional committee, where he favored a single-chamber legislature and supported a suspensive veto for the king. He presided over the **Constituent Assembly** in January 1790.

Target was a member of the **Jacobin club**, but no longer attended meetings after the fall of 1790. He supported the proposal of **Maximilien Robespierre** that deputies in the Constituent Assembly be declared ineligible for election to the **Legislative Assembly**. He withdrew from politics thereafter, and in August 1792 declined an invitation from **Louis XVI** to serve as defense counsel in his trial before the **National Convention**. Target grew increasingly alarmed as the Revolution entered its radical phase, and maintained a low profile through the period of the **Directory**. He supported **Napoleon Bonaparte's** seizure of power, was named to the Tribunal de Cassation in 1800, and participated in the drafting of Napoleon's criminal code. In 1802 he was named to the Tribunat.

TAXATION. Taxation under the Old Regime was both inefficient and unfair. A confusing array of both direct and indirect taxes varied from one part of the country to another, and the system of **privilege** meant that certain groups, provinces, and cities were exempt from particular taxes. The **aristocracy**, for example, was exempt from most direct taxes, as was the **clergy**, and the Church as an institution paid no taxes on its substantial landholdings. Among those who did pay the land tax, there was no guarantee that landowners of comparable estates in two different provinces would pay a similar amount. Much of the monarchy's revenue derived from indirect taxes, but the crown's reliance on tax farmers to collect those taxes meant that much of the money collected never reached the royal coffers. Taxes weighed more heavily on the **peasantry** than on other, generally wealthier, groups in French society. The whole system of taxation was thus the focus of bitter complaints in the *cahiers de doléances* that were drafted in 1789.

The challenge that the **Constituent Assembly** faced was to address the inequality of the old tax system at the same time that it addressed its inefficiency, and this proved an impossible task. As early as 15 September 1789, the deputies decreed that all future taxes would be equally applied, with no distinction for either person or place. Due to the financial crisis, the revolutionary governments were forced to resort, on several occasions, to **forced loans**, or patriotic contributions, and the first of these was levied on 6 October 1789. In November 1790 a new land tax was introduced, the *contribution foncière*, which was projected to yield just over 200 million *livres* per year. In January 1791 the Constituent Assembly created a new tax on movecable property, the *contribution mobilière*, which was projected to yield 60 million *livres* per year. The levy of the taxes was left to **departmental administrations**, however, which meant that the actual tax on property might still vary from one part of the country to another. In a climate of political uncertainty, some citizens simply refused to pay these new taxes, in the hope that they would eventually go away.

The *contribution foncière* and *contribution mobilière* were the two principal taxes introduced during the Revolution, but persistent financial shortfalls brought the addition of other forms of taxation. A tax on those practicing trades and professions, the *patente*, was created in March 1791, and was projected to yield 12 million *livres* per year (it brought in less than a tenth of that in its first year). The *patente* was abolished in 1793, and the *contribution mobilière* was repealed in May 1794, although both were later reintroduced. The **Directory** attempted to rationalize the taxation system in the summer of 1797, with some success, and in November 1797 introduced a new tax on doors and windows, which survived into the 20th century. Not until the regime of **Napoleon Bonaparte**, however, did the government reestablish financial solvency. *See also* SEIGNEURIAL DUES.

TEMPLES OF REASON. In towns and villages throughout France, churches were converted to Temples of Reason in the autumn of 1793, as the **deChristianization** campaign gathered force. Local **Jacobin clubs** took the initiative in most cases, often prodded by **representatives on mission**. The most celebrated Temple of Reason was Notre-Dame cathedral in **Paris**, where a **Festival of Reason** took place on 10 November 1793. Young **women** were typically selected to play the role of the goddess of Liberty or Reason, and those assembled sang revolutionary songs. This was an effort to introduce a civic religion, built on the ideals of the **Enlightenment**. But many Frenchmen, and particularly Frenchwomen, resented this usurpation of their churches. **Maximilien Robespierre** attempted to defuse the deChristianization campaign by introducing the **Cult of the Supreme Being**, but that effort, too, proved controversial and the Temples of Reason eventually reverted to their original function as Catholic churches.

TENNIS COURT OATH. The swearing of the Tennis Court Oath, on 20 June 1789, is among the most dramatic events of the French Revolution. Three days before, the deputies of the **Third Estate** had declared their intention to form a National Assembly, and were joined in this gesture by a number of **clergy**. On the morning of 20 June, those deputies found their meeting hall locked and guarded by royal troops, ostensibly to allow preparation for a royal session two days later. The deputies responded with anger and concern, convinced that the king planned to dissolve the National Assembly. At the suggestion of **Jean-Joseph Mounier**, they moved to a nearby indoor tennis court to swear an oath composed by **Emmanuel-Joseph Sieyès**, by which they pledged to remain together until a new constitution was written and firmly established. **Jean-Sylvain Bailly**, soon to become mayor of **Paris**, was the first to swear the oath, and he then administered it to the others gathered, who completed the ceremony by affixing their signatures to a copy of the oath. Among the 577 deputies present, only Martin Dauch, from Castelnaudary, refused to swear the oath. One week later, after initial resistance, **Louis XVI** accepted this initiative and ordered the three estates to meet in common as the National Assembly.

A substantial crowd witnessed the Tennis Court Oath, and revolutionaries almost immediately acclaimed it as a symbolic expression of social reconciliation, unity, and national **regeneration**. **Jacques-Louis David** declared his intention to capture the moment in a painted canvas, and in 1790 the **Jacobin clubs** launched a voluntary subscription campaign to subsidize the project. The effort fell short, and David never completed the painting, but the unfinished canvas remains a stirring evocation of the emotion and idealism that motivated the deputies that day.

TERROR. Terror became the "order of the day" in revolutionary France in the autumn of 1793, following the **uprising of 4–5 September**. Whether the Terror began with the execution of **Louis XVI** in January 1793, or with the creation of the **Revolutionary Tribunal** in March 1793, or with the consolidation of the **Committee of Public Safety** in July 1793 is open to debate, but generally speaking we think of the Terror as encompassing 1793–94, with its endpoint more precisely identified by the fall of **Maximilien Robespierre** on 9 **Thermidor**.

Revolutionary government, government by terror, meant essentially two things. First, it meant price controls on staple goods and the creation of an ***armée révolutionnaire*** to ensure an adequate supply of food to the cities. This was particularly important to the people of **Paris**, who had seen their city dangerously under-supplied in the summer of 1793. Second, the Terror involved the suspension of many civil liberties, and the repression of those believed to be enemies of the Revolution. The Terror was most severe in areas of civil war, **counterrevolution**, and in some of the departments near the frontier. In some departments the Terror claimed fewer than 10 victims. Seventy percent of the death sentences were handed down in just five departments. In some areas the Terror was particularly harsh. In Nantes, near the center of the **Vendée** rebellion, **Jean-Baptiste Carrier** ordered the drowning of 3,000 suspected counterrevolutionaries. In **Lyon** nearly 2,000 were executed, some by **guillotine** and others shot down by cannon. Under the **Law of Suspects**, some 70,000 people were arrested during the Terror, roughly 0.5 percent of the population. Our best estimates suggest that 40,000 people were executed during the Terror, but if one includes those who died in the repression of the Vendée rebellion, the death toll mounts considerably higher.

Prominent in the history of the Terror are the "show trials" of the **Girondin** deputies, of **Georges-Jacques Danton** and the **Indulgents**, and of **Jacques-René Hébert** and the *enragés*. Those trials did as much to discredit the revolutionary regime as the overall death tally of the Terror. Historians have long debated the meaning of the Terror. Some see it as an inevitable outcome of the ideology of the **Jacobin clubs** or the thought of **Jean-Jacques Rousseau**, while others interpret the Terror as an unfortunate, but understandable, response to the circumstances of war and counterrevolution. Supporters of the Revolution tend to downplay the scope of the Terror, while its opponents tend to exaggerate its scope. For virtually all who study the Revolution, however, the ideals of 1789 are tarnished by the violence of the Terror.

THEOPHILANTHROPY. Theophilanthropy emerged as a semi-official cult during a second campaign of **deChristianization** in the last years of the **Directory** regime. It was first proposed by Jean-Baptiste Chemin Dupontès, a bookseller in **Paris**, in a September 1796 pamphlet titled *Manuel des Théoanthrophiles*, later amended to *Théophilanthropes*, which literally means "lovers of God and man." The practices he described grew out of the deism of the **Enlightenment** and borrowed from the rituals of **freemasonry**. A number of prominent individuals took an interest in theophilanthropy, including **Marie-Joseph Chenier**, **Louis-Sébastien Mercier**, **Thomas Paine**, and **Pierre-Samuel Dupont de Nemours**. The first public service was held in January 1797 in the former chapel of Saint Catherine. With the support of **Louis-Marie La Révellière-Lépeaux**, one of the directors, the cult grew and soon enjoyed the use of more than a dozen Paris churches, including Notre-Dame cathedral.

The hope of those who practiced theophilanthropy was that it would succeed as a movement where the **Cult of the Supreme Being** had failed, as an alternative to Catholicism that would inculcate republican morality and patriotism while addressing the spiritual needs of the populace. In addition to services, held initially on Sundays and later on the *décadi*, the movement also published a **newspaper**, *l'Ami des théophilanthropes*. Though concentrated in Paris, there were pockets of support in the provinces as well, most notably in the department of the Yonne, southeast of the capital.

After the **Floréal coup** in 1798, the Directory withdrew some of its support for theophilanthropy, deeming it too closely associated with former **Jacobins**, and **Napoleon Bonaparte** banned the cult entirely in October 1801.

THERMIDOR. On 9 Thermidor II, **Maximilien Robespierre** was denounced before a session of the **National Convention** and toppled from power. It was more a coup than a *journée*. As **Bertrand Barère** would say the next day, "If the people made their revolution on 31 May 1793, the National Convention made its revolution on 9 Thermidor, and liberty applauded both equally."

Robespierre had been for some months a dominant force on the **Committee of Public Safety**, and the most prominent public defender of the policies of the **Terror**. Two assassination attempts against him in the spring of 1794 had resulted in the **Law of 22 Prairial** and a surge in the number of executions, at a time when many felt that revolutionary justice should be relaxed. The introduction of the **Cult of the Supreme Being** in early June 1794 convinced some that Robespierre aspired to dictatorial power, and when he spoke in the **Jacobin club** on 8 Thermidor about the need to expose more enemies of the Republic, those conspiring against him were galvanized into action.

Joseph Fouché and **Jean-Lambert Tallien** were prominent among those planning the coup, but **Jean-Marie Collot d'Herbois** and **Jacques-Nicolas Billaud-Varenne** also played important roles, along with a number of others. This was a coalition of deputies from both the left and the right, with a variety of conflicting motivations, but a common fear. Some among them hoped that the policies of the Terror would be extended, not curtailed. The conservative reaction against the Jacobin policies of the Year II, often referred to as the **Thermidorian** reaction, actually did not set in until some months later.

On 9 Thermidor those involved in the plot prevented Robespierre from speaking before the Convention. Others were denounced as well, most notably **Louis-Antoine Saint-Just**, **Georges Couthon**, and **Augustin Robespierre**. The accused took refuge in the Hôtel de Ville that evening, but the sections of **Paris**, so loyal to Robespierre in the past, did not rise in his support on this occasion. Robespierre went to the **guillotine** on 10 Thermidor, joined by 21 others. Dozens more would join them in the following days, 107 all told. Their execution marks the symbolic end of the Terror.

THERMIDORIANS. Narrowly defined, the Thermidorians were those men who led the coup of 9 **Thermidor** against **Maximilien Robespierre** and his supporters, men on both the left and the right of the political spectrum. More broadly speaking, the Thermidorians were those men, predominantly conservative republicans, who dominated the **National Convention** over the next 15 months, dismantling the institutions of the **Terror** and laying the groundwork for the regime of the **Directory**. They included ex-terrorists such as **Louis-Stanislas Fréron** and **Jean-Lambert Tallien**, as well as former Girondins such as **Jean-Baptiste Louvet**.

The Thermidorians brought a number of the most extreme terrorists to justice, including **Jean-Baptiste Carrier**, **Jacques-Nicolas Billaud-Varenne**, and **Jean-Marie Collot d'Herbois**; oversaw the closing of the **Jacobin clubs**; encouraged the *jeunesse dorée* in their tactics of political intimidation; dismantled much of the economic and social legislation introduced by the **Montagnards**; and created a liberal parliamentary regime that favored the interests of property owners and stifled popular democracy. Their policies were in some regards contradictory. They brought an end to the Terror and punished its perpetrators, but unleashed a **White Terror** against former Jacobins. They attempted to create a political system, in the **Consti-**

tution of 1795, that would preserve a moderate republic, but undermined its legitimacy by decreeing that two-thirds of their number would be guaranteed reelection to either the **Council of Ancients** or the **Council of Five Hundred**. To posterity, the term Thermidorian has come to seem synonymous with reactionary.

THÉROIGNE DE MÉRICOURT, ANNE-JOSEPHE (1762–1815). Théroigne de Méricourt was the daughter of well-to-do Belgian **peasants** in the countryside near Liège. At the age of 20 she moved to England, where she remained for some years, before traveling to Italy and then **Paris**, where she arrived in June 1789. Swept up by the events of that summer, Théroigne relocated to **Versailles**, where she assiduously followed the debates of the **Estates-General**. She joined the protests of the market **women** who marched to Versailles during the **October Days**, and subsequently followed the royal family back to Paris. Her continued attendance at sessions of the **Constituent Assembly** put her on familiar terms with a number of the leading deputies.

In May 1790 Théroigne was threatened with arrest for her participation in the October Days, and she fled to **Belgium**. In February 1791 she was seized by *émigrés* and held captive in the château of Kufstein for some nine months, by order of Joseph II. Théroigne returned to Paris in early 1792, and supported the war party of **Jacques-Pierre Brissot**. She called on women to join men at the battlefront, and made efforts to form a women's political club. Active in the **uprisings of 20 June 1792** and **10 August 1792**, Théroigne was presented a civic crown by the **Marseille** *fédérés* for her role in the latter. She supported the **Girondins** in their struggle with the **Montagnards**, and in May 1793 was beaten for her moderate views by a group of radical republican women outside of the central markets. Whether as a result of that beating, or of her nine months in an Austrian prison, Théroigne descended into madness and spent her final years in the Salpêtrière asylum.

THIRD ESTATE. The Third Estate consisted of the common people in Old Regime French society, the third of the three orders, the first two being the **clergy** and the **aristocracy**. The Third Estate thus constituted approximately 97 percent of the population. In response to the question posed by the title to his famous pamphlet, *What is the Third Estate?*, **Emmanuel-Joseph Sieyès** offered this answer: "Everything; but an everything shackled and oppressed. What would it be without the privileged order? Everything; but an everything free and flourishing."

Sieyès and others like him demanded in 1788 that the delegates of the Third Estate to the **Estates-General** be doubled in number, so as to equal the number of delegates of the first two estates. Once gathered at **Versailles** they demanded that votes be taken by head, rather than by order, and when the king and aristocracy balked at that demand, they took the lead in declaring a National Assembly. That being achieved, it was not long before the deputies abolished the system of **privilege** that had defined Old Regime society. In a nation of citizens, estates became obsolete. The clergy would survive as a profession, but with the abolition of aristocracy in 1790 the Third Estate disappeared as well. *See also* PEASANTRY.

TOULON. Toulon is a city on the southeast coast of France, near the Italian border, with a population of roughly 20,000 in 1789. It was the site of an important naval arsenal under the Old Regime and during the Revolution, and in 1790 was designated as the *chef-lieu* of the Var department. Municipal politics in Toulon were contentious in the early years of the Revolution, marred by frequent conflicts between local **Jacobins** and royalists, the latter finding their principal support among naval officers. Jacobins gained control of local politics in 1792, but were forced from power in July 1793 by rebels sympathetic to the **federalist revolt** in nearby **Marseille**. When Marseille fell to republican troops in August, royalists in Toulon turned the port over to the British, a treasonous act that sent shock waves throughout the country. The French army regained control of Toulon only after a three-month siege, during which the young **Napoleon Bonaparte** made his first mark as a commander of artillery. Toulon was severely damaged during the siege, and lost a substantial portion of its population to flight. A severe repression followed the recapture of the city, with more than 800 rebels summarily shot and another 300 later sentenced to death. The name of the city was temporarily changed to Port-la-Montagne. The city regained its vitality as a naval port in the years thereafter, attracting a growing population of immigrant workers, and remained politically quiescent as its population was restored.

TOULOUSE. Toulouse, located in south central France at the heart of a wheat-producing region, was the eighth largest city in France in 1789. It became a center of revolutionary enthusiasm over the ensuing decade. There was minor violence between **Protestants** and Catholics in spring 1790, on the eve of the troubles in nearby **Montauban**. By 1793 Toulouse was known as something of a **Jacobin** stronghold, although its inhabitants objected to the radicalism of **François Chabot** when he visited as a **representative on mission** in May 1793. One month later, local authorities flirted briefly with the **federalist revolt**, but took no active role in it. Despite this, the **Terror** was relatively harsh in the city, and local Jacobins actively pursued **refractory clergy** during the **deChristianization** campaign.

Toulouse could not turn to overseas sources of grain as easily as other large cities in France, so that when **peasants** withheld grain from the market in protest of the *maximum*, its urban populace suffered considerable hardship. The winter of 1795 was particularly difficult. Toulouse continued to be a Jacobin stronghold into the **Directory** period. In the summer of 1798, royalists in the region made it the target of a peasant uprising, but did not succeed in taking the city. Toulouse was one of the few cities in France in which Jacobins attempted a showing of opposition to **Napoleon Bonaparte** following the coup of 18 **Brumaire**.

TOUSSAINT-LOUVERTURE, FRANÇOIS-DOMINIQUE (1743–1803). Toussaint-Louverture was born a slave on the island of **Saint-Domingue**, but seems never to have worked as a manual laborer and gained his freedom in 1776. As a free man, he remained aloof from the early slave revolts, hopeful that the **Declaration of the Rights of Man and Citizen** would be applied to free blacks as well as whites. Disappointed in that hope, he eventually joined in the 1791 uprising, and emerged as a military leader of considerable skill in the years thereafter. He allied himself initially with the Spanish, then the British, but after the **National Convention** abolished **slavery** in 1794, he declared his loyalty once again to France. Toussaint played one European power off against the others in pursuing his ultimate goal of independence for the island, under black rule. By late 1797 he had emerged as the effective leader of Saint-Domingue, and in 1800 introduced a constitution that named him president for life, and which granted France only a nominal **sovereignty** over the island. Angered at this affront, **Napoleon**

Bonaparte dispatched an army of 10,000 men in 1802, under the command of General Victor-Emmanuel Leclerc. Toussaint was captured in November 1802 and transported to France, where he died in a fortress prison in the Jura the following year. French troops were forced to abandon Saint-Domingue in 1804, however, and the island, renamed Haiti, preserved its independence, a posthumous victory for Toussaint-Louverture.

TRIUMVIRATE. One can speak of at least three Triumvirates over the course of the French Revolution. The first was composed of the deputies **Antoine-Pierre Barnave**, **Adrien Duport**, and **Alexandre Lameth**, all active leaders in the **Jacobin club** and dominant figures in the **Constituent Assembly**. They led the campaign to restrict royal powers in the drafting of the **Constitution of 1791**, but grew more conservative in the aftermath of the king's flight to **Varennes**.

The second Triumvirate existed more in the minds of their accusers than as a real political force. Following the **September Massacres**, a number of **Girondins**, most notably **Jean-Baptiste Louvet**, accused **Maximilien Robespierre**, **Georges-Jacques Danton**, and **Jean-Paul Marat** of being a Triumvirate responsible for instigating the killings in the prisons and of aspiring to dictatorial power. There is little evidence that the three actively collaborated during this period, and they proved to be uneasy allies in the months that followed.

Finally, Maximilien Robespierre, **Louis-Antoine Saint-Just**, and **Georges Couthon** were denounced by their enemies as a dictatorial Triumvirate on the **Committee of Public Safety** as a prelude to the **Thermidor** coup that toppled all three from power and sent them to the **guillotine**.

TRONCHET, FRANÇOIS-DENIS (1726–1826). Tronchet was the son of a *procureur* at the **Parlement of Paris**, and followed in his father's footsteps by pursuing a legal career. He gained a reputation as a brilliant legal mind under the Old Regime, though not as a courtroom orator. In 1789 Tronchet was elected to the **Estates-General** by the **Third Estate** of **Paris**. He opposed the declaration of a National Assembly, but went on to preside over the **Constituent Assembly** in March 1791. Tronchet's principal contribution in that assembly was to legislation related to the suppression of **seigneurial dues**. Following the king's flight to **Varennes** he spoke in opposition to judicial proceedings, and after the **uprising of 10 August 1792** accepted an invitation to serve as defense counsel to **Louis XVI**. Tronchet styled himself a republican, but defended the king with energy and talent, retiring from public life after the king's execution. Following the proscription of the **Girondins** on 31 May 1793, Tronchet went into hiding in Paris until after 9 **Thermidor**. Thereafter he sat as a deputy from the Seine-et-Oise in the **Council of Ancients**, presided over the Tribunal de Cassation, and helped to draft the Napoleonic Civil Code. In 1802 he presided over the Senate, and was later named an officer in the Legion of Honor. At his death Tronchet left behind translations of the works of both John Milton and David Hume, and over 3,000 legal briefs and opinions. In 1806 his remains were interred in the **Panthéon**.

TUILERIES. When **Louis XVI** and his family returned to **Paris** following the **October Days** in 1789, they moved into the Tuileries palace, last inhabited by the royal family nearly a century before. Over the next two years, the king and **Marie Antoinette** felt like prisoners in their new home, forbidden even to travel to other royal residences in the Paris basin. On 20 June 1792, a crowd of **sans-culottes** invaded the Tuileries Palace, forcing Louis to don a **phrygian cap**, but failing in this first effort to topple the monarchy. They succeeded not quite two months later, in the **uprising of 10 August 1792**, led by the **Marseille** *fédérés*. The palace was severely damaged in this battle, but in May 1793 the **National Convention** made it its meeting place, and later that summer the **Committee of Public Safety** installed itself as well. Royal decoration now gave way to the symbols of the Revolution. Under the **Directory**, the **Council of Ancients** met in the Tuileries Palace, and **Napoleon Bonaparte** took up residence there in 1800 as first consul. The palace burned to the ground in 1871, during the repression of the Paris Commune.

– U –

UPRISING OF 10 AUGUST 1792. The uprising of 10 August 1792, one of the great *journées* of the Revolution, toppled the monarchy and eventually led to the trial of **Louis XVI**. Popular sentiment in

Paris turned increasingly against the king in the late spring of 1792 as the war against Austria went badly, and because the king refused to deal harshly with both the *émigrés* and the **refractory clergy**. The **sans-culottes** were particularly upset at the king's veto of legislation calling for the creation of a camp of *fédérés* in or near Paris, for the protection of the capital, and on 20 June 1792 an unruly crowd gained entry to the **Tuileries** Palace and forced Louis XVI to don a **phrygian cap**. The king was frightened, but he did not withdraw his veto, and this insult to royal authority drew a chorus of protests from **departmental administrations** throughout France.

In mid-July Prussia entered the war against France, and the **Legislative Assembly** declared *la patrie en danger*, calling for an additional 50,000 volunteers for the army. As apprehensions grew in Paris, **section assemblies** began to meet in permanent daily sessions, and radicals in those assemblies, as well as in the **popular societies**, most notably the **Cordeliers** and the **Jacobins**, began to call for an insurrection. In addition, the Legislative Assembly overturned the king's veto, and armed *fédérés* began to converge on the capital.

Early in August the majority of the sections delivered a petition to the Legislative Assembly calling for the king to be deposed. **Pierre-Victurnien Vergniaud** turned away that petition, claiming that it expressed the views of only a small portion of Frenchmen. **Maximilien Robespierre** now called for insurrection at a meeting of the Jacobin club, and **Georges Danton** played a prominent role in the planning of the uprising. Unlike 20 June, the uprising of 10 August was a planned assault, led by the *fédérés* from **Marseille** and Brittany. The battle quickly turned against the royal troops, and although the king called on them to lay down their arms, nearly all of the **Swiss Guards** were slaughtered by the crowd. Louis XVI and his family fled the palace and put themselves under the protection of the Legislative Assembly, which eventually ordered their arrest and transfer to the Temple. Robespierre characterized 10 August as a victory of the people, but it was a victory that would be tarnished by the **September Massacres** less than one month later, even as elections to the **National Convention** were being held throughout France.

UPRISING OF 31 MAY–2 JUNE 1793. The uprising of 31 May–2 June 1793 marked the end of the struggle between **Girondins** and

Montagnards within the **National Convention.** The two factions had been at odds with each other since the **September Massacres** the previous autumn, and that opposition expressed itself during the trial of **Louis XVI** and impeded the drafting of a new constitution for the young republic. The Girondins first attempted to break the stalemate by the impeachment of **Jean-Paul Marat** in April 1793, and then by the creation of the **Commission of Twelve**, called to investigate the alleged conspiracy of the **Paris Commune** and the sections of **Paris** against the National Convention.

Far from securing a victory by those actions, the Girondins were first stung by the acquittal of Marat by the **Revolutionary Tribunal**, and then watched helplessly as the **section assemblies** and the **popular societies** of Paris mobilized against them. An insurrectionary assembly convened at the bishop's palace on the Ile de la Cité, numbering some 500 delegates from throughout the city, including a substantial contingent of **women**. That assembly called for the proscription of 22 Girondin deputies, and eventually initiated the insurrection of 31 May. The deputies of the National Convention initially resisted the pressure of the crowd, but on 2 June 1793 François Hanriot led 80,000 **National Guards** to surround their meeting hall, and in the end 29 deputies and three ministers were proscribed from office.

This uprising brought the ascendancy of the Montagnards within a circumscribed National Convention, paving the way for the passage of the **Constitution of 1793**. But it also sparked the **federalist revolt** in provincial France, which ultimately ushered in the **Terror**. Most of the proscribed Girondin deputies perished on the **guillotine**. While the uprising of 31 May–2 June 1793 may be said to have initiated the most violent phase of the Revolution, it should be noted that the insurrection itself was remarkably peaceful.

UPRISING OF 4–5 SEPTEMBER 1793. The uprising of 4–5 September 1793 occurred in the context of rising bread prices and the news that **Toulon** had fallen to the British on 29 August. Calls for insurrection arose in **section assemblies** and were endorsed by the **Paris Commune. Jacques-René Hébert** and **Pierre-Gaspard Chaumette** played prominent leadership roles. On the first day of the uprising, large crowds gathered before the Hôtel de Ville, and on the second day marched on the **National Convention** to demand action against political suspects and hoarders.

These demonstrations had varied consequences. At the insistence of radicals, **Jacques-Nicolas Billaud-Varenne** and **Jean-Marie Collot d'Herbois** were added to the **Committee of Public Safety**. The National Convention finally approved the creation of the *armées révolutionnaires* and adopted the general *maximum*. **Terror** was declared the "order of the day," and in mid-September the **Law of Suspects** was passed. The Convention also mandated that section assemblies should meet twice weekly, and that the indigent should be paid 40 *sous* for attending, which some historians have argued had the unintended consequence of neutralizing the **sans-culotte** movement. In addition, the Committee of Public Safety ordered the arrest of **Jacques Roux**, a step clearly aimed at bringing the *enragés* to heel.

– V –

VADIER, MARC-ALEXIS-GUILLAUME (1736–1828). Vadier was born in the town of Pamiers, near the Spanish border, where his father was a collector of the *dîme* for the local **clergy**. He was educated at the Jesuit *collège* in Pamiers, went on to study law in **Toulouse**, but then enlisted in the army and saw combat in the Seven Years War. He returned to Pamiers in 1758, where he became a substantial landowner and in 1770 purchased the office of *conseiller* at the Présidial court. In that position, Vadier seems to have clashed with both the local **aristocracy** and the wealthy **bourgeoisie** of the area over the final 20 years of the Old Regime.

Vadier was elected to the **Estates-General** by the **Third Estate** of Pamiers in 1789. He played no prominent role in that assembly, and in 1791 returned to the Ariège as president of the district tribunal of Mirepoix. One year later he was elected from the Ariège to the **National Convention**, where he sat among the **Montagnards** and joined the **Jacobin club**. He voted for death in the trial of **Louis XVI** and against the *appel au peuple*. Vadier opposed the impeachment of **Jean-Paul Marat**, and following the proscription of the **Girondin** deputies returned to the Ariège to actively oppose the **federalist re-**

volt. In September 1793 he was elected to the **Committee of General Security**, over which he soon presided, and it was here that Vadier made his most dramatic contribution to the Revolution.

Vadier used his position on the Committee of General Security to settle scores with old enemies back home, more than 60 of whom would be brought before the **Revolutionary Tribunal** in **Paris**, 15 to be sentenced to death. Vadier was also among the principal antagonists of **Georges Danton**, initiating the decree of accusation against him and playing an active role in the courtroom proceedings. Two months later he turned against **Maximilien Robespierre**, jealous perhaps of the growing police powers being claimed for the **Committee of Public Safety**, but also adamantly opposed, as an atheist, to Robespierre's **Cult of the Supreme Being**. Vadier played a leading role in the coup of 9 **Thermidor**. It would not be long before Vadier found himself denounced, though he managed to escape prosecution for some time. In March 1795, however, he stood accused as a terrorist along with **Jacques-Nicolas Billaud-Varenne** and **Jean-Marie Collot d'Herbois** and went into hiding. He successfully eluded authorities until June 1796, when he was arrested near Toulouse, implicated in the **Conspiracy of Equals**. He went to trial and was acquitted, but remained in prison until 1799. Vadier lived quietly thereafter, always under police surveillance, was exiled in 1816 as a regicide, and died in Brussels.

VALMY. On 20 September 1792, the day of the first meeting of the **National Convention**, the French revolutionary army scored its first major victory over the Prussians at the Battle of Valmy. The Duke of Brunswick commanded the Prussian army, while the French forces were commanded by General François-Etienne Kellerman and General **Charles Dumouriez**. One day later the deputies of the Convention declared the first French Republic. Johann Wolfgang von Goethe, present at the battlefield, is reported to have said to the Prussian soldiers, "From this place and this time forth commences a new era in world history, and you can say that you were present at its birth."

VARENNES. Varennes is a small town near the eastern border of France, made famous by the king's attempted flight and arrest on

20–21 June 1791. The plan of escape, devised by **Axel Fersen**, called for **Louis XVI** and his family to leave the **Tuileries** Palace in the dead of the night on 20 June and to travel by coach, disguised as commoners, until they reached the safety of the *émigré* armies just across the border into Germany. The plan went awry almost from the beginning, however. The royal family was late leaving the palace and their planned escort, alarmed by the delay, failed to meet the coach en route. When the party stopped in Sainte-Menehould to change horses, the local postmaster recognized the king. The alarm was soon sounded, and when the coach reached the nearby village of Varennes a crowd of **National Guards** and concerned citizens surrounded it.

Back in **Paris**, the deputies of the **Constituent Assembly** were in a quandary. Louis XVI had left behind a note expressing his displeasure with the current state of affairs, in particular denouncing the excessive influence of the **Jacobin club**. Fearing the consequences should it become known that the king had fled, the deputies announced to Parisians that the king had been kidnapped and dispatched **Antoine-Pierre Barnave** and **Jérome Pétion** to "rescue" the royal family. Even given this official fiction, the king was temporarily suspended from his functions.

Radicals in Paris were now openly skeptical of the king's loyalty to the Revolution, and petitions calling for an end to the monarchy began to circulate in the capital. Moderates within the Constituent Assembly prevailed, however, and after hearing the King's deposition, the deputies returned him to his throne on 16 July 1791. Violence erupted on the **Champ de Mars** the following day, when **Marie-Joseph-Motier Lafayette** ordered the National Guard to fire on the crowd. The popularity of the crown was now severely tarnished, at least in Paris, but in September Louis XVI accepted the **Constitution of 1791** and the monarchy survived for one more year.

VARLET, JEAN-FRANÇOIS (1764–1832). Varlet was born in **Paris**. His mother was a widow, but the family was of comfortable means, so that he could attend the *collège* of Harcourt and live for some time without employment, though he eventually took a position at the *Poste*. Varlet was an ardent follower of **Jean-Jacques Rousseau**, and eagerly embraced the ideals of 1789. He joined both the **Jacobin club** and the **Cordelier club**, and with his portable podium soon became well-known in Paris as a popular orator, first in the **Palais Royal** and later in the **Tuileries** gardens. Varlet spoke out on behalf of the **sans-culottes**, a champion of the twin ideals of direct democracy and social equality, not only in his speeches but in numerous pamphlets as well.

In May 1793 Varlet was arrested along with **Jacques-René Hébert**, by order of the **Commission of Twelve**. Both were released within days, and Varlet was elected to the Central Revolutionary Committee that would lead and organize the **uprising of 31 May–2 June 1793** against the **Girondin** deputies. He was now associated with the *enragés*, and his extreme radicalism alienated the Jacobins, who expelled him from their club at the end of June. This scarcely fazed Varlet, and his intemperate words finally led to his arrest in September 1793. He remained in prison for just over a month, leaving little public record of his activities thereafter until being arrested once again after **Thermidor**. Released following the royalist uprising of **Vendémiaire** 1795, Varlet eventually rallied to **Napoleon Bonaparte** and left Paris for Nantes.

VENDÉE REBELLION. The most serious manifestation of **counter-revolution** occurred in the Vendée, a department located in western France, along the Atlantic seaboard, just to the south of **Nantes**. The rebellion began in March 1793, following the announcement of military recruitment to fill a levy of 300,000 men for the republican army. The Vendée was a predominantly rural area, with no major cities. The economy of the most important town, Cholet, had been seriously harmed by the textile treaty of 1786, and few of the local **peasantry** had benefited from the sale of *biens nationaux* in the early years of the Revolution. The peasants of the Vendée were intensely loyal to their priests, most of whom had been recruited locally, and most of whom refused to swear the **civil oath of the clergy**. Priests and local **aristocrats** took the lead in the rebellion, but it was largely a peasant movement.

The initial scattered uprisings quickly grew into something much larger, and the rebels formed what they called the Royal and Catholic Army. It was a force to be reckoned with. The city of Saumur fell to the rebels in early June, just as the **federalist revolt** was erupting in other areas of France, and by the end of the month Nantes was under siege. Republican volunteers rushed to the Vendée to combat the rebels, not only from **Paris** but also from cities such as **Caen** and **Bordeaux** that were themselves in revolt against the **National Convention**. The main rebel army was defeated in December 1793, with atrocities committed on both sides. In January 1794 General Louis-Marie Turreau unleashed his *colonnes infernales* to carry out a scorched-earth policy against the remnants of the rebel forces and their rural supporters. In Nantes, **Jean-Baptiste Carrier** oversaw the execution of approximately 3,000 people, most of them accused of having participated in the Vendée rebellion.

The severe repression may have shattered the capability of the rebels to mount a serious military challenge in the Vendée region, but it also inspired widespread resentment and perpetuated scattered resistance for years to come. A formal treaty was signed, ostensibly ending the rebellion, in February 1795, but the failed landing at **Quiberon** in June 1795 triggered renewed unrest. General **Lazare Hoche** pacified the region once again, without resorting to harsh repression, but it was not until the signing of the Concordat under **Napoleon Bonaparte**, in 1801, that peace returned permanently to the region. The cost of the rebellion to the Vendée was enormous, with the countryside laid waste and as much as one-third of the population killed in the fighting and the **Terror** that followed.

VENDÉMIAIRE. Vendémiaire is the first month in the **revolutionary calendar**, and 13 Vendémiaire IV (5 October 1795) is the date of the last popular uprising in **Paris** during the Revolution. One month before, the **National Convention** had submitted the **Constitution of 1795** to primary assemblies for ratification, along with two decrees mandating that two-thirds of the deputies elected to the new legislative bodies, the **Council of Ancients** and the **Council of Five Hundred**, be drawn from those currently sitting in the Convention. This effort on the part of the deputies to ensure stability and continuity encountered widespread opposition among voters, who felt that the decrees represented a denial of popular **sovereignty**.

Nearly all of the 48 sections in Paris voted against the two decrees. It should be noted that many radicals and "ex-terrorists" had been purged from **section assemblies** in the capital since the **Prairial riots**. Thirty-two of the sections simply reported that opposition to the decrees was unanimous, without counting votes, and the Convention chose to disqualify those votes from the total. The official announcement that the decrees had been approved, issued on 1 Vendémiaire, therefore elicited a widespread howl of protest in the capital. Section Lepelletier took the lead in organizing opposition, and a majority of the sections denounced the decrees and challenged their ratification. Deputies in the National Convention grew worried not only for their own safety, but for the future of the republic, and called upon five of their members, most notably **Paul Barras**, to prepare a defense. Others in Paris feared a return to the **Terror**.

Only 15 sections, principally located in the central and western sections of Paris, responded to the call for insurrection, and the crowd on the streets on 13 Vendémiaire numbered about 8,000. They were met, as they approached the **Tuileries**, by some 5,000 to 6,000 republican troops, under the command of seven generals recruited by Barras. Among them was **Napoleon Bonaparte**, though he did not play the leading role that history has ascribed to him. Nor were the insurgents dispersed by a simple "whiff of grapeshot." There were several hundred casualties on both sides, and the troops dispersed the crowd quite easily. The protesters were surprisingly young, drawn extensively from among the *jeunesse dorée*, who had been active in recent years. There were few arrests, since many fled the city immediately. The courts eventually sentenced some 49 of the leaders to death in absentia, but only two executions were carried out. This event is significant as the first occasion since 1789 that army troops had been used in Paris to suppress an uprising, and as the last occasion until 1830 that Parisians would take to the streets in political protest. It also brought Napoleon to the attention of the grateful deputies and to national prominence for the first time.

VENTÔSE DECREES. The Ventôse decrees, adopted by the **National Convention** on 8 and 13 Ventôse II (26 February and 3 March 1794), are generally considered the most egalitarian social legislation of the Revolution. **Maximilien Robespierre** reportedly initiated the legislation, and the proposals were read before the Convention by **Louis-Antoine Saint-Just**. The decrees essentially called for two things: sequestration of the land and other property of some 300,000 suspects, *émigrés*, and enemies of the people; and the distribution of that property to the indigent of France. Local authorities were to draw up the lists of potential beneficiaries, while popular commissions would oversee the actual redistribution of property.

This was considerably more radical than past policy regarding the *biens nationaux*, most of which had been sold at auction and rarely in plots small enough to benefit poor **peasants**. Indeed, anyone who had proposed in previous years anything resembling a redistribution of land ran the risk of being accused of calling for the **agrarian law**, or a virtual abolition of private property. The Ventôse decrees, however, were never fully implemented. Some property was confiscated, to be sure, but it was never distributed in the manner envisioned by the legislation. After the fall of Robespierre, on 9 **Thermidor**, the decrees became moot.

VERGNIAUD, PIERRE-VICTURNIEN (1753–1793). Vergniaud was born in Limoges, the son of a military provisioner who went bankrupt in 1770. Still, the family could afford to send Pierre to school, first to the Oratorien *collège* and then to the *collège* Duplessis in **Paris**. He went on to study at the Saint-Sulpice seminary, but did not take orders. After some years pursuing a literary career in Paris, with very modest success, he decided to study law in **Bordeaux,** where he began to practice in 1782. Although never known for his energy or diligence, his eloquence gained for him a considerable reputation by the eve of the Revolution.

Vergniaud took an active role in revolutionary politics from the outset, and was among the founders of both the **National Guard** and the **Jacobin club** in Bordeaux. He was elected to the first **departmental administration** of the Gironde, and was an ardent supporter of the **Civil Constitution of the Clergy**. Following the king's flight to **Varennes**, he called publicly for a trial, and was rewarded for his revolutionary ardor by election to the **Legislative Assembly**, along with his friends **Jean-François Ducos** and **Armand Gensonné**. Vergniaud quickly established a reputation for brilliant oratory with stirring speeches denouncing first the *émigrés* and then **refractory priests**. He allied himself closely with **Jacques-Pierre Brissot** and supported his call for war in the spring of 1792.

As the war went badly, Vergniaud became more and more vocal in his attacks on the monarchy. He initiated the vote declaring "*la patrie en danger*" in July 1792, but also grew increasingly wary at the prospect of yet another revolutionary upheaval in Paris. In late July he signed, along with Gensonné and **Margeurite-Elie Guadet**, the ill-considered letter to the court painter, Joseph Boze, which would later be interpreted as an effort to save **Louis XVI**. As president of the Legislative Assembly, he turned away the petition of the Mauconseil section on 4 August calling for the king's ouster, and then gave refuge to the king and his family in the midst of the **uprising of 10 August**. In the following weeks, he would be a harsh critic of the politics of the **Paris Commune**.

Vergniaud was reelected to the **National Convention** from the Gironde. He was among those deputies who proposed the declaration of the Republic on 21 September 1792, and was also among the first to drop the "veil of silence" surrounding the **September Massacres** and to call for the prosecution of those who had incited the violence. He spoke ominously about the danger of anarchy in the capital, and eventually abandoned the Paris Jacobins. Although Vergniaud distanced himself somewhat from the other **Girondins** in their bitter struggle with the **Montagnard** deputies, in virtually every major debate before the National Convention he assumed the role of oratorical sparring partner with **Maximilien Robespierre**. He sat on the constitution committee, led by **Marie-Jean Condorcet**, whose work the Montagnards would reject. In the trial of Louis XVI, he supported the *appel au peuple*, but ultimately voted for the sentence of death. Following the riots of March 1793, during which he had felt personally endangered, he denounced **Jean-Paul Marat** by name, though he regretted his impeachment in April. Even as the political struggle between Girondins and Montagnards heightened, however, Vergniaud remained a patron of the opera and theater, and was a particular fan of **François-Joseph Talma**. He opposed the creation of the **Revolutionary Tribunal**, but supported the creation of the **Committee of Public Safety**, and was among its first members. He also sat on the **Commission of Twelve** in May 1793, and this earned him a spot among the proscribed deputies following the **uprising of 31 May–2 June 1793**.

Vergniaud was placed under house arrest in June, but unlike many of the other proscribed Girondins chose not to flee the capital. He opposed the **federalist revolt** in the provinces, but did publish a pamphlet condemning the actions of the victorious Montagnards. In late July he was arrested and confined first in the Luxembourg palace, before being transferred to the **Conciergerie**. While in prison he wrote out elaborate notes in preparation for his courtroom defense, but at the trial was effectively silenced by the prosecutor, **Antoine-Quentin Fouquier-Tinville**. There is some evidence that Robespierre and **Georges Danton** would have preferred to spare Vergniaud, but he was convicted with the others, and joined them in singing the *Marseillaise* as they marched to the **guillotine**. Vergniaud would long be remembered as the greatest of the orators of the National Convention, most notably for his comment that the Revolution, like Saturn, devoured her children.

VERSAILLES. The magnificent palace at Versailles, built by Louis XIV after the rebellion of the Fronde in order to enhance the grandeur and security of the monarchy, served as the residence for French kings from 1664 until 1789. **Louis XVI** has been criticized by some for rarely leaving Versailles. Its significance during the Revolution is substantial. The **Estates-General** convened at Versailles, and it was the site of the swearing of the **Tennis Court Oath**, the declaration of the **Constituent Assembly**, and the **night of 4 August 1789**. In early October 1789 the market **women** of **Paris** marched to Versailles to protest rising prices and the insult to the Revolution made at a recent banquet of the queen's guards. Louis XVI and his family returned to Paris with the women, ending the monarchy's residence at Versailles. In September 1792 the city witnessed one of the worst episodes of provincial violence following the **September Massacres**, the killing of 44 prisoners en route from Orléans to Paris. Later in the Revolution some of the gardens at Versailles were seized as *biens nationaux* and given to **peasants** for cultivation.

VIEUX CORDELIER. The *Vieux Cordelier* was the third and final **newspaper** published during the Revolution by **Camille Desmoulins**. The title of the paper harkened back to the early days of the Revolution, to the patriots of 1789. The paper's motto, *Live free or die*, was a bold defense of civil liberties at a moment when they had come under severe assault. The first issues of the *Vieux Cordelier*, appearing on 5 and 10 December 1793, challenged the increasingly stringent economic measures then advocated by **Jacques-René**

Hébert and his followers. This polemical attack found favor with the **Committee of Public Safety** and **Maximilien Robespierre**, who were similarly wary of extremists on the left at that time. But the next two issues of the paper, published in January 1794, denounced the policies of the **Terror** as an infringement of liberty and called on the revolutionary government to offer clemency.

Desmoulins now came under attack at the **Jacobin club** and was expelled from the **Cordelier club**. Robespierre initially protected him, defending the revolutionary reputation of the friend he had first met at the *collège* Louis le Grand in **Paris**. Desmoulins took up his own defense in the last two issues of the *Vieux Cordelier*, published in late January and early February 1794, but continued to call for an end to the Terror. Now associated in the public eye with the **Indulgents**, he was abandoned in the end by Robespierre and arrested before the seventh issue of the paper could appear. Desmoulins went to the **guillotine** with **Georges-Jacques Danton** on 5 April 1794. Fragments of that seventh issue of the *Vieux Cordelier* were seized at the printers and published posthumously.

VINCENT, FRANÇOIS-NICOLAS (1767–1794). Vincent was born in **Paris** into a family of prison keepers. He worked for some time as a prosecutor's clerk before the Revolution, essentially living from hand to mouth. He joined the **Cordelier club** very early, and was soon among its leading activists. In 1792 Vincent was elected to the general council of the **Paris Commune**, and not long thereafter obtained a position as a minor clerk in the Ministry of War. When **Jean-Baptiste Bouchotte** became minister of war, in April 1793, he named Vincent his secretary-general, and from that key position Vincent staffed the ministry with a number of his Cordelier comrades. Vincent never hesitated to speak critically of the **Montagnard** government, either at his own club or at the **Jacobin club**, and he used his influence at the Ministry of War to further the radical Cordelier agenda. In the fall of 1793 he proposed that the authority of **representatives on mission**, who reported to the **Committee of Public Safety**, be curtailed, on the grounds that they were interfering with agents of the Ministry of War. He now found himself allied with General **Charles-Philippe Ronsin** and **Jacques-René Hébert**, whose fate he would eventually share. Vincent was arrested in December

1793, and although he temporarily regained his freedom he would be tried and executed with Hébert and a number of other leading Cordeliers on 24 March 1794.

VIZILLE. The château at Vizille, just outside Grenoble, was the site, on 21 July 1788, of an assembly of the three estates of Dauphiné. The assembly convened to protest the disbanding of the Parlement of Grenoble, ordered by decree in May 1788, and the judicial reforms that accompanied that decree. The representatives who met at Vizille, led by **Jean-Joseph Mounier**, called for the creation of provincial estates and the convocation of the **Estates-General**. The Vizille assembly is of particular significance because its delegates accepted a doubling of the representatives of the **Third Estate**, and the principle of voting by head, both of which would serve as powerful precedents when the Estates-General convened 10 months later at **Versailles**. The château at Vizille is today home to the National Museum of the French Revolution.

VOLTAIRE, FRANÇOIS-MARIE AROUET (1694–1778). Voltaire was perhaps the most influential of the French philosophes of the **Enlightenment**. Although he styled himself a nobleman, he was born in **Paris** to a middle-class family. Voltaire established his reputation early in life as a playwright, and served for a time as the court historian at **Versailles**. He twice alienated the crown, however, and spent time in the **Bastille** on two occasions. Following the second of those imprisonments, in the late 1720s, he spent three years in England. Voltaire is best known for his critique of religious intolerance and the institution of the Catholic Church, but his appreciation of English institutions, including the constitutional monarchy, was also influential. He spent most of the final three decades of his life outside France, at the court of Frederick the Great of Prussia from 1750 to 1753, and at his estate at Ferney, near Switzerland, from 1760 to 1778.

Voltaire's works were widely published in France during the first years of the Revolution, and his plays often performed. In July 1791 the **Constituent Assembly** ordered his remains returned to France to be interred in the **Panthéon**, in a majestic procession and ceremony choreographed by **Jacques-Louis David**. He thus became a sort of patron saint of the Revolution, celebrated in particular in **Jacobin**

clubs across the nation. Voltaire was no democrat, however. Conservatives and moderates also found support for their positions in his writings. The most direct impact of Voltaire's writings on the Revolution may have come in the **deChristianization campaign**, due to his harsh critique of the Catholic establishment.

VONCK, JEAN-FRANÇOIS (1743–1792). Born into a prosperous Belgian farming family, Vonck attended a Jesuit *collège* in Brussels and went on to study law at the University of Louvain. He excelled in his chosen profession and was soon among the leading lawyers in Brussels. An avid reader of **Enlightenment** philosophy, Vonck joined with another Brussels lawyer, Henri van der Noot, to lead a resistance movement against Austrian rule. Their uprising triumphed with surprising ease, and by November 1789 Austrian forces had withdrawn from **Belgium**. At that point, however, the movement split, with the more progressive supporters of Vonck calling for political reform, along the lines of what was now being proposed by the **Constituent Assembly** at **Versailles**, while the more conservative supporters of van der Noot, soon known as "statists," advocated a more moderate nationalism. Vonck enjoyed less support among the social elite of Belgium, and in May 1790 van der Noot and his allies forced him to flee to Lille. By the end of the year, Emperor Leopold had rallied Austrian troops, after securing the cooperation of Prussia, and van der Noot, too, was forced to flee the country. Vonck died in 1792, but the "Vonckists" continued to agitate for both national independence and progressive reform and in February 1793 would welcome the French revolutionary armies into their homeland.

VOTING. Voting was the principal means by which French citizens exercised their **sovereignty** during the Revolution, although the number of citizens eligible to vote and the manner in which they cast their ballots shifted over the decade. In 1789 all adult males 25 years of age and over whose names appeared on the tax rolls were eligible to vote in the election of delegates to the **Estates-General** for the **Third Estate**. This was very close to universal manhood suffrage. These were multi-stage, indirect elections for the Third Estate. For the other two estates, the **clergy** and **aristocracy**, elections were direct, but there were other restrictions on who might vote, so that not all clergy or nobility participated.

The **Constitution of 1791** amended that situation, creating two categories of citizens: **active citizens**, who were eligible to vote, and **passive citizens**, who were not. Elections for national deputies, **departmental administrations**, and district administrations were indirect, with an electoral assembly making the final decisions, whereas municipal elections were direct, and therefore the purest expression of popular sovereignty. To be an elector, one had to own a more substantial amount of property than required to be an active citizen. The manner of voting varied from one part of the country to another, secret ballot in some areas, voice vote in others.

After the **uprising of 10 August 1792**, the **Legislative Assembly** abolished the distinction between active and passive citizens and lowered the minimum voting age to 21, creating a system of virtual universal manhood suffrage. Despite that broadening of the suffrage, the voting turnout in the election of deputies to the **National Convention** was lower than in previous national elections, and that same trend held true for municipal elections later that year. Citizens also were called upon to vote for justices of the peace, for public prosecutors, for criminal juries, and for officers in the **National Guard**. Voting was also practiced in **popular societies** and in **section assemblies**. In all of these venues, the manner and means of voting were hotly debated. In municipal elections in **Marseille** and **Lyon**, for example, some citizens objected strongly to the fact that local **Jacobin clubs** had sponsored organized slates of candidates.

The **Constitution of 1793** preserved the principal of universal manhood suffrage and mandated voting by written ballot, but the constitution was never enacted, and there were no elections for public officials until 1795. By that time the National Convention had drafted a new constitution, which restored a property requirement for eligibility to vote, though not the distinction between active and passive citizens. The percentage of the population eligible to vote under the **Constitution of 1795** was almost identical to that which had prevailed under the Constitution of 1791. Electoral assemblies were once again introduced at the departmental level, and the secrecy of the ballot was mandated. This system prevailed until **Napoleon Bonaparte** came to power, at which time a distinction was made between the election of public officials and voting in plebiscites. In regard to the former, the franchise was restricted, elections were indirect, and the opportunity to exercise that franchise infrequent. Plebiscites were also relatively rare, but were conducted under the principle of universal manhood suffrage (although the results were often announced before the votes could be counted).

– W –

WARS. Wars had a dramatic impact on the French Revolution in a number of ways. The first years of the Revolution were free of war, but the departure of *émigrés*, and their congregation in Coblenz and Turin, fed rumors that they were preparing an army to march against the revolutionary regime. These rumors no doubt contributed to incidents of violence in 1790 and 1791, such as those in **Nancy** and **Lyon**, as well as the *Camp de* **Jalès**, but war did not break out. As the number of *émigrés* increased, however, and political tensions were heightened by the king's flight to **Varennes**, the pressures for war steadily grew. **Marie Antoinette** urged **Louis XVI** to declare war in the hope that her Austrian relatives would save the monarchy, and the leading **Girondin** deputies called for war in early 1792 out of conviction that this would force the king to reveal his true colors. Only a minority of deputies, led by **Maximilien Robespierre**, argued that war would be folly for the French. With so many parties eager for war for such disparate reasons, the **Legislative Assembly** declared war on Austria on 20 April 1792.

As Robespierre had warned, the war did not initially go well for French forces, wracked by divisions between the rank and file and the predominantly **aristocratic** officer corps. Soon Austrian and Prussian forces advanced onto French territory, and their march toward **Paris** helped trigger both the **uprising of 10 August 1792** and the **September Massacres** that followed. Bolstered by volunteers, however, the French army scored an impressive victory at **Valmy** on 20 September 1792, giving the deputies of the **National Convention** the confidence to declare the first French Republic the next day.

The trial and execution of Louis XVI expanded the war between the monarchies of Europe and the French Republic. France declared war on Great Britain and Holland on 1 February 1793, and on Spain just over one month later. The First Coalition formed under British leadership shortly thereafter, and although divisions within the Coalition interfered with the achievement of their common goal of defeating France, the French would remain at war with some version of a European coalition almost continuously for the next 20 years. Fortune on the battlefield turned initially against the French after British entry into the war, and the treason of General **Charles Dumouriez** in April 1793 brought a moment of crisis not only at the front but in Paris as well. The association of the Girondin deputies with Dumouriez led to their proscription in the **uprising of 31 May–2 June 1793**. The young republic now faced not only war abroad, and the **federalist revolt** in four of the country's most important cities, but internal war as well, as republican troops were kept from the front by the **Vendée rebellion** in the west.

The nation rallied, however, in the face of these challenges, and under the leadership of the **Committee of Public Safety** the republican armies triumphed over their enemies both at home and abroad. Rebellion and war also led to the **Terror**, however, and while the **Jacobin** government proved capable of withstanding the armies of Europe, it could not survive the internal political divisions sown by the seemingly relentless carnage wrought by the **guillotine**. While the Terror came to an end after 9 **Thermidor**, the war did not. The *levée en masse* introduced in 1793 soon increased the size of the army to over 800,000 troops, and the nation in arms proved to be a powerful force. The enthusiasm of the citizen army, joined to effective leadership, proved more than a match for the professional troops of Europe's monarchies, and the war that ebbed and flowed through the 1790s was largely fought away from French soil. There were setbacks for French forces, to be sure, most notably in the **Egyptian campaign**, but the man who led that fiasco, **Napoleon Bonaparte**, recognized the enormous power of the people in arms. Through victory at war over the next 15 years, Napoleon would spread the ideals and institutions of the Revolution across most of the European continent.

WHITE TERROR. There were two waves of violent reprisals against **Jacobins** and ex-terrorists, the first in the spring of 1795 and the second following the defeat of **Napoleon Bonaparte** at Waterloo in 1815, and together they are commonly referred to as the White Terror. The first wave consisted of a period of about three months and was concentrated in the Rhône valley and the southeast of France. **Lyon** and **Marseille**, where the **Terror** had been harsh, were particularly hard hit. In both cities angry crowds invaded the prisons, and there were mass killings of those who had been arrested after **Thermidor**. The return to France of *émigrés* after Thermidor, and the release of prisoners who had been arrested during the Terror, contributed to that first phase of the White Terror.

Vengeance tended to motivate the killings, however, rather than a conscious **counterrevolutionary** impulse. The fact that the violence was greatest in the southeast, where blood feuds were a tradition, is evidence of this. One might also note a continuity between the violence of the Wars of Religion and that of the White Terror in the department of the Gard, where the *bagarre de* **Nîmes** occurred early in the Revolution. There the White Terror was an opportunity for Catholics to take revenge against **Protestants**. It should also be noted that the first wave of the White Terror came during a period of economic hardship, following a particularly harsh winter and the abolition of the general *maximum*. The killings were more often isolated events, as opposed to the mass violence in Lyon and Marseille.

In some areas it appeared that local authorities were complicit in the violence of the White Terror. Only rarely, at any rate, were the perpetrators of the violence brought to justice. The second wave of killings, after the final defeat of Napoleon, was less extensive. All told, the White Terror claimed more than 2,000 victims.

WIMPFFEN, LOUIS-FÉLIX (1744–1814). Wimpffen was the son of Jean-George de Wimpffen, chamberlain to King Stanislas of Poland. Louis-Félix pursued a military career in France, participated in the **Corsican** campaign in 1760, was promoted to lieutenant-colonel, and decorated as a Chevalier of Saint-Louis. He fought in the American War of Independence, at the sieges of Mahon and Gibraltar, and retired to his estate in Normandy in 1788 with the rank of field marshal. In 1789 he was elected to the **Estates-General** as a delegate of the **Second Estate** of **Caen**. He sat among the liberal **aristocracy** in the **Constituent Assembly** and favored a constitutional monarchy. With the outbreak of war in April 1792, Wimpffen returned to active military duty and commanded at Thionville, defending the fortress successfully against the Prussians. Despite that victory, he was denounced by local patriots for alleged contacts with *émigrés*, and was eventually reassigned to command the Army of the Coast of Cherbourg.

In June 1793 General Wimpffen was invited by the **federalist** rebels in Caen to take command of the volunteer force that they proposed to march against **Paris**. Wimpffen accepted the post and sent a menacing letter to the **Montagnard National Convention**, promising to enter the capital city at the head of 60,000 brave Normans, unless the proscribed **Girondin** deputies were restored to their seats. Wimpffen's command of his troops was halfhearted, however, and they were routed on 13 July 1793 at Pacy-sur-Eure, near Evreux. The revolt quickly collapsed, and Wimpffen urged the fugitive Girondin deputies to approach England for support or refuge. They refused his advice, and Wimpffen went into hiding near his estate until after the **Terror**. He regained his military commission under the **Directory**, without active duty, and was later named a Baron of the Empire.

WOMEN. The French Revolution is seen by some as championing the rights of women, given the **Declaration of the Rights of Woman and Citizen** written by **Olympe de Gouges**, while it is seen by others as denying women access to the public sphere, given the overtly misogynistic attitudes expressed by a number of prominent **Jacobins** and the fact that no **constitution** of the revolutionary decade granted full citizenship or the right to vote to women. One might say, perhaps, that while the Revolution placed women's rights on the political agenda, it did relatively little to further their cause.

Women were certainly active participants in the political upheaval of the Revolution. Collectively, women participated in all of the *journées* of the Revolution and played the decisive role in the march to **Versailles** during the **October Days**. Women formed political clubs in 1790–91, most notably the **Society of Revolutionary Republican Women** in **Paris**, although these were forcibly closed by the Jacobins in 1793. Prior to that time, women were known to attend the meetings of the Jacobins and **Cordeliers**, and were often active in **section assemblies** as well. **Pauline Léon** and **Claire Lacombe** played active roles in the **sans-culotte** and *enragé* movements in Paris, as did **Théroigne de Méricourt**, who is better known, perhaps, for her desire to lead a battalion of women into battle against the enemies of revolutionary France. **Etta Palm d'Aelders** made an effort to export the ideals of 1789 beyond French borders, while **Germaine de Staël** came from abroad to support the revolutionary cause. Women were not spared by the **guillotine**: notable among its victims were **Charlotte Corday**, **Manon Roland**, and **Marie Antoinette**.

Women did make tangible legal gains during the Revolution. Divorce was legalized in 1792, and legislation passed in 1793 and 1794 made it possible for women to inherit property. Those gains were lost, however, under the Civil Code of **Napoleon Bonaparte**, who on this issue shared the view of **Jean-Jacques Rousseau** that wives should be subservient to their husbands. Not until after World War II would French women be granted the political and legal rights that most European women obtained in the years following World War I.

– Y –

YOUNG, ARTHUR (1741–1820). The celebrated traveler and writer was born in London, but his father was a gentry farmer in Suffolk. Arthur was an uninspired student as a youth, apprenticed in a commercial establishment, and dabbled a bit in theater. In his mid-twenties, however, he developed an interest in economics and agricultural reform, and in 1767 published his first major work, *The Farmer's Letters to the People of England*. One year later he published an account of his travels in southern England.

Young spent the next decade traveling throughout Great Britain and became well-known for his travelogues. In 1785 the French economist Claude-François Lazowski suggested to Young that he travel to France, and he followed that advice, making three separate trips in 1787, 1788, and 1789. Young's *Travels in France*, published in 1792, remain the best account we have of French agriculture and conditions in the countryside on the eve of the Revolution. He was a strong advocate of agricultural innovation and free trade in grain, and found the French to be lagging behind their English counterparts on both counts. Young was at **Versailles** in June 1789, and recounts the **Tennis Court Oath** and the royal session of 23 June. He left for eastern France shortly thereafter, and his final observations describe episodes of the **Great Fear** in those provinces. His work was translated into French in 1793, and the **National Convention** had 20,000 copies printed. The agents/observers sent into the provinces by Minister of the Interior **Dominique-Joseph Garat** in the summer of 1793 each carried a copy of Young's book.

Young was initially quite supportive of the Revolution, and became a corresponding member of the **Jacobin club**. He grew disenchanted after the fall of the monarchy, however, and in 1793 published *The Example of France a Warning to Britain*, which went through several editions in England and was also translated into French.

YSABEAU, CLAUDE-ALEXANDRE (1754–1831). Little is known of Ysabeau's youth or family, but he took orders as an Oratorien and served as a *préfet des études* in the 1780s, first at the military school of Vendôme and then at the *collège* of Tours. He was elected to the municipal council of Tours in 1790, swore the **civil oath of the clergy**, and was named a constitutional curé in Tours. In 1792 Ysabeau was elected to the **National Convention** from the Indre-et-Loire. He sat with the **Montagnards**, and voted for death in the trial of **Louis XVI** and against the *appel au peuple*.

In March 1793 Ysabeau went as a **representative on mission** to the departments of the Pyrenees with responsibility for recruitment and reorganization of the army. After the outbreak of the **federalist revolt**, he went on mission with **Jean-Lambert Tallien** to **Bordeaux**, one of the federalist centers. The two were chased out of town by young ruffians and took up residence in the nearby town of La Réole, returning to Bordeaux only in October, at the head of a republican army. In the months that followed, they established a Military Commission to judge the accused rebels, over 300 of whom were sentenced to death.

Following **Thermidor**, Ysabeau served on the **Committee of General Security**, and returned on mission to Bordeaux, where he now adopted a more moderate political stance. He was elected to the **Council of Ancients** under the **Directory**, and oversaw the creation of the Ecole Polytechnique. He went on to serve in the postal service in Rouen, a position that he retained under the Empire. In 1816 Ysabeau was exiled as a regicide and lived in Liège until 1830, returning to **Paris** just before his death.

Bibliography

INTRODUCTION

A vast amount has been written about the French Revolution over more than two centuries. Early in the 19th century, memoirs and political narratives began to appear, mostly in French but in English as well, many of them with little critical distance from the events themselves. In France, the revolutions of 1830, 1848, and 1871 each ushered in a new period of intense interest about the first, great revolution, and many of those who wrote about the 1789 revolution were politically active in the 19th century, including men such as Alphonse Lamartine, Jules Michelet, Louis Blanc, Hippolyte Taine, and Adolphe Thiers. Those who wrote about the Revolution often did so chiefly to champion the ideals of 1789 and the heroism of its actors or to denounce the excesses of popular violence and the Terror and decry the folly of popular democracy.

As the 19th century drew to an end and the Third Republic became a stable and widely accepted regime, published works on the Revolution took on a more scholarly tone. One thinks in particular of the books of Alphonse Aulard, the first historian to occupy a chair of the French Revolution at the Sorbonne, and Albert Mathiez, who succeeded him in that position. Aulard and Mathiez were unabashed republicans, to be sure, but their scholarship was firmly grounded in the voluminous archival material that was only beginning to be organized and classified in the French National Archives. We should also note here the multivolume history of the Revolution written by the socialist politician Jean Jaurès, who was assassinated on the eve of World War I.

The Russian Revolution in 1917 had a profound effect on the historiography of the French Revolution. The apparent success of a communist revolution in the 20th century prompted some historians to compare the Bolsheviks to the Jacobins of the French Revolution and others to look for the roots of modern communism in the Conspiracy of Equals led by Gracchus Babeuf in 1795–96. The new "mass politics" of the early 20th century also prompted historians to ask new questions in their research. Georges Lefebvre, writing in the 1930s and 1940s, focused his attention on the role of the peasantry in the French Revolution. George Rudé and Albert Soboul, both students of Lefebvre at the Sorbonne, wrote path-breaking studies of the Parisian crowd in the 1790s. Ernest Labrousse explored the economic origins of the Revolution. All of these men wrote within what soon came to be known as the Marxist tradition of revolutionary historiography, emphasizing social history, the importance of economic factors, and the role of class struggle in the politics of the French Revolution.

That tradition was first challenged by a British historian, Alfred Cobban, in his 1964 book *The Social Interpretation of the French Revolution*. Cobban's book triggered two decades of "revisionist" history, calling into question the Marxist paradigm that had interpreted 1789 as a "bourgeois revolution." Prominent among the revisionists were Colin Lucas and William Doyle in Great Britain, George Taylor and Elizabeth Eisenstein in the United States, and François Furet and Denis Richet in France. By 1989, the bicentennial of the French Revolution, the Marxist interpretation had been severely battered, if not quite dismantled, though the revisionists had not succeeded in putting a new interpretive framework in place. In recent years, however, two currents of historiography have made impressive contributions. On the one hand, a number of historians have interpreted 1789 as the "birth of modern democracy," emphasizing once again the importance of politics in the French Revolution. Keith Baker, Colin Lucas, and Lynn Hunt all deserve mention here. Lynn Hunt has also figured prominently in what has come to be called the "new cultural history" of the French Revolution, along with Roger Chartier, Mona Ozouf, and Antoine de Baecque. The past 20 years have also produced a substantial body of literature on the role of women in the Revolution, including works by Olwen Hufton, Joan Scott, Joan Landes, Dominique Godineau, and Dorinda Outram. As the bibliography to follow should make clear, these are only a few of the historians who might be mentioned as exemplary of the trends in scholarly work on the French Revolution. It is no less fascinating and significant a topic for research today than it has been over the past two centuries.

The bibliography begins with a section on documentary collections, including works (such as that by Alphonse Aulard on the Jacobins) that are essentially collections of archival documents and other collections that are intended for classroom use and offer an overview, through primary documents, of the events of the Revolution. Notable among the more recent of such collections are those edited by Keith Baker, Lynn Hunt, and Laura Mason and Tracey Rizzo.

Many general histories of the Revolution have been written over the past two centuries. For those new to the topic, the short histories by Albert Soboul, Alan Forrest, Jeremy Popkin, and David Andress would all be excellent points of departure. More substantial histories worthy of note include those by Donald Sutherland, William Doyle, Simon Schama, and François Furet. The older histories of Georges Lefebvre and Albert Soboul, as well as those by J. M. Thompson, Jean Jaurès, and Jules Michelet, remain valuable resources.

As with any major historical event, biography offers an interesting avenue into the complexities and contingencies of the period. Among those cited here, Norman Hampson's biographies of Danton and Robespierre deserve mention, as do Louis Gottschalk's works on Lafayette and Marat, David Jordan's biography of Robespierre, and John Hardman's study of Louis XVI. Among works on the Old Regime in crisis, Georges Lefebvre's *The Coming of the French Revolution* remains a classic. Also worthy of note are the works of C. B. A. Behrens, David Bell, Robert Darnton, Jean Egret, Daniel Gordon, Daniel Mornet, Daniel Roche, and Dale Van Kley.

For the period of the Constituent Assembly, the most important work is the recent book by Timothy Tackett. One might also look to the books by David Andress, Harriet Applewhite, Michael Fitzsimmons, Robert Griffiths, and Kenneth Margerison. Of particular note among the books listed in the section on the Legislative Assembly is Gary Kates's work on the *Cercle Social*. The National Convention has been the focus of considerable historical research. Notable among the works cited are those by Marc Bouloiseau, Lucien Jaume, David Jordan, Michael Kennedy, and Alison Patrick.

For the period of the Directory, Martyn Lyons's overview is indispensable. The books by Georges Lefebvre and Denis Woronoff on the Thermidorians are valuable, as are the studies of Gracchus Babeuf by both John Scott and Claude Mazauric. For 18 Brumaire, the article by Hunt,

Lansky, and Hanson is insightful, as is Lefebvre's classic study. For a treatment of the impact of Napoleon and his relation to the Revolution see the book by Louis Bergeron.

The remaining sections of the bibliography focus on particular historiographical approaches to the study of the Revolution or to thematic categories. The Terror remains a highly charged topic. Notable in this section are the short book by Daniel Arasse, the collection of essays edited by Keith Baker, the classic statistical study by Donald Greer, the sympathetic and nuanced book by Jean-Pierre Gross, and the highly regarded study of the Committee of Public Safety by R. R. Palmer. On the subject of religion and the Catholic Church, Suzanne Desan's book is noteworthy, as are the works of John McManners, Timothy Tackett, Dale Van Kley, and Michel Vovelle.

The cultural history of the French Revolution is a burgeoning area of historiography. Maurice Agulhon, Antoine de Baecque, Keith Baker, Roger Chartier, Thomas Crow, Robert Darnton, Paul Friedland, Lynn Hunt, Emmett Kennedy, Laura Mason, Dorinda Outram, and Mona Ozouf have all written noteworthy books that are included in this section. Excellent points of departure for the reader new to this area would be Lynn Hunt's *Politics, Culture and Class in the French Revolution* and Roger Chartier's *Cultural Origins of the French Revolution*.

Among the social and economic histories of the Revolution, Alfred Cobban's short book remains essential, as do the works of Ralph Greenlaw, Norman Hampson, Patrice Higonnet, Peter Jones, George Rudé, and Albert Soboul. Important recent works include those by John Markoff and Michael Sonenscher. Particularly significant books on women and gender include those by Dominique Godineau, Carla Hesse, Olwen Hufton, Joan Landes, Joan Scott, and the collections edited by Levy, Applewhite, and Johnson and Melzer and Rabine. Jean-Paul Bertaud, T. C. Blanning, Alan Forrest, John Lynn, and Samuel Scott are among the most important military historians of the Revolutionary period.

Edmund Burke leads the way on the subject of international reactions to the French Revolution, but see also the works by Geoffrey Best, Richard Cobb, Marvin Cox, and Eric Hobsbawm. Notable among the histories of Paris during the Revolution are the substantial article by Richard Andrews and the books by Pierre Caron, Richard Cobb, David Garrioch, Patrice Higonnet, Raymonde Monnier, Daniel Roche, and

Barry Shapiro. The 12-volume contemporary classic by Louis-Sébastien Mercier remains well worth a look.

Among historians of provincial France during the Revolution, Gail Bossenga, Malcolm Crook, Antonino de Francesco, W. D. Edmonds, Alan Forrest, Jacques Guilhamou, Paul Hanson, Maurice Hutt, Jean-Clément Martin, Claude Riffaterre, William Scott, Donald Sutherland, and Charles Tilly all merit attention. Among recent historiographical essays on the Revolution, see those by Suzanne Desan, Jack Censer, and Michel Vovelle, as well as the lengthy reflection on the bicentennial controversies by Steven Kaplan.

For the serious student of the French Revolution, the Bibliothèque Nationale in Paris and the National Archives in Paris are indispensable resources. Each French department has its own archival repository as well. The Public Record Office and the British Library in London also hold important collections. In the United States, the New York Public Library and the libraries of Yale University, Harvard University, the University of Pennsylvania, Florida State University, the University of Chicago, Stanford University, and the University of California at Berkeley all have impressive book collections and documentary materials. The Newberry Library in Chicago and the Lilly Library at Indiana University contain important collections of Revolutionary newspapers and pamphlets.

CONTENTS

DOCUMENTARY COLLECTIONS

Aulard, François-Alphonse. *La Société des Jacobins: Recueil de documents pour l'histoire du Club des Jacobins de Paris.* 6 vols. Paris: Librairie Jouaust, 1889–97.

——. *Recueil des actes du Comité de salut public.* 27 vols. Paris: Imprimerie Nationale, 1889–1923.

Bailly, J.S., and H. Duveyrier, eds. *Procès-verbaux des séances et délibérations de l'Assemblée Générale d'électeurs de Paris.* 3 vols. Paris: Imprimerie Nationale, 1790.

Baker, Keith Michael, ed. *The Old Regime and the French Revolution.* Chicago: University of Chicago Press, 1987.

Beik, Paul H., ed. *The French Revolution.* New York: Harper & Row, 1970.

Bloch, C., and A. Tuetey, eds. *Procès-verbaux et rapports du Comité de mendicité de la Constituante (1790–91).* Paris: Imprimerie Nationale, 1911.

Brette, Armand. *Recueil de documents relatifs à la convocation des Etats Généraux de 1789.* 4 vols. Paris: Imprimerie Nationale, 1894–1915.

Brunel, Françoise, and Sylvain Goujon. *Les Martyrs de prairial: textes et documents inédits.* Geneva: Georg, 1992.

Caron, Pierre. *Paris pendant la Terreur: Rapports des agents secrets du ministre de l'intérieur.* Paris: A. Picard, 1943.

Cobb, Richard, and John M. Roberts, eds. *French Revolution Documents.* 2 vols. Oxford: Oxford University Press, 1966, 1973.

Dawson, Philip, ed. *The French Revolution.* Englewood Cliffs, N.J.: Prentice-Hall, 1967.

Elyada, Ouzi, ed. *Lettres Bougrement Patriotiques de La Mere Duchêne* suivi du *Journal des Femmes février-avril 1791.* Paris: Les Editions de Paris/EDHIS, 1989.

Guillaume, James, ed. *Procès-verbaux du Comité d'Instruction publique de la Convention nationale.* 6 vols. Paris: Imprimerie Nationale, 1891–1907.

Hardman, John. *French Revolution Documents, (1792–95).* Oxford: Basil Blackwell, 1973.

Hunt, Lynn, ed. *The French Revolution and Human Rights.* Boston: St. Martin's, 1996.

Hyslop, Beatrice Fry. *A Guide to the General Cahiers of 1789 with the texts of unedited cahiers.* Morningside Heights, N.Y.: Columbia University Press, 1936.

——. *French Nationalism in 1789 According to the General Cahiers.* New York: Octagon Books, 1968.

Mason, Laura, and Tracey Rizzo, eds. *The French Revolution: A Document Collection.* New York: D.C. Heath, 1999

Mavidal, J., E. Laurent et al., eds. *Archives parliamentaires de 1787 à 1860. Première série (1789 à 1799).* 99 vols. to date. Paris: Paul Dupont, 1867–1913; Paris: Centre National de la Recherche Scientifique, 1961 —.

Michon, Georges. *Correspondance de Maximilien et Augustin Robespierre.* Paris, 1926.

Pouliquen, Monique, ed. *Doléances des peuples coloniaux à l'Assemblée Nationale Constituante.* Paris: Archives Nationales, 1989.

Roberts, J.M., and John Hardman, eds. *French Revolution Documents.* Oxford: B. Blackwell, 1966.

Sèze, Raymond de. *Défense de Louis.* Paris: Imprimerie Nationale, 1792.

Stewart, John Hall, ed. *A Documentary History of the French Revolution.* New York: Macmillan, 1951.

Walter, Gérard. *Actes du Tribunal révolutionnaire.* Paris: Gallimard, 1968.

Wickham Legg, L.G. *Select Documents Illustrative of the History of the French Revolution: the Constituent Assembly.* 2 vols. Oxford: Clarendon Press, 1905.

GENERAL HISTORIES

Abbott, John S.C. *The French Revolution of 1789 as viewed in the light of Republican institutions.* 2 vols. Boston, Mass.: Jefferson Press, 1887.

Acton, J.E.E.D. *Lectures on the French Revolution.* London: Macmillan, 1910.

Andress, David. *French Society in Revolution, 1789–1799.* Manchester: Manchester University Press, 1999.

Arbellot, Guy, and Bernard Lepetit, eds. *Atlas de la Révolution française.* Paris: Editions de l'Ecole des hautes études en sciences sociales, 1987.

Aulard, François-Alphonse. *Histoire politique de la Révolution française: origines et développement de la démocratie et de la République. 1789–1804.* Paris: A. Colin, 1909.

Beik, Paul. *The French Revolution Seen from the Right: Social Theories in Motion, 1789–1799.* New York: Howard Fertig, 1970.

Blanc, Louis. *Histoire de la Révolution française*. 12 vols. Paris: Langlois et Leclercq, 1847–62.

Blanning, T.C.W., ed. *The Rise and Fall of the French Revolution*. Chicago: University of Chicago Press, 1996.

——. *The French Revolution: Class War or Culture Clash?* Basingstoke, UK: Palgrave Macmillan, 1997.

Boroumand, Ladan. *L'Homme sans souveraineté. Droits de l'homme et droit de la nation dans les assemblées de la Révolution française, thèse de doctorat*. 2 vol. Paris: Éditions de l'EHESS, 1995.

Bosher, J.F. *The French Revolution*. New York: Norton, 1988.

Boursin, E. *Dictionnaire de la Révolution Française*. Paris, 1893.

Brinton, Clarence Crane. *The Jacobins: An Essay in the New History*. New York: Macmillan, 1930.

——. *A Decade of Revolution, 1789–1799*. New York: Harper & Row, 1934.

Carlyle, Thomas. *The French Revolution: A History*. New York: The Modern Library, 1934.

Censer, Jack R., and Lynn Hunt. *Liberty, Equality, Fraternity: Exploring the French Revolution*. University Park: Pennsylvania State University Press, 2001.

Challamel, Augustin. *Les Clubs contre-révolutionnaires. Cercles, comités, sociétés, salons, réunions, cafés, restaurants et librairies*. Paris: L. Cerf, 1895.

Chateaubriand, François-René. *An Historical, Political, and Moral Essay on Revolutions, Ancient and Modern*. English translation by anonymous translator. London: H. Colburn, 1815.

Cobb, Richard Charles. *A Second Identity: Essays on France and French History*. London: Oxford University Press, 1969.

——. *The Police and the People: French Popular Protest, 1789–1820*. Oxford: Oxford University Press, 1970.

Cobb, Richard, and Colin Jones, eds. *Voices of the French Revolution*. Topsfield, Mass.: Salem House Publishers, 1988.

Cobban, Alfred. *A History of Modern France: Old Regime and Revolution, 1715–1799*. Baltimore, Md.: Penguin Books, 1968.

——, ed. *Aspects of the French Revolution*. New York: George Braziller, 1968.

Cochin, Augustin. *La Crise de l'histoire révolutionnaire, Taine et Monsieur Aulard*. Paris: H. Champion, 1909.

——. *La Révolution et la libre pensée: la socialisation de la pensée (1750–1789); la socialisation de la personne (1793–1794); la socialisation des biens (1793–1794)*. Paris: Plon-Nourrit, 1924.

Cole, Alistair, and Peter Campbell. *French Electoral Systems and Elections Since 1789*. Aldershot, Hants, UK: Gower, 1989.

Cominel, George. *Rethinking the French Revolution: Marxism and the Revisionist Challenge*. London: Verso, 1987.

Connelly, Owen. *French Revolution/Napoleonic Era*. New York: Holt, Rinehart, and Winston, 1979.

Crook, Malcolm. *Elections in the French Revolution: an apprenticeship in democracy, 1789–1799*. Cambridge: Cambridge University Press, 1996.

——, ed. *Revolutionary France: 1788–1880*. Oxford: Oxford University Press, 2001.

Dalberg-Action, John Emerich Edward. *Lectures on the French Revolution*. Edited by John Neville Figgis and Reginald Vere Laurence. New York: Noonday Press, 1959.

Dartford, Gerald P. *The French Revolution*. Wellesley Hills, Mass.: Independent School Press, 1972.

Doyle, William. *Oxford History of the French Revolution*. Oxford: Oxford University Press, 1989.

Dunn, Susan. *Sister Revolutions: French Lightning, American Light*. New York: Faber and Faber, 1999.

Faÿ, Bernard. *L'esprit Révolutionnaire en France et aux États-Unis à la fin du XVIIIe siècle*. Paris: Librairie Ancienne Edouard Champion, 1925.

Fierro, Alfred, Jean-François Fayard, and Jean Tulard. *Histoire et Dictionnaire de la Révolution française: 1789–1799*. Paris: R. Laffont, 1987.

——. *Bibliographie de la Révolution française: 1940–1988*. Paris: Références, 1989.

Forrest, Alan. *The French Revolution*. Oxford: Blackwell, 1995.

Fox, Edward Whiting. *History in Geographic Perspective: The Other France*. New York: Norton, 1971.

Furet, François. *Penser la Révolution française*. Paris: Gallimard, 1978. Translated as: *Interpreting the French Revolution*. Elborg Forster. Cambridge: Cambridge University Press, 1981.

——. *La Révolution: de Turgot à Jules Ferry, 1770–1880*. Paris: Hachette, 1988. Translated as: *Revolutionary France, 1770–1880*. Antonia Nevill. Oxford: Oxford University Press, 1995.

Furet, François, and Denis Richet. *La Révolution*. Paris: Hachette, 1965–66.

Furet, François, and Mona Ozouf, eds. *Dictionnaire critique de la Révolution française*. Paris: Flammarion, 1988. Translated as: *A Critical Dictionary of the French Revolution*. Arthur Goldhammer. Cambridge, Mass.: Harvard University Press, 1989.

Gauchet, Marcel. *La Révolution des pouvoirs: La Souveraineté, le peuple et la représentation, 1789–1799*. Paris: Gallimard, 1995.

Gauthier, Florence. *Triomphe et mort du droit naturel en Révolution*. Paris: Presses Univérsitaires de France, 1992.

Gaxotte, Pierre. *La Révolution française*. 3e édition. Paris: Imprimerie Michels fils, 1928. Translated as: *The French Revolution*. Walter Alison Phillips. London: C. Scribner's Sons, 1932.

Gershoy, Leo. *The Era of the French Revolution, 1789–1799: Ten years that shook the world.* Princeton, N.J.: Van Nostrand, 1957.

——. *The French Revolution and Napoleon.* New York: Appleton-Century-Crofts, 1964.

Godechot, Jacques Léon. *Les Institutions de la France sous la Révolution et l'empire.* Paris: Presses Univérsitaires de France, 1951.

——. *La pensée révolutionnaire en France et en Europe, 1780–99.* Paris: A. Colin, 1964.

——. *Les Révolutions (1770–1799).* Paris: Presses universitaires de France, 1963. Translated as: *France and the Atlantic Revolution of the Eighteenth Century, 1770–1799.* Herbert H. Rowen. New York: The Free Press, 1965.

——. *La grande nation: l'expansion révolutionnaire de la France dans le monde de 1789 à 1799.* Paris: Aubier Montaigne, 1983.

Goodwin, Albert. *The French Revolution.* London: Hutchinson, 1953.

Greer, Donald. *The Incidence of the Emigration during the French Revolution.* Cambridge, Mass.: Harvard University Press, 1951.

Gueniffey, Patrice. *Le Nombre et la raison: La Révolution française et les élections.* Paris: Éditions de l'École des hautes études en sciences sociales, 1993.

Hampson, Norman. *The First European Revolution, 1776–1815.* New York: Harcourt Brace Jovanovich, 1969.

Higgins, E.L. *The French Revolution.* Boston, Mass.: Houghton Mifflin, 1938.

Higonnet, Patrice L.-R. *Goodness beyond Virtue: Jacobins during the French Revolution.* Cambridge, Mass.: Harvard University Press, 1998.

Jaurès, Jean. *Histoire Socialiste de la Révolution française.* Paris: Editions de la Librairie de l'humanité, 1922–27.

Jones, Colin. *The Longman Companion to the French Revolution.* London: Longman, 1988.

——. *The Great Nation: France from Louis XV to Napoleon.* London: Penguin Press, 2002.

Jones, Peter. *Reform and Revolution in France: The Politics of Transition, 1774–1791.* Cambridge: Oxford University Press, 1995.

——. *The French Revolution: Seminar Studies in History Series.* New York: Longman, 2003.

Kafker, Frank A., and James M. Laux. *The French Revolution: Conflicting Interpretations.* Malabar, Fla.: Robert E. Krieger Publishing, 1989.

Kaplow, Jeffry, ed. *New Perspectives on the French Revolution: Readings in Historical Sociology.* New York: John Wiley & Sons, 1965.

Kates, Gary, ed. *The French Revolution: Recent Debates and New Controversies.* London: Routledge, 1998.

Lamartine, Alphonse De. *History of the Girondists.* 3 vols. Translated by H.T. Ryde. London: Henry G. Bohn, 1856.

Le Bozec, Christine, and Eric Wauters, eds. *Pour la Révolution française: en hommage à Claude Mazauric.* Mont-Saint-Aignan: Publications de l'Univérsité de Rouen-IRED-CRHCT, 1998.

Lefebvre, Georges. *La Révolution française.* Paris: Presses Universitaires de France, 1951. Translated as: *The French Revolution.* 2 vols. Elizabeth Moss Evanson. New York: Columbia University Press, 1962–1964.

Lewis, Gwynne. *The French Revolution: Rethinking the Debate.* London: Routledge, 1993.

Livesey, James. *Making Democracy in the French Revolution.* Cambridge, Mass.: Harvard University Press, 2001.

Lucas, Colin, ed. *The Political Culture of the French Revolution.* Oxford: Pergamon Press, 1988.

——. *Rewriting the French Revolution.* Oxford: Clarendon Press, 1991.

Madelin, Louis. *The French Revolution.* London: William Heinemann, 1925.

Maistre, Joseph de. *Considerations on France.* Translated and edited by Richard A. Lebrun. Montreal: McGill-Queen's University Press, 1974.

Martin, Jean-Clément. *La France en Révolution, 1789–1799.* Paris: Belin, 1990.

——. *La Révolution française: étapes, bilans et conséquences.* Paris: Seuil, 1996.

——. *Contre-Révolution, Révolution et Nation en France, 1789–1799.* Paris: Seuil, 1998.

Mathiez, Albert. *La Révolution française.* Paris: A. Colin, 1922–1927. *The French Revolution.* Translated by Catherine Alison Phillips. New York: A.A. Knopf, 1929.

Matthews, Shailer. *The French Revolution.* New York: Longmans, Green, 1991.

Mazauric, Claude. *Sur la Révolution française: contributions à l'histoire de la révolution bourgeoise.* Paris: Editions sociales, 1970.

——. "Sur le *Dictionnaire critique de la Révolution française* de F. Furet et M. Ozouf." *Stanford French Review* 14 (1990): 85–103.

McLaughlin, J.P. "Ideology and Conquest: the Question of Proselytism and Expansion in the French Revolution, 1789–1793." *Historical Papers, Canadian Historical Association* (1976).

McPhee, Peter. *The French Revolution, 1789–1799.* Oxford: Oxford University Press, 2002.

Michelet, Jules. *Précis de l'histoire de France jusqu'à la Révolution française.* Paris: L. Hachette, 1834. Translated as: *Historical View of the French Revolution.* C. Cocks. London: H.C. Bohn, 1848.

——. *Histoire de la Révolution* française. Paris: Librairie internationale, 1868. Translated as: *History of the French Revolution.* Charles Cocks. Edited and with an Introduction by Gordon Wright. Chicago: University of Chicago Press, 1967.

Mignet, François-Auguste. *Histoire de la Révolution française: depuis 1789–*

jusqu'en 1814. Paris: Didier, 1880. Translated as: *History of the French Revolution.* Anonymous. London: G. Bell and Sons, 1902.

Morris, William O'Connor. *The French Revolution and First Empire.* New York: Charles Scribner's Sons, 1902.

Palmer, R.R. *The Age of the Democratic Revolution: A Political History of Europe and America, 1760–1800.* 2 vols. Princeton, N.J.: Princeton University Press, 1959–1964.

——. *The World of the French Revolution.* New York: Harper & Row, 1971.

Popkin, Jeremy. *A Short History of the French Revolution.* Upper Saddle River, N.J.: Prentice-Hall, 1995.

Ragan, Bryant T., and Elizabeth A. Williams, eds. *Re-creating Authority in Revolutionary France.* New Brunswick, N.J.: Rutgers University Press, 1992.

Roberts, J.M., and John Hardman, eds. *The French Revolution.* Oxford: Oxford University Press, 1978.

Rudé, George. *Revolutionary Europe, 1783–1815.* London, 1964.

——. *The French Revolution: Its Causes, its History, and its Legacy after 200 Years.* New York: Grove Weidenfeld, 1988.

Sa'adah, Anne. *The Shaping of Liberal Politics in Revolutionary France: a Comparative Perspective.* Princeton, N.J.: Princeton University Press, 1990.

Schama, Simon. *Citizens: A Chronicle of the French Revolution.* New York: Viking, 1989.

Scott, Samuel F., and Barry Rothaus. *Historical Dictionary of the French Revolution.* 2 vols. Westport, Conn.: Greenwood Press, 1985.

Skocpol, Theda. *States and Social Revolutions: A Comparative Analysis of France, Russia, and China.* Cambridge, Mass.: Cambridge University Press, 1979.

Soboul, Albert. *La Révolution française.* Paris: Editions Sociales, 1982. Translated as: *The French Revolution, 1789–1799.* Alan Forrest and Colin Jones. London: New Left Books, 1974.

——, ed. *Dictionnaire Historique de la Révolution française.* Paris: Presses Universitaires de France, 1989.

Solé, Jacques. *La Révolution en Questions.* Paris: Editions du Seuil, 1988.

Sorel, Albert. *Europe et la Révolution française: Les moeurs et les traditions politiques.* Paris: E. Plon, Nourrit, 1884–1904. Translated as: *Europe and the French Revolution: The Political Transitions of the Old Regime.* Alfred Cobban and J.W. Hunt. Garden City, N.J.: Doubleday, 1971.

Stephens, H. Morse. *A History of the French Revolution.* 3 vols. New York: Charles Scribner's Sons, 1886.

Stone, Bailey. *The Genesis of the French Revolution: A Global-Historical Interpretation.* Cambridge: Cambridge University Press, 1994.

Sutherland, Donald. *France 1789–1815: Revolution and Counter-Revolution.*

Oxford: Oxford University Press, 1986.

Sydenham, Michael J. *The French Revolution.* New York: Capricorn Books, 1965.

——. *The First French Republic, 1792–1804.* London: Batsford, 1974.

Taine, Hippolyte. *Les Origines de la France contemporaine.* 2 vols. Paris: Robert Laffont, 1952.

——. *The Origins of Contemporary France: The Ancient Regime, the Revolution, the Modern Regime: Selected Chapters.* Edited and with an introduction by Edward T. Gargan. Chicago: University of Chicago Press, 1974.

Thiers, Adolphe. *Histoire de la Révolution française.* Paris: Lecointe, 1834. Translated as: *The History of the French Revolution.* 5 vols. Frederick Shoberl. London: Richard Bentley, 1838.

Thompson, James Matthew. *The French Revolution.* London: Basil Blackwell, 1943.

Tocqueville, Alexis de. *L'Ancien régime et la Révolution.* In *Oeuvres complètes,* edited by J.-P. Mayer, vol. 2, pt. I. 18 vols to date. Paris: Gallimard, 1951–.

——. *The Old Regime and the French Revolution.* Trans. Stuart Gilbert. Garden City, N.Y.: Doubleday, 1955.

Vincent, K. Steven, and Alison Klairmont-Longo. *The Human Tradition in Modern France.* Wilmington, Del.: Scholarly Resources, 2000.

Vovelle, Michel. *La Chute de la Monarchie, 1787–1792.* Paris: Editions du Seuil, 1972.

——. *Les Images de la Révolution française: Actes du colloque des 25–26–27 octobre 1985, tenu en Sorbonne.* Paris: Publications de la Sorbonne, 1988.

——. *La Découverte de la politique: Géopolitique de la révolution française.* Paris: La Découverte, 1992.

——. *Révolution et république: L'Exception française.* Paris: Kimé, 1994.

——. *1789–1799, Nouveaux chantiers d'histoire révolutionnaire: Les Institutions et les hommes.* Paris: CTHS, 1995.

——, ed. *La Révolution française, images et récits, 1789–1799.* 5 vols. Paris: Messidor, 1986.

Waldinger, Renée, Philip Dawson, and Isser Woloch. *The French Revolution and the Making of Citizenship.* Westport, Conn.: Greenwood Press, 1993.

Walter, Gérard. *Histoire des Jacobins.* Paris: Gallimard, 1946.

Weiner, Margery. *The French Exiles, 1789–1815.* Westport, Conn.: Greenwood Press, 1960.

Woloch, Isser. *The New Regime: Transformations of the French Civic Order, 1789–1820s.* New York: W.W. Norton, 1994.

——. "Deputies, Voters, and Factions in French Revolutionary Political Culture." *Historical Journal* 42 (1999), 277–83.

BIOGRAPHIES AND MEMOIRS

Acomb, Frances. *Mallet du Pan (1749–1800): A Career in Political Journalism.* Durham, N.C.: Duke University Press, 1973.

Almeras, Henri d'. *Barras et son temps.* Paris: Albin Michel, 1929.

Bachaumont, Louis Petit de, et al. *Mémoires secrets pour servir à l'histoire de la République des lettres en France, depuis MDCCLXII jusqu'à nos jours; ou Journal d'un observateur.* 36 vols. London: John Adamson, 1780–89.

Badinter, Elisabeth, and Robert Badinter. *Condorcet (1743–1794): Un Intellectuel en politique.* Paris: Fayard, 1988.

Baecque, Antoine de. "Robespierre, monstre-cadavre du discours thermidorien." *Faces of Monstrosity* 21 (1997): 203–21.

Baker, Keith Michael. *Condorcet: From Natural Philosophy to Social Mathematics.* Chicago: University of Chicago Press, 1997.

Barbaroux. *Mémoires de Barbaroux.* Paris: Armand Colin, 1936.

Barentin, Charles-Louis-François de Paule de. *Mémoire autographe de M. de Barentin.* Paris: Comptoir des imprimeurs réunis, 1844.

Barruel, Augustin (abbé). *Mémoires pour servir à l'histoire du jacobinisme.* 1797. 2 vols. Vouillé: Diffusion de la pensée française, 1974.

Belloc, Hilaire. *Robespierre: A study.* New York: G.P. Putnam's Sons, 1927.

———. *Danton: A study.* New York: G.P. Putnam's Sons, 1928.

Bernard, Jack F. *Talleyrand: A Biography.* New York: Putnam, 1973.

Billaud-Varenne, Jacques-Nicolas. *Principes régénérateurs du système social.* 1795. Edited by François Brunel. Paris: Publications de la Sorbonne, 1992.

Blanc, Oliver. *Last Letters: Prisons and Prisoners of the French Revolution.* Translated by Alan Sheridan. New York: The Noonday Press, 1987.

Brissot, Jacques-Pierre. *Mémoires.* 2 vols. Paris: C. Perroud, 1911.

Brunel, Françoise. "L'Acculturation d'un révolutionnaire; L'Exemple de Billaud-Varenne (1786–1791)." *Dix-huitième siècle* 23 (1991): 264–74.

Caratini, Roger. *Dictionnaire des personnages de la Révolution.* Paris: Pré-aux-clercs, 1988.

Castries, Duc de. *La Fayette: pionnier de la liberté.* Paris: Hachette, 1974.

Chaussinand-Nogaret, Guy. *Mirabeau.* Paris: Seuil, 1982.

———. *Madame Roland: une femme en Révolution.* Paris: Editions du Seuil, 1985.

Cher, Marie. *Charlotte Corday and Certain Men of the Revolutionary Torment.* New York: D. Appleton, 1929.

Chevallier, Jean-Jacques. *Barnave ou les deux faces de la Révolution.* Paris: Payot, 1936.

Constant, Benjamin. *De la liberté chez les modernes: Ecrits Politiques.* Marcel Gauchet, ed. Paris: Le Livre de poche, 1980.

——. *Des réactions politiques.* 1797. In *De la force du gouvernement actuel de la France et de la nécessité de s'y rallier; Des réactions politiques; Des effets de la terreur*. Philippe Reynaud, ed. Paris: Flammarion, 1988.

Corday, Michel. *Charlotte Corday.* Translated by E.F. Buckley. New York: E.P. Dutton, 1931.

Crampe-Casnabet, Michèle. *Condorcet, lecteur des lumières.* Paris: Presses Universitaires de France, 1985.

Curtis, Eugene Newton. *Saint-Just: Colleague of Robespierre.* Morningside Heights, N.Y.: Columbia University Press, 1935.

Dobson, Austin. *Four Frenchwomen.* New York: Dodd, Mead, 1890

Dorigny, Marcel. *Oeuvres de Sieyès.* 3 vols. Paris: EDHIS, 1989.

Du Bus, Charles. *Stanislas de Clermont-Tonnerre et l'échec de la Révolution monarchique (1757–1792).* Paris: F. Alcan, 1931.

Egret, Jean. *Necker, ministre de Louis XVI (1776–1790).* Paris: Honoré Champion, 1975.

Eisenstein, Elizabeth. *The First Professional Revolutionary: Fillipo Michele Buonarroti, 1761–1837.* Cambridge, Mass.: Harvard University Press, 1959.

Ellery, Eloise. *Brissot de Warville: A Study in the History of the French Revolution.* Boston, Mass.: Houghton Mifflin, 1915.

Elliott, Grace Dalrymple. *Journal of My Life during the French Revolution.* London: R. Bentley, 1859.

Ellis, Geoffrey. *Napoleon.* London: Longman, 1997.

Fierro, Alfred. *Bibliographie Critique des mémoires sur la Révolution écrits ou traduits en français.* Paris: Service des travaux historiques de la ville de Paris, 1988.

Forsyth, Murray. *Reason and Revolution: The Political Thought of the Abbé Sieyès.* New York: Holmes and Meier, 1987.

Furet, François, and Ran Halévi, eds. *Orateurs de la Révolution Française.* Paris: Gallimard, 1989.

Gallo, Max. *Maximilien Robespierre, histoire d'une solitude.* Paris: Perrin, 1968. Translated as *Robespierre the Incorruptible: a psycho-biography.* Raymond Rudorff. New York: Herder & Herder, 1971.

Germani, I. *Jean-Paul Marat, Hero and Anti-Hero of the French Revolution.* Lewiston, N.Y.: E. Mellen Press, 1992.

Gershoy, Leo. *Bertrand Barère: A Reluctant Terrorist.* Princeton, N.J.: Princeton University Press, 1962.

Gerson, Noel B. *Statue in Search of a Pedestal: A Biography of the Marquis de Lafayette.* New York: Dodd, Mead, 1976.

Gottschalk, Louis Reichenthal. *Jean Paul Marat: A Study in Radicalism.* New York: Benjamin Blom, 1927.

——. *Lafayette between the American and French Revolution (1783–1789).* Chicago: University of Chicago Press, 1950.

Gottschalk, Louis, and Margaret Maddox. *Lafayette in the French Revolution: Through the October Days.* Chicago: University of Chicago Press, 1969.

——. *Lafayette in the French Revolution: From the October Days through the Federation.* Chicago: University of Chicago Press, 1973.

Guibal, Georges. *Mirabeau et la Provence en 1789.* Paris: A. Fontemoing, 1901.

Guilaine, Jacques. *Billaud-Varenne, l'ascète de la Révolution, 1756–1819.* Paris: Fayard, 1969.

Hampson, Norman. *The Life and Opinions of Maximilien Robespierre.* London: Duckworth, 1974.

——. *Danton.* New York: Holmes & Meier, 1978.

——. *Saint-Just.* Oxford: Basil Blackwell, 1991.

Hardman, John. *Louis XVI.* New Haven, Conn.: Yale University Press, 1993.

Harris, Robert D. *Necker: Reform Statesman of the Ancien Régime.* Berkeley: University of California Press, 1979.

Hayman, Ronald. *Marquis de Sade: The Genius of Passion.* London: Palgrave/ MacMillan, 2003.

Hearsey, John. *Marie Antoinette.* London: Constable, 1972.

Herold, Christopher J. *Mistress to an Age: A Life of Madame de Staël.* Indianapolis, Ind.: Bobbs-Merrill, 1958.

Heuer, Jennifer. "Adopted Daughter of the French People: Suzanne Lepeletier and Her Father, the National Assembly." *French Politics, Culture, and Society.* New York: Berghahn Books, 1999–.

Jean-Jacques Rousseau dans la Révolution Française, 1789–1801. Paris: Edhis, 1977.

Jordan. David P. *The Revolutionary Career of Maximilien Robespierre.* Chicago: University of Chicago Press, 1989.

Kintzler, Catherine. *Condorcet: L'Instruction publique et la naissance du citoyen.* 2d ed. Paris: Gallimard (Folio), 1987.

Lacour-Gayet, Robert. *Calonne: Financier, réformateur, contre-révolutionnaire, 1734–1802.* Paris: Hachette, 1963.

Lefebvre, Georges. *Napoleon: From Tilsit to Waterloo.* Translated by J.E. Anderson. New York: Columbia University Press, 1969.

Lever, Evelyne. *Louis XVI.* Paris: Fayard, 1985.

Levy, Darlene Gay. *The Ideas and Careers of Simon-Nicolas-Henri-Linguet: A Study in Eighteenth-Century French Politics.* Urbana: University of Illinois Press, 1980.

Ligou, Daniel. *Jeanbon Saint-André, Membre du Grand Comité du Salut Public.* Paris: Messidor, 1989.

Luttrell, Barbara. *Mirabeau.* Carbondale: Southern Illinois University Press, 1990.

Lyons, Martyn. *Napoleon Bonaparte and the Legacy of the French Revolution.* New York: St. Martin's Press, 1994.

Marat, Jean-Paul. *Oeuvres politiques 1789–1793.* Edited by Jacques de Cock and Charlotte Goetz. 10 vols. Brussels: Pôle Nord, 1989–1995.

Margerison, Kenneth. "P-L. Roederer: the industrial capitalist as revolutionary". *Eighteenth-Century Studies* 30 (Summer 1978), 473–88.

——. *P-L. Roederer: political thought and practice during the French Revolution*. Philadelphia, Pa.: American Philosophical Society, 1983.

May, Gita. *Madame Roland and the Age Of Revolution*. New York: Columbia University Press, 1970.

Ménétra, Jacques-Louis. *Journal de ma vie*. Daniel Roche, ed. Paris: Montalba, 1982.

Michon, Georges. *Essai sur l'histoire du parti feuillant: Adrien Duport*. Paris: Payot, 1924.

Morris, Gouverneur. *A Diary of the French Revolution*. Edited by Beatrix Cary Davenport. 2 vols. Boston, Mass.: Houghton Mifflin, 1939.

Mounier, Jean-Joseph. *Recherches sur les causes qui ont empêché les Français de devenir libres, et sur les moyens qui leur restent pour acquérir la liberté*. 2 vols. Geneva: Gattey, 1792.

——. *De l'influence attribuée aux philosophes, aux francs-maçons, et aux Illuminés sur la Révolution de France*. 1801. Paris: Ponthieu, 1822.

Necker, Jacques. *Oeuvres complètes*. Edited by Auguste-Louis de Staël-Holstein. 15 vols. Paris: Treuttel and Würtz, 1820–21. Reprint, Aalen: Scientia Verlag, 1970.

Oelsner, Conrad Englebert, and Emmanuel-Joseph Sieyès. *Notice sur la vie de Sieyès*. Paris: Maradan, 1794–1795.

Paganel, Pierre. *Essai historique et critique sur la Révolution française; ses causes, ses résultats, avec les portraits des hommes les plus célèbre*. 3 vols. Paris: Panckoucke, 1815.

Palmer, R.R. *From Jacobin to liberal: Marc-Antoine Jullien, 1775–1848*. Princeton, N.J.: Princeton University Press, 1993.

Rabaut Saint-Etienne, Jean-Paul. *Précis de l'histoire de la Révolution française (1792)*. Paris: Sevier, 1827.

Ravitch, N. "Liberalism, Catholicism, and the *Abbé* Grégoire." *Church History*, 36 (1996), 419–39.

Robespierre, Maximilien. *Oeuvres de Maximilien Robespierre*. Marc Bouloiseau, Jean Dautry, Eugène Desprez, Gustave Laurent, Georges Lefebvre, Émile Lesueur, Georges Michon, and Albert Soboul, eds. 10 vols. Paris: Ernest Leroux, Félix Alcan, Presses Universitaires de France, 1967.

Roland de la Platière, Marie-Jeanne (née Philipon). *Mémoires de Madame Roland*. 1795. Paul de Roux, ed. Paris: Mercure de France, 1966.

Rose, Robert Barrie. *Gracchus Babeuf: The First Revolutionary Communist*. Stanford, Calif.: Stanford University Press, 1978.

Rudé, George. *Robespierre, Portrait of a Revolutionary Democrat*. New York: Viking Press, 1975.

——, ed. *Robespierre.* Englewood Cliffs, N.J.: Prentice Hall, 1967.

Saint-Just, Louis-Antoine de. *Oeuvres complètes.* Edited by Michèle Duval. Paris: Gérard Lebovivi, 1984.

Sauvagé, René Norbert. "Les Souvenirs de J.-B. Renée sur la Révolution à Caen, 1789–93." *Normannia* VI (1933), 565–606, and VII (1934), 11–39.

Serna, Pierre. *Antonelle: Aristocrate révolutionnaire, 1747–1817.* Paris: Edition du Félin, 1997.

Sieyès, Emmanuel-Joseph (abbé). *Ecrits politiques.* Roberto Zapperi, ed. Paris: Éditions des Archives Contemporains, 1985.

Söderhjelm, Alma. *Fersen and Marie Antoinette.* Paris: Kra, 1930.

Staël, Anne-Louise-Germaine Necker, baronne de. *Des circonstances actuelles qui peuvent terminer la Révolution et des principes qui peuvent fonder la République en France.* 1798. Lucia Omacini, ed. Geneva: Droz, 1979.

Stephens, H. Morse. *Orators of the French Revolution.* 2 vols. Oxford: Clarendon Press, 1892.

Sydenham, Michael J. *Léonard Bourdon: The Career of a Revolutionary, 1754–1807.* Waterloo, Ontario: Wilfrid Laurier University Press, 1999.

Thomas, Donald. *The Marquis de Sade: A New Biography.* New York: Citadel Press, 1992.

Thompson, James Matthew. *Leaders of the French Revolution.* Oxford: B. Blackwell, 1929.

——. *Robespierre.* Oxford: Basil Blackwell, 1935.

Tulard, Jean. *Napoleon: The Myth of the Saviour.* Teresa Waugh, ed. London: Methuen, 1985.

Vaissière, Pierre de. *Lettres d'Aristocrates: La Révolution racontée par des correspondances privées, 1789–1794.* Paris: Perrin, 1907.

Van Deusen, Glyndon G. *Sieyès: His Life and His Nationalism.* New York: Columbia University Press, 1932.

Walker, E.J. "André Amar and His Role in the Committee of General Security." *Historian* (1961), 23.

Welch, Oliver J.G. *Mirabeau: A Study of a Democratic Moralist.* London: J. Cape, 1951.

Welvert, Eugène. *Lendemains révolutionnaires: les régicides.* Paris: C. Lévy, 1907.

Wendel, Hermann. *Danton.* New Haven, Conn.: Yale University Press, 1935.

Wood, Dennis. *Benjamin Constant: A Biography.* London: Routledge, 1993.

Zweig, Stefan. *Marie-Antoinette: The Portrait of an Average Woman.* New York: Viking, 1933.

THE OLD REGIME IN CRISIS

Alpert, M. "The French Enlightenment and the Jews: An Essay by Abbé Grégoire." *Patterns of Prejudice* 31 (1997), 31–41.

Ardascheff, Paul. *Les Intendants de province sous Louis XVI.* Translated by Louis Jousserandot. Paris: Alcan, 1909.

Barber, Elinor G. *The Bourgeoisie in 18th Century France.* Princeton, N.J.: Princeton University Press, 1973.

——. *Prélude idéologique à la Révolution française: Le Rousseauisme avant 1789. Annales littéraires de l'université de Besançon* 315. Paris: Les Belles lettres, 1985.

——. *Jean-Jacques Rousseau dans la Révolution française, 1789–1801.* Paris: Les Belles Lettres, 1995.

Barthélémy, Paul Bisson de. *L'Activité d'un procureur général au Parlement de Paris à la fin de l'Ancien Régime: Les Joly de Fleury.* Paris: Société d'édition d'enseignement supérieur, 1964.

Bates, David W. *Enlightenment Aberrations: Error and Revolution in France.* Ithaca, N.Y.: Cornell University Press, 2002.

Beach, V. "The Count of Artois and the Coming of the French Revolution." *Journal of Modern History* 30 (December 1958), 313–24.

Behrens, C.B.A. "Nobles, Privileges, and Taxes in France at the End of the Ancien Régime." *Economic History Review*, 2d ser., 15, no. 3 (April 1963), 451–75.

——. *The Ancien Régime.* London: Harcourt, Brace & World, 1967.

——. *Society, Government, and the Enlightenment: The Experiences of Eighteenth-Century France and Prussia.* New York: Harper & Row, 1985.

Bell, David A. *Lawyers and Citizens: The Making of a Political Elite in Old-Regime France.* New York: Oxford University Press, 1994.

——. "Lingua Populi, Lingua Dei: Language, Religion, and the Origins of French Revolutionary Nationalism." *American Historical Review* (1995), 1403–37.

Bickart, Roger. *Les Parlements et la notion de souveraineté nationale au XVIIIe siècle.* Paris: F. Alcan, 1932.

Bien, David. *The Calas Affair: Persecution, Toleration, and Heresy in Eighteenth-Century Toulouse.* Ontario, Canada: Wilfrid Laurier University Press, 1991.

Bluche, J. François. *Les Magistrats du Parlement de Paris au XVIIIe siècle (1715–1771).* Paris: Les Belles-Lettres, 1960.

Bosher, J.F. *French Finances, 1770–1795: From Business to Bureaucracy.* Cambridge: Cambridge University Press, 1970.

Bossenga, Gail. "Rights and Citizens in the Old Regime." *French Historical Studies* 20 (1997): 217–43.

Bouton, Cynthia A. *The Flour War: Gender, Class, and Community in Late An-

cien Régime France. University Park, Pa.: Pennsylvania State University Press, 1993.

Braesch, Frédéric. *1789, l'année cruciale*. Paris: Gallimard, 1941.

Carré, Henri. *La Fin des Parlements, 1788–1790*. Paris: Hachette, 1912.

——. *La Noblesse en France et l'opinion publique au 18e siècle*. Paris: E. Champion, 1920.

Censer, Jack R., and Jeremy D. Popkin, eds. *Press and Politics in Pre-Revolutionary France*. Berkeley: University of California Press, 1987.

Chaussinand-Nogaret, Guy. *Les Financiers de Languedoc au XVIIIe siècle*. Paris: S.E.V.P.E.N., 1970.

——. *La Noblesse au XVIIIe siècle: de la féodalité aux Lumières*. Paris: Hachette, 1976. Translated as: *The French Nobility in the Eighteenth Century: From Feudalism to Enlightenment*. William Doyle. Cambridge: Cambridge University Press, 1985.

Chérest, Aimé. *La Chute de l'Ancien Régime*. 3 vols. Paris: Hachette, 1884.

Chevallier, Pierre, ed. *Journal de l'Assemblée des Notables de 1787 par le Comte de Brienne et Etienne-Charles de Loménie de Brienne*. Paris: C. Klincksieck, 1960.

Church, Clive. *Revolution and Red Tape: the French Ministerial Bureaucracy, 1770–1850*. Oxford: Clarendon Press, 1981.

Dakin, Douglas. *Turgot and the Ancien Régime in France*. London: Methuen, 1939.

Darnton, Robert. *The Business of Enlightenment: A Publishing History of the Encyclopédie, 1775–1800*. Cambridge, Mass.: Harvard University Press, 1953.

——. *The Literary Underground of the Old Regime*. Cambridge, Mass.: Harvard University Press, 1982.

——. *The Corpus of Clandestine Literature in France, 1769–1789*. New York: W.W. Norton, 1995.

——. *The Forbidden Best-Sellers of Pre-Revolutionary France*. New York: W.W. Norton, 1995.

Dawson, Philip. "The Bourgeoisie de Robe in 1789." *French Historical Studies* 4 (Spring 1965), 1–21.

Doyle, William. "The Parlements of France and the Breakdown of the Old Regime, 1771–1788." *French Historical Studies* 6 (1970), 415–58.

——. "Was There an Aristocratic Reaction in Pre-revolutionary France?" *Past and Present* 57 (November 1972), 97–122.

——. *The Parlement of Bordeaux and the End of the Old Regime, 1771–1790*. London: E. Benn, 1974.

——. *The Ancien Regime*. Atlantic Highlands, N.J.: Humanities Press International, 1986.

——. *Origins of the French Revolution*. 2d ed. Oxford: Oxford University

Press, 1988.

Droz, Joseph. *Histoire du Règne de Louis XVI pendant les années où l'on pouvait prévenir ou diriger la Révolution française.* Paris: J. Renouard, 1839.

Egret, Jean. "L'Aristocratie parlementaire française à la fin de l'ancien régime." *Revue historique* 208 (1952), 1–14.

——. *La Pré-Révolution française (1787–1788).* Paris: Presses Universitaires de France, 1962. *The French Prerevolution 1787–1788,* trans. by Wesley D. Camp. Chicago: University of Chicago Press, 1977.

Eisenstein, Elizabeth. "Who Intervened in 1788? A Commentary on *The Coming of the French Revolution.*" *American Historical Review* 71 (October 1965), 77–103.

Emmanuelli, François-Xavier. "De la conscience politique à la naissance du 'provincialisme' dans la Généralité d'Aix à la fin du dix-huitième siècle." In C. Gras and G. Livet, eds. *Régions et régionalisme en France du 18e siècle à nos jours,* 117–138. Paris: Presses Universitaires de France, 1977.

Fairchilds, Cissie. *Domestic Enemies: Servants and Their Masters in Old Regime France.* Baltimore, Md.: Johns Hopkins University Press, 1984.

Faure, Edgar. *La Disgrâce de Turgot.* Paris: Gallimard, 1961.

Fitzsimmons, Michael. *The Parisian Order of the Barristers and the French Revolution.* Cambridge, Mass.: Harvard University Press, 1987.

Ford, Franklin L. *Robe and Sword: The Regrouping of the French Aristocracy after Louis XIV.* New York: Harper and Row, 1953.

Gagnebin, Bernard. "L'Etrange accueil fait aux *Confessions* de Rousseau au XVIIIe siècle." *Annales de la Société Jean-Jacques Rousseau* 38 (1969–71), 105–26.

Girault de Coursac, Pierette. *L'Education d'un roi: Louis XVI.* Paris: Gallimard, 1972.

Glasson, Ernst. *Le Parlement de Paris: Son rôle politique depuis le règne de Charles II jusqu'à la Révolution.* 2 vols. Paris: Hachette, 1901.

Godechot, Jacques Léon. *The Taking of the Bastille.* London: Faber & Faber, 1970.

Gomel, Charles. *Les Causes financiers de la Révolution française.* 2 vols. Paris: Guillaumin, 1892–93.

Goodwin, A. "Calonne, the Assembly of the French Notables of 1787 and the origins of the 'révolte nobilaire'." *English Historical Review* 61 (1946).

Gordon, Daniel. "'Public Opinion' and the Civilizing Process in France: The Example of Morellet." *Eighteenth-Century Studies* 22 (1989), 302–28.

——. *Citizens without Sovereignty: Equality and Sociability in French Thought, 1670–1789.* Princeton, N.J.: Princeton University Press, 1994.

Gruder, Vivian R. *The Royal Provincial Intendants: A Governing Elite in Eighteenth-Century France.* Ithaca, N.Y.: Cornell University Press, 1968.

——. "A mutation in elite political culture: The French notables and the defence of property and participation, 1787." *Journal of Modern History* 56 (December 1984) 598–634.

Halévi, Ran. "L'Idée et l'événement: Sur les origines intellectuelles de la Révolution française." *Le Débat* 38 (1986):145–63.

Hampson, Norman. *Will and Circumstance: Montesquieu, Rousseau and the French Revolution.* London: Duckworth, 1983.

Harris, Robert D. *Necker and the Revolution of 1789.* Lanham, Md.: University Press of America, 1986.

Higonnet, Patrice L.-R. *Sister Republics: the origins of French and American republicanism.* Cambridge, Mass.: Harvard University Press, 1988.

Hulliung, Mark. *Montesquieu and the Old Regime.* Berkeley: University of California Press, 1976.

Jacob, Margaret C. *The Radical Enlightenment: Pantheists, Freemasons, and Republicans.* London: G. Allen and Unwin, 1981.

——. *Living the Enlightenment: Freemasonry and Politics in Eighteenth-Century France.* New York: Oxford University Press, 1991.

Jacomet, Pierre. *Vicissitudes et chutes du Parlement de Paris.* Paris: Hachette, 1954.

Kaiser, Thomas E. "This Strange Offspring of *Philosophie:* Recent Historiographical Problems in Relating the Enlightenment to the French Revolution." *French Historical Studies* 15 (1988): 549–62.

Kaplan, Steven Laurence. *The Famine Plot Persuasion in Eighteenth-Century France.* Philadelphia, Pa.: American Philosophical Society, 1982.

——. *Provisioning Paris: Merchants and Millers in the Grain and Flour Trade during the Eighteenth Century.* Ithaca, N.Y.: Cornell University Press, 1984.

Katz, Wallace. "Le Rousseauisme avant la Révolution." *Dix-huitième siècle* 3 (1971), 205–22.

Kelly, Christopher. *Rousseau's Exemplary Life: The Confessions as Political Philosophy.* Ithaca, N.Y.: Cornell University Press, 1987.

Kors, Alan Charles. *D'Holbach's Coterie: An Enlightenment in Paris.* Princeton, N.J.: Princeton University Press, 1987.

Kwass, Michael. *Privilege and the Politics of Taxation in Eighteenth-Century France: Liberté, Egalité, Fiscalité.* Cambridge: Cambridge University Press, 2000.

Lardé, Georges. *Une Enquête sur les vingtièmes au temps de Necker: Histoire des remontrances du Parlement de Paris (1777–78).* Paris: Letouzey et Ané, 1920.

Lavergne, Léonce de. *Les Assemblées provinciales sous Louis XVI.* Paris: Michel Lévy Frères, 1864.

Lefebvre, Georges. *The Coming of the French Revolution.* Translated by R.R. Palmer. Princeton, N.J.: Princeton University Press, 1979.

Lucas, Colin. "Nobles, Bourgeois, and the Origins of the French Revolution."

Past and Present 60 (August 1973), 84–126.

Malesherbes, Guillaume-Chrétien Lamoignon de. *Mémoires sur la librairie et sur la liberté de la presse.* Edited by Graham E. Rodmell. Chapel Hill: University of North Carolina Press, 1979.

——. *Les "Remontrances" de Malesherbes, 1771–1775.* Edited by Elisabeth Badinter. Paris: Flammarion, 1985.

Marion, Marcel. *Le Garde des Sceaux Lamoignon et la réforme judiciaire de 1788.* Paris: Hachette, 1905.

——. *Histoire financière de la France depuis 1715.* vol. I: *1715–1789.* Paris: A. Rousseau, 1914.

Matthews, George T. *The Royal General Farms in Eighteenth-Century France.* New York: Columbia University Press, 1958.

Maza, Sarah. *Servants and Masters in Eighteenth-Century France: the uses of loyalty.* Princeton, N.J.: Princeton University Press, 1983.

——. "Politics, Culture, and the Origins of the French Revolution." *Journal of Modern History* 61 (1989), 703–23.

——. *Private Lives and Public Affairs: The Causes Célèbres of Prerevolutionary France.* Berkeley: University of California Press, 1993.

McCahill, M. "Open Elites: Recruitment to the French 'Noblesse' and the English Aristocracy in the Eighteenth Century." *Albion* 30 (1998), 599–629.

Mornet, Daniel. *Les Origines intellectuelles de la Révolution française, 1715–1787.* 6e édition. Paris: Armand Colin, 1967.

Mourlot, Félix. *Le Cahier d'observations et doléances du tiers-état de la ville de Caen en 1789.* Paris: Société de l'histoire de la Révolution française, 1912.

——. *La Fin de l'Ancien Régime et les débuts de la Révolution dans la généralité de Caen, 1787–1790.* Paris: Société de l'histoire de la Révolution française, 1913.

Mousnier, Roland. *Les institutions de la France sous la monarchie absolue, 1598–1789.* Paris: Presses Universitaires de France, 1974.

Murphy, Orville T. *Charles de Gravier, Comte de Vergennes: French Diplomacy in the Age of Revolution, 1719–1787.* Albany: State University of New York Press, 1982.

Necheles, Ruth F. "The curés in the Estates General of 1789." *Journal of Modern History* 46 (September 1974), 425–44.

Ozouf, Mona. "Public Opinion at the End of the Old Regime." *Journal of Modern History* 60, supplement (1988), S1–S21.

Palmer, R.R. "The National Idea in France Before the Revolution." *Journal of the History of Ideas* 1 (1940), 95–111.

Pomeau, René. *Politique de Voltaire.* Paris: A. Colin, 1963.

Renouvin, Pierre. *Les Assemblées provinciales de 1787: Origines, développements, résultats.* Paris: A. Picard, 1921.

Richet, Denis. "Autour des origines idéologiques lointaines de la Révolution française: Elites et despotisme." *Annales E.S.C.* 24 (1969), 1–23.

Robin, Régine. *La Société française en 1789—Semur-en-Auxois.* Paris: Plon, 1970.

Roche, Daniel. *Le Siècle des lumières en province: Académies et académiciens provinciaux, 1680–1789.* 2 vols. Paris: Mouton, 1978.

——. *Les Républicains des lettres: Gens de culture et Lumières aux XVIIIe siècle.* Paris: Fayard, 1988.

——. *La France des Lumières.* Paris: Fayard, 1993. Translated as: *France in the Enlightenment.* Arthur Goldhammer. Cambridge, Mass.: Harvard University Press, 1998.

Root, Hilton L. *Peasants and Kings in Burgundy: Agrarian Foundations of French Absolutism.* Berkeley: University of California Press, 1987.

Sénac de Meilhan, Gabriel. *Du gouvernement, des moeurs et des conditions en France, avant la révolution.* 1795. In Pierre Escoube, *Sénac de Meilhan (1736–1803): De la France de Louis XV à l'Europe des émigrés.* Paris: Librairie académique Perrin, 1984.

Sewell, William H., Jr. *A Rhetoric of Bourgeois Revolution: The Abbé Sieyès and "What is the Third Estate?"* Durham, N.C.: Duke University Press, 1994.

Shapiro, Gilbert, and John Markoff. *Revolutionary Demands: A Content Analysis of the Cahiers de Doléances of 1789.* Stanford, Calif.: Stanford University Press, 1998.

Shennan, J.H. *The Parlement of Paris.* London: Eyre and Spottiswoode, 1968.

Sieyès, Emmanuel-Joseph (abbé). *Qu'est-ce que le tiers-état?* 1789. Edited by Edme Champion. Paris: Presses Universitaires de France, 1982.

Starobinski, Jean. *1789: The Emblems of Reason.* Translated by Barbara Bray. Charlottesville: University Press of Virginia, 1982.

Stone, Bailey. *The Parlement of Paris, 1774–1789.* Chapel Hill: University of North Carolina Press, 1981.

——. *The French Parlements and the Crisis of the Old Regime.* Chapel Hill: University of North Carolina Press, 1986.

Swenson, James. *On Jean-Jacques Rousseau.* Stanford, Calif.: Stanford University Press, 2000.

Taylor, George V. "Types of capitalism in eighteenth-century France." *English Historical Review* 73 (1964).

——. "Noncapitalist Wealth and the Origins of the French Revolution." *American Historical Review* LXXII (1967), 469–96.

——. "Revolutionary and non-revolutionary content in the cahiers of 1789, an interim report." *French Historical Studies* (1972).

Van Kley, Dale K., ed. *The French Idea of Freedom: The Old Regime and the Declaration of Rights of 1789.* Stanford, Calif.: Stanford University Press, 1994.

Villers, Robert. *L'Organisation du Parlement de Paris et des Conseils Supérieurs d'après la réforme de Maupeou, 1771–74.* Paris: Jouve, 1937.

Weil, Éric. "J.J. Rousseau et sa politique." In *Essais et conférences,* 2:114–48. 2 vols. Paris: J. Vrin, 1991.

White, Eugene N. "Was There a Solution to the Ancien Régime's Financial Dilemma?" *Journal of Economic History* 49 (1989), 545–68.

Wokler, Robert. "The Influence of Diderot on the Political Theory of Rousseau." *Studies on Voltaire and the Eighteenth Century* 132 (1975), 55–111.

THE CONSTITUENT ASSEMBLY

Andress, David. "The Denial of Social Conflict in the French Revolution: Discourses around the Champ de Mars Massacre, 17 July 1791." *French Historical Studies* 22 (1999), 183–209.

——. *Massacre at the Champs de Mars: Popular Dissent and Political Culture in the French Revolution.* Woodbridge, UK: Royal Historical Society, 2000.

Applewhite, Harriet. *Political Alignment in the French National Assembly, 1789–1791.* Baton Rouge: Louisiana State University Press, 1993.

Barny, Roger. "Les Aventures de la théorie de souveraineté en 1789 (la discussion sur le droit de veto)." In *La Révision des valeurs sociales dans la littérature européenne à la lumière des idées de la Révolution française,* pp. 65–93. Paris: Les Belles lettres, 1970.

Braesch, Frédéric. "Les pétitions du Champ de Mars." *Revue Historique,* 1923.

Brette, Armand. *Les Constituants.* Paris: Au Siège de la Société, 1897.

Buchez, Philippe Joseph Benjamin. *Histoire de l'Assemblée Constituante.* Paris: Hetzel, 1846.

Caron, Pierre. "La Tentative de contre-révolution de juin-juillet 1789." *Revue d'Histoire Moderne* (1906–7).

Castaldo, André. *Les Méthodes de travail de la Constituante: les techniques delibératives de l'Assemblée nationale (1789–1791).* Paris: Presses Universitaires de France, 1989.

Censer, Jack R. *Prelude to Power: The Parisian Radical Press, 1789–91.* Baltimore Md.: Johns Hopkins University Press, 1976.

Chaussinand-Nogaret, Guy. *La Bastille est prise: la Révolution française commence.* Brussels: Complexe, 1988.

Diatkine, Daniel. "A French Reading of the *Wealth of Nations* in 1790." In *Adam Smith: International Perspectives,* Hiroshi Mizuta and Chuhei Sugiyama, eds., pp. 213–23. New York: St. Martin's Press, 1993.

Dodu, Gaston. *Le Parlementarisme et les parlementaires sous la Révolution (1789–1799), origines du régime représentatif en France.* Paris: Plon-Nourrit,

1911.

Dreyfus, J. "La manifeste royal du 20 juin 1791." *Revue Historique* 77 (1908).

Droits 2 (1985). Special issue on *La Déclaration de 1789*.

Duprat, Catherine. "Lieux et temps de l'acculturation politique." *Annales historiques de la Révolution française* 66 (1994), 387–400.

Egret, Jean. *La Révolution des notables: Mounier et les monarchiens, 1789.* Paris: Armand Colin, 1950.

Fauré, Christine, ed. *Les Déclarations de droits de l'homme de 1789.* Paris: Payot, 1988.

Fitzsimmons, Michael. *The Remaking of France: The National Assembly and the Constitution of 1791.* New York: Cambridge University Press, 1994.

———. *The Night the Old Regime Ended: August 4, 1789, and the French Revolution.* University Park, Pa.: Pennsylvania State University Press, 2003.

Gauchet, Marcel. *La Révolution des droits de l'homme.* Paris: Gallimard, 1989.

Girault de Coursac, Paul et Pierette. *Sur la route de Varennes.* Paris: Table Ronde, 1984.

Gooch, R.K. *Parliamentary Government in France: Revolutionary Origins, 1789–91.* Ithaca, N.Y.: Cornell University Press, 1960.

Grange, Henri. "Idéologue et action politique: Le Débat sur le veto à l'Assemblée constituante." *Dix-huitième siècle* I (1969), 107–21.

Griffiths, Robert. *Le Centre perdu: Malouet et les "monarchiens" dans la Révolution française.* Grenoble: Presses Universitaires de Grenoble, 1988.

Guilhamou, Jacques. *L'Avènement des porte-paroles de la République (1789–1792).* Villeneuve-d'Ascq: Presses Univérsitaires du Septentrion, 1998.

Hampson, Norman. *Prelude to Terror: The Constituent Assembly and the Failure of Consensus.* Oxford: Basil Blackwell, 1988.

Hanson, Paul R. "Monarchist Clubs and the Pamphlet Debate over Political Legitimacy in the Early Years of the French Revolution." *French Historical Studies* 21 (1998), 299–324.

Higonnet, P., and J. Murphy. "Les Députés de la noblesse aux Etats-Généraux de 1789." *Revue d'Histoire Moderne et Contemporaine* (1973).

———. "Notes sur la composition de L'Assemblée Constituante." *Annales Historiques de la Révolution Française* (1973).

Hood, James. "Revival and Mutation of Old Rivalries in Revolutionary France." *Past and Present* LXXXII (February 1979), 82–115.

Hutt, M.E. "The role of the curés in the Estates General of 1789." *Journal of Ecclesiastical Theory* (1955).

Kessel, Patrick. *La nuit du 4 août 1789.* Paris: B. Arthaud, 1969.

Lameth, Alexandre de. *Histoire de l'Assemblée Constituante.* 2 vols. Paris: Moutardier, 1828–29.

Le May, E. "La Composition de l'Assemblée Nationale Constituante: les hommes de la continuité." *Revue d'Histoire Moderne et Contemporaine*

(1977).

Lemay, Edna Hindie. *Dictionnaire des constituants, 1789–1791*. Paris: Universitas, 1991.

Ligou, D. "A propos de la Révolution municipale." *Revue d'Histoire Economique et Sociale* (1960).

Margerison, Kenneth. *Pamphlets and Public Opinion: The Campaign for a Union of Orders in the Early French Revolution*. West Lafayette, Ind.: Purdue University Press, 1998.

Mathiez, Albert. "Etude critique sur les journées des 5 et 6 octobre 1789." *Revue Historique* 67 (1898), 68 (1899).

——. *Le Club des Cordeliers pendant la crise de Varennes et le massacre du Champ de Mars*. Paris: H. Champion, 1910.

Mistler, Jean. *Le 14 Juillet*. Paris: Hachette, 1963.

Ozouf-Mariginier, Marie-Vic. *La Formation des départements*. Paris: Editions de l'École des Hautes Etudes en Sciences Sociales, 1989.

Ramsay, Clay. *The Ideology of the Great Fear: The Soissonnais in 1789*. Baltimore, Md.: Johns Hopkins University Press, 1992.

Rials, Stéphane. *La Déclaration des droits de l'homme et du citoyen*. Paris: Hachette, 1988.

Rodmell, Graham E. "Laclos, Brissot, and the petition of the Champ de Mars." *Studies on Voltaire and the Eighteenth Century* (1980).

Tackett, Timothy. *Becoming a Revolutionary: The Deputies of the French National Assembly and the Emergence of a Revolutionary Culture, 1789–1790*. Princeton, N.J.: Princeton University Press, 1996.

——. *When the King Took Flight*. Cambridge, Mass.: Harvard University Press, 2003.

Thompson, Eric. *Popular Sovereignty and the French Constituent Assembly*. Manchester: Manchester University Press, 1952.

Vingtrinier, Emmanuel. *La Contre-Révolution, première période, 1789–91*. 2 vols. Paris: Emile-Paul frères, 1924.

THE LEGISLATIVE ASSEMBLY

Bourderon, Roger, ed. *L'An I et l'apprentissage de la démocratie*. Saint-Denis: Editions PSD, 1995.

Chaumié, Jacqueline. *Les Relations diplomatiques entre l'Espagne et la France, de Varennes à la mort de Louis XVI*. Bordeaux: Féret et Fils, 1957.

——. *Le réseau d'Antraigues et la contre-révolution, 1791–1793*. Paris: Plon, 1965.

Kates, Gary. *The "Cercle Social," the Girondins, and the French Revolution*.

Princeton, N.J.: Princeton University Press, 1985.

Mitchell, C.J. *The French Legislative Assembly of 1791.* Leiden: E.J. Brill, 1988.

Reinhard, Marcel. *La Chute de la Royauté.* Paris: Gallimard, 1969.

Seligman, Edmond. *La Justice en France pendant la Révolution 1791–1793.* Paris: Plon-Nourrit, 1901.

THE NATIONAL CONVENTION

Baczko, Bronislaw. *Ending the Terror: The French Revolution After Robespierre.* Translated by Michel Petheram. Cambridge: Cambridge University Press, 1994.

Bienvenu, R.T. *The Ninth of Thermidor: The Fall of Robespierre.* New York: Oxford University Press, 1968.

Bouloiseau, Marc. *La République jacobine. 10 août 1792–9 thermidor an II.* Paris: Editions du Seuil, 1972.

Brunel, Françoise. *Thermidor: La Chute de Robespierre.* Brussels: Editions Complexe, 1989.

Colwill, Elizabeth. "Just Another Citoyenne? Marie-Antoinette on Trial, 1790–1793." *History Workshop* 28 (1989), 63–87.

Dunn, Susan. *The deaths of Louis XVI: regicide and the French political imagination.* Princeton, N.J.: Princeton University Press, 1994.

Dupuy, Roger, and Marcel Morabito, eds. *1795: Pour une République sans Révolution.* Rennes: Presses Univérsitaires de Rennes, 1996.

Gaulot, Paul. *Les grandes journeés révolutionnaires: histoire anecdotique de la convention nationale, 21 septembre 1792–26 octobre 1795.* Paris: E. Plon Nourrit, 1877.

Gendron, François. *The Gilded Youth of Thermidor.* Translated by James Cookson. Montreal: McGill-Queen's University Press, 1993.

Girault de Coursac, Paul et Pierette. *Enquête sur le procès du Roi Louis XVI.* Paris: Table Ronde, 1982.

Grall, Jeanne. "La France au lendemain du 31 mai 1793." *Bulletin de la Société des Antiquaires de Normandie* LV (1959–60), 513–24.

——. *Girondins et Montagnards: les dessous d'une insurrection, 1793.* Rennes: Edition Ouest-France, 1989.

Guérin, Daniel. *La lutte de classes sous la Première République: bourgeois et "bras nus," 1793–1797.* Paris: Gallimard, 1946. Translated as: *Class Struggle in the First French Republic: Bourgeois and Bras Nus, 1793–95.* Ian Patterson. London: Pluto Press, 1977.

Hanson, Paul R. "Revolutionary Violence, Political Legitimacy and the *journées* of 10 August and 31 May," In Robert Aldrich and Martyn Lyons, eds., *The Sphinx in the Tuileries and Other Essays in Modern French His-*

tory. Sydney: University of Sydney Press, 1999.

Higonnet, Patrice L.-R. "The Social and Cultural Antecedents of Revolutionary Discontinuity: Montagnards and Girondins." *English Historical Review* 100 (1985), 513–44.

Jaume, Lucien. *Le Discours jacobin et la démocratie.* Paris: Fayard, 1989.

Jordan. David P. *The King's Trial: Louis XVI versus the French Revolution.* Berkeley: University of California Press, 1979.

Kennedy, Michael L. *The Jacobin Clubs in the French Revolution, 1793–1795.* New York: Berghahn Books, 2000.

Kuscinski, Auguste. *Dictionnaire des conventionnels.* Paris: F. Rieder, 1916–19.

Mathiez, Albert. *Etudes sur Robespierre, 1758–1794.* Paris: Editions Sociales, 1958. Translated as: *The Fall of Robespierre and Other Essays.* New York: Augustus M. Kelley, 1968.

Mautouchet, Paul. *Le Gouvernement révolutionnaire (10 août 1792–4 brumaire an IV).* Paris: E. Cornély, 1912.

Patrick, Alison. *The Men of the First French Republic: Political Alignments in the National Convention of 1792.* Baltimore, Md.: Johns Hopkins University Press, 1972.

Rose, Robert Barrie. *The Enragés: Socialists of the French Revolution?* New York: Cambridge University Press, 1965.

Soboul, Albert, ed. *Actes du Colloque Girondins et Montagnards.* Paris: Société des Etudes Robespierristes, 1980.

Sydenham, Michael J. *The Girondins.* London: University of London, 1961.

Walter, Gérard. *La conjuration du neuf thermidor.* Paris: Gallimard, 1974.

Walzer, Michael, ed. *Regicide et Revolution: Speeches at the trial of Louis XVI.* Cambridge: Cambridge University Press, 1974.

Whaley, Leigh. *Radicals: Politics and Republicanism in the French Revolution.* Phoenix, Ariz.: Sutton, 2000.

THE DIRECTORY

Buonarroti, Filippo (Philippe). *Conspiration de l'égalité dite de Babeuf (1828).* Paris: Editions Sociales, 1957. Translated as: *Buonarroti's History of Babeuf's Conspiracy for Equality.* Bronterre O'Brian. New York: A.M. Kelley, 1965.

Dommanget, Maurice. *Sur Babeuf et la conjuration des Égaux.* Paris: F. Maspero, 1970.

Guyot, Raymond. *Le Directoire et la paix de l'Europe, 1795–1799.* Paris: F. Alcan, 1911.

Lefebvre, Georges. *The Directory.* Trans. Robert Baldick. New York: Vintage, 1964.

———. *The Thermidorians and the Directory: Two Phases of the French Revo-*

lution. Trans. Robert Baldick. New York: Random House, 1964.

Legrand, Robert. *Babeuf et ses compagnons de route.* Paris: Société des Etudes Robespierristes, 1981.

Lyons, Martyn. *France Under the Directory.* Cambridge: Cambridge University Press, 1975.

Mazauric, Claude. *Babeuf et la Conspiration pour l'égalité.* Paris: Editions Sociales, 1962.

Scott, John Anthony. *The Defense of Gracchus Babeuf.* Boston: University of Massachusetts Press, 1967.

Woloch, Isser. *Jacobin Legacy: The Democratic Movement Under the Directory.* Princeton, N.J.: Princeton University Press, 1970.

Woronoff, D. *The Thermidorian Regime and the Directory, 1794–1799.* Translated by J. Jackson. Cambridge: Cambridge University Press, 1984.

BRUMAIRE

Bergeron, Louis. *France under Napoleon.* Translated by R.R. Palmer. Princeton, N.J.: Princeton University Press, 1981.

Hunt, Lynn, David Lansky, and Paul Hanson. "The Failure of the Liberal Republic in France, 1795–1799: The Road to Brumaire," *Journal of Modern History* 51 (1979), 734–59.

Lefebvre, Georges. *Napoleon: From 18 Brumaire to Tilsit, 1799–1807.* Translated by J.E. Anderson and Henry F. Stockhold. New York: Columbia University Press, 1969.

Meynier, Albert. *Les Coups d'état du directoire.* 3 vols. Paris: Presses Universitaires de France, 1905.

Vandal, Albert. *L'avènement de Bonaparte.* 2 vols. Paris: Plon-Nourrit, 1902–1907.

THE TERROR

Arasse, Daniel. *La Guillotine et l'imaginaire de la Terreur.* Paris: Flammarion, 1987. Translated as: *The Guillotine and The Terror.* Christopher Miller. London: A. Lane, 1989.

Baecque, Antoine de. *La Gloire et l'effroi: Sept Morts sous la Terreur.* Paris: B. Grasset, 1997. Translated as *Glory and Terror: Seven Deaths Under the French Revolution.* Charlotte Mandell. London: Routledge, 2001.

Baker, Keith Michael, ed. *The Terror.* Oxford: Pergamon Press, 1994.

Cobb, Richard Charles. *Les Armées révolutionnaires, instrument de la Terreur dans les départements, avril 1793-floréal An II.* Paris: Mouton, 1961–1963. Translated as: *The People's Armies: the armées révolutionnaires, instrument of terror in the departments, April 1793 to floreal year II.* Marianne Elliott. New Haven, Conn.: Yale University Press, 1987.

Demerliac, M. "Une Ténébreuse Affaire à Limoges sous la Terreur." *Bulletin de la Société Archéologique et Historique du Limousin* LXXX (1943), 116–25.

Gobry, Ivan. *Joseph Le Bon: La Terreur dans le nord de la France.* Paris: Mercure de France, 1991.

Gough, Hugh. *The Terror in the French Revolution.* New York: St. Martin's Press, 1998.

Greer, Donald. *The Incidence of the Terror During the French Revolution.* Cambridge, Mass.: Harvard University Press, 1935.

Gross, Jean-Pierre. *Fair Shares for All: Jacobin Egalitarianism in Practice.* Cambridge: Cambridge University Press, 1997.

Kelly, George Armstrong. *Victims, Authority, and Terror: the Parallel Deaths of d'Orléans, Custine, Bailly, and Malesherbes.* Chapel Hill: University of North Carolina Press, 1982.

Le Bourguignon du Perré, Jacques-François. *Note d'un détenu de la maison de réclusion des ci-devant Carmélites de Caen pendant la Terreur.* Evreux: Imprimerie de l'Eure, 1903.

Lescure, M. de. *La Société française pendant la Révolution. L'Amour sous la Terreur.* Paris: Edition Dentu, 1882.

Loomis, Stanley. *Paris in the Terror: June 1793–July 1794.* Philadelphia, Pa.: Lippincott, 1964.

Lucas, Colin. *The Structure of the Terror: the Example of Javogues and the Loire.* Oxford: Clarendon Press, 1973.

Moore, Barrington Jr. "Misgivings about Revolution: Robespierre, Carnot, Saint-Just." *French Politics and Society* 16 (1998), 17–36.

Palmer, R.R. *Twelve Who Ruled: The Year of the Terror in the French Revolution.* Princeton, N.J.: Princeton University Press, 1996.

Paulhan, Jean. *Les Fleurs de Tarbes, ou, la terreur dans les lettres.* Paris: Galliamard, 1943.

Vivie, Aurélien. *Histoire de la Terreur à Bordeaux.* 2 vols. Bordeaux: Feret et fils, 1877.

Vovelle, Michel, ed. *Le Tournant de l'an III: Réaction et Terreur blanche dans la France révolutionnaire, Congrès national des sociétés historiques et scientifiques, Aix-en-Provence, 23–29 octobre 1995.* Paris: Commission d'histoire de la Révolution française, 1997.

RELIGION AND THE CHURCH

Desan, Suzanne. *Reclaiming the Sacred: Lay Religion and Popular Politics in Revolutionary France.* Ithaca, N.Y.: Cornell University Press, 1990.

Hoffman, Philip T. *Church and Community in the Diocese of Lyon, 1500–1789.* New Haven, Conn.: Yale University Press, 1984.

Hood, James. "Protestant-Catholic Relations and the Roots of the First Popular Counterrevolutionary Movement in France." *Journal of Modern History* XLIII (June 1971), 245–75.

Latreille, André. *L'Eglise catholique et la Révolution française.* Paris: Hachette, 1946.

Mathiez, Albert. *Les Origines des cultes révolutionnaires (1789–1792).* Paris: G. Bellais, 1904.

——. *Contributions à l'histoire religieuse de la Révolution française.* Paris: F. Alcan, 1907.

McManners, John. *The French Revolution and the Church.* New York: Harper & Row, 1970.

Préclin, E. *Les Jansenistes du dix-huitième siècle et la Constitution Civile du Clergé.* Paris: J. Gamber, 1928.

Sloane, William Milligan. *The French Revolution and Religious Reform.* London: Hodder and Stoughton, 1901.

Tackett, Timothy. *Priest and Parish in Eighteenth-Century France: A Social and Political Study of the Curés in a Diocese of Dauphiné, 1750–1791.* Princeton, N.J.: Princeton University Press, 1977.

——. *Religion, Revolution, and Regional Culture in Eighteenth-Century France: The Ecclesiastical Oath of 1791.* Princeton, N.J.: Princeton University Press, 1986.

Van Kley, Dale K. "Church, State, and the Ideological Origins of the French Revolution: The Debate over the General Assembly of the Gallican Clergy in 1765." *Journal of Modern History* 51 (1979), 629–66.

——. *The Religious Origins of the French Revolution: From Calvin to the Civil Constitution, 1560–1791.* New Haven, Conn.: Yale University Press, 1996.

Vovelle, Michel. *Piété baroque et déchristianisation en Provence au XVIIIe siècle.* Paris: Plon, 1973.

——. *Religion et Révolution: La Déchristianisation de l'an II.* Paris: Hachette, 1976.

——. *The Revolution Against the Church: From Reason to Supreme Being.* Translated by Alan José. Columbus: Ohio University Press, 1991.

CULTURAL HISTORIES

Agulhon, Maurice. *Marianne into Battle: Republican Imagery and Symbolism in France, 1789–1880.* Cambridge: Cambridge University Press, 1981.

Baecque, Antoine de. *Le corps de l'histoire: Métaphores et politique, 1770–1800.* Paris: Calmann-Lévy, 1993. Translated as: *The Body Politic: Corporeal Metaphor in Revolutionary France, 1770–1800.* Charlotte Mandell. Stanford, Calif.: Stanford University Press, 1997.

Baker, Keith Michael. *Inventing the French Revolution: Essays on French Political Culture in the Eighteenth Century.* Cambridge: Cambridge University Press, 1990.

Baker, Keith Michael, Colin Lucas, and François Furet, eds. *The French Revolution and the Creation of Modern Political Culture.* 4 vols. Oxford: Pergamon Press, 1987–94.

Barnard, H.C. *Education and the French Revolution.* Cambridge: Cambridge University Press, 1969.

Barny, Roger. "Jean-Jacques Rousseau dans la Révolution." *Dix-huitième siècle* 6 (1974), 59–98.

———. "Les Aristocrates et J.J. Rousseau dans la Révolution française." *Annales historiques de la Révolution française* 234 (1978), 534–64.

———. *Rousseau dans la Révolution: Le Personnage de Jean-Jacques et les débuts du culte révolutionnaire (1787–1791). Studies on Voltaire and the Eighteenth Century* 246. Oxford: Voltaire Foundation, 1986.

———. *L'Eclatement révolutionnaire du rousseauisme. Annales littéraires de l'université de Besançon* 378. Paris: Les Belles Lettres, 1988.

———. *Le Comte d'Antraigues, un disciple aristocrate de J.-J. Rousseau: De la fascination au reniement, 1782–1797. Studies on Voltaire and the Eighteenth Century* 281. Oxford: Voltaire Foundation, 1991.

Bianchi, Serge. *La Révolution culturelle de l'an II. Elites et peuple, 1789–1799.* Paris: Aubier, 1982.

Blum, Carol. *Rousseau and the Republic of Virtue: The Language of Politics in the French Revolution.* Ithaca, N.Y.: Cornell University Press, 1986.

Bollème, Geneviève, et al. *Livre et société dans la France du XVIIIe siècle.* 2 vols. The Hague: Mouton, 1965–70.

Bonnemaison, S. "Moses/Marianne Parts the Red Sea: Allegories of Liberty in the Bicentennial of the French Revolution." *Society and Space* 16 (1998), 347–65.

Calhoun, Craig, ed. *Habermas and the Public Sphere.* Cambridge, Mass.: MIT Press, 1992.

Carcasonne, Elie. *Montesquieu et le problème de la constitution française au XVIIIe siècle.* Geneva: Slatkine Reprints, 1970.

Censer, Jack R. *The French Press in the Age of Enlightenment.* London: Routledge, 1994.

———, ed. *The French Revolution and Intellectual History.* Chicago: The Dorsey Press, 1989.

Chartier, Roger. *The Cultural Origins of the French Revolution.* Translated by Lydia G. Cochrane. Durham, N.C.: Duke University Press, 1991.

Chisick, Harvey. *The Production, Distribution and Readership of a Conservative Journal of the Early French Revolution: the Ami du roi of the Abbé Royou.* Philadelphia, Pa.: American Philosophical Society, 1992.

———. *Historical Dictionary of the Enlightenment.* Lanham, Md.: Scarecrow Press, 2005.

Church, William F. *The Influence of the Enlightenment on the French Revolution.* Lexington, Mass.: D.C. Heath, 1964.

Cochin, Augustin. *L'Esprit du jacobinisme.* Paris: Presses Universitaires de France, 1979. [First published in 1921 as *Les sociétés de pensée et la démocratie.*]

Crow, Thomas. *Emulation: Making Artists for Revolutionary France.* New Haven, Conn.: Yale University Press, 1997.

Darnton, Robert. "In Search of the Enlightenment: Recent Attempts to Create a Social History of Ideas." *Journal of Modern History* 43 (1971), 113–32.

———. *The Great Cat Massacre and Other Episodes in French Cultural History.* New York: Basic Books, 1984.

Darnton, Robert, and Daniel Roche, eds. *Revolution in Print: The Press in France.* Berkeley: University of California Press, 1989.

Daumas, P. "Prénoms et révolution, 1775–1825: Propositions pour une nouvelle approche méthodologique." *Revue d'histoire moderne et contemporaine* 44 (1997), 109–32.

De Certeau, Michel, Dominique Julia, and Jacques Revel. *Une Politique de la langue: la Révolution française et les patois.* Paris: Gallimard, 1975.

DeJean, Joan. *Ancients against Moderns: Culture Wars and the Making of a Fin de Siècle.* Chicago: University of Chicago Press, 1997.

Denby, David. *Sentimental Narrative and the Social Order in France, 1760–1820.* Cambridge: Cambridge University Press, 1994.

Dorigny, Michel. *Montesquieu dans la Révolution française.* Paris: EDHS, 1990.

Dowd, David Lloyd. *Pageant-Master of the Republic: Jacques-Louis David and the French Revolution.* Lincoln: University of Nebraska Press, 1948.

Duprat, Catherine. *"Pour l'amour de l'humanité": Le Temps de philanthropes: La Philanthropie parisienne des Lumières à la monarchie de Juillet.* 2 vols. Paris: Edition du CTHS, 1993.

Dupront, Alphonse. *Les lettres, les sciences, la religion et les arts dans la société française de la deuxième moitié du XVIIIe siècle.* Paris: Centre de documentation univérsitaire, 1963.

Feher, Ferenc, ed. *The French Revolution and the Birth of Modernity.* Berkeley:

University of California Press, 1990.

Friedland, Paul. *Political Actors: Representative Bodies and Theatricality in the Age of the French Revolution*. Ithaca, N.Y.: Cornell University Press, 2002.

Furet, François. *Marx et la Révolution française*. Paris: Flammarion, 1986. Translated as: *Marx and the French Revolution*. Deborah Kan Furet. Chicago: University of Chicago Press, 1988.

Germani, Ian, and Robin Swales, eds. *Symbols, myths and images of the French Revolution: Essays in honour of James A. Leith*. Regina, Saskatchewan: University of Regina Press, 1998.

Godechot, Jacques Léon. "Nation, patrie, nationalisme, patriotisme en France au XVIIIe siècle." *Annales historiques de la Révolution française* 206 (1971).

——. *La Contre-Révolution: doctrine et action, 1789–1804*. Paris: Presses Universitaires de France, 1961. Translated as: *The Counter-Revolution: Doctrine and Action, 1789–1804*. Salvator Attanasio. Princeton, N.J.: Princeton University Press, 1981.

Goodman, Dena. *The Republic of Letters: A Cultural History of the French Enlightenment*. Ithaca, N.Y.: Cornell University Press, 1994.

Gordon, Daniel, David Bell, and Sarah Maza. "Forum: The Public Sphere in the Eighteenth-Century." *French Historical Studies* 17 (1992), 882–956.

Gough, Hugh. *The Newspaper Press in the French Revolution*. London: Routledge, 1988.

Guilhamou, Jacques. *La Langue politique et la Révolution française: de l'événement à la raison linguistique*. Paris: Méridiens/Klincksieck, 1989.

Habermas, Jürgen. *The Structural Transformation of the Public Sphere: An Inquiry into a Category of Bourgeois Society*. Translated by Thomas Burger and Frederick Lawrence. Cambridge, Mass.: MIT Press, 1989.

Halévi, Ran. *Les loges maçonniques dans la France de l'Ancien Régime: Aux origines de la sociabilité démocratique*. Paris: Armand Colin, 1984.

Hatin, Eugène. *Histoire politique et littéraire de la presse en France*. 8 vols. Paris: Poulet-Malassis et de Broise, 1859–1861.

Herbert, Robert L. *David, Voltaire, Brutus and the French Revolution: An Essay in Art and Politics*. New York: Viking, 1973.

Higgins, D. "Rousseau and the Pantheon: The Background and Implications of the Ceremony of 20 vendémaire Year III." *Modern Language Review* 50 (1955), 272–80.

Huet, Marie-Hélène. *Rehearsing the Revolution: The Staging of Marat's Death, 1793–1797*. Trans. Robert Hurley. Berkeley: University of California Press, 1982.

——. *Mourning Glory: The Will of the French Revolution*. Philadelphia: University of Pennsylvania Press, 1997.

Hulliung, Mark. *The Autocritique of the French Revolution*. Berkeley: University of California Press, 1994.

Hunt, Lynn. *Politics, Culture and Class in the French Revolution.* Berkeley: University of California Press, 1984.

——. *The Family Romance of the French Revolution.* Berkeley: University of California Press, 1992.

Julia, D. *Les Trois Couleurs de tableau noir: La Révolution.* Paris, 1981.

Kennedy, Emmett. *A Cultural History of the French Revolution.* New Haven, Conn.: Yale University Press, 1989.

Kennedy, Michael L. "The Foundation of the Jacobin Clubs and the Development of the Jacobin Club Network, 1789–91." *Journal of Modern History* LI (December 1979), 701–33.

——. *The Jacobin Clubs in the French Revolution.* 2 vols. Princeton, N.J.: Princeton University Press, 1982, 1988.

Kitchen, Joanna. *Un Journal "philosophique":"La Décade," 1794–1807.* Paris: Minard, 1965.

Koselleck, Reinhart. *Critique and Crisis: Enlightenment and the Pathogenesis of Modern Society.* Cambridge, Mass.: MIT Press, 1988.

Le Bihan, Alain. *Loges et Chapitres de la Grande Loge et du Grand Orient de France.* Paris: Bibliothèque Nationale, 1967.

Lee, Simon. *David (Art and Ideas).* London: Phaidon Press, 1999.

Leith, James A. *The Idea of Art as Propaganda in France, 1750–1799: a Study in the History of Ideas.* Toronto: University of Toronto, 1965.

——. *Media and Revolution.* Toronto: University of Toronto, 1968.

Levitine, G., ed. *Culture and Revolution: Cultural Ramifications of the French Revolution.* College Park: University of Maryland at College Park, 1989.

Lüsebrink, Hans-Jürgen, and Rolf Reichardt. *The Bastille: A History of a Symbol of Despotism and Freedom.* Translated by Norbert Schürer. Durham, N.C.: Duke University Press, 1997.

Marcetteau-Paul, Agnès, and Dominique Varry. "Les Bibliothèques de quelques acteurs de la Révolution." *Mélanges de la Bibliothèque de la Sorbonne* 9 (1989), 189–207.

Martin, Henri-Jean. *Le Livre français sous l'Ancien Régime.* Paris: Promodis, 1987.

Mason, Laura. *Singing the French Revolution: Popular Culture and Politics, 1787–1799.* Ithaca, N.Y.: Cornell University Press, 1996.

May, Gita. *De Jean-Jacques Rousseau à Madame Roland: Essai sur la sensibilité préromantique et revolutionnaire.* Geneva: Droz, 1964.

Maza, Sarah. "Women, the Bourgeoisie, and the Public Sphere: Response to Daniel Gordon and David Bell." *French Historical Studies* 17 (1992), 935–50.

Mazauric, Claude, and P. Goudard. "En quel sens on peut dire que la Révolution française fut une révolution culturelle." *Europa* (December 1978).

McDonald, Joan. *Rousseau and the French Revolution (1762–1791).* London: Athlone Press, 1965.

Melzer, Sara, and Kathryn Norberg, eds. *From the Royal to the Republican Body: Incorporating the Political in Seventeenth- and Eighteenth-Century France.* Berkeley: University of California Press, 1998.

Mercier, Louis-Sébastien. *De J.J. Rousseau considéré comme l'un des premiers auteurs de la Révolution.* 2 vols. Paris: Buisson, 1791.

Mornet, Daniel. "L'Influence de J.J. Rousseau au XVIIIe siècle." *Annales de la Société Jean-Jacques Rousseau* 8 (1912), 33–67.

Muchembled, Robert. *Culture populaire et culture des élites dans la France moderne (XVe-XVIIIe siècles).* Paris: Flammarion, 1991.

Murray, William James. *The Right-Wing Press in the French Revolution: 1789–92.* Suffolk, UK: Boydell Press, 1986.

Outram, Dorinda. *The Body and the French Revolution: Sex, Class and Political Culture.* New Haven, Conn.: Yale University Press, 1989.

Ozouf, Mona. "Innovations et traditions dans les itinéraires des fêtes révolutionnaires: l'exemple de Caen." *Ethnologie Française* VII (January 1977), 45–74.

——. *Festivals and the French Revolution.* Translated by Alan Sheridan. Cambridge, Mass.: Harvard University Press, 1988.

——. *L'homme régénéré: essais sur la Révolution française.* Paris: Gallimard, 1989.

Palmer, R.R. *The Improvement of Humanity: Education and the French Revolution.* Princeton, N.J.: Princeton University Press, 1985.

Parker, Noel. *Portrayals of Revolution: Images, Debates and Patterns of Thought on the French Revolution.* Carbondale: Southern Illinois University Press, 1990.

Perrot, Philippe. *Le Luxe: Une Richesse entre faste et confort, XVIIIe-XIXe siècle.* Paris: Editions de Seuil, 1995.

Perroud, C. "Le Roman d'un Girondin." *Revue du dix-huitième siècle* 2 (1914) and 3 (1915–16).

Phillips, Roderick. *Family Breakdown in Late Eighteenth-Century France.* Oxford: Clarendon Press, 1981.

Pocock, John Greville Agard. *The Machiavellian Moment: Florentine Political Thought and the Atlantic Republican Tradition.* Princeton, N.J.: Princeton University Press, 1975.

Popkin, Jeremy. *The Right-Wing Press in France, 1792–1800.* Chapel Hill: University of North Carolina Press, 1980.

——. *Revolutionary News: The Press in France, 1789–1799.* Durham, N.C.: Duke University Press, 1988.

Ravel, Jeffrey. *The Contested Parterre: Public Theatre and French Political Culture, 1680–1791.* Ithaca, N.Y.: Cornell University Press, 1999.

Revel, Jacques. "Marie-Antoinette and Her Fictions: The Staging of Hatred." In *Fictions of the French Revolution,* edited by Bernadette Fort, pp.111–29.

Evanston, Ill.: Northwestern University Press, 1991.

Ridehalgh, Anna. "Preromantic Attitudes and the Birth of a Legend: French Pilgrimages to Ermenonville, 1778–1789." *Studies on Voltaire and the Eighteenth Century* 215 (1982), 231–52.

Roberts, Warren. *Jacques-Louis David, Revolutionary Artist.* Chapel Hill: University of North Carolina Press, 1989.

———. *Jacques-Louis David and Jean-Louis Prieur, Revolutionary Artists: The Public, the Populace, and Images of the French Revolution.* Albany, N.Y.: State University of New York Press, 1999.

Rogers, Cornwell B. *The Spirit of Revolution in 1789: A Study of Public Opinion as Revealed in Political Songs and Other Popular Literature at the Beginning of the French Revolution.* New York: Greenwood Press, 1949.

Sewell, William H., Jr. *Work and Revolution in France: The Language of Labor from the Old Regime to 1848.* Cambridge: Cambridge University Press, 1980.

Shaw, Matthew. "Reactions to the French Republican Calendar." *French History*, 15 (March 2001), 4–25.

Shklar, Judith N. *Men and Citizens: A Study of Rousseau's Social Theory.* Cambridge: Cambridge University Press, 1969.

———. "Montesquieu and the New Republicanism." In *Machiavelli and Republicanism*, edited by Gisela Bock, Quentin Skinner, and Maurizio Viroli, pp. 265–79. Cambridge: Cambridge University Press, 1990.

Soboul, Albert. "Audience des Lumières: Classes populaires et rousseauisme sous la Révolution." *Annales historiques de la Révolution française* 170 (1962), 421–38.

Söderhjelm, Alma. *Le Régime de la presse pendant la Révolution française.* Geneva: Slatkine, 1971.

Sozzi, Lionello. "Interprétations de Rousseau pendant la Révolution." *Studies on Voltaire and the Eighteenth Century* 64 (1968), 187–223.

Staël, Anne-Louise-Germaine Necker, baronne de. *Lettres sur les ouvrages et le caractère de J.-J. Rousseau.* 1788. Geneva: Slatkine Reprints, 1979.

———. *Madame de Staël on Politics, Literature, and National Character.* Translated, edited, and with an introduction by Morroe Berger. Garden City, N.Y.: Doubleday, 1964.

Starobinski, Jean. *Jean-Jacques Rousseau: Transparency and Obstruction.* Translated by Arthur Goldhammer. Chicago: University of Chicago Press, 1988.

Swenson, James. "A Small Change in Terminology or a Great Leap Forward? Culture and Civilization in Revolution." *MLN* 112 (1997), 332–48.

Talmon, J.L. *The Origins of Totalitarian Democracy.* London: Secker and Warburg, 1952.

Tatin-Gourier, Jean-Jacques. *Le Contrat social en question: Échos et interprétations du Contrat social de 1762 à la Révolution.* Lille: Presses Universitaires de Lille, 1989.

Traer, James F. *Marriage and the Family in Eighteenth-Century France.* Ithaca, N.Y.: Cornell University Press, 1980.

Trahard, Pierre. *Les Maîtres de la sensiblité française au dix-huitième siècle.* 4 vols. Paris: Boivin, 1931–33.

Trenard, Louis. "La diffusion du *Contrat social*, 1762–1832." In *Etudes sur le Contrat social de J.-J. Rousseau,* pp. 432–38. Colloque de Dijon, May 3–6, 1962. Paris: Les Belles Lettres, 1964.

Viroli, Maurizio. *Jean-Jacques Rousseau and the "Well-Ordered Society."* Translated by D. Hanson. Cambridge: Cambridge University Press, 1988.

SOCIAL AND ECONOMIC HISTORIES

Ado, Anatoli. *Les paysans et la Révolution française: le mouvement paysan en 1789–1794.* Moscow: Moscow University Press, 1987.

Aftalion, Florin. *The French Revolution: An Economic Interpretation.* Cambridge: Cambridge University Press, 1990.

Blanning, T.C.W. *The French Revolution: Aristocrats versus Bourgeois?* Atlantic Highlands, N.J.: Humanities Press International, 1987.

Bosher, J.F. *French Finances, 1770–1795: From Business to Bureaucracy.* Cambridge: Cambridge University Press, 1970.

Cobban, Alfred. *The Social Interpretation of the French Revolution.* Cambridge: Cambridge University Press, 1964.

Dubois, Laurent. *Les Esclaves de la République: L'Histoire oubliée de la première émancipation, 1789–1794.* Translated by Jean-François Chaix. Paris: Calmann-Levy, 1998.

Forrest, Alan. *The French Revolution and the Poor.* Oxford: Basil Blackwell, 1981.

Garrioch, David. *The Formation of the Parisian Bourgeoisie, 1690–1830.* Cambridge, Mass.: Harvard University Press, 1996.

Greenlaw, Ralph W., ed. *The Economic Origins of the French Revolution: Poverty or Prosperity?* Boston, Mass.: D.C. Heath, 1958.

——. *The Social Origins of the French Revolution: The Debate on the Role of the Middle Classes.* Lexington, Mass.: D.C. Heath, 1975.

Hampson, Norman. *A Social History of the French Revolution.* London: Routledge and Kegan Paul, 1963.

Harris, S. E. *The Assignats.* Cambridge, Mass.: Harvard University Press, 1930.

Higonnet, Patrice. *Class, Ideology, and the Rights of Nobles during the French*

Revolution. Oxford: Clarendon Press, 1981.

Jones, Peter. *The Peasantry in the French Revolution*. Cambridge: Cambridge University Press, 1988.

Lafaurie, Jean. *Les Assignats: Et les papiers-monnaies émis par l'Etat au XVIIIe siècle*. Paris: Léopard d'or, 1981.

Markoff, John. *The Abolition of Feudalism: Peasants, Lords, and Legislators in the French Revolution*. University Park: Pennsylvania State University Press, 1996.

Maza, Sarah. "Luxury, Morality, and Social Change: Why There Was No Middle-Class Consciousness in Prerevolutionary France." *Journal of Modern History* 69 (1997), 199–229.

——. *The Myth of the French Bourgeoisie: An Essay on the Social Imaginary, 1750–1850*. Cambridge, Mass.: Harvard University Press, 2003.

Miller, Judith. *Mastering the Market: The State and the Grain Trade in Northern France, 1700–1860*. Cambridge: Cambridge University Press, 1998.

Patrick, A. "The Approach of French revolutionary officials to social problems." *Australian Journal of French Studies* 18 (1981), no. 1.

Peuchet, Jacques. *Statistique Elémentaire de la France*. Paris: Gilbert, 1805.

Roque, Louis de la, and Edouard Barthélemy. *Catalogue des Gentilhommes en 1789*. 2 vols. Paris: E. Dentu, 1866.

Rose, Robert Barrie. *The Making of the Sans-Culottes*. Manchester: Manchester University Press, 1983.

Rudé, George. *The Crowd in History: a Study of Popular Disturbances in France and England, 1730–1848*. New York: John Wiley, 1964.

——. *The Crowd in the French Revolution*. Oxford: Oxford University Press, 1972.

Sewell, William H., Jr. "Ideologies and Social Revolutions: Reflections on the French Case." *Journal of Modern History* 57 (1985), 57–85.

Skocpol, Theda. "Cultural Idioms and Political Idealogies in the Revolutionary Reconstruction to State Power: A Rejoinder to Sewell." *Journal of Modern History* 57 (1985), 86–96.

Soboul, Albert. *Les Sans-Culottes parisiens en l'an II: mouvement populaire et gouvernement révolutionnaire, 2 juin 1793–9 thermidor an II*. Paris: Clavreuil, 1958. Translated as: *The Sans-Culottes: The Popular Movement and Revolutionary Government, 1793–1794*. Rémy Inglis Hall. Princeton, N.J.: Princeton University Press, 1980.

Sonenscher, Michael. *Work and Wages: Natural Law, Politics, and Eighteenth-Century French Trades*. Cambridge: Cambridge University Press, 1989.

Tonnesson, K.D. *La défaite des sans-culottes*. Oslo: Presses Universitaires, 1959.

Vovelle, Michel. "Du tout social au tout politique." *Annales historiques de la Révolution française* 67 (1997), 545–54.

Wick, D. "The Court Nobility and the French Revolution." *Eighteenth-Century*

Studies 13 (Spring 1980), 263–84.

Williams, Gwyn A. *Artisans and Sans-Culottes: Popular Movements in France and Britain during the French Revolution.* New York: Norton, 1968.

WOMEN AND GENDER

Colwill, Elizabeth. "Pass as a Woman, Act like a Man: Marie-Antoinette as Tribade in the Pornography of the French Revolution." In *Homosexuality in Modern France,* Jeffrey Merrick and Bryant T. Ragan, eds., pp. 54–79. New York: Oxford University Press, 1996.

Davis, Natalie Zemon, and Arlette Farge, eds. *A History of Women in the West.* Vol. 3, *Renaissance and Enlightenment Paradoxes.* Cambridge, Mass.: Harvard University Press, 1993.

Desan, Suzanne. "'War Between Brothers and Sisters': Inheritance Law and Gender Politics in Revolutionary France." *French Historical Studies* 20 (1997), 597–634.

——. "Reconstituting the Social after the Terror: Family, Law, and Property in Popular Politics." *Past and Present* 164 (1999), 81–121.

DiCaprio, Lisa. "Women, Work, and Welfare in Old Regime and Revolutionary Paris." *Social Politics* (1998), 97–124.

Elshtain, Jean. *Public Man, Private Woman.* Princeton, N.J.: Princeton University Press, 1981.

Fauré, Christine, ed. *La Démocratie sans les femmes: Essai sur le libéralisme en France.* Paris: Presses Universitaires de France, 1985.

Fermon, Nicole. *Domesticating Passions: Rousseau, Woman, and Nation.* Hanover, N.H.: Wesleyan University Press, 1997.

Fraisse, Geneviève. *Muse de la raison: La Démocratie exclusive et la différence des sexes.* Aix-en-Provence: Alinéa, 1989. Translated as *Reason's Muse: Sexual Difference and the Birth of Democracy.* Jane Marie Todd. Chicago: University of Chicago Press, 1994.

Gelbart, Nina. *Feminine and Opposition Journalism in Old Regime France: "Le Journal des Dames."* Berkeley: University of California Press, 1987.

Godineau, Dominique. *Citoyennes tricoteuses: les femmes du peuple à Paris pendant la Révolution française.* Aix-en-Provence, Alinéa, 1988. Translated as: *The Women of Paris and Their French Revolution.* Katherine Streip. Berkeley: University of California Press, 1998.

Goldsmith, Elizabeth C., and Dena Goodman, eds. *Going Public: Women and Publishing in Early Modern France.* Ithaca, N.Y.: Cornell University Press, 1995.

Gutwirth, Madelyn. *The Twilight of the Goddesses: Women and Representation in the French Revolutionary Era.* New Brunswick, N.J.: Rutgers University Press, 1992.

Hesse, Carla. "Reading Signatures: Female Authorship and Revolutionary Law in France, 1750–1850." *Eighteenth-Century Studies* 22 (1989), 469–87.

——. "French Women in Print, 1750–1800: An Essay in Historical Bibliography." *Studies on Voltaire and the Eighteenth Century* 359 (1998), 65–82.

——. *The Other Enlightenment: How French Women became Modern.* Princeton, N.J.: Princeton University Press, 2001.

Heuer, Jennifer. "Adopted Daughter of the French People: Suzanne Lepeletier and Her Father, the National Assembly." *French Politics, Culture, and Society.* New York: Berghahn Books, 1999.

Hufton, Olwen H. *Women and the Limits of Citizenship in the French Revolution.* Toronto: University of Toronto Press, 1992.

Landes, Joan. *Women and the Public Sphere in the Age of the French Revolution.* Ithaca, N.Y.: Cornell University Press, 1988.

——. *Visualizing the Nation: Gender, Representation, and Revolution in Eighteenth-Century France.* Ithaca, N.Y.: Cornell University Press, 2001.

Levy, Darlene, Harriet Applewhite, and Mary Durham Johnson, eds. *Women in Revolutionary Paris, 1789–1795: Selected Documents.* Urbana: University of Illinois Press, 1979.

Melzer, Sara E., and Leslie W. Rabine, eds. *Rebel Daughters: Women and the French Revolution.* New York: Oxford University Press, 1992.

Montfort, Catherine, ed. *Literate Women and the French Revolution of 1789.* Birmingham, Ala.: Summa Productions, 1994.

Outram, Dorinda. " 'Le Langage mâle de la vertu': Women and the Discourse of the French Revolution." In *The Social History of Language,* Peter Burke and Roy Porter, eds. Cambridge: Cambridge University Press, 1987.

Pateman, Carole. *The Sexual Contract.* Cambridge: Polity Press, 1988.

——. *The Disorder of Women: Democracy, Feminism, and Political Theory.* Stanford, Calif.: Stanford University Press, 1989.

Rose, Robert Barrie. *Tribunes and Amazons: Men and Women of Revolutionary France 1789–1871.* Paddington, Australia: Macleay, 1998.

Scott, Joan Wallach. *Gender and the Politics of History.* New York: Columbia University Press, 1988.

——. *Only Paradoxes to Offer: French Feminists and the Rights of Man.* Cambridge, Mass.: Harvard University Press, 1996.

Stephens, Winifred. *Women of the French Revolution.* New York: E.P. Dutton, 1922.

Trouille, Mary. *Sexual Politics in the Enlightenment: Women Writers Read Rousseau.* Albany: State University of New York Press, 1997.

Vray, Nicole. *Les femmes dans la tourmente.* Rennes: Ouest–France, 1988.

Yalom, Marilyn. *Blood Sisters: The French Revolution in Women's Memory.*

New York: Basic Books, 1993.

MILITARY HISTORIES

Attar, Frank. *La Révolution française déclare la guerre à l'Europe. L'embrasement de l'Europe à la fin du XVIIIe siècle.* Brussels: Editions Complexe, 1992.

Baines, Edward. *History of the Wars of the French Revolution from the breaking out of war in 1792, to the Restoration of a general peace, in 1815; comprehending the civil history of Great Britain and France during that period.* New York: Bangs, Brother, 1855.

Bertaud, Jean-Paul. "Notes sur le premier amalgame." *Revue d'histoire moderne et contemporaine* (1973): 20.

——. *La Révolution armée: les soldats-citoyens et la Révolution française.* Paris: R. Laffont, 1979. Translated as: *The Army of the French Revolution: From Citizen-Soldiers to Instrument of Power.* R.R. Palmer. Princeton, N.J.: Princeton University Press, 1988.

Blanning, T.C.W. *The French Revolutionary Wars, 1787–1802.* New York: Arnold, 1996.

Chassin, Charles-Louis, and Léon Hennet. *Les Volontaires Nationaux pendant la Révolution.* 3 vols. Paris: L. Cerf, 1899–1906.

Forrest, Alan. *Conscripts and Deserters: The Army and French Society during the Revolution and Empire.* Oxford: Oxford University Press, 1989.

——. *The Soldiers of the French Revolution.* Durham, N.C.: Duke University Press, 1990.

Gérard, P. "L'armée révolutionnaire de la Haute-Garonne." *Annales historiques de la Révolution française* (1959), 31.

Hennet, L. *L'état militaire de France pour l'année 1793.* Paris: Au Siège de la Société, 1903.

Herlaut, Auguste-Phillipe. *Le général rouge Ronsin, 1751–1794.* Paris: Clavreuil, 1956.

Lynn, John. *The Bayonets of the Republic: Motivation and Tactics in the Army of Revolutionary France, 1791–94.* Urbana: University of Illinois Press, 1984.

Mitchell, Harvey. *The Underground War against Revolutionary France: The Missions of William Wickham, 1794–1800.* Oxford: Clarendon Press, 1965.

Moran, Daniel, and Arthur Waldron, eds. *The People in Arms: Military Myth and National Mobilization since the French Revolution.* Cambridge: Cambridge University Press, 2003.

Phipps, R.W. *The Armies of the First French Republic and the Rise of the Mar-*

shals of Napoleon the First. 5 vols. Oxford: Oxford University Press, 1926–39.

Regent, F. "Presse parisienne et expedition d'Egypte (9 mars 1798–novembre 1799)." *Revue historique des armées* 82 (1998), 21–39.

Richard, T. "La Logistique du corps expéditionnaire en Egypte." *Revue historique des armées* 82 (1998), 13–20.

Ross, Steven T. *Historical Dictionary of the Wars of the French Revolution.* Lanham, Md.: Scarecrow Press, 1998.

Scott, Samuel. "The Regneration of the Line Army during the French Revolution." *Journal of Modern History* (1970), 42.

——. *The Response of the Royal Army to the French Revolution.* Oxford: Clarendon Press, 1978.

Soboul, Albert. *Les Soldats de l'an II.* Paris: Livre Club Diderot, 1959.

Vovelle, Michel. *Combats pour la Révolution Française.* Paris: La Découverte, 1993.

Walter, Jakob. *The Diary of a Napoleonic Foot Soldier,* ed. Marc Raeff. New York: Penguin Books, 1993.

INTERNATIONAL REACTIONS TO THE REVOLUTION

Adams, Christine, Jack Censer, and Lisa Jane Graham, eds. *Visions and Revisions of Eighteenth-Century France.* University Park: Pennsylvania State University Press, 1997.

Althusser, Louis. *Montesquieu, Rousseau, Marx: Politics and History.* Translated by Ben Brewster. London: Verso, 1982.

Baker, Keith Michael, and Joseph Zizek. "The American Historiography of the French Revolution." In *Imagined Histories: American Historians Interpret the Past,* ed. Anthony Molho and Gordon S. Wood. Princeton, N.J.: Princeton University Press, 1998, 349–92.

Benot, Yves. *La Révolution Française et la fin des colonies.* Paris: La Découverte, 1988.

Best, Geoffrey. *Honour among Men and Nations: Transformations of an Idea.* Toronto: University of Toronto Press, 1982.

——, ed. *The Permanent Revolution: The French Revolution and its Legacy.* Chicago: University of Chicago Press, 1988.

Blackburn, Robin. *The Overthrow of Colonial Slavery, 1776–1848.* London: Verso, 1988.

Burke, Edmund. *Reflections on the Revolution in France.* London: J. Dodsley, 1790.

——. *A Letter to a Member of the National Assembly.* 1791. Oxford: Woodstock Books, 1990.

Cobb, Richard Charles. *Reactions to the French Revolution.* Oxford: Oxford University Press, 1972.

Cox, Marvin R., ed. *The Place of the French Revolution in History.* New York: Houghton Mifflin, 1998.

Droz, J. *L'Allemagne et la Révolution française.* Paris: Presses Universitaires de France, 1949.

Fick, Carolyn E. *The Making of Haiti: The Saint Domingue Revolution from Below.* Knoxville: University of Tennessee Press, 1990.

Fugier, André. *Histoire des relations internationales: La Révolution française et l'Empire napoléonien.* Paris: Hachette, 1954.

Gaspar, David Barry, and David Patrick Geggus, eds. *A Turbulent Time: The French Revolution and the Greater Caribbean.* Bloomington: Indiana University Press, 1997.

Geggus, David Patrick. *Slavery, War, and Revolution: The British Occupation of Saint-Domingue, 1793–1798.* New York: Oxford University Press, 1982.

Gilroy, Paul. *The Black Atlantic: Modernity and Double-Consciousness.* Cambridge, Mass.: Harvard University Press, 1993.

Goldhammer, Arthur. "From Project to Memory: The Crisis of Republican Civic Consciousness." *French Politics and Society* 16 (1998), 37–45.

Guilhamou, Jacques. "Un Débat franco-américain autour de la Révolution française." *Dix-huitième siècle* 30 (1998), 245–56.

Hayes, Richard. *Ireland and Irishmen in the French Revolution.* London: E. Benn, 1932.

Hobsbawm, Eric. *Echoes of the Marseillaise: Two Centuries Look Back on the French Revolution.* New Brunswick, N.J.: Rutgers University Press, 1990.

Hunt, Lynn. "Forgetting and Remembering: The French Revolution Now and Then." *American Historical Review* 100 (1995), 1119–35.

James, C.L.R. *The Black Jacobins: Toussaint L'Ouverture and the San Domingo Revolution.* 2nd ed. New York: Vintage Books, 1989.

Klaits, Joseph, and Michael H. Haltzel, eds. *The Global Ramifications of the French Revolution.* Cambridge: Cambridge University Press, 1994.

Lockitt, Charles Henry. *The Relations of French and English Society (1763–1793).* London: Longman, Green, 1920.

Macleod, Emma Vincent. *A War of Ideas: British Attitudes to the Wars against Revolutionary France, 1792–1802.* Aldershot, UK: Ashgate, 1998.

Markham, Felix. *Napoleon and the Awakening of Europe.* New York: Macmillan, 1965.

Paine, Thomas. *The Rights of Man: Being an Answer to Mr. Burke's Attack on the French Revolution.* 2 vols. London: J.S. Jordan, 1791.

Thompson, James Matthew. *English Witnesses of the French Revolution.* Port Washington, N.Y.: Kennikat Press, 1970.

Wahnich, Sophie. *L'Impossible citoyen: L'Etranger dans le discours de la Révolution française.* Paris: A. Michel, 1977.

PARIS

Andress, David. "Economic Dislocation and Social Discontent in the French Revolution: Survival in Paris in the Era of the Flight to Varennes." *French History* 10 (March 1996), 30–55.

Andrews, Richard M. "Paris of the Great Revolution: 1789–1796." In *People and Communities in the Western World,* Vol. II. Gene Brucker, ed. Homewood, Ill.: Dorsey Press, 1979.

———. "Social Structures, Political Elites, and Ideology in Revolutionary Paris, 1792–1794: A Critical Evaluation of Albert Soboul's *Les Sans-culottes parisiens en l'an II.*" *Journal of Social History* 19 (1985), 71–112.

Biver, Marie-Louise. *Fêtes révolutionnaires à Paris.* Paris: Presses Universitaires de France, 1979.

Burstin, H. *Le Faubourg St.-Marcel à l'époque révolutionnaire: Structure économique et sociale.* Paris: Société des Etudes Robespierristes, 1985.

Caron, Pierre. *Les Massacres de Septembre.* Paris: La Maison du Livre Français, 1935.

Chagniot, Jean. *Nouvelle Histoire de Paris: Paris au XVIIIe siècle.* Paris: Hachette, 1988.

Chauvet, Paul. *L'insurrection parisienne de la prise de la Bastille.* Paris: Domat-Montchrestien, 1946.

Cobb, Richard Charles. *Death in Paris: the records of the Basse-Geôle de la Seine, October 1795–September 1801 (Vendémiaire Year IV-Fructidor Year IX).* Oxford: Oxford University Press, 1978.

Crow, Thomas. *Painters and Public Life in Eighteenth-Century Paris.* New Haven, Conn.: Yale University Press, 1985.

Farge, Arlette. *Vivre dans la rue à Paris au XVIIIe Siècle.* Paris: Gallimard, 1979.

Fierro, Alfred. *Histoire et dictionnaire de Paris.* Paris: Laffont, 1996.

Freddi, F. "La Presse parisienne et la nuit du 4 août." *Annales Historiques de la Révolution Française*, 1985.

Garrioch, David. *Neighbourhood and Community in Paris, 1740–1790.* Cambridge: Cambridge University Press, 1986.

Gautier, Théophile. *Paris et les Parisiens.* Paris: Boîte à Documents, 1996.

Genty, Maurice. *Paris 1789–1795: L'Apprentissage de la citoyenneté.* Paris: Messidor-Editions Sociales, 1987.

Glotz, Marguerite. *Les Salons du XVIIIe siècle.* Paris: Hachette, 1988.

Hillairet, Jacques. *Dictionnaire historique des rues de Paris*. Paris: Minuit, 1963.

Hesse, Carla. *Publishing and Cultural Politics in Revolutionary Paris, 1789–1810*. Berkeley: University of California Press, 1991.

Higonnet, Patrice. *Paris, Capital of the World*. Cambridge, Mass.: Harvard University Press, 2002.

Isherwood, Robert. *Farce and Fantasy: Popular Entertainment in Eighteenth-Century Paris*. New York: Oxford University Press, 1986.

Johnson, James H. *Listening in Paris: A Cultural History*. Berkeley: University of California Press, 1995.

Kaplan, Steven Laurence. *The Bakers of Paris and the Bread Question, 1700–1775*. Durham, N.C.: Duke University Press, 1996.

Lenotre, Georges. *Les Massacres de septembre*. Paris: Librairie Académique Perrin, 1972.

McMahon, Darrin M. "The Birthplace of the Revolution: Public Space and Political Community in the Palais-Royal of Louis-Philippe-Joseph d'Orléans, 1781–1789," *French History* 10 (March 1996), 1–29.

Mercier, Louis-Sébastien. *Le tableau de Paris*. 1782–1788. Reprint, 12 vols. Geneva: Slatkine Reprints, 1989.

Monin, H. *L'État de Paris en 1789*. Paris: D. Jouaust, 1899.

Monnier, Raymonde. *L'Espace publique démocratique: Essai sur l'opinion à Paris de la Révolution au Directoire*. Paris: Kimé, 1994.

Palmer, R.R., ed. *The School of the French Revolution: a documentary history of the College of Louis-le-Grand and its director, Jean-François Champagne, 1762–1814*. Princeton, N.J.: Princeton University Press, 1975.

Ravel, Jeffrey S. "Seating the Public: Spheres and Loathing in the Paris Theaters, 1777–1788." *French Historical Studies* 18 (1993), 173–210.

Reinhard, Marcel. *Nouvelle histoire de Paris: La Révolution, 1789–1799*. Paris: Hachette, 1971.

Roche, Daniel. *Le peuple de Paris: essai sur la culture populaire au XVIIIe siècle*. Paris: Auber-Montaigne, 1986. Translated as: *The People of Paris: An Essay in Popular Culture in the Eighteenth Century*. Marie Evans. Berkeley: University of California Press, 1987.

Rousseau, Vigneron F. "Section de la Place des Fédérés pendant la Révolution," in *Contribution à l'histoire démographique de la Révolution française*, 3ème série, pp. 156–210. Paris, 1970.

Saint-Agnès, Yves de. *Guide du Paris Révolutionnaire, 1789–1795*. Paris: Perrin, 1989.

Serman, William. *La Commune de Paris*. Paris: Fayard, 1986.

Sevegrand, M. "La Section de Popincourt pendant la Révolution française," in *Contribution à l'histoire démographique de la Révolution française*, 3ème série, pp. 11–91. Paris, 1970.

Shapiro, Barry. *Revolutionary Justice in Paris, 1789–1790*. Cambridge: Cambridge University Press, 1993.

Slavin, Morris. *The French Revolution in Miniature: Section Droits-de-l'Homme, 1789–1795*. Princeton, N.J.: Princeton University Press, 1984.

Vovelle, Michel, ed. *Paris pendant la Révolution*. Paris: Sorbonne, 1989.

Wallon, Henri Alexandre. *Histoire du Tribunal Révolutionnaire de Paris*. 6 vols. Paris: Librairie Hachette, 1880–82.

PROVINCIAL HISTORIES

Agulhon, Maurice. *Pénitents et franc-maçons de l'ancienne Provence: Essai sur la sociabilité mériodionale*. 2d ed. Paris: Fayard, 1968.

Albert, Madeleine. *Le Féderalisme dans la Haute-Garonne*. Paris: J. Gamber, 1932.

Benoît, Bruno, ed. *Ville et Révolution française: Actes du colloque international: Lyon, mars 1993*. Lyon: Presses Universitaires de Lyon, 1994.

Berlanstein, Lenard. *The Barristers of Toulouse in the Eighteenth Century, 1740–93*. Baltimore, Md.: Johns Hopkins University Press, 1975.

Bonnet de la Tour, G. "Le fédéralisme normand; la bataille sans larmes (Brécourt, 13 juillet.)" *Le Pays d'Argentan* 132 (March 1964), 3–52.

Bossenga, Gail. *The Politics of Privilege: Old Regime and Revolution in Lille*. Cambridge: Cambridge University Press, 1991.

Boutier, Jean. "Jacqueries en pays croquant: les révoltes paysannes en Aquitaine, décembre 1789–mars 1790." *Annales: Economies, Sociétés, Civilisations* 34, 760–86.

Boutier, Jean, and Philippe Boutry. *Atlas de la Révolution française. Les Sociétés politiques*. Vol. 6. Paris: Editions de l'EHESS, 1992.

Brace, Richard Munthe. *Bordeaux and the Gironde, 1789–1794*. Ithaca, N.Y.: Cornell University Press, 1947.

Brelot, Jean. "L'Insurrection fédéraliste dans le Jura en 1793 (mars-août 1793)." *Bulletin de la Fédération des Sociétés Savantes de Franche-Comté* 2 (1955), 73–102.

Butet-Hamel, M. *La Société populaire de Vire pendant le Révolution*. Paris: Imprimerie Nationale, 1907.

Calvet, Henri. "Subsistances et fédéralisme." *Annales historiques de la Révolution Française* VIII (1931), 229–38.

Campion, M.A. *Les Fêtes Nationales à Caen sous la Révolution*. Caen: Imprimerie de Le Blanc-Hardel, 1877.

Chomel, Vital, ed. *Les Débuts de la Révolution française en Dauphiné, 1788–91*. Grenoble: Presses Universitaires de Grenoble, 1988.

Cochin, Augustin. *Les sociétés de pensée et la Révolution en Bretagne (1788–1789).* Paris: H. Champion, 1925.

Crook, Malcolm. "Federalism and the French Revolution: The Revolt in Toulon in 1793." *History* LXV (October 1980), 383–97.

———. *Toulon in War and Revolution.* Manchester: Manchester University Press, 1991.

Cubells, Monique. *Les Horizons de la Liberté: Naissance de la révolution en Provence, 1787–1789.* Aix-En-Provence: Edisud, 1987.

Daudet, R. *L'Urbanisme à Limoges au XVIIIe siècle.* Limoges: Imprimerie A. Bontemps, 1939.

Dawson, Philip. *Provincial Magistrates and Revolutionary Politics in France, 1789–1795.* Cambridge, Mass.: Harvard University Press, 1972.

De Francesco, Antonino. "Popular Sovereignty and Executive Power in the Federalist Revolt of 1793," *French History* 5 (March 1991), 74–101.

———. *Il Governo senza Testa.* Naples: Morano Editore, 1992.

Dollinger, Philippe, Philippe Wolf, and Simone Guenée. *Bibliographie d'histoire des villes de France.* Paris: C. Klincksieck, 1967.

Dorigny, Michel. *Autun dans la Révolution française.* Le Mée-sur-Seine: Edition Amatteis, 1988.

Dubreuil, Léon. "L'Idée régionaliste sous la Révolution." *Annales révolutionnaires* IX (1917), 596–609, and X (1918), 22–36, 230–45, 469–504.

———. "Evreux au temps du fédéralisme." *Révolution Française* LXXVIII (1925), 244–63, 318–48.

Dupuy, Roger, ed. *Pouvoir local et Révolution (1780–1850): La Frontière intérieure: Colloque international, Rennes, le 28 septembre-1er octobre 1993.* Rennes: Presses Universitaires de Rennes, 1995.

Edmonds, W.D. "Federalism and Urban Revolt in France in 1793." *Journal of Modern History* 55 (March 1983), 22–53.

———. *Jacobinism and the Revolt of Lyon, 1789–93.* Oxford: Clarendon Press, 1990.

Forrest, Alan. *Society and Politics in Revolutionary Bordeaux.* Oxford: Oxford University Press, 1975.

———. *The Revolution in Provincial France: Aquitaine, 1789–1799.* Oxford: Clarendon Press, 1996.

Forrest, Alan, and Peter Jones, eds. *Reshaping France: Town, Country and Region during the French Revolution.* Manchester: Manchester University Press, 1991.

Forster, Robert. *The Nobility of Toulouse in the Eighteenth Century.* Baltimore, Md.: Johns Hopkins University Press, 1960.

Fray-Fournier, Alfred. *Les Fêtes Nationales et les Cérémonies Civiques dans la Haute-Vienne pendant la Révolution.* Limoges: Imprimerie du Petit Centre, 1902.

——. *Le Club des Jacobins de Limoges, 1790–95.* Limoges: H. Charles-Lavauzelle, 1903.

——. *Le Départment de la Haute-Vienne, sa formation territoriale, son administration, sa situation politique pendant la Révolution.* 2 vols. Limoges: H. Charles-Lavauzelle, 1909.

Giraudot, Jean. *Le Département de la Haute-Saône pendant la Révolution.* 2 vols. Vesoul: Société d'agriculture, lettres, sciences et arts de la Haute-Saône, 1973.

Goodwin, Albert. "The Federalist Movement in Caen during the French Revolution." *Bulletin of the John Rylands Library* XLII (March 1960), 313–43.

Grall, Jeanne. "Le Fédéralisme: Eure et Calvados." *Bulletin de la Société des Antiquaires de Normandie* LV (1959–60), 133–53.

——. "L'Oeuvre de Robert Lindet dans le Calvados et le problème des subsistances (août-septembre 1793)." *Bulletin de la Société des Antiquaires de Normandie* LVI (1961–62), 339–57.

——. "Les foires de Caen pendant la période révolutionnaire." *Bulletin de la Société des Antiquaires de Normandie* LVII (1963–64), 525–38.

——. "La très courte carrière d'un procureur général syndic, Bougon-Longrais (1765–1794), procureur général syndic du Calvados." In *Droit privé et institutions régionales: Etudes historiques offertes à Jean Yver*, pp. 333–44. Paris: Presses Universitaires de France, 1976.

Guibal, Georges. *Le mouvement fédéraliste en Provence en 1793.* Paris: Plon-Nourrit, 1908.

Guibert, Louis. "Le Parti Girondin dans la Haute-Vienne." *Revue Historique* VIII (1878), 10–106.

——, ed. *Registres consulaires de la ville de Limoges, 1774–1790.* 6 vols. Limoges, 1897.

Guilhamou, Jacques. "Un Argument en révolution: La Souveraineté du peuple: L'Expérimentation marseillaise." *Annales historiques de la Révolution française* 66 (1994), 695–714.

Hall, Thadd. *France and the Eighteenth-Century Corsican Question.* New York: New York University Press, 1971.

Hanson, Paul R. "Les Clubs politiques de Caen pendant la Révolution française," *Annales de Normandie* 36 (Mai 1986), 123–141.

——. *Provincial Politics in the French Revolution: Caen and Limoges, 1789–1794.* Baton Rouge: Louisiana State University Press, 1989.

——. "The Federalist Revolt: An Affirmation or Denial of Popular Sovereignty?" *French History* 6 (September 1992), 335–55.

——. "Les Centres fédéralistes, avaieint-ils un projet commun?" In Bernard Cousin, ed., *Les Fédéralismes: Réalités et Représentations, 1789–1874.* Aix-en-Provence: Publications de l'Université de Provence, 1995.

——. *The Jacobin Republic under Fire: The Federalist Revolt in the*

French Revolution. University Park: Pennsylvania State University Press, 2003.

Hufton, Olwen H. *Bayeux in the Late Eighteenth Century.* Oxford: Clarendon Press, 1967.

Hunt, Lynn. "Committees and Communes: Local Politics and National Revolution in 1789." *Comparative Studies in Society and History* XVIII (July 1976), 321–46.

——. *Revolution and Urban Politics in Provincial France: Troyes and Reims, 1786–1790.* Stanford, Calif.: Stanford University Press, 1978.

Hutt, Maurice. *Chouannerie and Counter-Revolution: Puisaye, the Princes and the British Government of the 1790s.* 2 vols. Cambridge: Cambridge University Press, 1983.

Jessenne, Jean-Pierre. *Pouvoir au village et révolution: Artois, 1760–1848.* Lille: Presses Universitaires de Lille, 1987.

Jones, Peter. *Liberty and Locality in Revolutionary France: Six Villages Compared, 1760–1820.* Cambridge: Cambridge University Press, 2003.

Jouhaud, Léon. *Les Gardes nationaux à Limoges, avant la Convention.* Limoges: Imprimerie de Guillemot et de Lamothe, 1940.

——. *La Révolution Française en Limousin, pages d'histoire vécues, 1789–1792.* Limoges: Desvilles, 1947.

Kaplow, Jeffrey. *Elbeuf during the Revolutionary Period: History and Social Structure.* Baltimore, Md.: Johns Hopkins University Press, 1964.

Kennedy, Michael L. *The Jacobin Club of Marseille, 1790–1794.* Ithaca, N.Y.: Cornell University Press, 1973.

Lallié, Alfred. "Le Féderalisme dans le département de la Loire-Inférieure." *Revue de la Révolution* XV (May–August, 1889), 6–24, 357–76, 454–73, and XVI (September–December 1889), 126–38.

Lavalley, Gaston. "La Presse en Normandie: Journal de l'Armée des Côtes de Cherbourg." *Mémoires de l'Académie Nationale des Sciences, Arts et Belles-lettres de Caen* (1899), 205–75.

Lefebvre, Georges. *La Grande Peur de 1789.* Paris: Librairie Armand Colin, 1932. Translated as: *The Great Fear of 1789: Rural Panic in Revolutionary France.* Translated by Joan White. Princeton, N.J.: Princeton University Press, 1973.

Le Goff, T.J.A. *Vannes and its Region: A Study of Town and Country in Eighteenth-Century France.* Oxford: Clarendon Press, 1981.

Le Parquier, E. "Rouen et le Département de la Seine-Inférieure aux mois de juin et juillet 1793." *La Normandie* II (November 1895), 321–33, and (December 1895), 353–63.

Leroux, Alfred. *Les Sources de l'histoire de la Haute-Vienne pendant la Révolution.* Limoges: Ducourtieux et Gout, 1908.

Lewis, Gwynne. *The Second Vendée: The Constituency of Counter-Revolution in the Department of the Gard, 1789–1815.* Oxford: Clarendon Press, 1978.

Ligou, Daniel. *Montauban à la fin de l'Ancien Régime et aux débuts de la Révolution, 1787–1794.* Paris: M. Rivière, 1958.

Lucas, Colin, and Gwynne Lewis, eds. *Beyond the Terror: Essays in French Regional and Social History, 1794–1815.* Cambridge: Cambridge University Press, 1983.

Lyons, Martyn. *Revolution in Toulouse: An Essay on Provincial Terrorism.* Bern: Lang, 1978.

Margadant, Ted. *Urban Rivalries in the French Revolution.* Princeton, N.J.: Princeton University Press, 1992.

Martin, Jean-Clément. *La Loire-Atlantique dans la tourmente révolutionnaire: 1789–1799.* Nantes: Reflets du Passé, 1989.

———. *Blancs et bleus dans la Vendée déchirée.* Paris: Gallimard, 1996.

Marx, Roland. *Recherches sur la vie politique de l'Alsace prérévolutionnaire et révolutionnaire.* Strasbourg: Librairie Istra, 1966.

Mazauric, Claude. "A Propos de la Manifestation de la Rougemare (11–12 janvier 1793): Royalistes, Modérés et Jacobins à Rouen du 10 août 1792 au printemps 1793." *Cahiers Léopold Delisle* XV (1966), 43–76.

Mazière, Alfred. *Cour de l'appel de Caen. Le Tribunal Criminel du département du Calvados sous l'Assemblée Législative et la Convention.* Caen: Imprimerie de E. Lanier, 1902.

Mesaize, Jean-Baptiste-Michel. *Le Fédéralisme en Normandie: Journal du quartier-maître du 6e bataillon bis des volontaires du Calvados.* Caen: L. Jouan, 1909.

Montier, A. "Le Départment de l'Eure et ses districts en juin 1793." *Révolution Française* XXX (1896), 128–55, 198–226.

Nicolle, Paul. *Histoire de Vire pendant la Révolution (1789–1800).* Vire: Imprimerie J. Beaufils, 1923.

———. "Le Mouvement fédéraliste dans l'Orne en 1793." *Annales historiques de la Révolution Française* XIII (1936), 481–512; XIV (1937), 215–33; and XV (1938), 12–33, 289–313, 385–410.

Perrot, Jean-Claude. "Documents sur la population du Calvados pendant la Révolution et l'Empire." *Annales de Normandie* XV (March 1965), 77–128.

———. "Introduction à l'emploi des registres fiscaux en histoire sociale: l'exemple de Caen au XVIIIe siècle." *Annales de Normandie* XVI (March 1966), 33–65.

———. "Rapports sociaux et villes au XVIIIe siècle." *Annales: Economies, Sociétés, Civilisations* XXIII (1968), 241–67.

———. *Genèse d'une ville moderne: Caen au XVIIIe siècle.* 2 vols. Paris: Mouton, 1975.

Peterson, Stephen M. "The Social Origins of Royalist Political Violence in Directorial Bordeaux," *French History* 10 (March 1996), 56–85.

Peyrard, Christine. *Les Jacobins de l'Ouest: Sociabilité révolutionnaire et formes de politisation dans le Maine et la Basse-Normandie.* Paris: Publications de la Sorbonne, 1996.

Plantadis, Johannès. *L'Agitation autonomiste de Guienne et le mouvement fédéraliste des Girondins en Limousin, 1787–1793.* Tulle: Imprimerie Crauffon, 1908.

Renard, Charles. *Notice sur les Carabots de Caen.* Caen: Legost-Clérisse, 1858.

Riffaterre, C. *Le Mouvement antijacobin et antiparisien à Lyon et dans le Rhône-et-Loire en 1793.* 2 vols. Lyon: A. Rey, 1912–1928.

Sauvage, René Norbert. *Rapports d'un agent du Conseil exécutif sur le Calvados à l'époque du fédéralisme.* Caen: H. Delesques, 1908.

———. "La Loge maçonnique la Constante Fabert à Caen, en 1785." *Mémoires de l'Académie Nationale des Sciences, Arts, et Belles-lettres de Caen* (1918–20), 397–406.

———. "Les Souvenirs de J.-B. Renée sur la Révolution à Caen, 1789–93." *Normannia* VI (1933), 565–606, and VII (1934), 11–39.

Scott, William. *Terror and Repression in Revolutionary Marseilles.* London: Macmillan, 1973.

Secher, Reynald. *La Génocide franco-français: la Vendée vengé.* Paris: Presses Universitaires de France, 1986.

Sée, Henri. "Notes sur les Foires en France et particulièrement sur les Foires de Caen au XVIIIe siècle." *Revue d'Histoire économique et sociale* XV (1927), 366–85.

Sheppard, Thomas F. *Lourmarin in the Eighteenth Century: A Study of a French Village.* Baltimore, Md.: Johns Hopkins University Press, 1971.

Sirich, John Black. *The Revolutionary Committees in the Departments of France, 1793 1794.* Cambridge, Mass.: Harvard University Press, 1943.

Soullier, Charles. *Histoire de la Révolution d'Avignon et du Comtat Venaissin en 1789 et années suivantes.* 2 vols. Paris: Seguin Aîné, 1844.

Stone, Daniel. "La Révolte fédéraliste à Rennes." *Annales Historiques de la Révolution Française* XLIII (1971), 367–87.

Sutherland, Donald. *The Chouans: The Social Origins of Popular Counter-Revolution in Upper Brittany, 1770–1796.* New York: Oxford University Press, 1982.

Sydenham, Michael J. "The Republican Revolt of 1793: a Plea for Less Localized Local Studies." *French Historical Studies* XI (Spring 1981), 120–38.

Tilly, Charles. *The Vendée: A Sociological Analysis of the Counterrevolution of 1793.* Cambridge, Mass.: Harvard University Press, 1964.

Verynaud, Georges. *Histoire de Limoges.* Limoges: Centre régional de recherche et de documentation pédagogiques, 1973.

Wallon, Henri Alexandre. *La Révolution du 31 mai et le fédéralisme en 1793.* 2 vols. Paris: Hachette, 1886.

——. *Les Représentants du peuple en mission et la justice révolutionnaire dans les départements en l'an II (1793–1794).* Paris: Hachette, 1889.
Yver, Jean. "Une Administration municipale 'orageuse' à Caen à la fin de l'Ancien Régime: La Mairie de M. de Vendoeuvre." *Mémoires de l'Académie Nationale des Sciences, Arts, et Belles-lettres de Caen* (1931), 241–68.

HISTORIOGRAPHY

Aberdam, S., Serge Bianchi, and R. Demaude, eds. *Voter, élire pendant la Révolution française, 1789–1799: guide pour la recherche.* Paris: CTHS, 1999.
Ben-Israel, Hedvah. *English Historians on the French Revolution.* Cambridge: University Press, 1968.
Caldwell, Ronald J. *The Era of the French Revolution: A bibliography of the history of western civilization, 1789–99.* New York: Garland, 1985.
Caron, Pierre. *Manuel pratique pour l'étude de la Révolution française.* Paris: A. Picard et Fils, 1947.
Censer, Jack R.. "The Coming of a New Interpretation of the French Revolution." *Journal of Social History* 21 (1987), 295–309.
——. "Commencing the Third Century of Debate." *American Historical Review* 94 (1989), 1309–25.
——. "Social Twists and Linguistic Turns: Revolutionary Historiography a Decade after the Bicentennial." *French Historical Studies* 22 (1999), 139–67.
Desan, Suzanne. "What's After Political Culture? Recent French Revolutionary Historiography." *French Historical Studies* 23 (2000), 163–96.
Goodman, Dena. "Public Sphere and Private Life: Toward a Synthesis of Current Historiographical Approaches to the Old Regime." *History and Theory* 31 (1992), 1–20.
Hatin, Eugène. *Bibliographie historique et critique de la presse périodique française.* Paris: Fimin-Didot Frères et Fils, 1866.
Kaplan, Steven Laurence. *Adieu 89.* Paris: Fayard, 1993.
——. *Farewell, Revolution: 1789–1989.* 2 vols. Ithaca, N.Y.: Cornell University Press, 1995.
Monglond, André. *La France révolutionnaire et impériale: Annales de bibliographie méthodique et description des livres illustrés.* Grenoble: Arthaud, 1933.
Offen, Karen. "The New Sexual Politics of French Revolutionary Historiography." *French Historical Studies* 16 (1990), 909–22.
Orr, Linda. *Headless History: Nineteenth-Century French Historiography of the Revolution.* Ithaca, N.Y.: Cornell University Press, 1990.
Vovelle, Michel. "L'Historiographie de la Révolution française à la veille du bicentenaire." *Annales historiques de la Révolution française* 60 (1988),

113–26 and 306–15.

———. *Recherches sur la Révolution: Un Bilan des travaux scientifiques du Bicentenaire.* Paris: La Découverte, 1991.

Walter, Gérard. *Répertoire de l'histoire de la Révolution française. Travaux publiés de 1800 à 1940.* 2 vols. Paris: Bibliothèque Nationale, 1941–51.

About the Author

Paul R. Hanson attended college at Stanford University and earned his Ph.D. at the University of California, Berkeley, where he wrote his dissertation under the direction of Lynn Hunt. He has taught at Arizona State University, Linfield College, and since 1984 at Butler University, where he is now Professor of History and Dean of the College of Liberal Arts and Sciences. Professor Hanson teaches courses on both French and Chinese history, but has published principally on the subject of the French Revolution. His books include *Revolutionary France* (Indianapolis, Ind., 1987), *Provincial Politics in the French Revolution: Caen and Limoges, 1789–1794* (Baton Rouge, La., 1989), and *The Jacobin Republic under Fire: The Federalist Revolt in the French Revolution* (University Park, Pa., 2003).